CALIFORNIA STUDIES IN THE HISTORY OF ART
Walter Horn, General Editor
Advisory Board: H.W. Janson, D. Posner, J.R. Martin

French Gothic Architecture
of the 12th and 13th Centuries

JEAN BONY

French Gothic Architecture
of the 12th and 13th Centuries

UNIVERSITY OF CALIFORNIA PRESS

BERKELEY   LOS ANGELES   LONDON

FRENCH GOTHIC ARCHITECTURE OF THE 12TH AND 13TH CENTURIES
is a volume in the
California Studies of the History of Art Series
sponsored in part by the Samuel H. Kress Foundation
University of California Press
Berkeley   Los Angeles
University of California Press Ltd
London, England
© 1983 by the Regents of the University of California
Designed by DAVE COMSTOCK

Library of Congress Cataloging in Publication Data
Bony, Jean.
    French Gothic Architecture of the 12th and 13th Centuries.

    (California studies in the history of art; 20)
    Bibliography: p.
    Includes index.
      1. Architecture, Gothic—France.   2. Church architecture—
France.   I. Title.   II. Series.
    NA5543.B66   726'.5'0944   74-82842
    ISBN 0-520-02831-7

To the memory of Henri Focillon, 1881–1943

Foreword

A SERIES of public lectures given in New York in 1961, as the Charles T. Mathews Lectures, under the joint auspices of Columbia University and the Metropolitan Museum of Art, gave me the opportunity of first presenting in this form my view of the historical development of French Gothic architecture in the age of its beginnings and of its major creations. Many parts of the original text have been expanded, and sometimes largely rewritten, but the leading thread has remained unchanged and I have tried all along to preserve something of the tone of the spoken word.

In the material presentation of this book a few points should perhaps be explained. The graphic illustration has been treated as an integral part of the reasoning, and it is as such that plans of buildings are most often given as 'original reconstructed plans,' with all the elements of hypothesis that such reconstructions entail. Plans placed side by side or in close proximity have been established on the same scale, but the differences of actual size between buildings ruled out as unrealistic the use of a single, consistent scale for all plans throughout the book. Sections and elevations, when used, are of a rather diagrammatic nature. The maps, on the other hand, have been made to hold elements of information not to be found in the text or even in the notes; for it has been thought that, when plotted on a map, series should appear as complete as possible, to transmit an image of their geographical distribution. The outlining of specific areas on the maps may of course seem a questionable mode of simplification; but the risk has been taken of offering such schemas, if only to strike the eye and invite reflection.

vii

A travel grant from the Samuel H. Kress Foundation enabled me to revisit a number of essential buildings in France in 1970, and for this my special thanks go to Miss Mary M. Davis, Vice-President of the Foundation. Assistance has come over the years from the Regents of the University of California through their programs of support for research, providing me with periods of time in which to carry out revisions and assemble additional documentation.

The extensive illustration of this book could not have been put together without help from many quarters. Kind consideration from the Archives Photographiques and Caisse Nationale des Monuments Historiques et des Sites, Paris, from the Courtauld Institute of Art, University of London, and from the National Monuments Record (England) has greatly aided me in the task. Quite a few items of illustration, belonging to the Clarence Ward Medieval Archive have been supplied by courtesy of the Photographic Archives of the National Gallery of Art in Washington, D.C. Mrs. Shirley Prager Branner has put at my disposal photographs from the collection of the late Robert Branner. Mr. Sumner McKnight Crosby has made a series of photographs of Saint-Denis available to me. Mr. Neil Stratford has been kind enough to give me prints of his photographs of Saint-Martin-aux-Bois. Monsieur Pierre Bougard, Directeur des services départementaux d'archives du Pas-de-Calais, has provided me with photographs of rare drawings of the destroyed cathedral of Arras. Monsieur François Hébert-Stevens has supplied me with photographs of Troyes and Strasbourg cathedrals from the archives of the Editions Arthaud, Paris. Monsieur J.R. Haeusser of the Oeuvre Notre-Dame at Strasbourg has sent me a photograph of an engraving of the Cathedral by Isaac Brunn. Monsieur Henry Goüin has granted me permission to take photographs of the remains of Royaumont Abbey. The right to freely make use of photographs from their collections has been accorded me by Walter Horn, Virginia Jansen, Vivian Paul and Sarah Pearson. And the aid of Mademoiselle Jeanne Vinsot of the Service des Monuments Historiques in the compilation of photographic documentation has been a positive element in the achieving of this book, to be acknowledged with much gratitude.

In the matter of graphic illustration, I have debts of a very special nature. Mr. C.L. Wysuph has made the most generous gift of his time and skill in the preparation and drawing of reconstructed plans of Saint-Denis, Notre-Dame and Bourges and in the reproducing of a set of diagrams. Mrs. Margaret Burke has executed a great number of drawings with an expertise and a care for exactness going far beyond her duties as illustrator—to which she has added the outright gift of a splendid piece of draughtsmanship, an isometric reconstruction of Laon Cathedral. The many maps, most demanding in their detail, have been transcribed by Mrs. Adrienne Morgan, with an attention and a technical virtuosity which greatly enhance their usefulness.

Mr. August Frugé, former Director of the University of California Press, gave me great encouragement by his unstinting approval of my aims in this work. It has been my good fortune to have in Lorna Price an editor of uncommon understanding and capabilities, who has clarified many problems for me; and in David Comstock a designer of great sensitivity to the presentation of architecture. And my wife, Mary, has given me the most precious collaboration at every stage in the making of this book.

The advice of fellow medievalists, especially Robert Branner, Sumner Crosby, Louis Grodecki, Pierre Héliot, Peter Kidson and Robert Mark, has been of the greatest help to me. Finally, and most fundamentally, the director of this series, my colleague and friend, Walter Horn, through his critical judgment and constant interest, has made a reality of this long-standing enterprise.

ix

Contents

xi

Illustrations

All photographic credits are entered in this list. The following abbreviations are used:

A.C.L., Bruxelles
> Archives centrales iconographiques de l'art national, Institut Royal du Patrimoine Artistique, Ministère de l'Education nationale et de la Culture, Brussels

Arch. Phot. Paris/ S.P.A.D.E.M.
> Archives Photographiques, Caisse Nationale des Monuments Historiques et des Sites, Ministère des Affaires Culturelles, Paris

Bibl. nat., Paris
> Bibliothèque nationale, Paris

Court. Inst.
> Courtauld Institute of Art, University of London

Marburg
> Bildarchiv Foto Marburg im Forschungsinstitut für Kunstgeschichte, Philipps-Universität, Marburg-an-der-Lahn

N.M.R.
> National Monuments Record, Royal Commission on Historical Monuments, England

Ward Archive, National Gallery
> Photograph Clarence Ward Medieval Archive, courtesy of the Photographic Archives, National Gallery of Art, Washington, D.C.

xvii

xviii

xxii

xxiv

xxv

xxvii

xxix

xxxvii

xxxix

xl

xlii

Introduction

THIS BOOK has been written in the conviction that the true significance of Gothic architecture can be captured only if one does not lose sight of the unexpectedness of the course of history. The art we call Gothic was the assertion of a spirit of modernity which went on renewing itself for centuries, almost ceaselessly; and what matters is to perceive again the vitality of that movement and the accidental quality of its development.

The driving force of human inventiveness being a critical dissatisfaction with the immediate past, each generation of Gothic builders in turn had to reassess its aims, each time redefining Gothic in its own terms and often changing dramatically the direction of the movement. There was a time when Gothic was viewed as a predetermined development, as the unfolding through time of a sort of theorem guided by an inner necessity. This implied the belief that a long sustained movement of civilization could be condensed into one short phase of supposed perfection and the whole movement then defined in terms of that moment alone. But such schematizations deny the life of history. In fact, each work of art (or group of closely related works) is meant as a final statement for its moment in time and each moment has its right to be considered ultimate. So the only productive line of approach for the historian is to try to uncover the urges which at each stage dictated the new orientations that were taken by the Gothic movement, and to see how the creations of art both expressed and fashioned the turns of thought and the sensibility of their age. The past must be relived as what it was when it was happening: as a sequence of distinct and unforeseeable presents.

When the emphasis is placed on this open-endedness of history and on the shifting nature of its configurations, one soon becomes aware that the term "Gothic" is generally made to designate not one historic age but two; and the history of Gothic makes sense only when that succession of two essentially different cycles of development is accepted as a principle of periodization. Those great divisions we adopt to categorize history are not just a matter of convention: they are meant to correspond to major changes in the reality of historical life, and the later part of the thirteenth century is commonly recognized in practically all domains of medieval civilization as representing one of those times when everything seems to take a new turn. That the concept of a break taking place at this point has not been applied more often to architectural history is due to a superficial continuity in the vocabulary of forms. But behind that surface the transformation was no less real than in the other fields of life: the forces which support artistic creation also were changing rapidly and even the geography of art centers was soon to be completely altered.

It is from an objective examination of such basic data and their confrontation with the other orders of facts that I have come to believe in the significance of that break (progressive, not sudden, but a break all the same) in the overall history of medieval architecture and in its importance as an element of understanding. The evaluation thus arrived at has determined the chronological framework of this book, which is conceived as a study of that first era of Gothic which terminates shortly before the end of the thirteenth century: an age characterized in its very structure by the preponderance of the northern French milieu. For all along the first cycle of its history, from its Parisian beginnings in the 1130s to the decisive shift of the late thirteenth century, Gothic architecture remains a French thing, dominated as it is by the power of invention of a constellation of centers in northern France, which held their artistic initiative unchallenged for one hundred and fifty years. It was north French leadership which conferred its unity on the age; and it is this phenomenon of continued inventiveness, this process of creation and renewals emanating repeatedly from the same human environment over an extended period of time that constitutes the main theme of this study. Our effort will therefore focus on identifying what gives Gothic its forward thrust, while another most interesting but less operative aspect of that age—the reactions triggered in the rest of Europe, in areas of different cultural background, by the artistic inventions of northern France—will of necessity receive rather cursory treatment. Only briefly, in Chapter VIII, will these other, "peripheral", lines of Gothic be referred to and discussed in some of their aspects, but mainly inasmuch as they relate to the central Gothic movement. For how could one give an idea of the pace of artistic life in periods of great inventiveness, if not by placing the stress firmly on the dynamics of change and on the unpredictability of stylistic invention? Approached from that angle, Gothic architecture will perhaps recover for us some of the intensity of meaning it had for the men who created it and who kept rethinking and reimagining it, following no preestablished destiny and guided by no other necessity than that of constantly revitalizing the power and the originality of their vision.

1. SOISSONS CATHEDRAL, work begun late 1190s, choir completed 1212

CHAPTER I

The Technical Bases of Gothic Architecture

Every age of architecture can be characterized, on a rather elementary level, by a few obvious and fairly constant features which result from the general acceptance of certain basic solutions to technical problems and of certain preferences in the shaping of space. A first hold can thus be gained on some essential aspects of the reality that builders had to face in a given age; and if Gothic architecture is to be initially approached along these lines, it is perhaps simplest to turn to some building of the early years of the thirteenth century—such as the cathedral of Soissons[1] (Fig. 1)—because works of that date are still close enough to the beginnings of the movement to preserve much of its original spirit and yet advanced enough to give a clear image of the new tendencies which, by then, had been at work for two generations.

At Soissons Cathedral one of the most obvious features is the use of a certain type of vaulting: the rib vault, in which the criss-cross lines of penetrations, which remained plain and somewhat indistinct in groin vaulting, are underlined by a system of ribs clearly dividing the surface of the vault into triangular compartments or cells. Another typical feature is the pointed shape given to all the arches and present everywhere in the structure: in the vaults, in the windows, as well as in the main arcade and in the smaller arcading of the triforium. The third characteristic is a deliberate

2. RIVOLTA D'ADDA, SS. MARIA E SIGISMONDO, nave, ca. 1120

insistence on height, which affects all the proportions of the building: not only the general shape of the interior volume but the divisions of all the stories and the architectural members which articulate them, whether piers or shafts or arches or windows. This becomes particularly evident in the narrow bays of the apse—or, rather, in the hemicycle, since this is the term to be used when the semicircular termination of the choir is surrounded by an ambulatory making, with its crown of chapels, that complex composition of volumes which is known as a chevet. Finally, the whole building gives an impression of openness, for the solid masses, the solid surfaces especially, are here reduced to a minimum. The size of the windows,

6

the brightness of light in this interior are particularly striking; and that skeletonization of the structure, that thinning out of its constructional substance add the final touch to what we feel makes the Gothic quality of this work.

ROMANESQUE ANTECEDENTS

Now it must be recognized that all of these features were already present in some measure in Romanesque architecture. However tempting, it would be a diversion of intent to give too much time to a quest for distant origins; but the direct Romanesque sources must of necessity be briefly reviewed.

By 1100, the rib vault was already in use in both England and Italy. The north Italian group[2] can be represented by the church of Rivolta d'Adda (Fig. 2) where the choir, begun quite probably by 1099, was still simply barrel vaulted, while the nave built soon after was rib vaulted in large units, domed in the center and covering two bays each. The proportions and the size of the resulting spatial units give an impression of massive power. But it is very likely that some church in Milan was in fact the initiator of the whole series: either S. Nazaro, the remodeling of which may have been begun by 1093, or some other church later destroyed, perhaps in the earthquake of 1117. In the early 1120s Milan, Novara, and Pavia were the three main centers of this new method of vaulting; but the famous nave of S. Ambrogio in Milan was begun only after 1128 and its vaults were not designed much before 1140.[3]

In England, rib vaulting made its appearance at Durham Cathedral, begun in 1093, where the oldest vaults are those of the choir aisles (Figs. 3, 4), certainly completed before 1100; and it is known that by 1104 the main span of the choir was rib vaulted, in a particular type of double-bay unit without a transverse rib to divide the two bays. These original vaults of the main choir are gone, replaced by a thirteenth-century rebuilding; but an identical type of double-bay vaulting is still preserved in the slightly later north transept (Figs. 5, 6), which must have been vaulted at the latest by 1115—since the ribs still lack the zig-zag ornament which was introduced at about that date in the building of the nave, starting

3. DURHAM CATHEDRAL, N side of choir, begun 1093

5. DURHAM CATHEDRAL, N transept vaults, ca. 1110–1115

6. DURHAM CATHEDRAL, E side of N transept, ca. 1093–1115

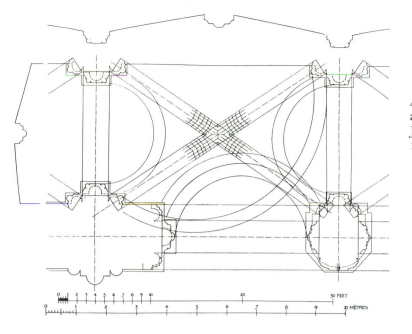

4. DURHAM CATHEDRAL, N aisle of choir, plan of vault, by J. Bilson, *Journal of the RIBA*, 1898–1899

7. DURHAM CATHEDRAL, nave from W, mostly ca. 1115–1133

with the main arcade and aisle vaults (ca. 1115–1125). Next came the vaulting of the south transept (ca. 1125–1128) and then the central space of the nave (Fig. 7), which again is known to have been vaulted between 1128 and 1133. This chronology of the construction of Durham was established by John Bilson more than 80 years ago and remains unshakable in its factual sequence.[4] The rib had appeared at Durham in association with a number of other unusual features, one of which would seem to be of special significance, as it is clearly linked with the use of the rib itself. In both choir and transepts, the diagonal ribs of the vault are supported on a very distinctive grouping of short vaulting shafts starting from tribune level only, in emphatic contrast to the tall vertical shafts rising from ground level in strong projection on alternate piers, which carry the heavy transverse arches and which seem not to be intrinsically related to the vaulting system but rather to pursue across the space of the nave the double-bay organization of the elevation. This absence of integration between the pattern of vaults and that of bays was not repeated outside England, but the principle of rib vaulting as initiated at Durham did spread rapidly across the Channel.

By 1120 or 1125, the system of diagonal ribs was adopted in Normandy. Three early examples can be identified: at Evreux, Lessay and Jumièges. The Romanesque cathedral of Evreux is still partly preserved, since the lower story of the nave was incorporated into the Gothic rebuilding; and excavations have proved that the choir was rib vaulted.[5] Evreux had been destroyed by Henry I of England in 1119 and rebuilding was actually started about five years later. At Lessay (Fig. 8), in the Cotentin peninsula, the abbey church was begun in all probability in 1105, with groin-vaulting only in mind and that restricted to the choir; but by the time the clerestory had been reached, it was decided to use the new type of vault over the whole church, and this must again have happened about 1120.[6] The other example is the chapter-house of Jumièges (Fig. 9), now ruined but preserving clear indications of its original rib vaulting. Urso being the first abbot to have been buried there, this chapter-house is assumed to have been built during his rule,

8. LESSAY, choir and N transept, begun ca. 1105, vaulted ca. 1120

9. JUMIÈGES, Chapter House, NE respond, ca. 1120–1127

10. MOISSAC, lower story of porch tower, ca. 1125–1130.

1101–1127. Georges Lanfry, who gave the first accurate reconstruction of its vaulting system,[7] placed it in the first years of Urso's abbacy, before the war of 1106; but it seems more likely to have been built in the period of peace following 1120, especially if one bears in mind the stylistic analogies of the Jumièges chapter-house with the choir of Saint-Paul at Rouen, the crossing of Duclair, or even the transept and nave of Christchurch (Dorset), all datable in the 1120s at the earliest. By that time, large rib vaults (of a different type) were also being used in the south of France at Moissac (Fig. 10), in the porch-tower generally attributed to Abbot Roger (1115–1131): the new technique of vaulting was already giving rise to a growing number of interpretations.

No one claims now that the use of the rib vault is sufficient to make a building Gothic. There is a whole Romanesque history (Fig.

11. SOISSONS CATHEDRAL, nave vaults being rebuilt after 1914–1918 war

12) to that method of vaulting, which goes back to distant oriental sources transmitted to Islamic Spain as early as the second half of the tenth century.[8] But it is difficult to establish an absolutely convincing connection between the Islamic examples and the two main Romanesque series, which applied the principle of intersecting ribs to a totally different type of vault based on the Western practice of groin-vaulting.[9] Some other suggestions must also have acted on the minds of Romanesque builders; and, at least in the case of the Lombard series, it is quite possible that some knowledge of the Roman methods of incorporated brick ribbing[10] intervened in the elaboration of that system of large square vaulting units. However, it does not seem pure accident that, both in England and Italy, the first systematic experiments in rib-vaulting started within ten years of the capture of Toledo (1085), where could be seen—on a reduced scale but in a rich variety of types—some of the finest examples of Islamic rib-vaults.

13

12. MAP: Distribution of Early Rib Vaults

LEGEND

Symbols used

- □   Early rib vaults, up to the later 1130s
- ■   Early rib vaults, late 1130s to early 1150s
- ✖   Ribbed cloister vaults, up to the later 1130s
- ✕   Ribbed cloister vaults, late 1130s to early 1150s

Limits indicated

--------   Area of formation of Gothic architecture

Places not named on map
Great Britain (from N to S)
Warkworth, Heddon-on-the-Wall, Selby (aisles), Stow,
Southwell (aisles), Warwick (St. Mary's, crypt),
Cambridge (St. Sepulchre, aisle), Avening,
Malmesbury, Reading (Founder's Chapel), Exeter
(aisles)

Northern France: see Fig. 112
Northern Italy (from W to E)
Sannazzaro-Sesia, Novara, Pavia, Piacenza

13. Map: Distribution of Early Pointed Arches

What were the actual material advantages derived by Romanesque builders from the use of that framework of ribs? This is not perfectly clear on all points. The theory advanced by Viollet-le-Duc in mid-nineteenth century, on the basis of an apparent analogy with iron construction and still widely accepted fifty years ago, has since been shown to be simplistic and unfounded:[11] the ribs do not carry the mass of the vault compartments, their presence does not change radically the mechanics of masonry vaults. The action they exercise is rather one of reinforcement; they stiffen in particular the haunches of the vault, where the creasing of the vault surface is most accentuated, important stresses thus being created. Otherwise rib vaults continue to function very much in the same manner as plain groin vaults. They are merely groin vaults which, being better reinforced, can be made thinner. It is also fairly evident that, through the fragmentation of their surface into triangular cells, the rib vaults became much easier to build and even to conceive than unribbed groin vaults, since the shape of the vault ceased to be thought of in terms of three-dimensional curvature—an almost impossible approach in the state of medieval geometry—and became reduced to a simple combination of two-dimensional arches which had only to be covered by a mantle of masonry (Fig. 11). The use of regular ashlar masonry instead of rubble in the construction of vault cells is another characteristic of Gothic vaulting. But this important new feature developed only after some time, in a few well-defined regions, and does not relate with the earliest diffusion of rib vaulting. When the rib was first adopted, the vaults were still built of rubble and the most important changes seem to have affected the methods of centering.[12] All arches and vaults are built over a temporary wooden support called formwork or center, which is removed once the stone arch or vault is finished. Unfortunately, very little is known as fact about the types of formwork normally used in the Romanesque period. But one thing at least seems certain: since the framework of ribs had to be built before the rest of the vault, a skeleton timber centering had to be erected first to support the ribs alone while they were being set in place; after which timber and ribs together must have served as an armature for the full centering which was required

16

for the filling in of the vault cells. This means that the procedure of vault construction was henceforth divided into two distinct stages, and this change of procedure was probably what started the whole sequence of further technical experiments, simplifications and improvements, at the end of which the fully Gothic types of vaults became possible. Any break or new departure in the accepted routine of building operations is a stimulus to invention and may have unexpected and far-reaching consequences.

The pointed arch also was known to Romanesque builders (Fig. 13) before the end of the eleventh century. It had been adopted first in Islamic architecture of the Near East in the course of the eighth century and had propagated itself through Egypt and Tunisia to Sicily, then under Arab domination.[13] The exact course of its transmission to western Christendom is uncertain. It is commonly thought that the pointed arch must first have been adopted at Amalfi, then the main center of trade with the Islamic countries, and that from there it passed to Monte Cassino at the time of Abbot Desiderius who rebuilt the main church of the monastery between 1066 and 1071. Nothing remains of the eleventh century buildings at Amalfi or Monte Cassino, both victims of recurrent destructions, and it had been thought until recently that the west porch of the church of S. Angelo in Formis near Capua, also built under Desiderius, was a contemporary replica of that of Monte Cassino and gave an idea of the style practiced there in the 1070s. But that west porch has now been proved to be a rebuilding of the end of the twelfth century. As there are no early examples (dating from the late eleventh or early twelfth century) standing in mainland Italy, it cannot now be conclusively proved that transmission of the pointed arch took place via Campania. On the other hand, it has recently been suggested that transmission could equally well have been made directly from Sicily, where the pointed arch was surely in use before the conquest of the island in the 1060s and 1070s by the Normans, who most likely adopted it at once and used it in the first cathedrals they founded on Sicilian soil between 1086 and 1093.[14] Whatever the case, the pointed arch made its appearance in a properly Romanesque context at Cluny, in southern Burgundy, at an early stage in the construction of the new church, begun by Saint Hugh of Semur in 1088, the church known as Cluny III and destroyed in great part in the wake of the French Revolution.[15] The surviving south transept of Cluny (Fig. 14) and the church of Paray-le-Monial (Fig. 42, p. 47)—a small-scale replica of Cluny III—, both of which were completed ca. 1120, manifest the importance that was assumed in Burgundy by the pointed arch from the moment of its arrival, since it was not used only in the main arcade and in the groin vaults of the aisles but also in the large pointed barrels thrown over the main spans in both structures. This new way of tracing vaults and arches reduced the thrusts appreciably, by about 20 percent,[16] and this technical advantage explains its rapid diffusion in some areas of Romanesque Europe.

14. CLUNY, remains of S transept looking N, pointed barrel vault ca. 1100–1120, terminal wall modern

15. SOISSONS, NOTRE-DAME, begun ca. 1130, drawing by Tavernier (Paris, Bibl. nat.)

By 1130 or 1135 the pointed arch had already spread to many parts of France: Burgundy, the Rhône valley, Provence, Poitou, Aquitaine; and it was beginning to affect the Paris region and even some centers in England, where the nave vaults of Durham (Fig. 7), completed in 1133, antedate by a few years the Cistercian examples of Rievaulx and Fountains.[17] In northern France—or more exactly in those plains which spread from Burgundy to Artois and are by nature geographically centered on Paris—the Romanesque buildings of the 1130s and early 1140s show the arrival of the pointed arch in a variety of contexts. Until the Revolution, Soissons possessed, not far to the east of the cathedral, a richly decorated Romanesque abbey church dedicated to Notre-Dame. Begun probably soon after 1130, that church had an unvaulted nave, not even divided into bays but having pointed arches throughout the main arcade story (Fig. 15); and a pointed barrel ending in a pointed semidome seems to have covered the choir.[18] It is clear that Notre-Dame of Soissons had a considerable following in the area for fifteen to twenty years (Urcel, Lhuys, Trucy, Bruyères); and the slight pointing of the arches of the ambulatory of Morienval (also datable to the early 1130s) may well be connected with the early work at Notre-Dame of Soissons. Closer to Paris, at Villers-Saint-Paul (Fig. 16), another unvaulted building, the main arcades again are pointed and so was in all probability the diaphragm arch that originally divided the nave into two sections. The somewhat later church of Grez-sur-Loing, near Fontainebleau, has preserved, still recog-

16. Villers-Saint-Paul, N side of nave, mid 1130s   17. Seraincourt, crossing, ca. 1135–1140

nizable in spite of its later vaulting, a similar type of pointed diaphragm arch spanning the nave on alternate bays. Pointed barrels
and pointed groin vaults became also quite common shortly before
1140 around Paris: in the Vexin, west of Paris, as at Seraincourt
(Fig. 17) near Meulan; south of Paris, in the plains of Beauce, at
Etampes for instance, in the nave of the church of Notre-Dame
(Fig. 34); while in Paris itself the pointing of vaults and arches had
certainly been adopted as early as at Soissons and was well established by the mid 1130s, witness the east end of Saint-Martin-des-
Champs (Fig. 47, p. 51) or the narthex of Saint-Denis (Fig. 37). The
diffusion of the pointed arch is therefore to be seen as one of the
general developments of Romanesque architecture in the second
quarter of the twelfth century, and in the late 1140s and early 1150s
a persistent Romanesqueness continued to accompany the spreading
use of that new type of arch, as at Lillers (Fig. 18) in Artois, Berteaucourt in Picardy and in Cistercian churches, which mostly went on
acting as an advance guard in the propagation of the pointed arch.

The tendency to stretch the naves in height—and at the same
time to emphasize the vertical lines of the bay pattern—was no less
clearly inherited from Romanesque times: it was very much in evidence in the churches of the "Pilgrimage Road" group, such as Santiago, Conques or Saint-Sernin at Toulouse (Fig. 19) (all begun
before 1085), and was no less marked at Cluny III (Fig. 43, p. 47)
in its final design (datable in the later 1090s). But it was already
present, before 1050, in the larger vaulted churches of southern
France and Catalonia, as at Sant Vicens de Cardona (begun before
1040) or soon after at Saint-Guilhem-le-Désert; and a similar tendency can be traced back also to the first half of the eleventh century
in the timber covered tribune churches of northern France. Even
roofless and partly ruined, the great church of Jumièges (Fig. 21)
in Normandy (1040–1067) remains as a most typical example of
that ideal of loftiness, which was soon to receive its vaulted version
in the Pilgrimage Road Churches. Ile-de-France builders at first
seem to have favored simpler and lower types of structures, such as
the nave of Saint-Germain-des-Prés in Paris. But they caught up
with the taste of the time a little before 1100: the destroyed abbey

church of Saint-Lucien at Beauvais (Fig. 20), begun about 1090, is known to us particularly through a fine engraving of the nineteenth century, which shows a tall and narrow nave reminiscent of Jumièges in its proportions.[19] The presence of such a building at Beauvais at that date should be taken as the sign of a much wider movement, which can be perceived soon after in Flanders, even in Hainault, and which probably touched all the northern provinces of France.

As for the skeletal quality of the structures, which might seem to be the most specifically Gothic of all these general features, this also had its roots in the past: a whole sequence of Romanesque experiments had already prepared the ground. Various types of structural openness were in fact possible and had been attempted

18. LILLERS, nave to W, late 1140s or early 1150s

19. TOULOUSE, SAINT-SERNIN, choir begun by 1083, nave from ca. 1100

20. BEAUVAIS, SAINT-LUCIEN, begun 1090, ruins in early 19th c. by A. Van den Berghe

21. JUMIÈGES, NOTRE-DAME, nave and W walls of transept: transept ca. 1040–1050, nave ca. 1050–1067

in the course of the eleventh century. They did not all lead in the direction in which Gothic was to develop some time later: in the west choir of Essen for instance—now dated after 1040—the large openwork panels are framed by powerful arches which give an impression of roundness and solidity, recalling the massive openness of the *exedrae* of Late Antique and early Byzantine architecture. With their regular gridwork of bays and their use of wall passages, particularly that of the triforium, Gothic buildings appear on the other hand rather closely related to the system evolved in Normandy (Fig. 22) and England in the later part of the eleventh century.[20] The type of the Gothic triforium[21] was actually created at Caen, in the lantern tower of the church of Saint-Etienne (Fig. 23),

22. CAEN, SAINT-ETIENNE, analysis of nave elevation by G. Bouet, showing state of upper stories before and after rib vaulting of ca. 1130–1135

État ancien. État actuel.

23. CAEN, SAINT-ETIENNE, crossing and nave from S transept, ca. 1067–1083, originally unvaulted (Ward Archive)

24. PETERBOROUGH CATHEDRAL, N transept, ca. 1117–1140

between 1067 and 1079, and was first applied to a full-scale elevation in the choir and transept of St. Albans (begun in 1077). The
loggia treatment of the clerestory, initiated also at Saint-Etienne at
Caen, achieved the most striking effect of two-layer openness at
Cerisy-la-Forêt (begun ca. 1090) and in the nave of Ely (begun in
1102). Another remarkable development was the multiplication of
the windows in such structures as the transepts of Norwich (1096–
1119) or the apse and transepts of Peterborough (Fig. 24) (after

25

1117). From ca. 1070 the basic principle of Norman building was to reduce all walls to a thick but open skeleton of arches.

That this Norman system itself was initially derived from distant Roman prototypes[22] is interesting but not of special moment here, for what matters is rather the novelty of the reinterpretation and the potentialities it contained for the future. But these were not discovered until much later. For a long time the double-wall methods of Norman builders had no appeal outside the limits of England and Normandy. The first signs of an expansion are nowhere earlier than 1130,[23] and in the whole of the Ile-de-France area, stretching from Laon to Orléans, a single example only can be detected before 1150: the apse of the destroyed church of Notre-Dame at Soissons, where the opened-up treatment of the walls reduced on the inside to a two-story screen of thin detached arches (Fig. 15), was a direct reflection of the system followed not so many years before in the remodeling of the apse of La Trinité at Caen. But nothing followed this isolated attempt for another twenty years; only in the second half of the twelfth century, when Gothic architecture was already well defined, was a systematic effort made along the lines indicated by these Anglo-Norman anticipations.

The Ile-de-France Milieu

In this rapid survey of Romanesque sources a name has been cited again and again: that of Normandy, and there is no doubt that a strong case exists for a theory of Norman origins as providing the key to the beginnings of Gothic architecture. This appears particularly true when one tries to trace how rib vaulting started in the Ile-de-France area. The ambulatory of Morienval (Figs. 26, 27), often mentioned as showing the earliest rib vaults in the Paris region, does not deserve that distinction: the presence of slightly pointed arches, and a profile of ribs (Fig. 29) similar to that of the second campaign of vaulting at Saint-Etienne at Beauvais, are enough to prove that Morienval did not come first.

Rib vaulting seems to have entered Ile-de-France from Normandy along two roads. One of these axes of penetration passes north of Paris, running in an easterly direction from Beauvais to the middle valley of the Oise and beyond, rapidly reaching Morienval and the plain of Valois but touching also southern Picardy (Airaines, on the road from Beauvais to Abbeville, is one of the signs of that northward diffusion). The earliest rib vaults in that area are probably those of the easternmost bay of the nave aisles of Saint-Etienne at Beauvais (Fig. 25), which belong to the same campaign of construction as the old choir, destroyed and rebuilt in the sixteenth century but recently recovered through excavation. This part of the building may go back to the mid or late 1120s, and it was certainly based on Norman and even English models: the plan of the choir, for one thing, was almost a replica of that of Romsey.[24] Simultaneously another penetration of the rib-vaulting process was taking place directly west of Paris, on the axis of the middle valley of the Seine. Two early representatives of that advance are the choir of the little church of Verneuil-sur-Seine (Fig. 30) between Meulan and Poissy, and the remnants of the old crossing of Jouy-le-Moutier, south of Pontoise: the presence in both buildings of heavy soffit rolls under the main arches is a sure sign of the influence of that crucial recent Norman building, the cathedral of Evreux (Fig. 28) (begun ca. 1125). The rich plastic style of chevron decoration which had just been evolved in England followed the same path, reaching Paris at the same time as the rib-vault in the mid-1130s.[25] Norman sources are indeed obvious at the start of the Ile-de-France movement.

But is it enough to say that Ile-de-France Gothic was the result of an invasion of English forms transmitted through Normandy? If that was enough, how could the no less obvious fact be explained that these new features, and rib vaulting especially, were finally of so little consequence in England and Normandy, while they suggested so much more to the master-builders of that restricted area around Paris? Why had the rib vault to come as far as Ile-de-France to bring about the birth of a new architecture? There must surely have been some essential difference of architectural outlook between Norman and Ile-de-France builders. The addition of the pointed arch, which happened then to reach Paris from the other direction, coming from Burgundy, was not sufficient to make all

25. BEAUVAIS, SAINT-ETIENNE, view into nave and S aisle from transept: easternmost bay ca. 1130, rest of nave from ca. 1140 (Ward Archive)

26. MORIENVAL, choir: hemicycle and ambulatory ca. 1130–1135 (upper parts restored), straight bay late 11th c. with rib vaults of ca. 1145 (Ward Archive)

that difference either: it reached England also at about the same time and nothing fundamental occurred.[26] This fact suffices to demonstrate the danger of purely additive reasoning where problems of origins are concerned. Things do not happen by mere addition in history: forces have to be released, an impetus has to be created for art movements to take shape. And this is where we come to grips at last with the real problem of the beginnings of Gothic.

Rib vaulting, in the Ile-de-France region, found itself in a new technical environment. Racial explanations are of no avail here (they have often been discreetly hinted at, in self-flattery): the Frenchmen of the Ile-de-France were not, by virtue of birth, more logical or clear-minded than their neighbors; they did not, as the cliché goes, see at once all the consequences that could be derived from the new vaulting technique. They simply placed themselves in an impossible situation and had to extricate themselves from it. But here, instead of considering the vault alone, it becomes necessary to look also at the walls and see in what way they affected the vaulting or were affected by it.

27. MORIENVAL, E end from N, ca. 1130–1135 (Ward Archive)

28. EVREUX CATHEDRAL, N side of nave, E bays ca. 1125–1135

29. MORIENVAL, vault of an ambulatory bay, ca. 1130–1135

30. VERNEUIL-SUR-SEINE, chancel vault, probably ca. 1130–1135

No decisive change was likely to take place in England or Normandy as a result of the practice of vaulting[27] because Norman structures were too safe. At Durham or Lessay the walls were so heavy, so thick all the way down (roughly seven feet, or 2.13m, in both cases), that their stability was not seriously affected by the presence or absence of a stone vault: the thrusts of the vaults were easily absorbed by the bulk of the wall structure. In these conditions vaulting was not really adventurous, and this is why no technical advance followed their adoption of rib vaulting. In the Ile-de-France, on the other hand, architectural practice had remained comparatively archaic and the builders of that region stuck to the principle of lightweight construction, using thin walls still very much in the manner which had been current all over the northern half of France (Fig. 31) in the first half of the eleventh century.[28] When these Ile-de-France builders received from Normandy the method of rib vaulting and decided to use it, they refused to accept with it the heavy Norman walls, which they probably disliked intensely; and as a consequence vaulting became a more adventurous enterprise. To Norman minds it must have seemed an absurd gamble to try to combine in the same building the two contradictory ideas of total vaulting in stone on the one hand, and a systematic thinning out of the wall structure on the other. But Gothic architecture was the result of this inner contradiction. Attempting the absurd is a powerful stimulus—danger at any rate is one—and the pattern followed in the invention of Gothic was one of challenge and response: a sharp response to a self-made challenge.

The sector northwest of Paris, which was the sector of entry of rib vaulting, shows a first very typical series of reactions. If the wall itself was too weak, the piers at least could be made strong enough to receive the thrust of the vault without being pushed apart. Thus the first thing to do was to reinforce the piers by increasing their projection on the surface of the wall (Fig. 32), on the inside in the form of strong groups of engaged columns, on the outside in the form of bigger buttresses, the purpose being to give more depth to the supports. That was achieved from the very start at Saint-Etienne at Beauvais (Fig. 25), and repeated or improved upon soon

31. PARIS, SAINT-GERMAIN-DES-PRÉS, nave mid 11th c., originally unvaulted (17th c. vaults)

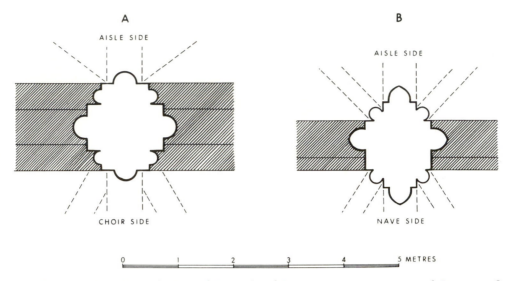

32. Comparative plans of piers of *A*. choir of Lessay, ca. 1105–1125, and *B*. nave of Saint-Etienne at Beauvais, E bay ca. 1130–1140. Hatching indicates thickness of walls.

after at Poissy, Bury, Airaines (Fig. 33) and in a long sequence of similar buildings,[29] stretching in time into the thirteenth century. In that way began the neat differentiation of Gothic structures into a framework of strong vertical members and a series of thin, rather unremarkable panels of wall between them: the combination of thinness with vaulting resulted in a much increased accentuation of the bay pattern of Romanesque times. At the same time, efforts were made to reduce the thrust of the vaults. The adoption of the pointed arch and of a pointed shape for the vault cells was a first step toward that end. But the thickness of the vault could be reduced too, and the best way of doing it was by building the vault in courses of well-cut stones of comparatively thin ashlar, instead of the thick rubble conglomerate normally used until then, particularly in England and Normandy. With thinner vaults it became possible to cover wider spans or, if the nave remained narrow, to reduce the size of the piers. Many such experiments were made in the early rib-vaulted buildings of Ile-de-France.

34

But the extremes of thinness are not found in the north-western sector (Beauvaisis, Vexin, and the meeting valleys of the Oise and Seine): they are found only in Paris itself and, to the south of Paris, in the plains of Beauce. The nave of Notre-Dame at Etampes (Fig. 34), which seems to have been covered from the start with pointed groin vaults just about the time (the mid 1130s) when the rib vault was arriving in that area, has almost paper-thin walls

33. AIRAINES, NOTRE-DAME, nave, ca. 1140

and round piers of small section, indicating a remarkably bold approach to the problems of stability.[30] In Paris, at Saint-Pierre de Montmartre (Fig. 35) (begun in 1133), that amazing thinness which goes—as at Etampes—with a very wide spacing of the piers, is compensated by heavily reinforced piers; but very soon after, in the central part of the choir of Saint-Martin-des-Champs, the piers again tend to become lighter. This is the tendency which came to a sudden climax with the choir of Saint-Denis (Fig. 38) (1140–1144),

34. ETAMPES, NOTRE-DAME, nave from S aisle, ca. 1135–1140 (enlarged clerestory windows a 19th c. modernization)

35. PARIS, SAINT-PIERRE-DE-MONTMARTRE, S side of nave: church founded 1134, dedicated 1147 (nave vaults rebuilt in 15th c.)

where the piers are reduced to thin columns and where the walls of the ambulatory chapels, whether seen from inside or from outside, appear unbelievably light, not only because of the vast windows which reduce the solid masonry to a mere margin in each bay panel but perhaps even more because everything the eye perceives is so thin in section: the windowsills and jambs, the applied colonnettes, the buttresses, the few spare moldings, and the shallow recesses of the relieving arches which on the outside bite into the remaining zones of wall. This lightness is all the more remarkable for the contrast it makes with the weightiness and plasticity of the narthex and façade (Figs. 36, 37).[31] Designed only a few years before, completed

36. SAINT-DENIS, W façade, begun ca. 1135, completed 1140

37. SAINT-DENIS, S side of narthex, ca. 1135–1140   38. SAINT-DENIS, N side of ambulatory, 1140–1144

in June 1140, five weeks before the choir was begun, this first work of Saint-Denis, which consisted in the building of a monumental western entrance to the church, belonged to another world of architectural expression. It was still part of that very first stage of Gothic experimentation, in which the emphasis was placed on the accentuation of the structural framework and the vigorous projection of the piers, achieved there with an exuberance of plastic richness which went back directly to English and Norman models;[32] while in the choir (Fig. 38) the old Ile-de-France ideal of light-weight construction emerged more than ever triumphant, freed

39

from all concessions to bulkiness, so radical even in its new solutions as to give an impression of slight unreality, as if matter had lost some of its normal ponderousness. This was the vindication of the attitude taken from the start by the builders of the Paris region: a new approach to the exploitation of rib vaulting was indeed possible.

In that architecture of thinness the problems of buttressing were bound to become of prime importance, since the walls had not enough bulk to absorb the thrusts of the vault. Buttresses of the ordinary type did not suffice: other, more powerful buttressing devices had to be imagined and fitted at the back of the nave walls, perpendicularly behind the points where the thrusts converged, to stay them. These new means of abutment were generally hidden under the aisle roofs, which came up to the level of the springers of the high vaults; but they took a variety of forms. Triangular spurs of wall falling on the inner half of the aisle vaults were used in the choir of Saint-Martin-des-Champs in Paris (Fig. 39) ca. 1140; that may have been a Burgundian idea, as the same method was also applied at Avallon at about the same date and survived for some time in that area, as in the nave of Pontigny. Another type of strengthening became more common after 1150: built over the transverse arches of the aisle or tribune vaults and completely hidden from sight under the lateral pent-roofs, triangular screens of wall acted as a transverse stiffening to bolster the head of each pier and link it with the corresponding buttress in the outer walls. This device, which may have been initiated at Saint-Denis itself, had the added advantage of simplifying the roof structure, since these screens of wall took the place of the principal rafters. The cathedral of Laon is a good example of that system, which was in fact widespread in the second half of the twelfth century and survived well into the thirteenth, when more modern techniques had been invented.

More interesting by reason of the new principle it involved and of its later developments was the system of quadrant arches which was used in the early 1160s at Saint-Germer (Fig. 124, p. 129), and in all probability also in Paris in the choir of Notre-Dame (1163–1180)

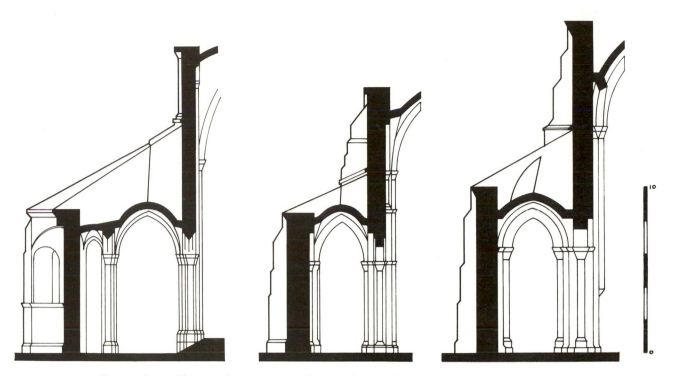

39. Comparison of buttressing systems (redrawn after A. Choisy): *1.* Paris, Saint-Martin-des-Champs, choir; *2.* Avallon, Saint-Lazare, nave; *3.* Pontigny, nave

before the alterations of the thirteenth century.[33] The idea of opposing a quadrant arch to the thrust of the vault for maximum economy in buttressing was the principle out of which the flying buttress was born; and these concealed arches were already hidden flying buttresses, although low placed and as a result less efficacious than the exterior flying buttress of later times.[34] But at that stage in the middle and in the third quarter of the twelfth century, Gothic builders had not yet come to realize that the point at which the vault thrusts acted most dangerously on the fabric, was situated higher than the level of the vault springers. When they became aware of the fact that their vaults tended to break at the point where the radius of the curve reaches an angle of about thirty degrees with the horizontal (this they realized about 1180), it became apparent to them that their buttressing devices were placed too low and could no longer remain hidden under the roofs of the aisles.[35] A radical step had to be taken and the first exterior flying-buttresses were built, thrown high over the roofs to apply their pressure against the walls at the height required.

This step marked the beginning of a second period of technical progress in the development of Gothic architecture. The first one had taken place between 1130 and 1145, when the problem of combining thinness with vaulting had had to be solved. The new challenge now was how to evolve the perfect system of buttressing, at once powerful and light. By 1180 or 1185, the first flying buttresses were being added to the choirs of Saint-Germain-des-Prés in Paris, of Saint-Leu-d'Esserent (Fig. 176, p. 182) in the Oise valley, in the form of a single arch at the head of each pier.[36] Fifteen years later, when the cathedrals of Chartres and Bourges were under construction, the flying-buttress had developed into full buttressing screens composed of two, three or even four quadrant arches, supported in the air by tall detached buttresses and combining their thrusts and their power of resistance to make possible heights hitherto impossible. Gothic engineering had achieved another major step forward. And this advance made the break between two periods of Gothic art, for all technical discoveries have a profound effect on the working of the artistic imagination. The invention of the flying buttress was implicit from the first in the approach taken by the builders of Ile-de-France to the problems of vaulted structures: their lightweight walls were so transparent to the thrusts that a transverse exterior counter was the natural answer; its direction, its movement were already written on the building in terms of threats to be opposed. Even before Gothic had really taken shape, the bold triangular spurs of Saint-Martin-des-Champs (Fig. 39) pointed already at the coming problem; after that, it was just a matter of finding the means of maximum efficiency. Reduced to an extreme of material thinness (sheets of glass and the skeleton of stone required to canalize the thrust), the architecture of the early thirteenth century, as symbolized by the choir of Soissons or the nave of Saint-Pierre at Chartres (Fig. 188, p. 194), shows the ultimate results of that initial postulate. Viollet-le-Duc was probably right in his general conception of Gothic as an art of visionary engineering.

42

What must, however, also be kept in mind is the uniqueness of historical situations. None of those experiments would ever have been made and Gothic, as a consequence, would never have taken shape if the Ile-de-France masters of the 1130s had been disposed to play safe or compromise and had accepted, together with the rib vault, the system of heavy Norman masonry. The part played by the Norman sources must therefore not be exaggerated. England and Normandy may have already possessed most of the component elements of Gothic architecture; but they did not possess the essential, that Ile-de-France obsession with thinness. And that obsession did not simply alter the solutions to a number of technical problems: by engendering a sense of danger and urgency, it provided the stimulus without which the invention of a new world of forms could not have happened.

40. SENS CATHEDRAL, choir, ca. 1145–1164 (Ward Archive)

CHAPTER II

Gothic Spaciousness

THERE IS a particular fascination in the study of the beginnings of a movement of art, of the moment when a few men suddenly feel that a new road can perhaps be opened in some unexpected direction, and that no choice is left to them but to start on that venture. We have all seen this happen, sometimes more than once, in our own day and we have always felt involved in it. But even with our contemporaries it is only too easy to miss some of their most deeply felt intentions; and when it comes to reliving the avant garde movements of eight hundred years ago, how can we be sure that we do not overlook something essential? Were the creators of Gothic interested only in vaulting impossibly thin structures? Were they caught up only by the excitement of daring technical experiments? Or was that just a means towards achievements of another order, and toward exactly what kind of achievements?

In nearly all great ages of architecture the final aim has been one of spatial magnificence: the creation of some new style of spaciousness. Often these new ideals were best expressed in the vastness of a single unified space, as in the colossal dome of Hadrian's Pantheon, in the combination of domes and semi-domes of Hagia Sophia, or, in later times, in the centralized compositions of Brunelleschi's dome of Florence or Michelangelo's dome of St. Peter's. Gothic architecture stands at the opposite end of the scale, for its approach to volume is through fragmentation and multiplicity. This was due, in a sense, to comparatively recent developments, such as the system of rib vaulting and the strong rhythm of bays

41. COMO, S. ABBONDIO, interior to E, nave ca. 1070–1095

evolved at the beginning of the Romanesque period. But it went back to the more fundamental fact that medieval architecture was based essentially on the basilican type of structure in which the interior is cut into parallel longitudinal vistas running on each side of a tall axial nave and separated by long repetitive sequences of identical piers and arches, so that the total space can be perceived only as the result of an addition of parts, a complex cumulative assemblage of distinct and numerous units. That original formula of longitudinal repetitions had simply been articulated further by the recent addition of a strong crosswise pattern of transverse bay divisions.

In the Romanesque period, effects of spaciousness had been achieved most commonly in that basilican class of building, by

46

42. PARAY-LE-MONIAL, view across nave from
S aisle, ca. 1110–1120

43. CLUNY, interior, ca. 1100–1130, by Lallemand
(Paris, Bibl. nat.)

enlarging the main arcade and thereby making the side aisles
merge as much as possible into the space of the nave. At Tournus
or in the nave of S. Abbondio at Como (Fig. 41), the height of the
arches was the preponderant factor; at Cluny III (Fig. 43) this basic
effect had been exploited on a much grander scale and given a
further dimension by the depth of the double aisles,[1] as already
suggested at S. Abbondio. In the absence of Cluny III, we can at
least get some idea of the Cluniac sense of space by looking at the
church of Paray-le-Monial (Fig. 42), where the aisles make an impression of total openness. What becomes there almost as noticeable as the height of the arches is their width: an element which was
to take particular prominence in certain groups of late Romanesque buildings, for instance in the Limousin (Beaulieu) or in the

47

southern part of Ile-de-France (nave of Notre-Dame at Etampes). In a totally different context, with heavy plastic forms and none of the sharpness of Paray, the nave of Durham (Fig. 44) is no less remarkable for the height and width of its arcades and for the way in which the tall volume of the aisles seems to be drawn towards the nave, instead of just simply running alongside it. And this was still the method followed in the first work of Saint-Denis, in the narthex of the late 1130s (Fig. 37, p. 39), which shows how an exceptionally tall arcade[2] was used to counteract the enormous bulk of the piers (they had to be heavy to carry the towers) and to establish a close relationship between the different spatial compartments.

44. Durham Cathedral, S side of nave, ca. 1115–1133

The Genesis of the Gothic Chevet:
Saint-Martin-des-Champs

But the new Gothic line of development as it manifested itself in the choirs of Saint-Martin-des-Champs and Saint-Denis was based on a completely different principle: instead of drawing the aisles inward towards the center and of concentrating for that effect on the treatment of the main arcade, the new Paris masters turned to a systematic enlargement of the lateral volumes by doubling the depth of ambulatory and aisles and changing their simple passage-like structure into an agglomeration of small vaulted units gravitating in a wide sweep around the choir. The new approach to spaciousness was one of expansion in width and its direct result was the creation of the wide Gothic *chevet* (Figs. 45, 46).

Most remarkable in these new Parisian designs of ca. 1140 was the location chosen within the building for that expansion of the interior space. Until then, the nave had been the enlargeable part of the church, the only part in fact which could be given double aisles. Common in the large basilicas of the Early Christian period, the five-aisled plan had been revived in Italy at the end of the tenth century, spreading rapidly around 1020 to places as far apart as Ripoll, Ghent and Orléans. A further revival was marked later in the eleventh century by the construction of Pisa Cathedral and of Cluny III, which started in France a whole series of double-aisled naves: Saint-Sernin at Toulouse, Souvigny, La Charité-sur-Loire, Saint-Martin at Tours, and even such comparatively small churches as Notre-Dame-du-Puy at Figeac in the mid-twelfth century. But in all these buildings it was only the nave that was affected by these enlargements—or, at most, the straight bays of the choir—while the east end remained untouched, surrounded only by a plain ambulatory on which opened a discontinuous series of small chapels.

At Saint-Martin-des-Champs on the other hand, when the choir was rebuilt under Prior Hugues I, between 1130 and 1142,[3] a double ambulatory was for the first time created, tracing a wide semicircle around the choir; and for the first time the chevet, that eastern termination of the church, was given more width than the nave itself. Since this was to become the rule in Gothic plans, the

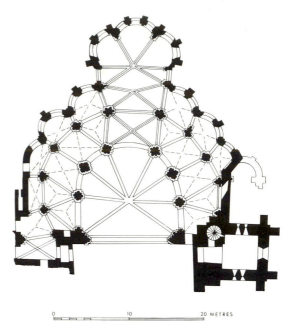

45. Paris, Saint-Martin-des-Champs, choir, ca. 1130–1145 (redrawn after H. Deneux)

0   10   20 METRES

46. Paris, Saint-Martin-des-Champs, choir, ca. 1130–1145

47. PARIS, SAINT-MARTIN-DES-CHAMPS, vaulting of axial bays of ambulatory, ca. 1135–1140

change which occurred then at Saint-Martin-des-Champs in the relative size of nave and choir takes on a truly historic significance. But one fact has to be stressed here, because it contradicts a commonly accepted opinion: the double ambulatory was not the outcome of the new ease afforded by the rib in handling vaults of complex shapes, since at Saint-Martin-des-Champs, where this enlargement was initiated, both ambulatories are groin vaulted (Fig. 52). The rib is used there too, but only in the central space of the choir, which was built last,[4] and in the axial chapel and the bays leading to it (Fig. 47). This shows that once again the rib has been made to explain too much in the genesis of Gothic architecture and that another essential element, that urge for spaciousness that was one of the motive forces in the creation of the new style, was ini-

51

tially unconnected with rib-vaulting. The urge has to be treated as an independent factor which was already at work in the Paris milieu when the rib arrived there in the mid-1130s. These two elements, rib and spaciousness (plus the element of lightness already discussed), became intimately linked in 1140 in the choir of Saint-Denis. It is therefore an appreciable piece of historical luck to find them appearing separately just before that momentous meeting, so that they can be discerned for what they actually were: distinct sources at the origins of the Gothic movement.

At Saint-Martin-des-Champs, the second ambulatory—the outer one—was not functionally an ambulatory at all, since it was not used for circulation: it fulfilled the rôle of a succession of contiguous chapels, the only difference being that they were linked laterally by open arches instead of being separated by solid walls; and certainly when seen from outside the general aspect of the volumes can be assimilated to that of a continuous series of chapels. This would seem to establish a connection between Saint-Martin-des-Champs and a type of chevet elaborated in Normandy at the end of the eleventh century: at the abbey church of Fécamp, dedicated in 1106, where the original structure survives on one side of the choir (Figs. 48, 49), and soon after that at the now destroyed cathedral of Avranches, dedicated in 1121, the ambulatory had been surrounded by an uninterrupted sequence of radiating chapels leaving no gaps between them, and differing in that respect from the usual Romanesque formula. Whatever their exact date (a dedication took place in 1133), the niche-like chapels of the old chevet of Thérouanne were most probably derived from that Norman series, even if their stylistic connections may have been more complex. But none of these buildings[5] possessed that essential feature of spatial openness, unencumbered by the earlier partitioning into separate chapels, which altered so profoundly the interior effect in the choir of Saint-Martin-des-Champs. The only way in which that essential change can be described is by using the term "double ambulatory," since a new zone of continuous space was added to the normal ambulatory space, beyond a second semicircle of piers; and surely the mere routine uses to which this

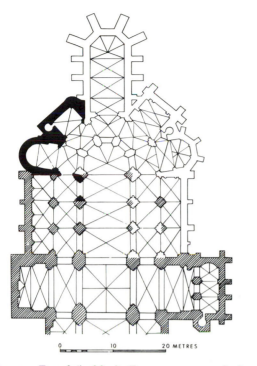

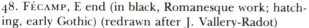

48. FÉCAMP, E end (in black, Romanesque work; hatching, early Gothic) (redrawn after J. Vallery-Radot)

49. FÉCAMP, E end from NE, chapels 1082–1106

new zone of space was put are less significant than the spatial purpose which alone can explain that interior redesigning of the whole chevet.

Without trying to reduce the rôle of invention, which seems to have been very great at Saint-Martin-des-Champs, the question of possible antecedents or at least of some first suggestions has to be raised. Can this idea of widening the choir in preference to the nave be traced back to some earlier experiments? It does not appear likely to have originated in Normandy or anywhere in the northern sector of France: it seems rather to have come to Paris from the Loire Valley, where it can be detected in a rather rudimentary form ca. 1130; and its sources lead beyond the Loire to the middle and southern section of France. Beside the ambulatory plan, the other classic method of composing the east end of a church, in Romanesque architecture, was the system of staggered apses initiated at Cluny II between 955 and 981.[6] In the richest

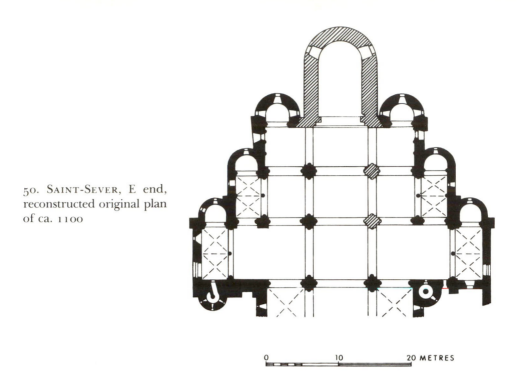

50. Saint-Sever, E end, reconstructed original plan of ca. 1100

0   10   20 METRES

51. Fontgombault, ambulatory and chapel on S side of choir, ca. 1125–1141

variant of this family of chevets, the seven-apse type, the first bays (or at least the first bay) of the choir were flanked on either side by two deep chapels; and if arches were opened between these chapels laterally, to make them communicate with each other and with the central part of the choir, a double-aisle effect was created. This never happened in the English branch of the series (St. Albans, York St. Mary's, or Binham), but it was done south of the Loire: at Châteaumeillant for instance (ca. 1120–1130) or, in the extreme south-west of France, at Saint-Sever (Fig. 50) on the river Adour, the first traceable example of that solution, begun before 1100.[7] Saint-Sever lies very far to the south and in a rather isolated position, although situated on one of the routes leading to Santiago; but it was the work of a Cluniac reformer and appears to have reflected direct Burgundian sources: not only Cluny II, but also the

52. PARIS, SAINT-MARTIN-DES-CHAMPS, S side of ambulatory, ca. 1130–1140

53. FONTGOMBAULT, E end, ca. 1125–1141

Carolingian crypts of Saint-Germain at Auxerre, which suggested the type of dual side-openings of the lateral chapels.

A more generalized effect of spaciousness was achieved when this partial widening of the choir, still restricted to its very first bays, became combined with the arcaded hemicycle of the ambulatory plan. This happened just before 1130 in the region of the plains of the Loire, at Fontgombault (Fig. 51), dedicated in 1141, and was repeated a few years later in the choir of Saint-Laumer (now Saint-Nicolas) at Blois, begun in 1138.[8] The choir of Saint-Martin-des-Champs was, in a sense, only a step further in that direction,

56

54. PARIS, SAINT-MARTIN-DES-CHAMPS, E end, ca. 1130–1145

and its exterior silhouette (Fig. 54) would seem to confirm that relationship: rather squat and short, two stories only in height, it appears close to Fontgombault (Fig. 53) and even to Fontgombault's prototype, the choir of Saint-Benoît-sur-Loire, in matters of volumes and proportions. But at Saint-Martin-des-Champs the space left vacant between the chapels has now been filled in, the volume has become continuous, with only slight indentations to suggest that it is still basically made up of chapels; and on this continuous volume the dominant motif is a continuous zone of windows.

This continuity of the lower zone of windows was an innova-

57

tion of considerable importance, since it was taken up again and further developed in the choir of Saint-Denis (1140–1144) and was considered by Abbot Suger himself as the most significant feature of the new style. In one of the few passages in which Suger refers specifically to the architecture of the buildings erected under his care, he selects for special praise "the wonderful and uninterrupted light of most sacred windows" which was diffused through the whole of the new choir.[9] At Saint-Martin-des-Champs the large axial chapel, which takes the shape of a trefoil, is surrounded by a sequence of nine windows separated only by narrow piers (Fig. 55), and ten more windows open on the curving bays of the ambulatory. From the center of the choir the eye follows the spreading curve of this long succession of windows to gain thereby an awareness of the

55. PARIS, SAINT-MARTIN-DES-CHAMPS, axial chapel, ca. 1130–1140

56. Saint-Denis, E end, lower stories 1140–1144, upper
stories rebuilt from 1231

57. Paris, Saint-Martin-des-Champs, E end, ca. 1130–
1145, by A. Lenoir

depth to that outer limit, which serves in turn to give a measure of the whole interior expanse. To this first perception must be added the actual spaciousness of the central part of the choir and the engulfing effect produced by the enlargement both in height and width of the axial arch of the hemicycle, opening on the disproportionately amplified eastern chapel, as if the choir was bursting open in the middle under the pressure of the expanding space of the building. This irregular, untidy but powerful vision stands on the threshold of the new architecture as a reminder of the end it was meant to achieve (Fig 46).

58. SAINT-DENIS, N side of ambulatory, 1140–1144

THE CHOIR OF SAINT-DENIS

Gothic architecture has often been defined, in the essence of its effort, as an architecture which aimed at being at the same time colossal and light, and the first manifestation of this dual character is generally considered to be the choir of Saint-Denis (Figs. 58, 59) as designed at Abbot Suger's request in 1140. As a statement of basic intents this formula can stand; it requires only two qualifications. The first is that size was not, for the men who conceived these structures, an abstract numerical value: the interest they took in increased dimensions was gauged in terms of the space enclosed.

59. SAINT-DENIS, S side of ambulatory, 1140–1144

The other necessary correction is that the new Gothic sense of spatial freedom, achieved so typically through the thinning out of all the elements of the structure, existed already at Saint-Martin-des-Champs. The choir of Saint-Denis has thus to be viewed as a second stage in a development which had already been started in another Parisian workshop a few years before. What remains now of Suger's choir at Saint-Denis is only the lower story: the ambulatory and chapels (and the crypt that carries them). Above that, instead of the present thirteenth-century superstructure (Fig. 56), has to be imagined something very much like the long roofs and short upper story of Saint-Martin-des-Champs (Fig. 57): somewhat taller but not so very different in silhouette.[10] What differs profoundly at Saint-Denis is the style of execution: the clear articulation of the surfaces and the elegant handwriting of moldings, jambs and buttresses; a dry rather than plastic style, sharp in its formal delineation. Otherwise, the effect of continuity of the windows, the wide sweep of the volumes, even the scallop-like outline of the outer walls were already to be found in the chevet of Saint-Martin-des-Champs.

These similarities should not however be too exclusively emphasized: the choir of Saint-Denis marked a decisive step forward, the passage from experiment to ultimate formulation. It was larger and more spacious, and more unified, the whole peripheral area of ambulatories and chapels now being on the same level as the choir itself (whereas at Saint-Martin-des-Champs five steps lead down into that outer zone). It was also more orderly and regular, with larger windows descending much lower and taking up the whole width of the bay, and with a uniform system of rib vaulting; and most noticeable of all was the consistent use in all its parts of the neatest and most concise of pier types: thin monolithic columns only 52 centimeters (20½ inches) in diameter (Fig. 58). The piers of the central part of the choir were altered in the 1230s, when they had to be made stronger to carry a much taller upper story; but originally the two colonnades, of twelve columns each, were almost certainly identical. Columns always accentuate the effect of spaciousness: being circular with no linear articulations and no axes, they do not break up the interior space, which turns around them, uninterrupted. This effect is further increased at Saint-Denis by the thinness of the columns and by their spacing, which tends to be very wide, except in the hemicycle. The choice of the column as the new form of support was another stylistic decision of the first importance: within ten years, it had become the usual type of Gothic pier and it remained so for at least fifty years, up to the end of the twelfth century; and even after Chartres had invented its new type of "quartered" columns (the *cantonné* pier), the plain cylindrical column was preserved in many series of buildings, well into the middle of the thirteenth century.

It has sometimes been said that the column, at Saint-Denis and in the buildings that followed, was a survival from Romanesque times.[11] But this is a complete historical error. In Romanesque architecture the normal type of support was the compound pier. The column belongs to a much older world; and the questions which have to be asked here are rather: what can explain that deliberate revival of the columnar supports of Antiquity? and more precisely, what sources are likely to have intervened? The immediate source appears to have been, at Saint-Denis, the Carolingian nave, which was considered Early Christian by Suger himself and by all his contemporaries. As early as the 1130s, when he was engaged in rebuilding the western parts of the church, Suger had been anxious to preserve this ancient type of support in the bays which were then added to the old Carolingian nave to link it with the new façade, built a little further forward.[12] When it came to enlarging the choir in 1140, the same idea remained valid and the same form of pier was repeated; but here the doubling up of the ambulatory created two concentric colonnades in the semicircular termination of the chevet and four parallel rows of columns in the straight bays. This repetition of colonnades had not been practised in Carolingian architecture; but it was common in Early Christian buildings and at Saint-Denis it seems to hark back to definite Roman models. Rome· had double colonnades in the aisles of its most famous fourth-century basilicas, S. Giovanni in Laterano, Old St. Peter's and S. Paolo fuori le mura; and with its columns arranged in concentric circles, the church of S. Stefano Rotondo, built in the second half of the fifth century, could also provide a suggestion, although on a

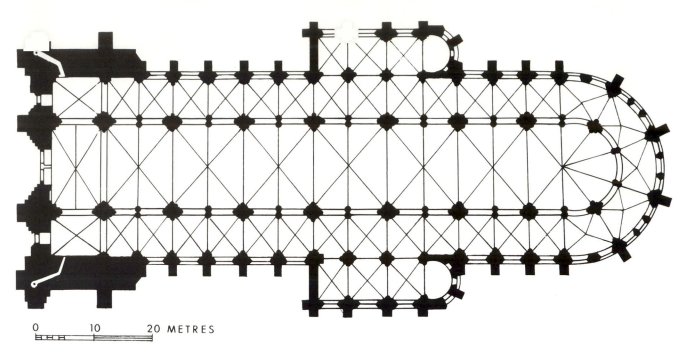

0   10   20 METRES

60. SENS CATHEDRAL, reconstructed original plan
See ADDENDUM following page 623.

much larger scale, for the double hemicycle of the chevet at Saint-Denis. A deliberate return to such prototypes seems all the more likely since at Sens Cathedral, a few years only after Saint-Denis, twin columns were used in a manner reminiscent of another Roman rotunda, this one of Constantinian date, the church of S. Costanza.[13] In view of these converging hints, it can probably be said that, in their desire to build spacious lightweight structures, in spite of stone vaulting and with the help of more refined methods of vault construction, the initiators of the new architecture became suddenly attracted by the solutions evolved in the thin timber-covered structures of the late Roman age; and this introduced a rather unexpected element into the pattern of speculations of early Gothic builders.

THE INTERIOR DESIGN OF SENS CATHEDRAL

Such was at least the Saint-Denis interpretation of the new feeling for spaciousness which was then developing. But this was not its only possible interpretation: in fact the first leaders of the Gothic movement seem to have used almost any form of increased spaciousness, and the building which stands out as the other major

64

creation of the 1140s, the cathedral of Sens (Fig. 40), was remarkably different from the choir of Saint-Denis in the handling of space. Instead of laying the stress, as had been done at Saint-Denis, on an effect of lateral expansion with double aisles and double ambulatories, Sens gave an absolute preponderance to the central space which was enlarged to a width of 15.25 m. (50 feet),[14] while the side volumes were reduced to a single aisle continued around the east end as a single ambulatory, probably without any chapel at all. The principle applied here was one of central, not of peripheral spaciousness; and to further concentrate the volumes, this wide nave was meant to remain unbroken in its longitudinal movement, since originally Sens had no transept (Fig. 60). The present transepts date only from the end of the fifteenth century and an effort should be made to forget their presence and recapture the obsessive singleness of purpose of the original structure. Halfway down the length of the building, in the position where a transept could have been expected, Sens had only two little side chapels flanking the aisles: a peculiarity which was to be repeated soon after in the church of Saint-Père at Chartres[15] but which was not unknown in the area, since it was present already in the choir of Saint-Thomas

61. SAINT-RÉVÉRIEN, nave, ca. 1130–1140

at Epernon, built ca. 1125. Actually the very type of these churches designed with an ambulatory but without transepts seems to have been a regional formula, particularly favored in the country south of Paris, between Seine and Loire, where it had begun a century before, in the Romanesque cathedrals of Chartres and Auxerre, and from where it had started spreading further afield in the early twelfth century, going as far as Avranches to the west[16] and Saint-Révérien (Fig. 61) (near Nevers) to the south.

It appears therefore that the cathedral of Sens should be linked to a wide background of still ill-identified tendencies. The building is actually less simple than it looks and even the chronology of the work raises some disconcerting problems. The local Chronicle of Saint-Pierre-le-Vif lists the rebuilding of Sens Cathedral among the first acts of Archbishop Henri le Sanglier, which suggest the possibility of an early start;[17] and this would seem confirmed by the successive changes of design which have left traces in

62. SENS CATHEDRAL, chapel of Saint Jean (lateral chapel on N side of choir), showing style of first design of Sens, ca. 1140

63. SENS CATHEDRAL, N side of ambulatory, showing pre- and post- 1145 work (Ward Archive)

the fabric. The outer walls of the aisles were obviously built first, at a time when no rib vaulting was contemplated over the aisles; the little side chapel which is preserved on the north side of the choir (the chapel of Saint Jean) still has a purely Romanesque character (Fig. 62); and it is quite evident that before the aisle walls were finished, their height was altered several times (Fig. 63). Even in their present form, after these alterations, these outer walls are in striking disagreement with the central structure of the choir and nave, which represents a new design in a decidedly Gothic style

67

certainly not earlier than the mid-1140s. The arrival of a new arch-bishop in 1142[18] would seem to correspond to that major change in the project. But the starting point should not be pushed back too far: ten years at most separated the two designs, and the essential break between them was made not so much by a time lag as by a change of stylistic allegiance: the most modern of styles succeeded what had been no more than a somewhat renovated version of the local Romanesque tradition. Certainly the final conception inher-ited from the first design some of its most remarkable features, such as the enormous width of the nave[19]—which was probably not meant at first to be vaulted—and the very idea of a plan without transept. The two successive layers of thought became inevitably interlocked. But once its existence has been recognized and its con-tribution defined, the first design should not be given an exagger-ated importance: what really counts at Sens, what creates the whole interior effect, is the treatment given to the central space, and that was the invention of the man who redesigned Sens Cathedral in the mid-1140s.

Compared with Saint-Denis, that vast nave of Sens assumes a particular significance, because it shows that no single formula and not even the prestige of Suger's Saint-Denis could exhaust the crea-tive power of the new Gothic urge for ordered spaciousness. What becomes at Sens the principle of the whole interior organization is the exact and regular delineation of huge blocks of space, almost square in plan and defined by the jutting out, on every second pair of piers, of strongly projecting groups of engaged columns and, joining them across the nave, of heavy transverse arches in two or-ders (Fig. 64). These colossal spatial units were just a new version of an old and prestigious form: the large square bays of Roman groin-vaulted structures, such as the Basilica of Maxentius or the *frigidaria* of the great Roman baths, a type of building common not only in Rome but in many cathedral cities of western Europe, since these were nearly all of Roman foundation (in Paris a fine example of such vaulting is still preserved, incorporated into the Musée de Cluny). Ever since the 1090s, the square Roman bay had haunted the imagination of the North Italian builders; and in its revived Lombardic form, rib vaulted and embracing two bays of the lower

64. SENS CATHEDRAL, nave. ca. 1145–1164 (Ward Archive)

elevation (Fig. 2, p. 6), it was already spreading in the early 1140s not only along the Rhine but also right across France, in the zone of plains which runs south of Paris from southern Champagne to the border of Brittany. The influence of Lombard architecture, of Rivolta d'Adda or of some similar structure of the 1120s or 1130s, seems fairly evident in the nave of Saint-Loup-de-Naud (Fig. 66), which has the same square four-part vaults over the main span, corresponding to two bays of aisles, and the same semicircular arches and low proportions as in Lombardy. The same type again basically, but this time with pointed arches and vaults, is found around 1145 or just after that date much further west, in the nave of Le Mans Cathedral (Fig. 65) and at Avénières (Fig. 67), outside Laval.[20] Closely related buildings of similar or later date, some obviously influenced by Sens, can be identified at Chartres, Corbeil, Provins, Voulton, Troyes and even, at the other end of the line, at Vannes in Brittany, making a remarkably consistent group which bars the map of France from east to west some fifty miles south of Paris, with Saint-Loup-de-Naud and Sens as its stylistic extremes.

65. Le Mans Cathedral, nave to W, ca. 1145–1158 (Ward Archive)

66. SAINT-LOUP-DE-NAUD, W bays of nave, ca. 1150–1160 (Ward Archive)

67. AVÉNIÈRES, choir ca. 1150, E bay of nave ca. 1160–1170

When placed against that historical background, it becomes quite clear that the final design of Sens was, in a sense, only the Gothic transfiguration of that popular regional formula which at that moment was just in the process of establishing itself in that area. All the other works which belonged to that movement were still Romanesque in character, although they were already touched in most cases by a proto-Gothic tendency to increase the openings and reinforce the supports. The transformation which took place at Sens involved the intervention of definitely Norman elements, such as the sexpartite vault and a well identifiable type of triforium, which can eventually be traced to the nave of Mont-Saint-Michel. The system of alternating piers also has often been treated as representing at Sens another of these ideas of Norman origin: and it is true that Normandy too had, since about 1050, her own tradition

71

of alternating supports. But this must not lead to a misreading of the evidence. At Sens the idea came from the local environment. This is proved by the use throughout the building of a most significant detail of constructional and spatial design: the heavy transverse arches of rectangular section which separate so firmly, at Sens, the double bays of vaulting. These heavy arches are absolutely unknown in the sexpartite vaults of Normandy, while on the other hand they constitute one of the constant characteristics of the Lombard double-bay formula; and their presence is sufficient to indicate from which direction the master of Sens received, in this matter, his initial impulse. Similar traditions of bay rhythm and of pier treatment simply made the insertion of certain Norman forms particularly easy to achieve.

But the importance of these Norman borrowings should not be overrated. The essential transfiguration of the structure was of another nature and came from a different source: it was due to the Parisian formation of the designer and to his complete adherence to the new Gothic movement. Sens is in many ways connected with Saint-Denis, it seems even to have combined in its design formal features which came from the two works of Saint-Denis: the narthex suggesting the very tall aisles and the plastic vigor of the major piers; while the more recent choir gave the columnar type of the intermediate piers, the brittle thinness of shafts and moldings, and the principle of destruction of all solid surfaces. In this sense and from the point of view of the development of the new style, the significance of Sens seems finally to be that, through the accident of a given program in which some basic dimensions were already fixed, and through the further accident of a late Romanesque movement touching that spot at that moment, a man who counted among the creators of the new architecture was made to conceive and materialize in bold technical terms a new vision of colossal spaciousness, which went far beyond anything attempted before that date in the Paris milieu.[21] But it must be remembered that in this new adventure the stress had remained on the conquest of space in width (not in height), as in all the early works of Gothic architecture.

68. Angoulême Cathedral, nave, ca. 1125–1150   69. Angers Cathedral, nave, begun ca. 1149–1152

The Importance of Width

If it was necessary to prove even more conclusively that this new spaciousness was really the basic revelation of Gothic architecture when it appeared on the European scene, it would suffice to take a glance at the first arrival of the new building system in western France—more precisely in Anjou and Poitou. These Angevin lands provided an ideal testing-ground, since an original set of building traditions prevented there the transplantation pure and simple of the architectural types used in the Ile-de-France sector. Begun ca. 1150, the cathedral of Angers[22] represents the gothicization of the type of the domed churches of Aquitaine (Figs. 68, 69), which had reached the Loire Valley at Fontevraud some ten or fifteen years before and constituted there the most modern form of

73

70. Comparative sections of Angoulême and Angers cathedrals

building. A simple comparison of size between Angers and Angoulême (Fig. 70), of which Fontevraud was the mere replica, shows such a change of scale that it is at first sight evident that the new style meant primarily an increased technical power and a much enlarged space. In the same way, when Gothic touched the hall-type church[23] of Poitou, as happened in 1162 when the new cathedral of Poitiers was begun, the volume enclosed by those tall triple naves of hall-churches became so continuous and disencumbered that the impression achieved was one of overwhelming spatial unity (Fig. 71). In this line of development, the climax was reached in the early thirteenth century when tall and thin columns, as in the choir of Saint-Serge at Angers (Fig. 280), took the place of the compound piers at Poitiers Cathedral.

We tend all too often to think of Gothic in terms of height, of vertical elongation, of an upward surge affecting the whole structure; but this seems to have been a secondary feature in the de-

74

71. POITIERS CATHEDRAL, choir, ca. 1162–1180

velopment of the new architecture. What Gothic meant at first was an ambitious conquest of width in a great multiplicity of manners: it was an art of wide, open volumes, in which light could play unhindered by walls or by solid partitions. It was only when width had been achieved that the next generation of architects embarked on the conquest of height. But throughout the Gothic centuries the greatest and most progressive architects were probably those who refused to become fascinated exclusively by the movement in height and were still attracted, in the terms used by Abbot Suger in the 1140s, by "the beauty of length and width."[24] This happened time and again, each time Gothic architecture had a chance to start afresh with a renewed sense of its original vitality: at Bourges and Chartres, at Albi and Barcelona, at Ely, at Schwäbisch-Gmünd. The whole history of Gothic invention could be reduced to an essential pulsation from periods of expansion in width to periods of ascension and tension in height. But all the major steps forward, all the great renewals of Gothic architecture, coincide with the ages of width.

72. Saint-Denis, angle of N transept and nave: transept and first three bays of nave ca. 1235–1245, rest of nave ca. 1260–1280

CHAPTER III

The Early Gothic Grid

OF THAT UNIQUE combination of tendencies which could not be found assembled anywhere else in Romanesque Europe and which by their convergence happened to turn Paris just before 1140 into a natural center of architectural invention, two basic components have so far been identified: one an ideal of lightweight construction applied to the handling of vaulted structures, and the other a yearning for increased spaciousness, with the feeling of freedom and power which results from the achievement of that kind of spatial conquest. But there was still another important tendency, a third aspect which was certainly no less essential in the minds of the men who created Gothic architecture: and that other element was a certain sense of architectural rhythm, a certain way of dividing and accenting constructed forms in space. Gothic is an architecture of multiplicity, it seems to have been guided throughout its history by a principle of fragmentation, and one of the characteristics of its development was the elaboration of a succession of grid systems. Expressions such as "network", "repetitive series", "all-over pattern" come up constantly in the analysis of Gothic forms. But finally all these various terms and concepts simply reflect the different facets of one and the same order of reality: the linear quality of the new architecture and the uses that could be made of it for purposes of formal expression.

79

That linear tendency was to reach a remarkable climax in the skeletal structures of the style known as Rayonnant Gothic, in the middle and second half of the thirteenth century; and it might be useful to look for a moment at one of these later buildings, the nave of Saint-Denis (Fig. 72) for instance, as it was rebuilt under Saint Louis from the 1230s.[1] In such buildings as this, one becomes immediately aware that the innumerable lines which seem to compose the whole fabric are not all of the same nature. They belong quite clearly to several different types. One type is represented by the tall vertical lines—actually groups of three thin shafts—which go right up from the ground to the vault: these mark the essential division of the nave into bays, that is, into a series of identical units, slices of space and vertical panels of elevation, which by addition make up the whole length of the nave. A second type, quite different in nature, is represented by the thin arches or ribs which underscore the shape and curvature of the vault. These lines are the outcome of the technique of rib vaulting, a method of vault construction which simplifies the actual building process of vaults of complex shape by dividing the vault surface into sections separately and successively built. A third element of linearity is introduced into the building by the window tracery, which fills the upper half of the nave elevation. This is another type of network again: a mere screenwork of mullions, a spiderweb of stone, which corresponds to a particular mode of treatment—or rather of negation—of the wall surface. And finally there is also a fourth type of lines: those which surround the piers up to the level of the main arcade. These tight clusters of verticals which make up the whole lower story of the structure are the product, this time, of a certain method of modeling in the round, which aims at hiding the actual volume of the piers by breaking them up into a repetition of very thin components.

It may be questionable from the point of view of historical method to insert into an account of the very beginnings of Gothic art the analysis of a building which was to come only one hundred years later and was unimaginable in 1140: this rather hazardous historical procedure may perhaps be excused on the grounds that it presents so convenient a way of demonstrating the multiplicity of different things we tend to cover under the terms "lines" or "linear values." But this anticipation must be wiped out of our minds and we must make the effort of becoming again men of the 1140s, when Gothic was just beginning to appear as an amazingly modern architecture and one which gave an increasing importance to linear effects and to all means of linear expression.

THE BASIC PATTERN OF BAYS

At that date the linear tendency was not new in the architecture of western Europe, for it had been building up for nearly a century and a half. Its first decisive manifestation was the division of naves into bays, which had been one of the first expressions of the novelty of Romanesque.

The appearance of a system of bays in the architecture of western Europe raises a tricky problem of origins, for the bay concept seems to have had two separate sources. On the one hand, it had been announced by a series of Late Antique experiments starting in the middle of the fourth century and common to many areas of the Roman Empire, from Africa to Syria and to the north Adriatic coastland, which had tended to impose a definite cadence of divisions upon the interior space of basilican structures by way of vertically rising pilasters or columns applied against the wall at equal intervals, in rhythms which varied from region to region.[2]

On the other hand, the bay concept seems to have been closely connected with the patterns of structural framework which had been evolved through the centuries in the utilitarian timber architecture of northern Europe.[3] By its very nature any wooden structure in length is formed of two parallel lines of timber uprights linked transversely across the median space (by tie beams) as well as in their longitudinal succession (by plates), the transverse linkage being by far the more strongly marked. The importance of the timber element has not always been recognized, but it seems difficult to deny that, by providing a ready model for a system of three-dimensional framing, the timber structures of northern Europe were bound to imprint in the mind of builders the image of a regular and increasingly gridlike division of space. The influence of that mental pattern seems to have proceeded in stages, affecting at first only the ground plan, then spreading its action into the third dimension and suggesting even perhaps the cadence of spacing of interior divisions. But the most decisive step in that development appears to have been the one that was taken in the Loire Valley shortly before 1000, when it was decided to divide all the main elevation walls throughout the larger stone buildings into clearly legible bay units by way of projecting pilasters or engaged columns rising vertically from the ground to the top of the walls.

The oldest building of that type, begun in the last decade of the tenth century, was the old Romanesque cathedral of Orléans,[4] known to us through two series of excavations and through a few drawings of the seventeenth century showing the old transept in 1623, just before its destruction (Fig. 73). Orléans marked the beginning of the systematic exploitation of linear accentuations in the stone architecture of medieval Europe, which was to transform the whole interior appearance of the traditional basilica by the addition of that new element of rhythm and of insistent regular repetition; and in this key building those two lines of origin seem to have converged. For if the grid-like nature of the new system of bays has close analogies with the regularity of pattern of timber structures— no doubt current then in that area as in the whole of northern France—the way in which the bay divisions were inscribed in space, the very type of those rectangular pilasters barring vertically the elevation, is most likely to have come from some late tenth-century building of northern Italy, such as the first Romanesque cathedral of Vicenza which was itself reviving a form used in the area four centuries earlier, in the churches of Grado.[5] So it appears that the stimulus of a contact with the Late Antique experiments had probably intervened decisively to initiate in late tenth-century France that new kind of instantly legible visual organization now imposed on the basilican structure. The attractiveness of this early bay formula is proved by its progressive propagation during the first half of the eleventh century in two large sectors of Europe. From the Loire Valley it soon started spreading in a north and northwesterly

73. ORLÉANS, old Romanesque cathedral, ruins of S transept in 1623, drawing by E. Martellange (Paris, Bibl. nat.)

74. JUMIÈGES, parish church, late 11th c. survival of earliest type of bay articulation

direction toward Normandy (Fig. 74) and the Ile-de-France (choir of Bernay, Jumièges, nave of Mont-Saint-Michel in Normandy; nave of Saint-Germain-des-Prés in Paris), occasionally reaching as far as the Rhineland (nave of Speyer as redesigned ca. 1050), then passing to England, where it took a firm hold as a result of the Norman Conquest.[6] But simultaneously another line of propagation can be observed, which spread the bay concept in a strip of countries around the western Mediterranean, from Catalonia to northern and central Italy.

In its earliest form the bay pattern remained purely two-dimensional, applied only to the flat surface of the nave walls; no visual link was yet established between the two sides of the nave, which ran their parallel courses unconnected. But while the diffusion of this first type was under way, the rhythm of the bays began to be extended three-dimensionally across the space of the nave: either (in the more southerly areas) through the use of barrel vaults with transverse arches which made the link between the elevations of the two walls, or (when a vaulted structure was not contemplated) through the use of diaphragm arches spanning the nave at intervals and dividing it into a succession of firmly boxed spaces. This last method of overall organization was the one that

75. JUMIÈGES, NOTRE-DAME, abbey church, reconstruction of nave with diaphragm arches, ca. 1052–1067 (choir begun ca. 1040)

was followed in the nave of the abbey church of Jumièges (1052–1067) (Figs. 75, 76), which preserves in the height of its walls clear indications of its original disposition.[7] On the other hand the bay-divided barrel-vaulted nave, which had been initiated in Catalonia and Burgundy in the 1030s and 1040s,[8] became the basis in the 1070s for the most impressive display of monumentality, both in scale and cadence, in the series known as the Pilgrimage Road Churches. At Santiago de Compostela, begun in 1078, at Saint-Sernin at Toulouse, begun a few years later, the regular beat of the transverse divisions which cut these tall naves into a succession of identical slices, reveals itself a most powerful principle of unification.[9]

76. Jumièges, Notre-Dame, ruins of nave, ca. 1052–1067

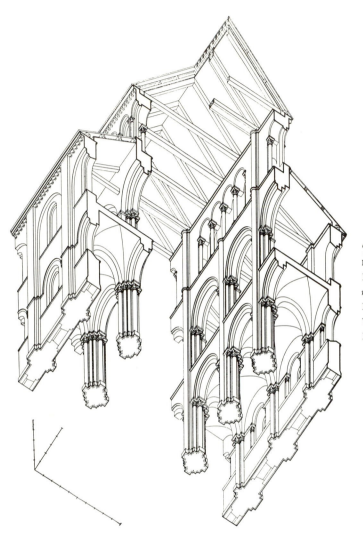

77. Caen, Saint-Etienne, iso-
metric reconstruction of nave bays
From E. Gall, *Die gotische Baukunst in Frank-
reich und Deutschland,* Leipzig, Klinkhardt &
Biermann Verlag, 1925 (drawing by P.
Walther), by kind permission of Klinkhardt &
Biermann, Braunschweig

An Increasing Linearization

But by that time Normandy and England were already adding to
the architectural vocabulary new elements of linear accentuation.
In the church of Saint-Etienne at Caen (Fig. 77), begun by Lan-
franc in 1067 and completed ca. 1085, the fragmentation of the
piers was very much increased (each pier being now composed of
ten members instead of four), the curve of the arches became
vigorously underlined by a marked recession in two orders, and an
upper loggia running along the top story of the elevation made a
little grille of detached colonnettes in front of the clerestory win-

dows.[10] Then, in the last years of the eleventh century, intervened the decisive innovation of rib vaulting, which made the vaults take a predominant part in the process of linear expression and, by subdividing each vault unit into four triangular compartments, introduced into Romanesque architecture a new principle of fragmentation.

How should the rib vault be viewed, and its effect evaluated? Was it merely one step further taken toward another kind of self-explanation? In some of its early versions, in Lombardy for instance, where the divisions of the nave are generally square in plan and where the vaults are domed in shape and therefore rather centered upon themselves, the ribs become essentially an element of tighter bay definition, binding within themselves more firmly than ever the individual double-bay units (Fig. 2, p. 6). However, in its most usual forms the rib vault is characterized by a particular ambivalence of expression, for it has the simultaneous effect of clearly separating the bays, by way of its transverse arches (or *doubleaux*), and at the same time of interweaving the bays in their succession in depth through the movement of their diagonals which, zigzagging from one side to the other, unify under that network of intersections the totality of the nave space (Figs. 7, 8, pp. 9, 11). With that combination of clarity and complexity, of division and unification, the rib vault opened to architecture a whole range of new possibilities in the handling of interior space.

But the relationship between space and line is not the only thing to be considered here: of equal importance were the relationships between line and mass, and between the vault ribs and the linear accents of other kinds that may appear on the other solid parts of the structure. Actually those other aspects seem to have been given great weight by the first users of the rib vault, at least in the English and north French series, and preoccupation with texture and with overall surface treatment was clearly in the mind of the man who took the momentous step of designing the first rib-vaulted building in the north Romanesque world, the master of the choir of Durham.

The subtle modeling that was given to the ribs themselves (an axial roll flanked on either side by a widely hollowed-out *chamfer*) shows that at Durham the linearization of the vault was only one aspect of a much more generalized display of linear expression. All parts of the structure were affected by it: the simple half-columns which separated the double bays of the elevation in the nave of Jumièges have grown at Durham into groupings of three engaged columns; a complete system of additional short shafts has been inserted at the level of the tribune story to support, independently from all other shafting, the diagonal ribs of the main vault; the arches of the main arcade are treated pictorially in a succession of small-scale moldings which pile up line after line on their undersurfaces, concealing the simple structure of the arches beneath bundles of fibrous stripings; even the big round piers, deliberately incised with colossal abstract motifs of spirals, chevrons and other ornamental patterns, have been turned into a field for further linear enrichment (Fig. 78).

Durham is an example of particular interest because here, at the very start of the movement which among other things was to lead to Gothic, one is made aware of the fact that in the matter of linear values the truly essential point is the relation between line and bulk. At Durham the linear accentuations remain on the surface; they do not penetrate deeply into the heavy masses of masonry which lie behind and which obviously constitute the real, solid structure. This is also evident, in a more simplified context, at Norwich Cathedral (begun in 1096), where shafts and moldings are a mere surface accident, a sort of cloak applied on a solid mass of piers and arches of wide rectangular section. This kind of surface modeling does not create a linear architecture and furthermore is entirely un-Gothic; whereas at Saint-Martin-des-Champs, a generation later, the effect is instantly recognizable as Gothic, because the projecting vertical members have almost exactly the same section as the wall itself (as can be judged from the thickness of the main arcade) and appear for that reason as essential components of the structure (Fig. 79). Thus it can probably be said that for linear accents to be properly Gothic they have to represent, and be conceived as representing, the very framework of the structure.

It would of course be wrong to imagine that all the earliest

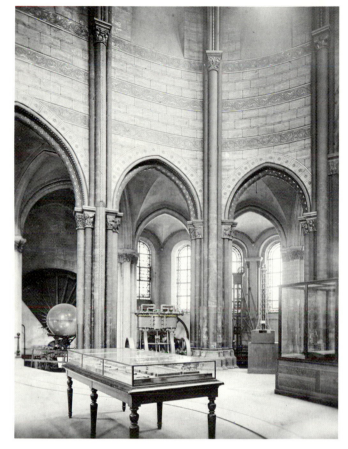

78. DURHAM CATHEDRAL, E side of N transept, main arcade and tribune story 1093–1104, vaulted ca. 1110–1115

79. PARIS, SAINT-MARTIN-DES-CHAMPS, piers of hemicycle, ca. 1140–1145

Gothic buildings were quite as thin as the choir of Saint-Martin-des-Champs. At Saint-Denis the two westernmost bays, generally known as the narthex, which are the oldest part of Abbot Suger's rebuilding (they were completed by 1140), are treated in a heavy, repetitive linear style (Fig. 80), with an apparently countless number of shafts compressed around the voluminous piers that carry the towers. But there again it is not just pure surface modeling: certain shafts stand out in bolder relief because they have to carry the diagonal ribs of the vault and are thus part of the essential framework.[11] Even in this early and rather untypical work the Gothic element of self-explanation was present.[12]

A Stereometric System

The first great masterpiece in which the new style of linearity can be clearly recognized is the choir of Saint-Denis, built only a few years later, between 1140 and 1144. The ideal of spaciousness expressed in that famous structure has been discussed in the preceding chapter, but what must be examined now is the use made there of linear values. Instead of the heavy insistence of the older work in the narthex, the ambulatory shows in its vaults a restrained, an almost purified use of single tubular delineations (Fig. 81), which articulate the vault with great clarity and finally converge in their downward movement onto the larger tubular forms of the columns. The same simplicity of line and of spacing is evident also on the outside (Fig. 82); and what can be perceived already in that outer sequence of windows is the impeccable regularity of the scanning, which provides a real optical module: a unit of measurement for the eye. Within, in the double ambulatory around the choir (Figs. 83, 84), this modular system progresses from two dimensions to a third, since it must now regulate the shape and structure of a

80. SAINT-DENIS, piers in narthex, ca. 1135–1140

81. SAINT-DENIS, ambulatory vaults, 1140–1144

82. SAINT-DENIS, exterior of chevet chapels, crypt and choir levels, 1140–1144

hollow volume, scanning it in depth as well as in its curvature. What emerges is a regular cagelike organization of the supports, imposing its pattern on the space enclosed and dividing it into an agglomeration of analogous intercommunicating units; and the viewer feels that he has been given the yardstick by which to measure in all direc-

91

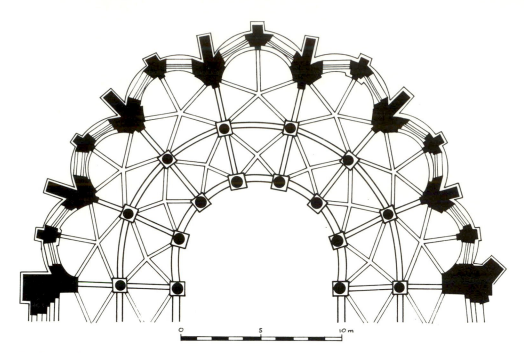

83. SAINT-DENIS, E end, 1140–1144

84. SAINT-DENIS, double ambulatory, 1140–1144

tions the continuous space around him.[13] This three-dimensional grid is stereometric in intention; it is a system of measurable spacing in width and depth, within a zone of unvarying height. As a linear system, it is obviously far removed from the surface networks then used in Norman England, in the chapter house of Much Wenlock, of ca. 1150 (Fig. 85) for instance;[14] and there is no mistaking the new intellectual quality given by the Gothic masters to that way of handling lines.

Was this beautiful clarity of the horizontal distribution of space matched by a similar regularity in the treatment of the elevation in height? The answer will always be a mystery since the upper stories of the choir vanished entirely in the thirteenth-century rebuilding and what remains of the twelfth-century structure is only its lower story: main arcade and aisles. However, the elevation of that Saint-Denis of Suger is not totally unknowable: some definite facts relating to some elements of it are on hand. Following the extensive excavations made by Sumner Crosby in the late 1940s, it has become possible to reconstruct fully the ground plan of the church as it had been conceived by Suger's architect (Fig. 86). The founda-

85. MUCH WENLOCK, chapter house, blind arcading on N wall, ca. 1150

tions uncovered west of the transept all along the walls of the present nave prove that at some time between 1144 and 1151 work had been started on a new nave (never completed) which was planned as a double-aisled structure as wide as the choir itself; but the bays of that projected nave were made much narrower than those of the choir, in order to preserve on either side of the central space of the nave the original sequence of columns of the old Carolingian basilica.[15] A reconstruction of that intended plan of the twelfth-century church reveals, on the one hand, that Saint-Denis, in the alignment of its volumes and the continuity of its five-aisled interior, was the prototype of the plan which was to be followed some twenty years later in Paris in the cathedral of Notre-Dame, that model of spatial regularity. On the other, a no less striking feature of the twelfth-century plan is the marked change in the rhythm of bays between the choir, conceived in terms of wide spacings, and the much tighter grid of the projected nave, commanded by the narrow Carolingian intercolumniations. As that change of rhythm coincided also with a change in height—the pavement of the choir, raised upon a crypt, being 3.18 m (10′5″) above that of the nave—it is obvious that a considerable difference of aspect must have been intended between the two elevations of the choir and nave. A sketch is necessary to make these differences clear (Fig. 87), and even if the figuration of the upper stories is of necessity hypothetical,[16] at least the dimensions of the main arcade story are documented, the bays of that story being short and broad in the choir—8.25 meters (27 feet) high for a width of 5.50 meters (18 feet), representing a 1:1.5 ratio—, tall and narrow in the nave—11.43 meters (37½ feet) high for a width of only 4 meters (13 feet), i.e. a 1:2.85 ratio. A full analysis of all the available data gives for Saint-Denis an overall image of greater complexity and a picture of more changeable patterns than would have seemed likely at first, on the mere consideration of what remains of the choir. On such an old historic site as the abbey of Saint-Denis the past was inevitably weighing upon the present, and it is not surprising that the twelfth century design had had to combine and interrelate, within the remarkable continuity of its composition of volumes, two different systems of regularity.[17]

94

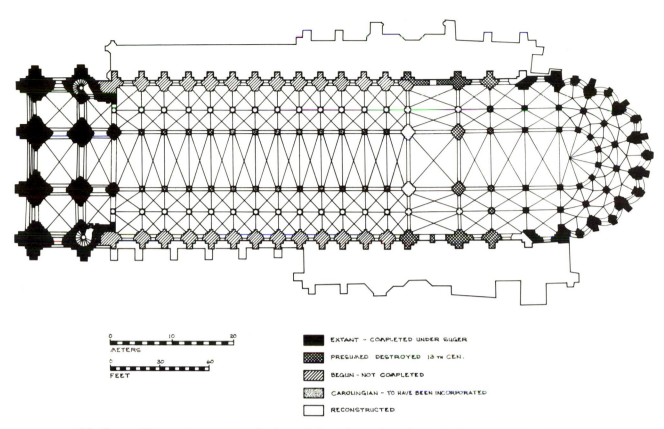

METERS

FEET

86. SAINT-DENIS, reconstructed plan of Suger's projected total rebuilding (vaulting hypothetical)

87. SAINT-DENIS, tentative reconstruction of elevation of Suger's church

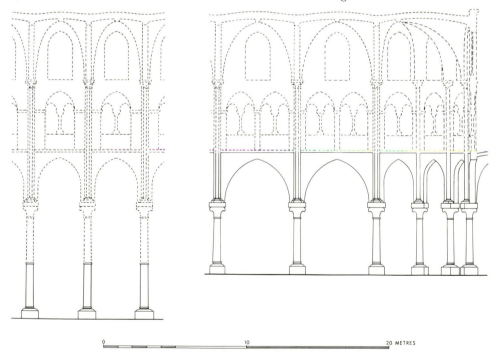

0   10   20 METRES

If Saint-Denis was the most decisive creation of its age, it left the door open for further invention. Other concepts of architectural ordering were elaborated by other builders, and they can be studied in slightly later buildings all situated within eighty miles to the south or to the north of Paris.

One of the most typical of these new compositions and the most elegant in the lightness of its linearity is the west façade of Chartres Cathedral—or rather, that façade as it was originally designed around 1145 (Figs. 90, 91).[18] Much more inventive in the

88. Saint-Denis, W façade, ca. 1135–1140

89. Saint-Denis, W façade in early 17th c., drawing by E. Martellange (Paris, Bibl. nat.)

arranging of its parts than the façade of Saint-Denis (Figs. 88, 89), which remained fairly close to the type of the Norman façades, the west front of Chartres shows the new love for line as such. The conventional two-tower pattern loses its weightiness to become multiplied in all its components, developing into a screen of vigor-

90. CHARTRES CATHEDRAL, W façade

91. CHARTRES CATHEDRAL, reconstruction of 12th c. façade, before fire of 1194

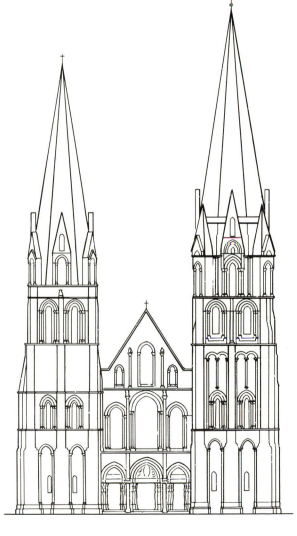

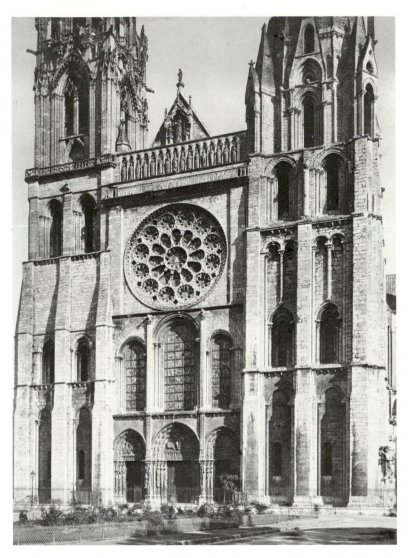

92. CHARTRES CATHEDRAL, W façade, showing rhythm of divisions in design of ca. 1145 (rose added ca. 1200)

ous vertical bars, which asserts itself as a principle of order (Fig. 92); and the sense of cadence that controls these repetitive series of forms and the intervals at which they are set recalls not the west front of Saint-Denis, but the exterior treatment of its east-end chapels (Fig. 82).

No less original in the implications of its mode of visual organization is Sens Cathedral (Fig. 93) which represents, in the main longitudinal body of its structure, another new design of the mid-

98

93. SENS CATHEDRAL, nave, ca. 1145–1164 (originally without transept)

1140s.[19] What has been analyzed so far has been the importance of Sens as defining one of the early forms of Gothic spaciousness in the succession of vast spatial units composing its nave. In matters of style, Sens has often been explained as being essentially Norman in conception because it uses the sexpartite vault, which had been invented at Caen (Fig. 94) some ten or fifteen years earlier and never before used outside Normandy; and because the type of its triforium in series of twin openings, known also in Norman England, derived in the final analysis from the nave of Mont-Saint-Michel (Fig. 95).[20] But those Norman ideas were employed at Sens in a new and specifically Gothic manner, and no earlier architect had anticipated the subtle way in which the master of Sens was to resolve the conflict between the double bays of the nave and the single bays of the aisles.

Sens Cathedral is the first Gothic building in which can be observed the systematic application of a simple numerical formula in the designing of a complex elevation. But first the original disposition of the upper stories must be restored (Fig. 96), and in particular the size and shape of the windows, which were increased in height in the thirteenth century. The pattern of the elevation is commanded by the number two and proceeds by dichotomy: the basic unit of spatial division being two bays coupled beneath a single vaulting unit, the nave walls on either side necessarily become organized into a succession of twin bay panels; and each individual bay is made to repeat that same principle of duality at different levels in its smaller-scale divisions. Above the tall arches of the main arcade, in the upper stories, the perforations of the wall seem to multiply themselves irresistibly in series of twos and fours, the clerestory having been composed in its original state of a pair of windows in each of its panels, while the triforium—which carries the formula to a climax—becomes a sequence of two groups of two openings per bay and repeats that arrangement twice in the length of each double bay unit. That mode of subdivision, which gives a distinct cadence to each story, with a metrical inversion in their progression, creates a pattern which is not just a play of lines but which reflects a concept of intellectual ordering. Even the intermediate piers on which the diptychs of bays of the elevation hinge

94. CAEN, SAINT-ETIENNE, sexpartite vaulting of nave, ca. 1130–1135 (Ward Archive)

95. MONT-SAINT-MICHEL, S side of nave, begun 1062

96. SENS CATHEDRAL, reconstruction of original elevation

are made up of two columns back to back, so that the binary grouping is extended to the very structure of the supports.

There is also at Sens another kind of subtlety which has to be taken into account in any attempt to assess the nature and inner structuring of this very first Gothic of the 1140s. In most of the other types of double bays, as in the nave of Le Mans Cathedral (Fig. 97), an ambiguous merging takes place within the bay when the eye travels from the lower to the upper stories: the main arcade shows two bays; but higher up, under the simple units of large quadripartite vaulting, the whole width of these two bays is gathered into one, so that each spatial unit becomes self-centered

97. LE MANS CATHEDRAL, N side of nave, ca. 1145–1158

98. SENS CATHEDRAL, N side of nave, ca. 1145–1164 (westernmost bay after 1170)

and detached from its neighbors, breaking the continuity of movement of the nave. But at Sens (Fig. 98) the whole elevation flows smoothly in a procession of single narrow bay units seeming to pass behind the reinforcements of the heavy piers required to support the vast vault units. This continuity of movement is made possible only by the use of the sexpartite vault, the intermediate rib of which splits the double bay in two from top to bottom and thereby preserves the autonomy of each single bay, in spite of their regular regrouping in twos for the purpose of spatial composition. The two rhythms are superimposed but are not made to merge; and this is probably why the sexpartite vault enjoyed such a success in the fifty years that followed: it gave a sort of contrapuntal movement of large divisions overlying the faster pace of the suite of single bays.[21] The later nave of Mantes (Fig. 147, p. 153) could be taken as another good illustration of this property of the sexpartite design.

THE FOUR-STORY GRID

However, the dominating formula of twelfth-century Gothic elevations was to be quite different in concept and pattern from the lengthwise pull of the rows of arches along which Sens had organized its rhythmical interweavings of forms, and that other pattern took another ten to fifteen years to develop. This delayed development means that it was not a product of the initial stage of Gothic that we have followed so far but of a second stage, in which a change of emphasis was already taking place, the main effort passing from extension of the building in width and length to its extension in height. This first Gothic conquest of height was achieved by the absorption of the type of the great Romanesque tribune churches, which had ceased well before 1140 to enjoy current use in its original centers of the Loire Valley and Normandy but had become increasingly popular in the northern provinces of France.[22] And actually the new formula of the Gothic tribune elevations was not invented in the Paris milieu, where Gothic had been born, but came from the northern fringe of the Ile-de-France and even from the still-Romanesque countries which lay north of Beauvais and north of the Aisne Valley.

The architecture which was developing at Soissons in the 1140s was in no way Gothic: the abbey church of Notre-Dame (Fig. 99) was still timber-roofed and its rich decoration was more plastic than linear, as can be seen from the type of its sculpted buttresses, documented in eighteenth-century drawings, which was repeated at Bruyères (Fig. 100) near Laon as late as 1160 or 1165. The development of the thin linear quality which marked the more advanced works of the Paris group met a considerable resistance in that area, which remained for a while half-way between the surface accentuations of the Anglo-Norman tradition and the sharp precision which had prevailed at Saint-Denis as early as 1140. The vanished east end of Mont-Notre-Dame (of which Courmelles is a reflection) (Figs. 101, 102), built probably ca. 1160, still displayed a great bulk of heavy masonry as one of the major elements of architectural power, in spite of the sharp linear subdivisions used particularly at tribune level.[23] It is in this intermediate style (Fig. 103), only half Gothic, that the tribune churches with their tall silhou-

99. SOISSONS, NOTRE-DAME, 17th c. drawing by M. Tinguy (Paris, Bibl. nat.)

100. BRUYÈRES-LES-LAON, E end, ca. 1160

101. MONT-NOTRE-DAME, ruins of chevet of ca. 1160, 18th c. water color (Paris, Bibl. nat.)

102. COURMELLES, apse, ca. 1160–1170

103. CHÂLONS-SUR-MARNE, NOTRE-DAME-EN-VAUX, end wall of S transept, ca. 1160–1170 (upper story ca. 1190)

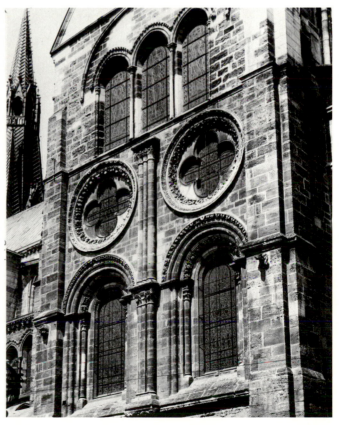

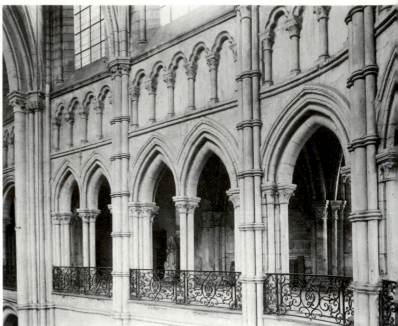

105. NOYON CATHEDRAL, tribune story of choir, designed ca. 1160, built mostly ca. 1175–1185

104. NOYON CATHEDRAL, chevet, ca. 1150–1185

ette—so different from the rather squat proportions of Saint-Martin-des-Champs, Sens, and no doubt also Saint-Denis—came to be entirely rib vaulted and turned progressively to a more orthodox Gothic style. But even at Noyon (Fig. 104), which is in some ways so closely related to Saint-Denis, the treatment of the windows as rich motifs enclosed in heavy linear frames slightly staggered in depth, the repetitive moldings of the cornices and string courses, and inside in the choir, the sculptural profiles of the tribune arches (Fig. 105) and of the hood molds that underline them, still recall the old concepts of the linear values as inseparable from plastic enrichment and as surface ornament rather than as the direct reflection of an articulated structure.[24] It was only much later, perhaps just a few years before 1170, that the ideal of thin linearity gained currency in that northern sector of France. The choir of Noyon was actually completed only in 1185, but the design of the upper stories went back to ca. 1160 at the latest and was rather self-consciously followed twenty years later. And the interesting thing is that this design already included an elevation in four stories (Fig. 106): main arcade, tribunes, triforium, and clerestory windows; that is, the formula which was to provide the ideal gridwork for the development in height of buildings.

The four-story elevation was not a new invention at that date, but it had been until then a rare solution. It had made its first ap-

106. Noyon Cathedral, choir, ca. 1150–1185, elevation designed ca. 1160

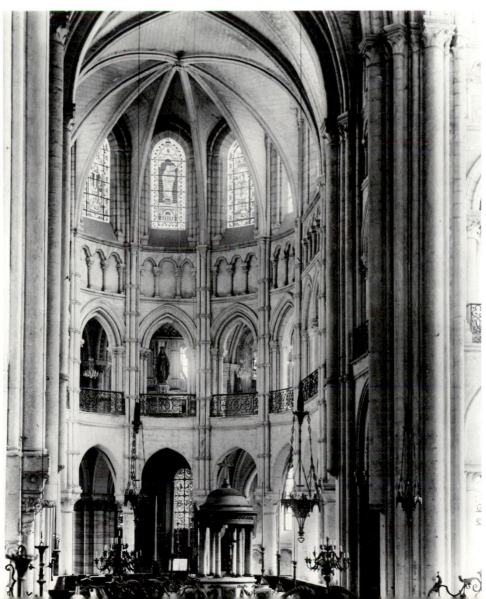

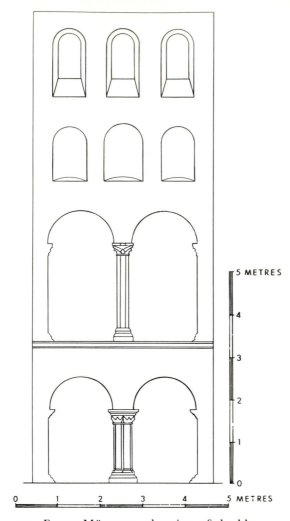

107. ESSEN MÜNSTER, elevation of double bay of choir, ca. 1039–1051
Redrawn after W. Zimmermann, *Karolingische und Ottonische Kunst*, Wiesbaden, 1957, 153, fig. 35, by kind permission of Franz Steiner Verlag

108. TEWKESBURY, E side of S transept, ca. 1090–1120

pearance, as an exceptional variation on a late Ottonian type of east end, in the short choir of Essen (Fig. 107) in the mid-eleventh century.[25] Following the Norman Conquest, which had opened England to all kinds of artistic influences, the principle of the four-story elevation had been imported into the west of England late in the eleventh century and adapted there both to vaulting and to the technique of thick Norman construction, in the ambulatory choir of Tewkesbury (Fig. 108), begun ca. 1090.[26] A generation or so later, in the second quarter of the twelfth century, it suddenly took a firm hold in what is now western Belgium, on both sides of the Scheldt River in the counties of Flanders (then attached to the French kingdom) and Hainault (then part of the Holy Roman Empire): the destroyed church of Sint Donaas (Saint-Donatien) at Bruges (begun probably around 1130 and built from west to east), the nave (begun ca. 1135–1140) of Tournai Cathedral (Fig. 109) and the transepts (Fig. 110) built immediately after (ca. 1160) initiated the decisive extension of the four-story elevation from end to end of vast buildings. There were considerable differences in the handling between Bruges and Tournai of the formula, and at Tournai itself between the nave and the transepts: differences that involved proportions, pier types, the whole elevation pattern, even the nature and appearance of the inserted fourth story. The idea was thus in a state of active experimentation. It has been proved that in the church of Sint Donaas at Bruges—one more of those churches which were pulled down during the French Revolution— the triforium story was made up of a succession of semicircular niches,[27] very much in the manner of the choir at Essen. In the nave of Tournai, the additional story is a continuous horizontal

109. TOURNAI CATHEDRAL, nave, begun ca. 1135–1140

110. TOURNAI CATHEDRAL, N transept, begun ca. 1160

arcading, the whole nave elevation being treated in successive horizontal zones of heavy arches which recall a Roman viaduct. But in the transepts, raised some twenty years later, the elevation is quite different, and not only because the main arcade is so much taller and the proportions therefore altered: the triforium which surmounts the tribunes has become a wall passage in the English manner, as it was to be in most of the great Gothic churches of the 1160s and 1170s.[28]

It was from Bruges and Tournai that this four-story elevation passed to northern France and became, within a very short time, assimilated into the new Gothic vocabulary—largely, we can imagine, because it gave a possibility of greater height and provided, with its additional horizontal divisions, the elements of a richer grid. The first example of a four-story elevation in a Gothic context was probably the nave of a building now destroyed, the old cathedral of Cambrai,[29] first Gothic outpost on the banks of the Scheldt River. Begun in 1150, the nave of Cambrai was very tall (32 meters or 105 feet); we know that its structure was thin, which rules out the possibility of a wall passage; but in the absence of any graphic document giving a view of the interior, it is impossible to say what was the appearance of its fourth story. The two surviving examples of the early adoption of the four-story pattern in Gothic workshops, the choirs of Saint-Germer and Noyon, both slightly later than Cambrai,[30] show the diversity of solutions that still prevailed up to the early 1160s. At Saint-Germer (Fig. 111) the additional story, which is composed of a succession of isolated rectangular openings (now blocked), one in each bay, is accentuated by a bold horizontal cornice running immediately above, at the foot of the clerestory windows; and in the choir of Noyon, where the additional story becomes a blind arcading, two horizontal stringcourses outline it above and below, insisting on the presence of that new element added to the traditional sequence of stories. But in neither case is the structure made thick enough to admit of a two-layer treatment at the level of that new triforium story.

It was only after 1160 or even 1165 in such buildings as the cathedrals of Arras and Laon, that the system applied in the transepts of Tournai, with the play in depth of its triforium passage, influenced Gothic builders. Begun in the mid-1160s, Laon[31] provides the classic type of this new formula of tribune elevations (Fig. 114, p. 116), in which the multiplicity of stories gave the means of answering in height, in the vertical plane of the nave walls, the regular gridwork in width of the plan of Saint-Denis. And the rapid success of that satisfying new pattern is probably the reason why Gothic entered, in the course of the 1160s, a period of comparative stabilization. The principle of analytical partitioning, that Gothic idea of a tight-woven network of small units, could now easily be applied to the extension of the naves in height, as well as to their horizontal extension on the ground: a complete and consistent system was now at hand, and it was to dominate for more than twenty years the vision and the experiments of Gothic architects.

111. SAINT-GERMER, choir, begun shortly before 1160

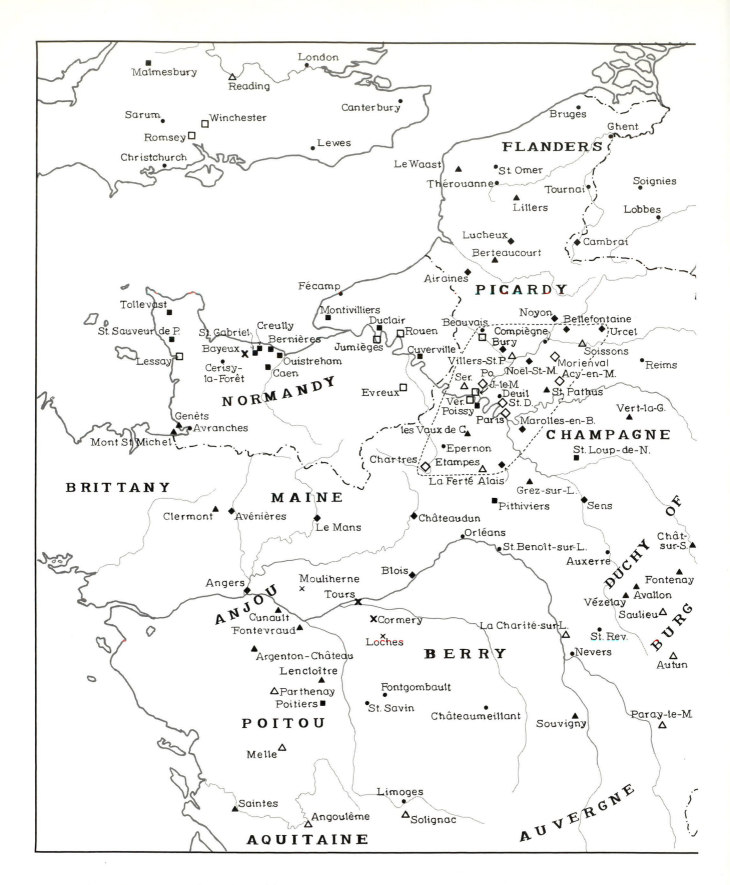

112. MAP: The Genesis of Gothic Architecture (up to ca. 1150)

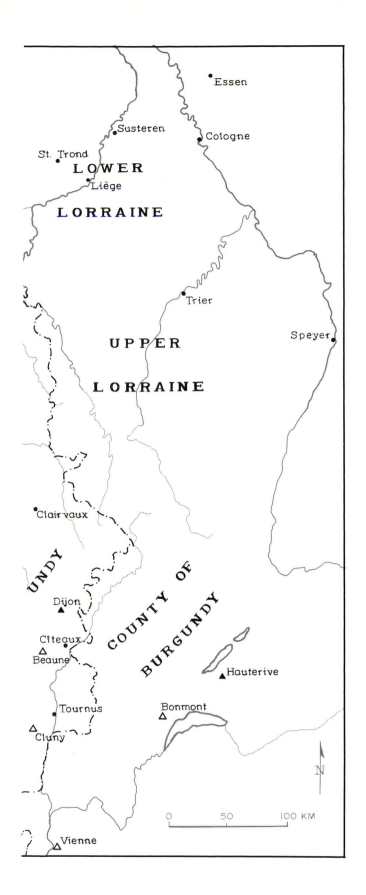

LEGEND

Symbols used

△   Early pointed arches, up to later 1130s

▲   Early pointed arches, late 1130s to early 1150s

□   Early rib vaults, up to the later 1130s

■   Early rib vaults, late 1130s to early 1150s

✕   Ribbed cloister vaults, up to the later 1130s

✗   Ribbed cloister vaults, late 1130s to early 1150s

•   Other Romanesque buildings

◇   Buildings combining pointed arch and rib vault, up to ca. 1140

◆   Buildings combining pointed arch and rib vault, 1140s and early 1150s

Limits indicated

—·—·   Limits of the Holy Roman Empire and of the Anglo-Norman kingdom

-------   Area of formation of Gothic architecture

Abbreviations

Acy-en-M.	Acy-en-Multien
La Charité-sur-L.	La Charité-sur-Loire
Chât.-sur-S.	Châtillon-sur-Seine
Grez-sur-L.	Grez-sur-Loing
J.-le-M.	Jouy-le-Moutier
Marolles-en-B.	Marolles-en-Brie
Noël-St.-M.	Noël-Saint-Martin
Paray-le-M.	Paray-le-Monial
Po.	Pontoise
St.Benoît-sur-L.	Saint-Benoît-sur-Loire
St.D.	Saint-Denis
St.Loup-de-N.	Saint-Loup-de-Naud
St.Rev.	Saint-Revérien
St.Sauveur-de-P.	Saint-Sauveur-de-Pierrepont
Ser.	Seraincourt
les Vaux-de-C.	les Vaux-de-Cernay
Ver.	Verneuil-sur-Seine
Vert-la-G.	Vert-la-Gravelle
Villers-St.P.	Villers-Saint-Paul

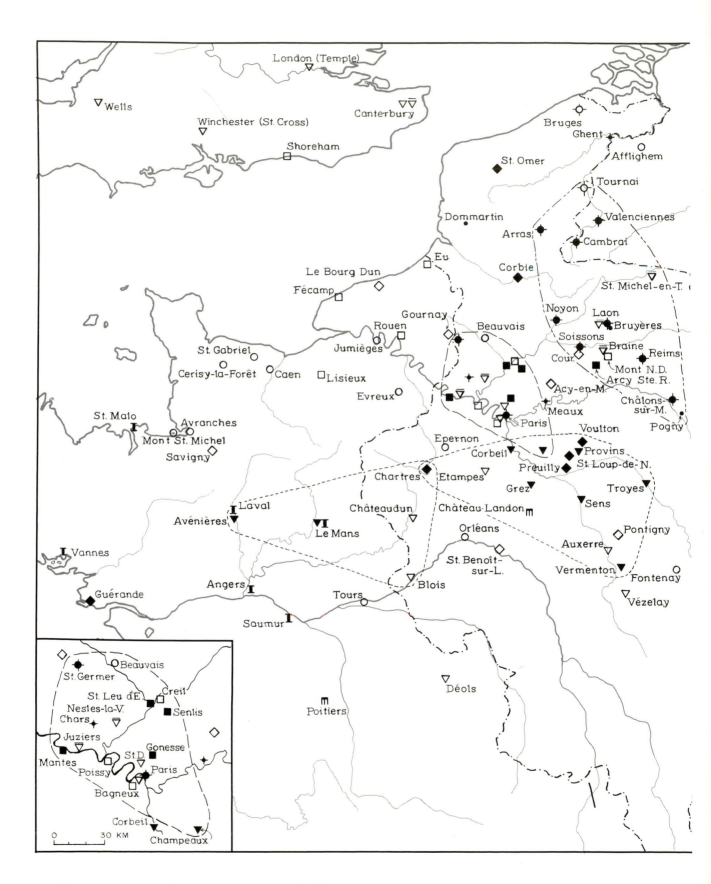

113. MAP: Early Gothic Architecture (second half of the 12th century)

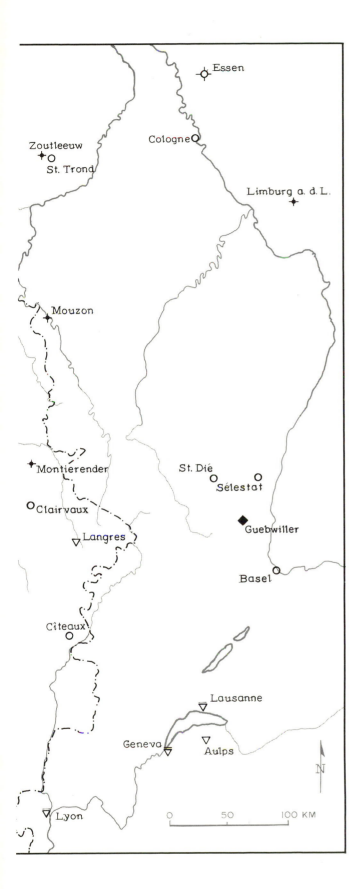

LEGEND

In this map the stress has been placed on two main features: the four-story elevation and the alternation of supports.

Symbols used

○	Romanesque buildings
◇	Romanesque examples of the four-story elevation
✦	Gothic four-story elevations up to ca.1190–1195
✚	Later examples of the four-story elevation
■	Tribune (or false-tribune) elevations with alternation of supports
□	Tribune (or false-tribune) elevations without alternation
▼	Triforium elevations with alternation
▽	Triforium elevations without alternation
▽̄	Triforium elevations of the Braine type
◆	Two-story elevations with alternation
◇	Two-story elevations without alternation
•	Other early Gothic buildings
I	Aisleless naves
⊓	Hall structures

Limits indicated

—·—·— Limits of the Holy Roman Empire and of the Angevin lands, ca.1155–1160

——·—— Limits of the Northern Group, ca.1190

— — — Limits of the Central (Paris) Group, ca.1190

------- Limits of the Southern Group proper (with plan and triforium of the Sens type), ca.1190, and of its westerly variant

Abbreviations

Acy-en-M.	Acy-en-Multien
Arcy-Ste.-R.	Arcy-Sainte-Restitue
Châlons-sur-M.	Châlons-sur-Marne
Cour.	Courmelles
Limburg a.d.L.	Limburg-an-der-Lahn
Mont N.D.	Mont-Notre-Dame
Nesles-la-V.	Nesles-la-Vallée
St.Benoît-sur-L.	Saint-Benoît-sur-Loire
St.D.	Saint-Denis
St.Leu d'E.	Saint-Leu d'Esserent
St.Loup-de-N.	Saint-Loup-de-Naud
St.Michel-en-T.	Saint-Michel-en-Thiérache

114. Laon Cathedral, S side of choir and S transept from crossing, ca. 1165–1175

CHAPTER IV

A First Gothic System, ca. 1160-1180

THE BEGINNINGS of Gothic architecture have to first be analyzed in purely architectural terms: in terms of light-weight structures, of spaciousness increased and reorganized, and of a new play of linear rhythms involving new kinds of repetitive effects. This technical and formal approach of necessity takes precedence, because it is in such terms that new concepts of art take shape in the mind of their inventors. Art is, after all, the creation of artists, not of statesmen or philosophers. But art is closely linked, and at a very deep level, with all the other aspects of historical life and it would be wrong to neglect these connections.

The many studies which have been made in the last forty years on the personality of Abbot Suger and on the historic significance of the choir of Saint-Denis[1] have all placed insistence on the direct relationship which must be recognized between that great architectural work—the first articulate manifestation of the new ideal in art—and the religious and philosophical ideas expressed by Suger in his writings. Not that Suger was a philosopher, but he crystallized from the complex metaphysics he found in the writings then attributed mistakenly to Saint Denis a concept of spiritual ascension toward the understanding of God through the physical medium of the contemplation of light. And it is this radiance of light, diffused through an uninterrupted sequence of unusually large windows, that Suger extols as the great splendor of the new choir built at his command and certainly with the intention of materializing the Dionysian metaphysics of light.

It was a fortunate superimposition of errors which assembled at that time in the figure of a single Saint Denis, patron saint of Paris, a composite of three historical personages: Dionysius the Areopagite, convert and disciple of Saint Paul in the first century; Dionysius, first bishop of Paris and a martyr, in whose honor the abbey of Saint-Denis had been founded; and a great theologian, then believed to have been Dionysius the Areopagite, but now known to be a late fifth-century Syrian, thereby attracting to himself the scholarly nickname of the Pseudo Areopagite. This overlay of Areopagite and Pseudo-Areopagite and their identification with Dionysius, martyred bishop of Paris, furnished the abbey of Saint-Denis with the most prestigious background of culture of medieval times and reflected its brilliance upon the nascent Gothic.

Further elements could be added to the picture, and one should be aware in particular of the importance of the political conjuncture which surrounded the rebuilding of Saint-Denis.[2] In the hands of Suger, the abbey and its patron saint were then becoming the center of an elaborate ideological system which was in fact as political as religious in intent, for Suger used it as a tool to establish the unquestioned pre-eminence of the Capetian monarchy and widen its popular appeal. Although the use of political explanations has always to be handled with caution in art history, it seems fairly evident that Saint-Denis under Suger-the-Abbot could not escape being influenced by the grand design of Suger-the-Statesman; and this is what gave in those days to everything connected with the abbey of Saint-Denis an exceptional significance. The renewed interest taken in Dionysian thought, particularly its theology of light; the image created by Louis VI when he decided to dramatize his alliance with the Church by proclaiming Saint Denis the special patron of his kingdom, in a sense his overlord, going to battle under his banner; the fact that Louis, taking full advantage of Suger's abilities, had made the abbey a main center of decision in the realm; the great historical compilations written at Saint-Denis under Suger's initiative, and the additions made to the legend of Charlemagne, who was now consciously pictured as the prototype of the ideal Capetian king: all this aura of inspired leadership created around Saint-Denis is indeed likely to have sharpened the imagination of the artist who had to design a building as new and exciting as this revitalized concept of allied spiritual and political power.

Certain combinations of circumstances undoubtedly favor artistic creation; and here an even wider view should be taken of the political situation in northern France, since it was not only Saint-Denis but the whole of Capetian Ile-de-France that was involved in this sudden release of inventiveness. Coming on top of the progressive realization of the results achieved through the policy of Louis VI and his curbing of feudal anarchy, a feeling of particular optimism seems to have crystallized around the year 1137, when the son of Louis VI—who became Louis VII a few months later—married Eleanor, heiress of the vast domains of Aquitaine. Through this marriage, which was the greatest political success of the Capetian monarchy, an unexpected fusion between North and South appeared to bring within the limits of a near future the unification of the whole kingdom of France. We know now that the attempt was to fail after only fifteen years, but for the generation of the 1140s this idea that a new era was opening must have been a very real stimulant; and the boldness and confidence of the first Gothic creations (Saint-Martin-des-Champs, Saint-Denis, Sens) should probably be placed against that background of fast-growing power.

On the other hand, after 1152, that is, after the divorce of Eleanor and Louis VII, when the dream dissolved, Paris and its region lost their exclusive leadership in the development of the new style, which was more and more attracted toward the north and northeast margins of the Royal Domain and beyond them toward the industrial towns of southern Flanders and the chain of smaller commercial centers which linked them with southern Champagne and its Fairs: after the 1150s the great trade routes drew toward the north the creative power which in the 1140s was centered around Paris. Of course the geographical location of art centers is the result of a complex interaction of forces and it would be vain to pretend that the facts just mentioned are a sufficient explanation. But it remains true that in the period which followed the first flash of creation, between approximately 1160 and 1180, when Gothic architecture enjoyed a first golden age, the pattern of distribution of the new architecture (Fig. 113, p. 114) was quite different from what it had been some fifteen or twenty years before.[3]

THREE SCHOOLS OF GOTHIC

One of the remarkable characteristics of that period—apart from the great number of works which by then were being produced in the new style—was the breaking up of the original Gothic milieu as it began to expand into what should be recognized as three distinct architectural schools. In the southern part of Ile-de-France and Champagne, in a zone stretching west to east from Chartres to

115. Château-Landon, Notre-Dame, hall choir, ca. 1160

Troyes, the influence of Sens remains supreme for nearly fifty years. This did not exclude the existence of other kinds of structures, such as the choir of quasi-hall type of Notre-Dame at Etampes or the full hall type of Château-Landon (Fig. 115); but most of the churches of some importance repeated the principal features of the Sens formula. They favored the plan without transept, which brought about a massive simplification of the buildings by reducing them to a continuous longitudinal movement, without even the momentary break of a crossing. Examples of this plan are: Saint-Père (now Saint-Pierre) at Chartres (Fig. 116.A), the lower parts of which are still of mid-twelfth century date; Saint-Quiriace at Provins, founded in 1157 by Count Henry I of Champagne; Voulton near Provins, of ca. 1180; and at Troyes, the now destroyed church of Saint-Etienne, another foundation of Henry I of Champagne.[4]

Derived from Sens also was the general use of alternating supports, stressing the division of the interior space into large double-bay units.[5] In a few cases (at Provins, Saint-Père at Chartres, Voulton) one of these spatial units was even further enlarged to make it encompass three bays instead of two; and in the same way as sexpartite vaults had to be used to cover the more usual double bays, octopartite vaults had to be invented to cover these triple bays (Figs. 117, 118). As these enlarged triple units were always restricted to the choir and never repeated in other parts of the church, it seems fairly clear that they had a precise symbolic significance and were meant to represent the Trinity.

The last feature of that Sens group was a preference for rather wide and low general proportions. These churches do not rise very high: repeating the Sens pattern of elevation, they insert only a narrow triforium between the main arcade and the upper windows;[6] not one building in all that area south of Paris used the tribune elevation which was so popular further north and gave so much more height to the buildings. Practically uninfluenced by the developments which were taking place elsewhere,[7] this southern sector of Gothic Ile-de-France, after its initial originality, settled into set formulas which allowed only for minor embroideries upon its dominant themes.

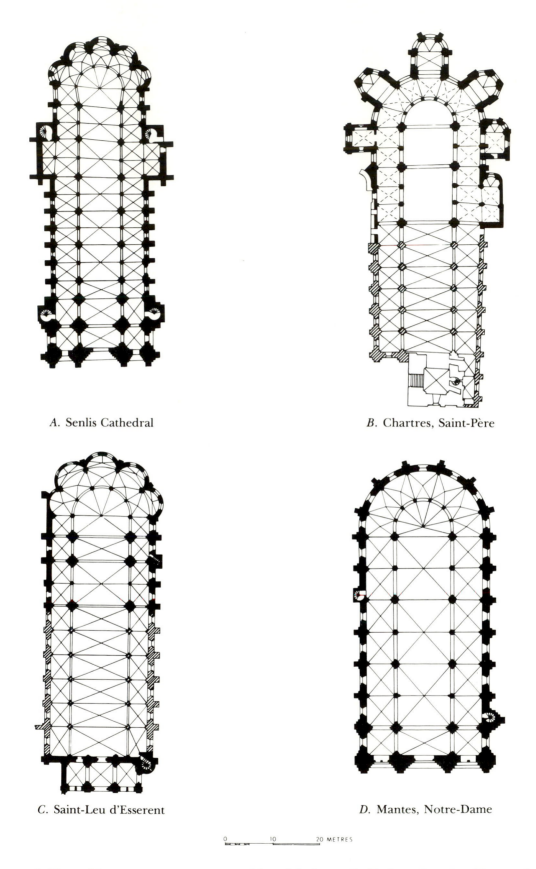

A. Senlis Cathedral

B. Chartres, Saint-Père

C. Saint-Leu d'Esserent

D. Mantes, Notre-Dame

0   10   20 METRES

116. Plans without transept, reconstructed in original state (in black, 12th c.; hatching, 13th c.):

117. Provins, Saint-Quiriace, choir, begun 1157
(transept added ca. 1230) (Ward Archive)

118. Voulton, N side of nave and choir, begun ca.
1180

The other two schools which had taken shape in the course of the 1150s could be called the Paris School and the Northern School or School of the Northern Trade Routes. The first one was rather restricted in its spread, extending not much further around Paris than Mantes, Senlis or Melun; while the other one stretched diagonally across the map for nearly two hundred miles, from Arras, Valenciennes and Cambrai to Reims, Châlons-sur-Marne and Montierender, to include on the way on the northern edge of

123

119. SAINT-GERMER, view from SE, begun shortly before 1160 (Ward Archive)

Ile-de-France, the bishoprics of Noyon, Laon and Soissons. Paris group and Northern group had in common the same constructional formulas, they had the same interest in the conquest of height and had the same way of achieving it, by means of a multi-storied framework incorporating tribunes as an additional zone in the elevation. And this basic identity of approach is what gives validity to the notion of a first Gothic system.

A CONSTRUCTIONAL SYSTEM: THE TRIBUNE CHURCH

How to define the characteristics of this first Gothic system? The first essential is to train the eye to subtract all the later additions and especially the flying buttresses, for this external device had not yet been invented and has changed considerably the silhouette of most

124

120. NOYON CATHEDRAL, chevet, begun ca. 1150, completed 1185 (additional buttressing, 15th and 18th c.)

of these early Gothic buildings. Thus stripped and re-established in their original state, the compactness of the exterior volumes becomes evident and particularly clear in the majestic march of the three recessed tiers of the chevets. Saint-Germer (Fig. 119), archaic in style,[8] has preserved almost unchanged its original aspect, and even at Noyon (Fig. 120) it is a fairly easy operation to blot out the fifteenth- and seventeenth-century buttresses and the conical roofs of the radiating chapels, in order to retrieve the simple flow of the horizontal masses (Fig. 273.B, p. 297).

Next to be borne in mind is the fact that in this first Gothic system the topmost volume could not be pushed to the great height achieved in later Gothic architecture: twelfth-century buildings tend to have a hunched look. That the clerestory remained short

125

was due to the constructional method by means of which the stability of the building was secured (Fig. 121). At that stage in the development of Gothic technology the only way of preventing the thrusts of the central vaults from pushing apart their supports and the whole of the wall structure with them, was by making the lateral volumes rise high enough to shore up the piers to the point where they received the thrust of the central vaults. This stiffening process was performed partly by the vaulting of these lateral volumes (particularly when they were composed of two stories: aisles and tribunes, giving two levels of vaulting), which supplied a strong cagelike armature on each side of the nave walls. But even more important in terms of constructional technique were the specific organs of abutment hidden from view above these lateral vaults and concealed beneath the slanting roof which covered the whole side masses of the structure (Fig. 123).

The type of concealed buttressing most commonly employed by twelfth-century builders was that of spurs of wall applied against the upper part of each pier, mounted upon the back of the side vaults and housed within the roof space above them. At first, as in

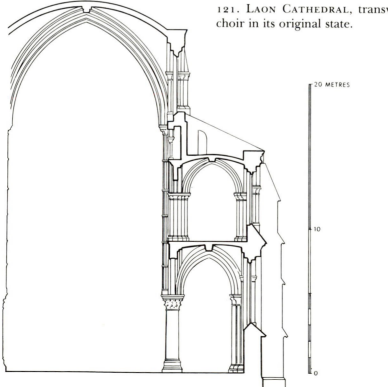

121. LAON CATHEDRAL, transverse section of choir in its original state.

20 METRES

10

0

122. LAON CATHEDRAL, wall buttresses concealed under tribune roofs, S side of choir, ca. 1165–1175 (Ward Archive)

123. CANTERBURY CATHEDRAL, segmental buttressing under aisle roof of Trinity Chapel, 1179–1184

the choir of Saint-Martin-des-Champs, these buttressing members descended onto only half of the width of the aisle vaults; but from about 1160 it became the practice to expand them into triangles of wall, pierced simply to allow passage but otherwise occupying the entire width of the roof-space which was thereby divided into separate compartments, one to each bay of the aisles or tribunes below. This is what French archaeologists have called *murs boutants* (buttressing walls), a device which can be observed at Laon Cathedral (Fig. 122) where it represents the original mode of buttressing of ca. 1170 (the external flying buttresses are an addition of the thirteenth century, later by some forty years). The old cathedral of Arras (Fig. 129), destroyed in the first years of the nineteenth century, used a very similar type of buttressing walls[9] and they performed their function so well that it was never considered necessary to supplement them by flying buttresses.

Another method of buttressing, which can be traced back to Anglo-Norman sources,[10] consisted in placing under the side roofs a succession of quadrant arches: a device reflecting another technical approach, based on the principle of skeletalization, since the buttressing members were then reduced to mere arches spanning the width of aisle or tribune vaults instead of loading them, and slanted at a sufficient angle to act as struts and block the heads of the piers in position. Saint-Germer (Fig. 124), where the remains of such concealed flying buttresses can still be seen under the roof space which surmounts the groin vaults of the tribunes in both choir and nave, seems to have been one of the earliest examples of that solution within the context of Gothic architecture. A very similar system was probably used (at a date that must have been very close to that of Saint-Germer) in the nave of the old cathedral of Cambrai (Fig. 128), now vanished,[11] and also originally (i.e., before the alterations of ca. 1225/30) in the choir of Notre-Dame in Paris (Fig. 178, p. 184): in all buildings where the roof of the tribune story was given a steep slope in the order of 45 degrees, there is a strong presumption that quadrant arches constituted the original system of buttressing.

These organs of buttressing had obviously to be placed quite

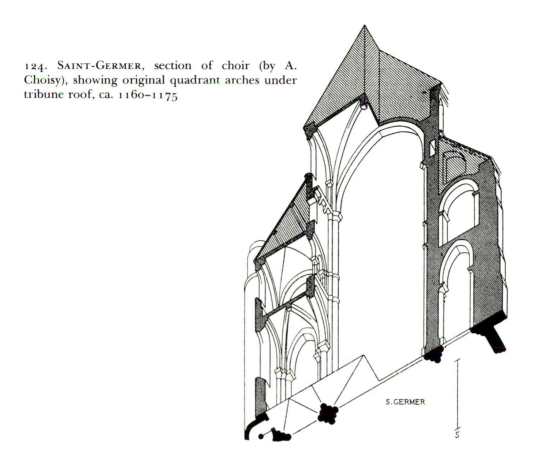

124. SAINT-GERMER, section of choir (by A. Choisy), showing original quadrant arches under tribune roof, ca. 1160–1175

S.GERMER

high on the sides of the naves to be of any value; and right through the third quarter of the twelfth century it was considered that they should be brought (together with the roofs which hid them and the aisles which supported them) up to the exact level at which the nave vaults began. The raising of the lateral volumes with their concealed buttressing to the springing line of the central vaults left little height in the upper nave walls in which windows might be pierced. And this is why the clerestory remained a compressed story, restricted to the height of the nave vault itself, the windows enclosed within the curve of the side cells of the vault (Fig. 125).

The consequence of all this was that taller naves—or, in other words, the conquest of height—could be achieved only by piling up one above the other two stories of lateral volumes: a lower story of vaulted aisles (of the same height as the chapels of the chevet) and on top of them a second story of vaulted tribunes. Only in this way

129

125. LAON CATHEDRAL, view into choir from tribune of N transept, ca. 1165–1175 (Ward Archive)

could the devices of buttressing lodged under the pent roof of the tribunes be brought to a sufficient height to shore up the crowning vaults of a tall central space. Height and interior loftiness could be achieved only by the superimposition of horizontal zones in the lateral structure and consequently in the elevation: verticality had to be achieved through horizontality.

In these conditions it is not surprising that the four-story elevation became so popular with Gothic architects in the second half of the twelfth century. By inserting in the interior elevation an additional story of triforium between the top of the tribune arches and the base of the clerestory windows (in place of the undefined zone of wall corresponding to the height of the tribune roof on the outside) an effect of multiplication of horizontal stories was created which emphasized most tellingly the character of the constructional system employed; and the importance of the zone of concealed buttressing, which was lodged above the tribune vaults under the high lateral roofs, was also given its full architectural expression. It was logical to mark that level as a definite and independent story in the delineation of the component parts of the structure.

Contrast between Parisian and Northern Group (1)
Volumes and space

But these general trends and common principles could be used to erect churches quite different in aspect, shape and composition, and reflecting different modes of artistic sensibility. In the Paris group there was a marked preference for compact plans, in the Northern group for articulated cruciform plans (Fig. 126.A-D). The simplified plan without transepts had spread fairly early from Sens to the Paris area. Its first appearance north of the Marne River was at the cathedral of Senlis (Fig. 116.A), begun in 1153, where the double bay rhythm created by the alternation of strong and weak piers leaves no doubt that Sens was the model followed by the architect, the only difference being that the short dark triforium story of Sens has been replaced at Senlis by a taller, open and vaulted story of tribunes (Fig. 127): a change which alters profoundly the character of the elevation. The colossal clerestory that now tops the

A. Arras

B. Noyon

C. Cambrai

D. Soissons

0   10   20 METRES

126. Plans of the Northern Group, reconstructed in original state (in black, 12th c.; hatching, 13th c.)

elevation of Senlis is the result of a great heightening of the early
sixteenth century: in the twelfth century the vaults were much lower
and the clerestory much shorter, as evidenced by the occasional
presence of the old capitals. This type of unarticulated plan was
repeated after Senlis in a number of buildings around Paris, for
instance at Mantes,[12] the purest of the series (Figs. 116.D and 147),
or at Saint-Leu d'Esserent (in the lower Oise Valley), the interior of
which provides an impressive example of the inexorable longitudinal movement of an unbroken suite of bays, even though the
exterior is interrupted by the presence of two towers which were
meant to mark the separation between choir and nave (Figs. 116.C
and 301, p. 326).

In the Northern area, by contrast, the plans point in the four
directions of the compass, and often there is also a lantern tower
pointing upward over the crossing. This principle of vigorous articulation of plan implies that the transepts have to be enlarged and

127. SENLIS CATHEDRAL, N side of choir, main arcade and tribune ca. 1153–1170
[heightened upper story 16th c.]. (Ward Archive)

given a more monumental character; and there are only two ways of monumentalizing the transepts: they can either be treated as if they were two other choirs emanating from the crossing, or as if they were two other naves converging on the crossing. The triple repetition of the choir pattern or trefoil plan can be traced back to the Early Christian period.[13] In its most perfect Gothic form it meant that each transept had not only a semi-circular termination but was further surrounded by an ambulatory like the choir itself, and all three were given the same depth. The best representatives of the trefoil plan in the second half of the twelfth century were the cathedral of Cambrai (Fig. 126.B) and Notre-Dame-la-Grande at Valenciennes, both destroyed at the time of the French Revolution.[14] The church of Valenciennes was the more typical, as the original plan (established after the fire of 1171) had been followed throughout; while at Cambrai the choir, as may be seen on the fine seventeenth-century drawing by van der Meulen (Fig. 128), did not conform to the typical trefoil plan, having been built later than the transepts to a much enlarged thirteenth-century design. These two major examples now vanished, the only survivor of the series is the south transept of Soissons Cathedral (Figs. 126.D and 143), now attached to an edifice of much larger proportions: a fragment only of a trefoil plan but a precious one, giving as it does the possibility of experiencing the effect achieved in the whole series, with the multiplicity of windows on three levels and the spatial enlargement provided by the big two-story chapel which flanked the east side of all these transepts. Noyon, although it too has rounded transepts (Figs. 149 and 159, pp. 156, 168), is a special case, for there the tall and narrow aisleless transepts were never meant to balance the swelling expanse of the chevet.[15]

It has often been said that the immediate source of this Gothic series of trefoil plans was the cathedral of Tournai (Fig. 138), which is slightly older than all these French buildings and which is known to have been influential in many other ways. But in the matter of the groundplan and of the whole organization of exterior volumes Tournai must be recognized as belonging to an entirely different filiation, harking back to some definite Early Christian models.[16]

128. CAMBRAI CATHEDRAL, 17th c. drawing by A. Van der Meulen (Paris, Musée des Gobelins): nave ca. 1150–1180, transept ca. 1175–1200, choir ca. 1220–1250

The real prototype of the Gothic series was the (destroyed) Romanesque church of Saint-Lucien at Beauvais, earlier than Tournai since it was begun in 1090, and built on a type of trefoil plan which had already the proportions of Cambrai and Valenciennes; and with even (as proved by the recent excavations) the characteristic big chapel on the east side of the transepts.[17]

Side by side with these trefoil plans the Northern group also used in some of its major buildings another type of widely articulated layout: that of large cruciform plans in which, as at Laon and Arras cathedrals, the deep rectangular transepts are flanked on both sides by aisles and tribunes in the same manner as the nave; their termination can even take, as at Laon, the form of a two-tower

135

129. ARRAS CATHEDRAL, late 18th c. drawing (Arras, Archives du Pas-de-Calais): lower story of choir ca. 1160–1170, upper stories ca. 1170–1185, transept ca. 1190

façade, repeating the treatment normally reserved for west façades. These large aisled transepts were another of those formulas of spatial amplification which had been first conceived in Early Christian times; but this one had been revived from the very beginning of the Romanesque period and used in many regions,[18] including northern France. The eleventh century churches of Saint-Remi at Reims, of Saint-Bertin at Saint-Omer may have acted locally as reminders of the interest of that solution; but the Gothic masters of the 1160s seem to have been particularly interested in outdoing their Romanesque forerunners: Laon by its three façades, Arras by its immense wingspan (Figs. 126A and 129). With its transepts of six bays each, Arras could be compared only with Santiago de

136

Compostela and with Old St. Paul's in London, the largest and most ambitious representatives of the two major series of Romanesque cruciform plans at the end of the eleventh century.

This confrontation of plans, taken on the one hand from the Paris area and on the other from the Northern Gothic group, is already proof that between the architects of these two schools there was a profound difference of taste, and that it affected even the general principles of architectural composition. But the best way of understanding to what extent these two major schools of the 1160s and 70s differed in their intentions and in their conception of architectural beauty, is to compare the most outstanding works of these two schools: namely, Notre-Dame in Paris,[19] begun by 1163 at the latest, and its almost exact contemporary, the cathedral of Laon,[20] begun in all probability around 1165 (Fig. 130).

Notre-Dame was the most colossal building of its generation: colossal in length and area as well as colossal in height.[21] The Gothic masters of the thirteenth century were to build on an even larger scale, but a knowledge of Amiens or Cologne does not diminish the impact of Notre-Dame and the impression on entering is still one of amazement at the sheer size of that nave and the loftiness of its proportions (Fig. 131). But Notre-Dame is not just a feat of building in height: it combines height and width into a vast yet compact composition. Its plan is packed tightly within the restraining limits of a continuous outline, and even the transept does not project beyond this limit: Notre-Dame has all the spaciousness in width of Saint-Denis but on a larger scale. It is the only twelfth-century building in which the double ambulatory of Saint-Denis was repeated, at least prior to the 1190s when Bourges and Chartres initiated what is in fact the architecture of the thirteenth century. To a multiplicity of small spatial units spreading horizontally in the ground plan, Notre-Dame adds a similar multiplicity in height (Fig. 132): the tribune story adds a second layer of cubicles of space of the same size as the small square bays of the aisles; and in the transept, which offers a magnificent cross section of the building, one becomes immediately conscious of the systematic quality of this three-dimensional gridwork. It looks as if space had crystallized

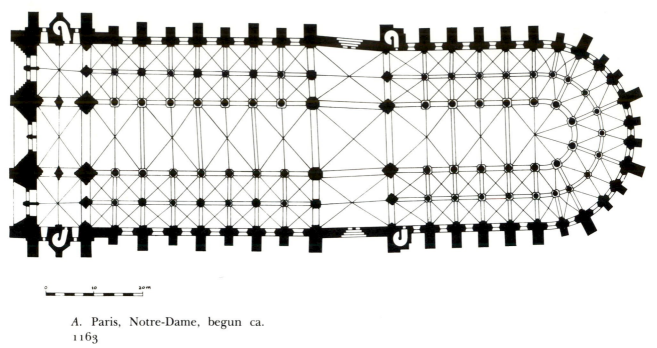

A. Paris, Notre-Dame, begun ca. 1163

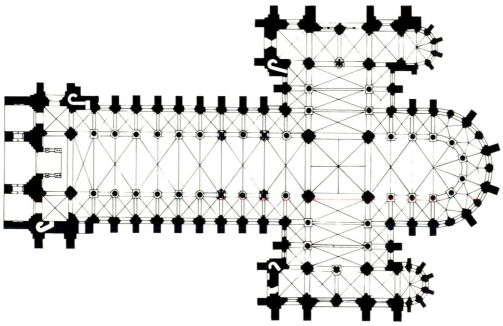

B. Laon, Notre-Dame, begun ca. 1165–1170

130. Reconstructed original plans of the cathedrals of Paris and Laon

131. PARIS, NOTRE-DAME, general view: choir ca. 1163–1180, nave ca. 1175–1195, clerestory windows extended downward ca. 1225–1230

132. PARIS, NOTRE-DAME, view from transept tribune, looking W into nave and its N aisles and tribunes, ca. 1175–1195

naturally into a honeycomb of little hollowed blocks, from which the central space is sliced out cleanly, leaving exposed sheer faces imprinted with a surface grid on which one reads the partitioning of the lateral volumes into the modular cages which encase the whole building and sustain it. Here lies the key to the ordered spatial vision of Notre-Dame. A diagram is perhaps the best means of explaining this mode of spatial composition (Fig. 133). The austere beauty of this nave reflects the intellectual tension which alone could produce such a complex and perfectly regulated universe.

The spatial magnificence of Laon is of an entirely different order: far from being compact, Laon stretches in all directions. The crossing is the center from which emanate five divergent movements, pointing north, south, east, west, and to the zenith (Fig. 135). Triforium and clerestory windows are repeated at two levels: at the top of the nave walls and again in the lantern. Laon is remarkable now for its enormous length, cut right in the middle by the transept and by the great shaft of light that falls from the lan-

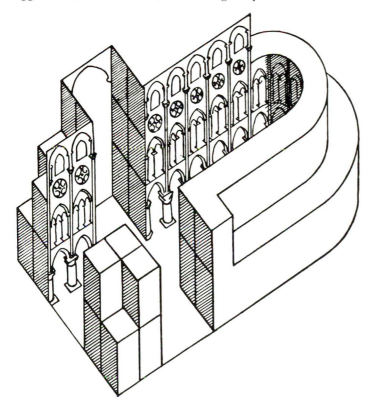

133. PARIS, NOTRE-DAME, structuring of space

134. CHARS, choir, built in imitation of original elevation of Notre-Dame, ca. 1190–1200

135. LAON CATHEDRAL, crossing and lantern, ca. 1175–1190

tern (Fig. 136). But the present very long choir is an addition of the first years of the thirteenth century and originally, when the church had a short and rounded east end, the interior aspect must have been quite different, the crossroad effect of the transept being even more strikingly marked. No doubt the design of the original east end had been conceived to some extent as an enlarged version of a neighboring late Romanesque composition, the chevet of Notre-Dame at Soissons, built some thirty years earlier. But to this Laon added another major element, in its multiplication of the towers (Fig. 137); and this feature came from another direction, from that same building which had already inspired the four-story pattern of elevation, the cathedral of Tournai (Fig. 138). The transept of Tournai may have been started not even ten years before Laon and, although it had not risen to its full height when Laon was designed, it did provide the idea for the amazing cluster of towers

142

136. LAON CATHEDRAL, general view: nave and W bays of choir ca. 1165–1200, extension of choir to
E from ca. 1205

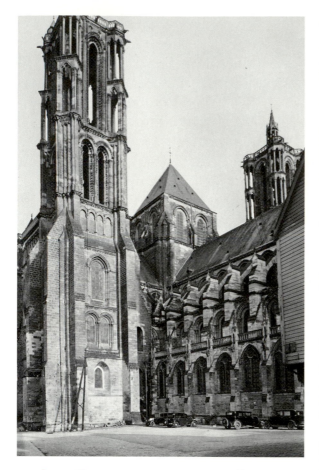

137. Laon Cathedral, transept towers from NW, ca. 1175–1200 (Ward Archive)

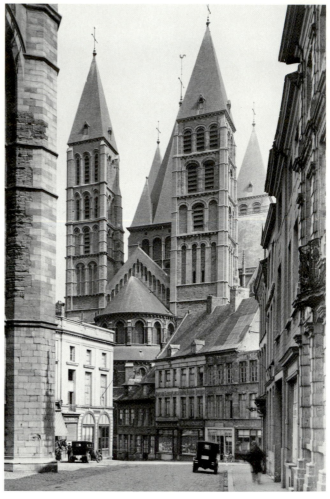

138. Tournai Cathedral, cluster of transept towers from S, ca. 1160–1200

139. Laon Cathedral, reconstruction of projected composition of volumes as of ca. 1175–1180

planted over the transept at Laon.[22] Two of these towers have been left unfinished; but even if the five towers had been completed they would not have repeated the tight massing of Tournai: more air would have circulated between and around them. Here also the Gothic sense of space was at work and it tended to openness.

Another particularity of Laon is the presence on the east side of the transepts of tall chapels (Fig. 180, p. 186), clearly intended to flank the short original east end rather than the present one. They fall in a steep cascade from the height of the unfinished towers, and their modeling in the light of day perhaps gives a useful clue to the intentions of the master of Laon (Fig. 139): for him the play of volumes was not just a matter of compact and rigorous order as at Notre-Dame, it was an art of sculpture on the grand scale.

CONTRAST BETWEEN PARISIAN AND NORTHERN GROUP (II)
Surfaces and light

Even in the regularity of the interior elevation, at Laon there is the same sense of the plastic quality of matter: the linear frame-work is substantial, it stands out in the round and defines itself in terms of light and shadow, in contrast to the almost abstract quality of the thin shafts which separate the bays at Notre-Dame. Depth at Laon is not so much an element to be evaluated and measured in terms of a cubic system of space units: depth becomes, rather, a dramatic element of contrast between successive planes; it is a background against which the gridwork of the elevation becomes more meaningful. The triforium passage, with the recession of planes it involves, is perhaps the motif which expresses most clearly that exploitation of depth as a mere background for a detached linear framework.[23]

This is the moment when the Northern group assimilated and incorporated into the Gothic tradition the Anglo-Norman tech-nique of the thick wall hollowed out by longitudinal passages, which in England had already led during the first half of the twelfth century to a remarkable reduction in the substance of the walls, as in the apse and transepts of Peterborough cathedral.[24] The transept of Tournai, as far as can be judged, was the first in-

140. LAON CATHEDRAL, N side of choir showing elevation in tiers of arches, first bays ca. 1165–1175, rest after 1205

strument of transmission of this method of building walls in two layers; but once introduced to this new constructional technique, the North Gothic masters turned directly to England where they found a rich fund of architectural experimentation along this line. Of special attraction to them was the realization that by means of a thickening of structure it was possible to achieve an extraordinary degree of openness, the wall resolved into tier on tier of arches and further lightened by the presence of cushions of space within its two-layered structure.[25] This treatment of the elevation as a mere trellis of arches (Fig. 140) susceptible to rhythmic ordering after a simple numerical sequence (e.g. at Laon one arch per bay in the lower story, two at tribune level, three at triforium level) shows itself as one of the basic laws of architecture in the Northern group of the 1160s and 1170s.

The choir of Saint-Remi at Reims (ca. 1170–1180) is quite different from Laon in many ways:[26] it reflects a taste for wide and almost massive spaciousness, it expands in width so greatly that it seems about to burst open on its outer edges. In the outer wall of the tribune story, which is all windows, the middle lancet of each bay thrusts upward to shatter the roofline, creating an illusion of structural insecurity. The heavy flying-buttresses underline the effect; but they were added some years after completion of the choir and must not be taken into account. This building too speculates on rhythms and numbers: on the outside (Fig. 142) one finds three variants of the triplet, three ways of making groups of three openings. It is again the number three which regulates the form of the screen of narrow arches separating ambulatory from chapels, and which in the tribunes determines the system of vaulting. And in the interior elevation (Fig. 141) the formula resolves itself into the

141. REIMS, SAINT-REMI, choir during restoration

142. REIMS, SAINT-REMI, two bays of chevet, ca. 1170–1180

143. Soissons Cathedral, S transept, 1177 to ca. 1185

same three-two-one sequence as at Laon; but differently, because this time three stands for the clerestory windows themselves, the triforium having become integrated into the design of the clerestory, as an accelerated variant of its pattern of arches. As the supreme example of those elegant gridwork elevations was to come soon after, in the late 1170s, the south transept of Soissons (Fig. 143): all in threes, thinner and more regular than ever, with hardly any spandrel of wall remaining—a pure linear cross ruling, all voids.[27]

In this respect again the Paris group offers the most striking contrast with its Northern counterpart. Originally at Notre-Dame the additional story was not a triforium, not a continuous horizontal zone of arcading, but a succession of round openings or oculi, dark because they gave onto the roof space above the tribunes and separately spaced one to each bay, to be read vertically in the context of the bay entity as much as horizontally in the story sequence. These oculi disappeared as early as the thirteenth century, absorbed by the enlargement of the clerestory windows; but in the mid-nineteenth century Viollet-le-Duc effected a partial restoration of the original four-story elevation in the transepts and in the bays immediately adjacent (Fig. 144). This restoration of oculi and small clerestory windows makes it possible to realize how important the wall is to the balance of this Parisian architecture, where the flat wall surface flows in a unifying presence from story to story around all the openings, which look as if they had been punched out of it. The smooth, taut, parchmentlike quality of the thin wall of this Paris group is due not only to its actual thinness (walls that often rise to a hundred feet or more are only two to three feet thick) but also to the absence of those plastic effects of projection and recession which played such an essential part in the textured surfaces of the Northern style.

The beauty of these thin screens of pale stone, the peacefulness of these flat surfaces of wall are everywhere in the Paris group: on a small scale they are seen at work in the nave of Champeaux for instance (Fig. 145), where traces of round openings like those of Notre-Dame are still faintly discernible under a light plastering;

149

and on a much larger scale at Mantes.[28] And if Mantes is confronted with a building of the Northern group employing the same rhythm of alternate supports, such as the nave of Noyon (of almost identical date), then the two systems of architectural aesthetics can be perceived at one glance: at Mantes an art proclaiming mural values, at Noyon a sophisticated play of perforated screens (Figs. 146, 147).

A no less significant comparison can be made between the exterior of Mantes (Fig. 148) and an exterior view of the chevet of the old cathedral of Arras (Fig. 129). Instead of the thin lacework of

144. PARIS, NOTRE-DAME, W side of S transept, showing four-story elevation of ca. 1175–1185, as restored by Viollet-le-Duc

145. CHAMPEAUX, nave, ca. 1190–1205, blocked circular openings of original intermediate story faintly discernible on wall surface

lines and fragmented surfaces of the tribune story and of the picturesque zigzagging of its pointed gables over each bay, which gave to that east end of Arras a character of such delicate elaboration, Mantes displays another form of refinement, that of the most rigorous simplicity. Originally there were no chapels and the wall fell straight to the ground, with just one small window in the lower story. The wall which is only 42 cm. (16½ inches) thick at tribune level is here, truly supreme and in the most unorthodox manner. It has taken on an almost abstract quality, its large round windows staring outward and not registering in their shape, as windows usually do, the direction and pull of gravity. Furthermore, at the top this wall stops short on a sharp edge, without the normal slope of roofs to soften the outline. But the hard geometry of this simplified form did not express the reality behind it: until quite recently each

151

146. NOYON CATHEDRAL, S side of nave from crossing, first double bay ca. 1170–1185, rest of nave ca. 1185–1205

147. MANTES, NOTRE-DAME, showing Parisian mural style, lower story ca. 1170–1180, upper stories ca. 1180–1200

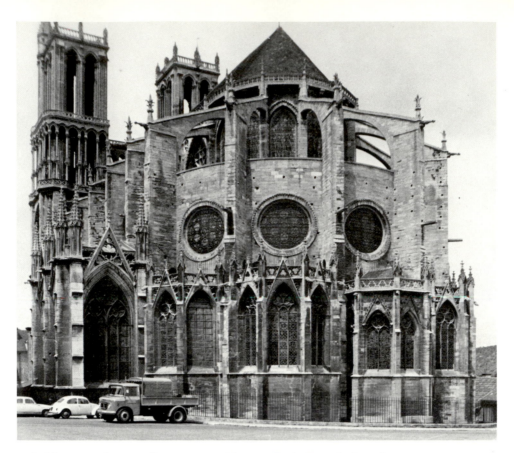

148. MANTES, chevet, tribune story with round windows designed ca. 1180–1185

tribune bay was capped by a small ridge roof, somewhat in the manner of Arras; and that broken roofline was deliberately masked by an austere screen of wall, in a manifest declaration of aesthetic choice. Here at Mantes is something as pure and abstract as a Le Corbusier of the 1920s, and yet Gothic in that Parisian Gothic style of the late twelfth century which has such a paradoxical flavor of intellectual absolutism.

PLURALITY WITHIN THE GOTHIC MOVEMENT

If this first Gothic system was uniform in its basic constructional principles, it obviously admitted of a diversity of artistic interpretations: living movements in art are always subject to the attraction of contradictory tendencies. Often these reflect nothing more than the instinctive preferences of different artistic personalities; but the interest of the period which has just been considered is that its variations cannot be reduced to a simple question of individual temperaments. What happened then was a much more complex and

154

far-ranging phenomenon: the crystallization of artistic tendencies into separate geographical entities, and the splitting up of the original Gothic milieu of the 1140s into three distinct art milieux, each following its own line of development. The forces at work were not the same in all three cases. The character of the Southern group, focused as it was on Sens, resulted essentially from a static outlook, an attitude of mere fidelity to a much admired prototype which had supposedly given the final solution of all problems. But between the other two milieux, which remained progressive and experimental in their approach, the difference was one of attitudes of mind; it was the conflict of two philosophies, invention in these two groups being aimed in different directions.

The key to that major split within the Gothic movement and the dualism that ensued is probably to be found in the attitude of the Paris milieu, where a decisive step was taken with the design of the choir of Notre-Dame. While the Northern milieu, where Gothic was still a recent and exciting revelation, was attracted by all forms of picturesqueness and ready to absorb a constant influx of ideas borrowed from late Romanesque sources, Paris in the 1160s refused both the picturesque and that extreme openness to suggestions from outside. Instead, it turned in upon itself to discover in its own traditions the guide to further advances. Not only did the masters of this Paris group defend the values of the 1140s, seen as the authentic Gothic values (thinness of structure, compactness of plan, insistence on spatial expansion); they even went much further than the Parisian masters of the preceding generation in their attachment to the tradition of thin wall construction with all the visual effects that accompanied it.[29] Turning deliberately for inspiration toward the great works of the previous century, in which the logic of the system had first been defined, they undertook to revive—in a much modernized form—the mural style (Figs. 20 and 21, p. 23) of Jumièges (nave begun in 1052) and of Saint-Lucien at Beauvais (choir begun in 1090), and also to explore what reinterpretations would be required to create a new Gothic style of mural values. And so a great controversy was engaged, which intensified the inner tensions within the creative circles of Gothic architectural thought, preparing it for further renewals.

149. NOYON CATHEDRAL, S transept, showing Gothic version of double-wall structure, ca. 1170–1185

CHAPTER V

Late Twelfth-Century Changes

By the late 1160s Gothic architecture had reached a high degree of systematic organization. Its technical power was remarkable: the space enclosed was not only wider but much taller than before; and in the great tribune churches the gridlike elevation with its repetitive units gave a most impressive and convincing explanation of the structure of the building. But Gothic architecture did not stop at this point, for the urge to give a new accent to their creations and to imagine more powerful designs continued to drive forward the more inventive minds, and as early as 1180 it became obvious that problems were shifting and that familiar features of recent Gothic buildings were gradually undergoing change. These changes can be classified under two headings: some were refinements, significant but based upon principles already established; others were radical innovations, pathfinders toward the future.

Among the more evident cases of refinement was a general tendency to further accentuate the linear skeleton of Gothic structures, to make it appear thinner, to increase the sharpness of its lines and make it stand out more vigorously from the background against which it was drawn. For the first time these linear values were consciously exaggerated. But the methods then evolved were quite different from those which were to develop two generations later, in the mid-thirteenth century, culminating in the reduction of

157

the wall substance to a spiderweb of traceried windows. In the last quarter of the twelfth century the Gothic architects did not work to annihilate all sense of substance; rather, they ran a fine surface network over the inner face of the building to give the impression of a coherent and self-sufficient armature which, in spite of its thinness, appears to actually stiffen and support the whole fabric: an illusory effect but not an irrational one, for the network expresses to the eye the forces at work in the masonry behind. Various constructional processes were used to create that effect and must be clearly distinguished.

METHODS OF DETACHED SHAFTING

One of these processes, which became the point of departure for a great variety of experiments, consisted in the use of detached shafts applied against the masonry of the walls to receive and to continue downward vertically the ribs of the vault. This building device had been systematically employed as early as 1140 in the choir of Saint-Denis (Fig. 38, p. 39), where the shafts which support the vault springers against the outer wall of the ambulatory are mounted distinct from the wall itself, each shaft being composed of two lengths only, with a narrow bronze band to link them together and hook them to the masonry.[1] In the French technical vocabulary, these detached shafts are said to be constructed *en délit*. *Lit* being the French for bed, *délit* means against the bed: a term which applies adequately here, since these long shafts are necessarily cut out of a horizontal bed of stone or stratum in the quarry but then placed vertically (i.e. against their natural position in the quarry bed) when mounted in the building. They are stones placed at right angle to bed, whereas in regular coursed masonry the stones are laid flat and preserve the position they had in the rock strata of the quarry. It might be simpler to speak of monoliths, of detached monolithic shafts, though of course a long shaft is always composed of several such monolithic sections put end to end, and the term "oligolithic" would be more accurate. This way of assembling responds or other groups of shafts was not universally followed at first: at Notre-Dame in the choir (1163–1182) the responds placed against the outer wall of the aisles and the tall verticals in the major elevation were still built with the wall in courses continuous with those of the wall itself; it was only in the nave, begun shortly before 1178, that thin detached shafts *en délit* were used.[2] On the other hand, from the early 1160s in the choir of Noyon (Fig. 106, p. 107) and from the late 1160s at Laon (Fig. 114, p. 116), the vertical lines were already made up of applied shafts in short monolithic sections and banded at regular intervals (eight sections in the choir of Noyon, six sections at Laon).

A further refinement, which started a particularly persistent fashion in England, was the practice of employing dark marbles for the applied vertical shafts and of extending their use to the horizontal components of the linear grid, so that abaci of capitals and string courses above and below the triforium or the tribune were also treated in dark stone. A classic example of this practice, and the earliest Gothic example extant, is the choir and presbytery of Canterbury Cathedral (Fig. 150), built between 1175 and 1178 by the French architect William of Sens, and supplemented by a further eastern extension, the Trinity Chapel, built in the six years that followed by his successor William the Englishman.[3] The idea of contrasting dark shafts against white masonry came from the region of Tournai, where a hard darkish blue stone (a near marble) was quarried and had been used architecturally for a long time. The Romanesque nave of Tournai Cathedral, begun probably in the late 1130s, shows an extensive but archaic use of blue Tournai marble in the form of octagonal shafts, which surround the windows on the exterior of the building (Fig. 158) and which appear in the composition of the piers on three of the four stories of the interior elevation (Fig. 109, p. 109).[4] But since the nave of Tournai was conceived as a mere superposition of self-contained horizontal stories, these different series of shafts do not even link together and create no overall pattern. The use of marble had to be first translated into Gothic; and that translation was made not at Tournai but in the nearby city of Valenciennes, in the choir of the church of Notre-Dame-la-Grande,[5] which was begun in 1171, that is, four years before Canterbury. The only graphic document that

150. CANTERBURY CATHEDRAL, choir, presbytery and Trinity Chapel, 1175–1184

survives to give us some idea of the interior appearance of the building is a very poor drawing of the eighteenth century, which shows at least that it was a purely Gothic structure closely related to Noyon; and the descriptions of the church before its destruction all state that the shafts were of dark Tournai stone. In these conditions Valenciennes appears as the most likely source for that important element of the design of Canterbury; and a confirmation of that likelihood is the fact that William of Sens brought with him to Canterbury a most distinctive style of capital carving which had just been developed at Arras in the early 1170s, indicating that William himself had been working in the area of southern Flanders or Hainault immediately before coming to England and that he had called former collaborators to join his workshop at Canterbury. The use of the dark marble never gained wide acceptance in French Gothic circles and remained a fashion of marginal areas;[6] but its appearance at that precise moment has the value of a

151. LAON CATHEDRAL, piers of easternmost bays of nave, ca. 1175–1185 (Ward Archive)

152. BLOIS, SAINT-LAUMER, pier in N choir aisle, ca. 1160

153. PARIS, NOTRE-DAME, double aisles on S side of nave, ca. 1175–1180

symptom, since the use of dark marble added to the sharpness of the monolithic treatment of the pier shafts the accentuation of a contrast of color, to stress further—and even with an almost excessive insistence—the linear quality of the style.

Another possible line of development of this method of detached shafting was the addition of applied shafts around the lower part of the piers which, ever since Saint-Denis, had generally been treated as plain round columns. This was done for instance in the four easternmost bays of the nave of Laon Cathedral (Fig. 151), which were probably built shortly before 1180. In these four bays plain columns alternate with piers composed of a column encaged by five monolithic shafts; and a very similar alternation is also found, with an increased number of shafts, in the aisles of the nave of Notre-Dame in Paris (Fig. 153) at about the same date. The first Gothic example so far identified of such piers composed of a columnar core surrounded with monoliths, is a pier, datable to ca. 1160, which stands in the north aisle of the choir of Saint-Laumer

162

(now Saint-Nicolas) at Blois (Fig. 152): a building which in its lower story is still half-Romanesque and shows some definite connections with Burgundy. That hint of a possible Burgundian origin is not without meaning because in fact throughout the Romanesque period Burgundian builders had frequently used groupings of monoliths, generally in much shorter piers, as a persistent survival of very early modes of pier composition; and it seems most likely that Gothic architects received that idea through contacts with Burgundy, the Cistercians acting often as one of the agents of transmission (though not in the particular case of Saint-Laumer).

But once assimilated into the context of Gothic architecture and of its increasing linear insistence, piers with monoliths took on a new significance: they provided a way of harmonizing the supports with the ribbed texture of the vault and with the sharp vertical accentuations of the interior elevation, while at the same time guarding to a large degree the plastic value[7] and autonomy of composition of the plain column; and the horizontal banding, so frequently employed, simply added a further overtone by reflecting the storied organization of the whole building. In this respect the piers which stand at the entrance to the chapel of the south transept of Soissons Cathedral (Fig. 155) are most typical. The chapel is a rather voluminous two-storied adjunct placed on the east side of the rounded south transept, the lower story opening onto the ambulatory, the upper one onto the tribunes above. Globular in plan, this large chapel recalls the unusual shape of the radiating chapels of Saint-Remi at Reims, from which it has also borrowed its triple opening on the ambulatory and the detached piers such an arrangement demands. On the lower story, these piers have a quatrefoil-shaped core with thin shafts *en délit* in the angles, the whole being composed into a clustered pier. On the upper story there is no more coursed masonry core to be seen in the piers; instead, eight monolithic shafts are grouped into a tight cluster under an octagonal abacus.

Another set of interesting variations, quite different in their emphasis because of the black and white effect of the marble shafts (and also because of their greater thinness), can be observed in the later half of William of Sens' work at Canterbury Cathedral: the east crossing and the presbytery (Fig. 154). The term "presbytery" applies to that part of the chevet complex which is situated east of the choir proper, between the east transept and the "Pilgrims' Steps" which lead up to William the Englishman's addition, the Trinity Chapel. Some of the piers there—those of the east crossing—have eight shafts around an octagonal core; in the presbytery itself some have four shafts placed on the axes and there is even a pair of piers of a different type, composed of twin columns with two shafts only, placed one on each side to mask the junction of the two rounded surfaces. The great advantage of Canterbury to the modern historian is that every pier there is exactly dated, thanks to the wonderful precision of mind of Gervase of Canterbury, the chronicler, who recorded in great detail the sequence of the building operations. In that way we know that the west piers of the east crossing were built in 1177 and that the east piers of the

154. CANTERBURY CATHEDRAL, piers on S side of presbytery, 1178

155. SOISSONS CATHEDRAL, piers at entrance to S transept chapel, ca. 1177–1180

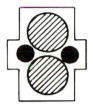

CANTERBURY
presbytery, 1178

CAMBRAI
S transept, ca. 1175–80

SOISSONS
S transept, ca. 1177–80

LAON
nave, ca. 1175–80

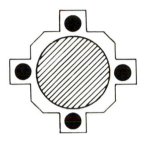

YORK
crypt, ca. 1170–75

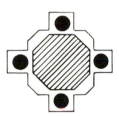

CANTERBURY
presbytery, 1178

CANTERBURY
E crossing, 1177

PARIS, NOTRE-DAME
nave, ca. 1175–80

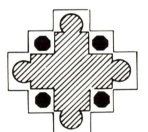

TOURNAI
nave, ca. 1145

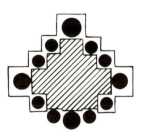

NOYON
choir tribunes, ca. 1180

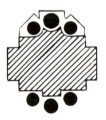

PARIS, NOTRE-DAME
nave tribunes, ca. 1180

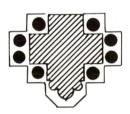

BOXGROVE
nave, ca. 1190

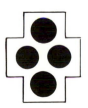

YORK
crypt, ca. 1170–75

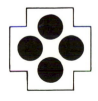

BAGNEUX
choir, ca. 1180–85

LONDON, TEMPLE
ca. 1180–85

SOISSONS
transept tribunes, ca. 1180

156. Early examples of piers with detached shafts, France and England (free shafts in black, coursed core in hatching)

crossing and the presbytery followed in 1178. Strangely enough Laon, Soissons, Notre-Dame point also to the same years: all these examples seem to have been designed within a few months. The great diversity of shapes and patterns which were imagined by the builders of that time for the central core and for the placing of the monolithic shafts is illustrated on Fig. 156,[8] which also gives the approximate dates of these piers; and it will be seen that there was an especially inventive period between 1178 and 1185.

THE DOUBLE-WALL SYSTEM

Even more powerful perhaps than these diverse uses of the technique of applied shafts to express the linear nature of the new architecture was the other major constructional refinement of that period: the full Gothic exploitation of the double-wall system. Of course the adoption of a triforium of the wall-passage type, as had been done some years before in the choirs of Laon (Fig. 125) and Arras, was enough to create a two-layer effect[9] at one level in the elevation: and the whole concept had already been extensively elaborated for as much as a hundred years in the Anglo-Norman style of architecture, since its first adoption of that line of experiment ca. 1067 in the design of Saint-Etienne at Caen (Fig. 22, p. 24). From the very start, this mode of building thick had even led in specific cases to the superposition of two passages one above the other (as in the lantern tower of Saint-Etienne at Caen), making structures in two layers on some considerable height. But the architect who started in ca. 1170 the transept of Noyon cathedral (Fig. 157) gave a remarkably gothicized version of the Norman thick wall with passages, reducing it for the first time to something of a skeleton of thickness, in accordance with the Gothic compulsion to lightness. In this new interpretation, the insistence was not so much on depth or on the cavities opened within the thickness of the masonry as on the open-web surface pattern of thin shafts and arches detached in front of the passages. And in the transepts of Noyon this fine grid encloses three passages one above the other: a small triforium running at the level of the tribune floor, an intermediate story of windows just above, also pierced by a passage, and

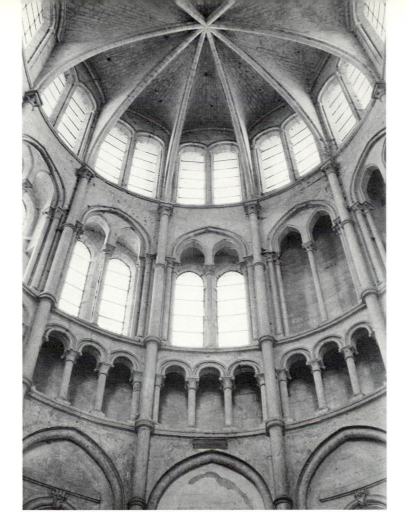

157. Noyon Cathedral, N transept, looking upward to show wall passages, ca. 1170–1185

an exterior passage behind an outer screen of arches in the upper story (Fig. 159); so that this tall vertical elevation is split into two layers, not exactly from top to bottom, but on two-thirds of its total height.[10] The exterior passage at clerestory level clearly came from Tournai (Fig. 158), which had provided in the preceding decades, in two successive variants, a most original version of the thick Anglo-Norman structures hollowed by passages—the source of these variants, and of the exterior passages in particular, being eventually traceable to northern Italy.[11] But the novelty of Noyon was the thinness of the two layers as well as their fragmentation into twin openings in each bay, and the effect of repetition of the two upper stories. Rather than a double wall, there was now a two-layer grid in openwork: for the eye is unaware of the thickness of the

167

158. TOURNAI CATHEDRAL, S side of nave showing exterior passage at clerestory level, ca. 1135–1160

159. NOYON CATHEDRAL, S transept showing exterior passage at clerestory level, ca. 1170–1185

rings of arches which stiffen the structure in its heights by linking in depth the inner and outer layers of the two upper stories, registering the existence of solid masses of masonry only at the base of the walls and in the deep splays of the lowest story of windows.

This treatment in detached layers was soon extended to the side walls as well, and this was a remarkable innovation, for never before had the Norman or English builders (or those of Tournai for that matter) applied to the aisle walls the mode of double-wall treatment they used in the major elevation.[12] The variant of the double-wall technique that became most common in aisle walls in the thirteenth century, the so-called "Champenois passage," which splits the wall at the height of the windows while the base of the wall remains solid and heavy, was invented ca. 1170 at Saint-Remi at

Reims (Fig. 161), in the deeper axial chapel (the Lady Chapel). This formula however was not repeated for at least a generation.[13] Much more characteristic for the period of the 1180s was the articulation of the walls of aisles or chapels by means of a system of applied arches, framing the heads of the windows and supported on detached responds, behind which a man could pass. This full-height layering of the lateral walls was used for instance in the upper chapel of the south transept of Soissons, in single arches per bay in its seven-sided hemicycle; and at Canterbury in the ambulatory of the Trinity Chapel (Fig. 160), in a regular pattern of two arches per bay.

The most striking example of these skeletal structures playing on two planes is the one found at Laon Cathedral, at the back of the

160. CANTERBURY CATHEDRAL, ambulatory of Trinity Chapel, showing double-wall treatment with passage at floor level, 1181–1182

161. REIMS, SAINT-REMI, axial chapel with champenois passage above solid dado, ca. 1170–1180

162. LAON CATHEDRAL, transept to N, ca. 1170–1190 (Ward Archive)

163. LAON CATHEDRAL, tribune story at end of N transept, looking into E chapel, ca. 1180–1190 (Ward Archive)

transept façades (Fig. 162) and in the chapels that adjoin them. At the end of the transepts, from the level of the platform linking the tribunes (Fig. 163), the terminal bay opens up laterally into the tall volume of the hollowed out tower bases which flank it, creating there in the heights a most amazing effect of transverse spatial expansion, which pursues its movement on the east into a diminutive apse of a singular delicacy. At this upper level, which corresponds to the tribunes in the rest of the building, all the shafts and responds are detached from the walls by some two feet and are used to support two kinds of constructional arrangements. In the apsidal ends of the upper chapels (Fig. 165), sets of two slender monolithic shafts combined to form stiff little piers carry a miniature two-

164. Laon Cathedral, N transept, terminal wall at tribune level, ca. 1180–1190

165. Laon Cathedral, S transept chapel at tribune level, ca. 1180–1190

storied elevation, the clerestory stage of which continues the vertical plane of the inner screen of the two-layered lower story, while the deep arches which unite the two layers and frame the lower windows give the impression of a foreshortened main arcade and aisle: a most unusual and subtle play on the mobility of the limit and on suggested effects of space. On the other hand, against the flat terminal wall of the transept the detached colonnettes support little bridges of stone which appear suspended at mid-height and carry another level of upper passages running at the foot of the rose and of the windows that accompany it (Fig. 164). In this way is created a system of small alveoles of space, lining the surfaces of wall and reminiscent in their three-dimensional precision of the

171

aedicular constructions of Pompeian painting.[14] This continuous layer of compartmented space, evenly hugging the wall, looks as if it had been hollowed out of the wall itself, suggesting an originally heavy wall eaten away by some powerful erosion and now reduced to the mere shell of its primitive thickness. This combined effect of structural lightness and spatial interpenetration was considered so successful that it was repeated with little change more than thirty years later on the inside of the façade of Mantes, with the same hollowing out of the towers which open internally in the same manner onto the west bay of the nave.[15]

A Simplified Elevation: the Braine Type

It so happens that at the very moment when all these new methods were being evolved, which aimed at stressing with the utmost clarity the grid-work of these multi-storied structures, Gothic architects were beginning to weary of the tight pattern of the tribune churches and of their principle of insistent repetitions. They began to yearn for simpler formulas, especially for fewer stories; and after the south transept of Soissons there came as the next step forward, in the 1190s, the simplified pattern of Saint-Yved at Braine (Fig. 166): a widened grid in two major stories only, separated by the horizontal belt of a triforium. Braine is still very close to Laon, the triforium in particular being of the Laon type in two layers with a wall passage: what has vanished is the tribune story.

Braine is a building of such harmony and definition that it was bound to be very influential in its own time; and it has since been commonly treated as the model of its type. But it would be a mistake to imagine that it was necessarily the first example of the series it has been made to represent. One of its supposed copies, Saint-Michel-en-Thiérache, now appears to have been started a few years before Braine itself[16] and even to have initiated its most characteristic feature of plan, the diagonally planted chapels (Fig. 305.A, p. 331). As for the new kind of triforium elevation that Braine so effectively illustrates (substituting a double-wall triforium story for the openness to the roof space of the earlier triforium types), this went back further still, at least to the early 1170s: the abbey-church

166. BRAINE, SAINT-YVED, choir and transept, ca. 1190–1216 (Ward Archive)

167. Laon, destroyed abbey church of Saint-Vincent, begun ca. 1174, drawing by Tavernier (Paris, Bibl. nat.)

168. Juziers, choir, ca. 1170

of Saint-Vincent at Laon (Fig. 167), begun soon after 1174, had adopted this pattern of stories a good fifteen years before Braine;[17] and the existence at Juziers, near Mantes, of a choir (Fig. 168) of similar design at a date which, from the style of capitals and moldings, cannot be much after 1170, seems to indicate that even Saint-Vincent at Laon was not the first building of the type. The formula rapidly became so popular that in the early 1190s, when Braine was probably designed, it had already developed into several distinguishable variants. Braine itself was an emanation of the Laon style; but a Flemish variant can also be spotted, characterized by an exterior clerestory passage running behind a screen of open arches. Strangely enough the oldest example of that Flemish variant (ca. 1190) is found at Lyon Cathedral (Figs. 169, 170), far away

170. LYON CATHEDRAL, N side of choir, ca. 1190–1200

169. LYON CATHEDRAL, choir, mostly ca. 1190–1200

171. CANTERBURY CATHEDRAL, Trinity Chapel, by William the Englishman, 1181–1184

172. CANTERBURY CATHEDRAL, S side of Trinity Chapel, crypt story 1179–1180, main structure 1181–1184

173. Lausanne Cathedral, choir and S transept, ca. 1190–1230

from Flanders certainly, but on one of the main roads from Flanders to Italy.[18] A third variant, adapted to English usage with the interior clerestory passage of the Norman tradition superposed on top of a two-layer triforium in the Laon manner, had been created a few years before at Canterbury in the Trinity Chapel (Figs. 171, 172) by the English William; and this Kentish variant also was to be repeated very soon (just after 1190) far on the other major road to Italy: at Lausanne Cathedral,[19] in sight of the Alps (Fig. 173). The explosive expansion of these two variants of the new type of eleva-

178

tion from England and Flanders to the last halting places before the Alpine passes, along the great trade routes of the time, shows quite clearly that in the 1190s the triforium elevation of the Braine type, that latest creation of the Northern French group, was considered to express the most recent fashion in Gothic design. The age of the tribune churches was over, a simpler grid-work was now favored; and this is an essential fact to remember, for it shows what prepared the advent of the grander formula which was finally to be created at Chartres in 1194.

Of course, before a new architecture could be conceivable other deeper changes had to take place: the guiding principles of the 1160s had to lose their power to stimulate creation and become regarded as the inheritance of a dead past; and that change in attitude could occur only under the influence of some far-reaching innovations, affecting engineering practice as well as engendering new visions of forms in space. But precisely—and this is why the period of the 1180s and 1190s is so fascinating to study at close quarters—these deep changes were already manifesting themselves and beginning to disrupt the old order. And they were taking place (as one might perhaps have expected) in the two greatest workshops of the preceding generation: those of Paris and Laon.

INVENTION OF THE FLYING BUTTRESS

What Paris invented was the new constructional device which was to change everything some twenty years later: the external flying-buttress. Quadrant arches had been used before then for purposes of buttressing, but always under the roofs of the aisles or tribunes, as at Saint-Germer (Fig. 124, p. 129) (which is the classic early Gothic example of this method) and, as has been noted in the preceding chapter,[20] it is most likely that hidden flying-buttresses of a very similar kind had been employed also in the nave of Cambrai and the choir of Notre-Dame (Fig. 178A). Thus the question that arises here is simply: when was it decided to make those quadrant arches rise above the lateral roofs of the aisles and tribunes? or, in other words, when and where were the first external flying buttresses employed?

179

It is often said that the flying buttresses which were added soon after 1180 around the chevet of Saint-Germain-des-Prés (Fig. 174) in Paris are the oldest external flying buttresses still in existence; and this may be so, although it must be borne in mind that all the roofs and buttresses of Saint-Germain-des-Prés were restored or touched up in some manner in the seventeenth century. Perhaps equally early are the flying buttresses of the east end of Saint-Leu d'Esserent (Fig. 176), which must also be the result of an addition, since they are not planted in exactly the same line as the buttresses of the lower story on top of which they stand. The system of buttressing planned originally consisted simply in quadrant arches placed at a lower level, so that they would have been hidden as usual under the roof of the ambulatory. But the use of external flying buttresses rising above the roofs was decided in all probability before that part of the building was even completed, perhaps when the choir vaults were being built (as was done in the Trinity Chapel at Canterbury Cathedral [Fig. 172] in 1184). The flying buttresses of Saint-Leu d'Esserent are of a more typically early shape than those of Saint-Germain-des-Prés, since they display a most awkward way of passing from the greater width of the free-rising pier buttress to the lesser width of the quadrant arch itself: the slope of the back of the arch being continued onto the head of the pier buttress, an indentation occurs on each side of the point of contact between arch and buttress, which is marked by a clear vertical recession. This frank admission of an unsolved snag was less exceptional than might be imagined, for the same form was used at Champeaux (Fig. 175), at Gonesse with only a slight vertical break, most probably also at Mantes;[21] it may have been quite common in the Paris region in the 1180s and 90s.

The existence of that early group clearly centered around Paris seems to confirm what has often been suggested: namely, that the first structure ever conceived and built with exterior flying-buttresses was the nave of Notre-Dame—which would place the invention ca. 1175–1178, when the nave of Notre-Dame was designed. In its original state there were flying-buttresses against only every other nave pier, as extra buttressing was considered neces-

174. PARIS, SAINT-GERMAIN-DES-PRÉS, chevet with flying buttresses added ca. 1180–1185

175. CHAMPEAUX, S side of nave, buttressing on alternate piers, ca. 1190–1205

176. SAINT-LEU D'ESSERENT,
flying buttresses of chevet, ca.
1180–1190

sary only at those points where the sexpartite vaults operate the
greatest concentration of thrusts; and this explains why, in the
aisles of Notre-Dame, alternate piers had to be reinforced by a ring
of twelve additional shafts. The nave of Champeaux still preserves
that method of buttressing on alternate piers (Fig. 175): a perfectly
logical and sound arrangement, since in sexpartite vaulting the
thrust received by the intermediate supports is only two-fifths of
the thrust concentrated on the points where the diagonal ribs converge.[22] The huge flying-buttresses which now flank the nave of
Notre-Dame date, in their present form, from Viollet-le-Duc's restoration and, in their pre-restoration state, from the alterations of
ca. 1230. But there remains one indication of what must have been
the curve of the original flying buttresses: behind the south-west
corner of the south transept façade (which was brought forward
and totally redesigned between 1259 and 1267), the original angle

182

buttress of the transept is preserved (Fig. 177). When he restored the building Viollet-le-Duc noticed that the original slope of the tribune roof (which before the changes of ca. 1230 was situated at a higher level than it is now) was still clearly marked in the masonry. Above that line there was—and still is—a relieving arch of quadrant form which undoubtedly was established with that curve at that level to repeat the curve and level of the original flying buttresses of the nave, the west walls of the transept having been built with the nave. And this remnant of the original external buttressing system suggests that the nave of Notre-Dame must have been designed with flying-buttresses of the simplest kind; but in view of its complex structural type, there must have been two tiers of such flying buttresses (Fig. 178.B), one at the height of the tribune windows and the other at the height of the clerestory.[23]

It was certainly quite natural that the need for more accuracy in the positioning of the members that sustained the upper walls should have been felt at Notre-Dame, where the walls were both very tall and very thin, rather than in the buildings of the Northern group, where the presence of a heavier framework of walls, articulated in depth in their upper parts and often loaded at the top (as in Noyon transept and nave) by substantial masses of masonry, made it less imperative to maximize the efficacy of the constructional devices employed to resist the thrusts of the vaults. It is worth noting that these earliest flying buttresses apply their action against the wall pretty well at the place where it is most required: i.e., at the height at which the radius of the vault makes an angle of about 30 degrees with the horizontal, this being the point where the vault tends to break if it is not sufficiently buttressed.[24] This degree of exactness, in what was just a guess at the mechanics of masonry vaults, was possible only in the very thin structures of the Paris group, in which distortions due to faulty buttressing must have been especially apparent, demonstrating along what lines improvements needed to be made. There seems to have been a gap of some five to ten years between the earliest flying buttresses of the Paris region and the first examples found in the Northern group: at Saint-Remi at Reims, the south transept of Soissons, the naves of

177. PARIS, NOTRE-DAME, SW
angle buttress of S transept, ca.
1175–1185, drawing by Lassus and
Viollet-le-Duc

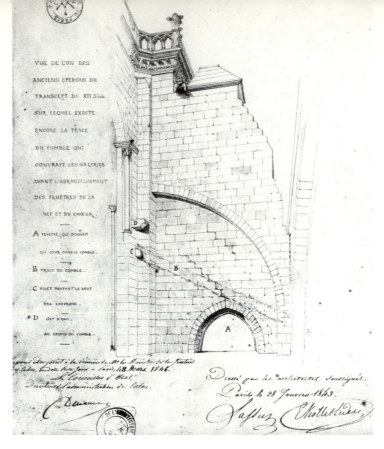

178. PARIS, NOTRE-DAME, reconstructed original sections of:

    A. choir, begun ca. 1163   *B.* nave, begun ca. 1175

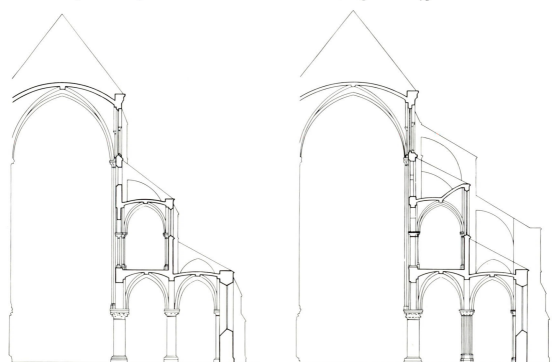

179. MANTES, NOTRE-DAME, flying buttresses of chevet, ca. 1180–1200, but modified late 13th c.

Noyon and Laon. As for the claim that has sometimes been put forward in favor of the flying-buttresses of the abbey-church of Cluny, it must be remembered that no one knows when these were added to the original structure and that there is no way of studying them, since the whole church was pulled down more than one hundred and fifty years ago; but from drawings of the seventeenth and eighteenth centuries they would seem to have belonged to a type which was common in Burgundy ca. 1200 or 1210.

The invention of the flying-buttress did not change at once the vision of Gothic architects. They went on applying the same methods of design as before, and Mantes is a good example of this first conservative stage in the use of the new constructional device (Fig. 179). The flying buttresses there were planned from the moment the building had reached the level of the tribune floor, from ca. 1185,[25] but they were used only to give more height and even thinner walls to a building conceived according to the principles of the previous generation, with the same storied structure and the same large expanses of flat wall; the deep buttresses required to carry the flying buttresses were even visualized as radial walls of the same surface value as the outer wall of the tribunes, spreading its mural quality into a further dimension. It took more than fifteen years for the flying buttress to act upon the creative imagination of two very great architects and to lead them to imagine a different world of forms—a new Gothic architecture in fact—at Chartres and Bourges, ca. 1194–1195.

FINAL INNOVATIONS AT LAON

However, the elements of a new vision were already developing in another area, at the cathedral of Laon, and in a way quite unconnected with the flying-buttress. One sign of this change was the exterior treatment of the chapels which jut out towards the east from the terminal bay of the Laon transepts (Fig. 180). Seen from outside, these tall apselike chapels rise vertically in three zones of windows. But inside there are two chapels only, one above the

180. LAON CATHEDRAL, transept from NE, ca. 1175–1190

other: at the ground story, a plain and fairly heavy-looking chapel, with a wall-arcading below the window sills as at Noyon or Saint-Germain-des-Prés; and above, at tribune level, corresponding to the two upper zones of windows, the tall and lightly built chapel which has already been described for its double-wall structure.[26] In the apse of that upper chapel, the double wall method having been applied to only the lower half of the elevation (Fig. 165), the upper story is built in a single layer, flush with the inner face of the double wall structure below it; which leaves a deep recess on the outside, carrying an exterior passage that cuts through the heads of the buttresses at the topmost level of the exterior elevation.

This displacement of the limit from one side of the double wall to the other had been practised already in the transepts of Noyon, where the upper passage also opens on the outside. But there the wall remained double in its structure and of the same thickness right to the top; and seen from the outside the rounded ends of the transepts make a huge half cylinder rising on all its height as a sheer vertical surface (Fig. 182): the ideal followed was still the creation of simple geometrical forms. In the chapels of Laon on the other hand the treatment of the wall changes suddenly in the upper story as the double wall loses its outer layer (Fig. 181), so that all that remains is the thin inner layer, in which the windows are set, and a substantial ledge on which the upper passage emerges open to the elements.[27] Obviously, the exterior volume of the chapel is profoundly altered as a result of that change from thick to thin in the wall structure: wider at the base, the chapel recedes to a much diminished and attenuated top story. And a very similar treatment is applied to the exterior of the lantern-tower, where a broad ledge running below the windows represents the depth of wall that has been discarded in the upper story.

Playing on effects of recession, on recessed planes and recessed volumes, to modulate the exterior appearance of a building was a very bold and new idea. It gives an impression of mobility in depth — but also of mobility in height by creating a telescopic effect of volumes which could be elongated or compressed, as if they could slip one into the other (Fig. 183). This play on recession combines in

181. Laon Cathedral, E chapel of N transept, showing recession of upper story, ca. 1180–1190

182. Noyon Cathedral, end of S transept, showing vertical rise of wall, ca. 1170–1185

the apse of the Laon chapels with the use of an overall polygonal shape, creating a faceted volume of sharply defined bay panels in place of the usual continuous semicircular form. And if you look carefully at the transept chapels of Laon, you will see that their volume does not change only in its upper part, but all the way down: it widens progressively toward the base, and even below the lower windows the wall becomes considerably thicker than just above them (a difference that can be judged from the comparative projection of the buttresses). This progressive downward swelling of the volumes gives an illusion of elasticity and explains to a certain extent

183. LAON CATHEDRAL, E chapels of N transept, upper stories ca. 1180–1190

184. LE MANS CATHEDRAL, radiating chapel, ca. 1217–1230

the false notion Viollet-le-Duc had of an actual quality of elasticity in Gothic structure. These chapels seem to possess an organic life, like great tree trunks; while in fact the effect results simply from the application of an old principle of building practice based on the notions of gravity and stability. But what remains true is that there is at Laon, in these works of the 1180s, a new quality of suppleness and a fluidity of treatment which were to become characteristic of Gothic architecture in the thirteenth century. This was probably a much modernized expression of a plastic feeling inherited from the earlier, semi-Romanesque stage of the architecture of the Soissannais in the early 1160s, from such works as the east end of Mont-Notre-Dame for instance, which was also, according to the drawings that have survived, very much modeled in diminishing bulk. As for the

189

185. SENLIS CATHEDRAL, W façade, ca. 1170–1180

influence on the following generation of architects of that art of large-scale modeling, two examples will suffice: the radiating chapels of the choir of Le Mans (Fig. 184), begun in 1218, which are simply an enlargement of the upper stories of the transept chapels of Laon; and the exterior elevation of the nave of Chartres (begun in

190

1194), the very source of thirteenth century architecture, where the progressive thickening of the buttresses (Fig. 211) reflects most clearly the same feeling about matter and the art of weighting down the mass of a building.

All this would be quite enough to give to the workshop of Laon in the last decades of the twelfth century a very special position in the history of Gothic architecture. But the west façade, which was begun in the same years, was no less remarkable. The façades of the 1170s, that of Senlis (Fig. 185) for instance, were still arid in their vertical surfaces: the large motif of the rose window had not yet been adopted as the normal center-piece for a façade.[28] This was done, as far as can be judged, in the transept façades of Laon (Fig. 186) by 1180 or 1185; but in spite of its many openings the north transept façade at Laon (which alone has preserved its original character) remains rather bare and dry. It was in the west front (Fig. 187), designed very soon after, that a transfiguration took place, again under the stimulus of the desire for strong plastic effects: two zones of cavernous openings, one of projecting porches, one of deep-set arches enclosing the rose and its flanking windows, establish a colossal pattern of large forms underlined by dark patches of

186. Laon Cathedral, N transept façade, ca. 1180–1190 (Ward Archive)

187. Laon Cathedral, W façade, ca. 1190–1205

shadow, which organizes in one stroke the whole block of the façade and imposes the most striking vision of order. The formula thus created on the west front of Laon was to become the general principle of composition of all Gothic façades after that date, although the particular visionary quality of Laon remained unique.

But there is more to that façade than just the use of vast perforations as a principle of large-scale composition. All sorts of new motifs are created there too, and treated simultaneously on different scales and sizes, making series of homologous forms repeated at different logical levels:[29] the porches are gabled like small autonomous buildings; they are separated by pinnacles which are spires in miniature; smaller pinnacles rise out of the upper arcading; and the towers themselves are surrounded by clusters of smaller towers and seem to pivot on their base, to face simultaneously in all directions. This breaking up of the volumes, this mobility, these families of smaller forms repeating the larger ones, all this expressed for the first time a new architectural vision which was to guide the following stage in the development of Gothic architecture.

The sensibility of this master of Laon (conjectured to be the second master) was certainly no less important than the technical invention of the flying-buttress by the Paris builders, in bringing about the great stylistic mutation of the mid-1190s. Out of the strict order of the previous generation and of its almost too regular system of multi-storied structures, after a short period of experimentation, something quite unexpected and new was beginning to emerge—pointing in various directions, still rather unconnected, but already moving far away from what had constituted a first universe of established Gothic forms. A great effort of lucidity and concentration was now required to revise and integrate again the whole language of architecture; and it was only with Chartres and Bourges that the great jump forward was made that started Gothic architecture on its new course.

188. CHARTRES, SAINT-PÈRE (now Saint-Pierre), view from interior of nave, showing abutment of flying buttresses, ca. 1205–1230

CHAPTER VI

The Flying Buttress and the Second Gothic System

THE LAST six or seven years of the twelfth century mark in the history of Gothic architecture in France the beginning of a new age: with Chartres begun just after the fire of 1194,[1] with Bourges where work seems to have been started in 1195,[2] the potentialities of the flying buttress became suddenly understood and visualized by architects as a revolutionary element. In its simplest form, as a single quadrant arch rising above the lateral roofs to hold the building at a higher level, the exterior flying buttress had been known already for some twenty years (Figs. 174–176, p. 181), although it had never been viewed as anything more than a useful addition to a pre-existing architectural system which remained otherwise unaltered. But from the mid-1190s the flying buttress became the basis for all kinds of changes that affected profoundly the whole conception and designing of the constructional organism. Many things which before had been impossible became possible and were soon to be accepted as the norm; and the size and appearance of buildings were transformed. The pre-eminent position taken by the flying buttress in the imagination of the architects of that generation is so manifest that the architecture of northern France in the

195

early part of the thirteenth century would probably be best described as the architecture of the flying buttress.

THE WORKINGS OF THE FLYING BUTTRESS

The most telling symptom of change was the way in which the flying buttresses were suddenly multiplied and their scale enlarged. It was from the mid-1190s that they began to be doubled up in height in batteries of two arches placed one above the other, as in the choir of Soissons Cathedral (Fig. 189); and in the larger buildings such as Chartres or Bourges, they were further duplicated in two successive flights one behind the other (Fig. 196) so as to have them stride over double aisles or double ambulatories. From the status of an accessory member and something of an emergency solution, the flying buttress had developed into one of the dominant elements in the organization of Gothic structures, systematically applied and particularly striking visually for the way in which it

189. SOISSONS CATHEDRAL, flying buttresses of E end, ca. 1200–1210

imprinted on the exterior of the building with the greatest immediacy the repetitive pattern of the bays. But however far-ranging the aesthetic consequences which were to be derived from this whole-hearted acceptance of the new mode of buttressing, it was not on aesthetic grounds that the flying buttress won its new eminence: it had won its place in the minds of Gothic builders on its value as a powerful device of structural engineering.

How did those screenlike assemblages of buttressing piers and arches function as stabilizing devices? They worked essentially as a system of struts applied high against the main walls of the structure just above the heads of the piers, at the back of the vault springers (Fig. 188); and by transmitting the excess thrust of the vaults to a line of solid pier buttresses planted on the outer edges of the building, they did with the necessity of enlarging the interior piers (which should normally have followed from any increase in the height of the high vaults). The function of lateral bracing, which until then had been achieved through the superposition of vaulted stories on either side of the main vessels of Gothic churches (Fig. 121, p. 126), was now performed by autonomous members which could rise with the main vaults, independently of the rest of the fabric; and Gothic builders soon realized the degree of technical freedom they had thus acquired.

Of course to treat flying buttresses as mere struts or props is a simplification of the constructional reality. Being made not of timber but of masonry, these struts had to be built as combinations of slanting arch units of quadrant shape which by definition, being arches, exert a thrust of their own.[3] At the points where their heads abut on the tall central structure, they apply against it a counter thrust, the force of which varies according to their own weight, their curve and their span. This inherent thrust force is not negligible, although recent calculations using the most modern methods of structural analysis have proved that it can never be more than a fraction of the thrust force generated by the high vaults themselves;[4] and the difference in magnitude between these opposing forces means that it is essentially as struts that the flying buttresses function. It is through the rigidity of their assemblages that they block in position the upper parts of the structure, relaying the thrusts of the vaults out to an external row of pier buttresses, which alone can be given sufficient bulk and depth to finally absorb those retransmitted thrust forces.

Obviously the architects of the late twelfth and early thirteenth century experimented on the use of these buttressing members in a manner which was not always the most logical, and when faced with alternative hypotheses they did not necessarily choose what appears to us now the better one technically:[5] everything depended on the judgment of individual architects and on chains of educated guesses. But a process of trial and error was for many centuries the path by which engineering progressed. Whatever deficiencies there may have been in their interpretation of the play of mechanical forces, the Gothic masters had become aware of having made a great technological advance, which put into their hands a most versatile instrument with which to achieve the stability of complex vaulted structures. It was the consciousness of this augmented power that made them take a fresh look at the organization of their buildings and submit the most basic concepts to a thorough re-evaluation. What were those major changes that so renewed architecture in the mid-1190s? How did they come about and what new visions of order did they reflect? These are the points on which a close analysis must now be focused in order to understand in what manner, within so short a time, a new kind of Gothic came to define itself.

The Start of a Great Renewal: The Bourges-Chartres Contrast

The use of the flying buttress seems to have given a new start to all the basic Gothic desires for reduced bulk, for spaciousness, for linear expression. And when one looks at the buildings of the extreme end of the twelfth century and the first years of the thirteenth, one feels that Gothic simply starts all over again, repeating the same program of width and height and openness and scanning—but this time on a larger scale and with much more powerful technical means.

The most obvious advance is probably that of size. The buildings become larger than ever in height and width and, significantly,

190. BOURGES CATHEDRAL, reconstructed original plan: E half of building 1195–1214, W half ca. 1225–1255 (N tower of façade hypothetically reconstructed similar to S tower)

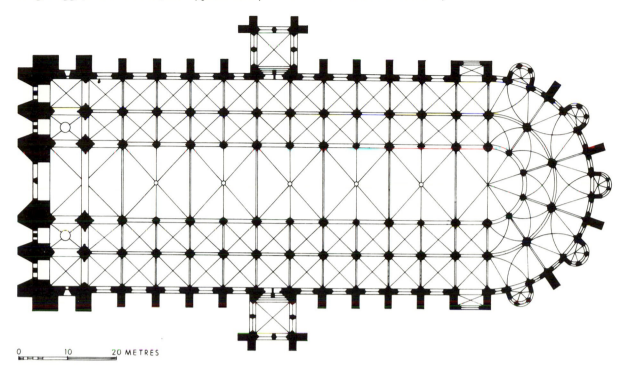

0   10   20 METRES

191. CHARTRES CATHEDRAL, reconstructed original plan: W façade and towers ca. 1135–1160, rest of cathedral built from 1194, nave and choir completed 1220, transept ends ca. 1235

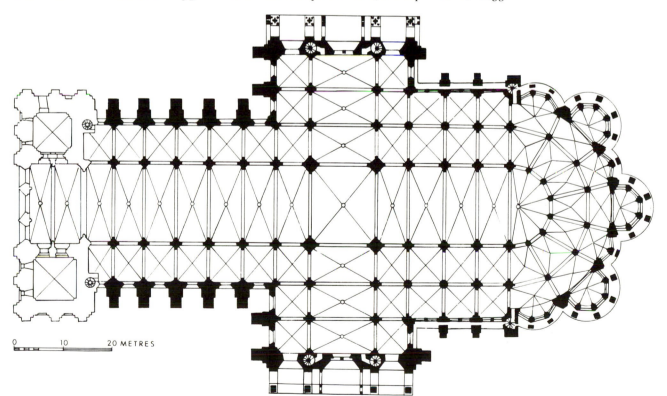

0   10   20 METRES

the plans of both Bourges and Chartres (Figs. 190, 191) show a simultaneous return to the grand pattern of double aisles and double ambulatory, which had been used only exceptionally in the twelfth century (for, after Saint-Denis, it had been repeated only once, at Notre-Dame). The revival of the double ambulatory in the two great cathedrals of the mid-1190s began a trend which affected a whole generation, and for about forty years it became more frequent as a feature of the more ambitious churches than it had been before or than it was to be for the next two centuries.[6] The success of the double ambulatory plan was of course the sign of a renewed interest in the achievement of maximum spaciousness as one of the main aims of architecture; and it should also be noted that, at both Bourges and Chartres, the total width is relatively great when compared with the total length of the building. The effect of expanding space is particularly striking in the choir of Chartres, where three deep chapels projecting beyond the two zones of ambulatories spread out the building even further on the surrounding landscape. No such attempt at further peripheral expansion is found at Bourges where the tiny nichelike chapels, added only as an afterthought, do not affect the movement of the volumes: from inside they look rather like oriel windows and from outside they are hardly more important than the buttresses. The idea of the double ambulatory was obviously not exploited in at all the same way at Bourges and Chartres. Indeed, apart from the very general similarities which have just been noted, the two buildings are so completely different in style and intentions that it would be difficult to claim that they be considered together as two expressions of the same idea. The fact is that what developed around 1195 was not one but two new architectures, formed at the same time but independently of each other, one being Bourges and the other Chartres.

In plan the concepts that these two revolutionary works materialize are almost perfect opposites. At Bourges the plan is continuous, without a transept, dominated by the single movement of a large double-aisled nave running from end to end without interruption and folding upon itself in the semicircle of the chevet. Bourges should therefore be seen as resulting from the fusion of two traditions, for it is from the Sens series that it inherits the total elimination of the transept, while it is from Notre-Dame (and behind Notre-Dame, from the early project of Saint-Denis) that it takes its two other ruling principles: the extension to the whole building of the five-aisled plan of the choir, and the enclosure of that complexity of structure within the rigorous limit of an unbroken outline. By fusing these two traditions Bourges arrives at an extreme of nonarticulation. Chartres, on the other hand, is the very model of a clearly articulated plan composed of well differentiated elements: a nave flanked only by single aisles; then the strong crosswise break of the transept, which is conceived in itself as a nave running north and south, each transept also flanked with aisles and terminating in a façade; then the much wider and more spatially magnificent ensemble of the choir (or chevet), which covers even more surface than either of the other major components of the plan and which gives the impression of being short only because it is so wide. If at both Bourges and Chartres the plan is colossal, the type of layout chosen by each master is absolutely different.

Exterior photographs show perhaps even more clearly than the flattened geometry of a plan the difference of intention between the two works. Bourges is one long uninterrupted roofline, a single continuous volume (Fig. 192), while Chartres, as can instantly be perceived in an aerial view, has the shape of a huge cross (Fig. 193), ending toward the east in the rich and complex composition of a swelling chevet. A no less striking view can be had from the north spire of the façade: from there the great cruciform expanse of the structure, facing in the four directions of space,[7] can be measured on a more real scale; and what underlines most powerfully that articulation in space is the added element of a whole series of towers, which were left unfinished but which, had they been completed, would have given to Chartres very much the same sort of skyline silhouette as the cathedral of Laon as planned with its seven towers. Chartres would even have had eight, plus probably a thin central spire over the crossing.[8]

Between Bourges and Chartres there is something of the same contrast as between Notre-Dame and Laon Cathedral in the 1160s. They differ not only in their design but also in what they accept or reject of the recent past: they do not share the same artistic allegiance. While Laon features largely in the background of Chartres, it seems almost unknown to the master of Bourges who, on the other hand, had a great familiarity with the Parisian milieu—although the likeness between Bourges and Notre-Dame must not be overdrawn. When the two plans are compared, Bourges immediately shows itself to be somewhat greater in width and Notre-Dame to be relatively long and narrow (Fig. 130, p. 138); but the major difference is that Notre-Dame does have a transept, even if a non-projecting one, while at Bourges all notion of a transept has vanished. However, some typical details of designing show that Notre-Dame is indeed part of the ancestry of Bourges, and not only in matters of plan or volumes.

THE WORLD OF BOURGES

One of the strangest features of Notre-Dame is the mode of vaulting adopted in the curved section of the double ambulatory: combinations of small triangular units describe a sequence of W patterns

192. BOURGES CATHEDRAL, view from SE

in the inner ambulatory and of M patterns in the outer one (Fig. 130, p. 138). The basic intention behind this unusual vaulting arrangement was the desire to achieve on the outside and at all levels an even regularity of divisions, irrespective of the widening of the circumference of the volumes as the building spreads downward in three regular tiers in the semicircular sweep of the east end. That effect could be accomplished only by inventing a system of vaulting which would produce a progressive multiplication of the piers in the three concentric semicircles of supports of the double ambulatory. That system of triangular vault patterning—passing from five bays in the center at clerestory height to ten on the outer curve of the tribune and finally to thirteen bays on the periphery of the outer ambulatory—succeeded in creating at Notre-Dame a unique effect of all-over equidistance in the definition of the bay panels at all heights. At Bourges this system of subdivision is not applied with the same purposefulness and the same consistency: at the lowest level triangular compartments of vaulting are present in the outer ambulatory (Fig. 190) but, being confined to the sides of each bay

193. CHARTRES CATHEDRAL, aerial view from SE

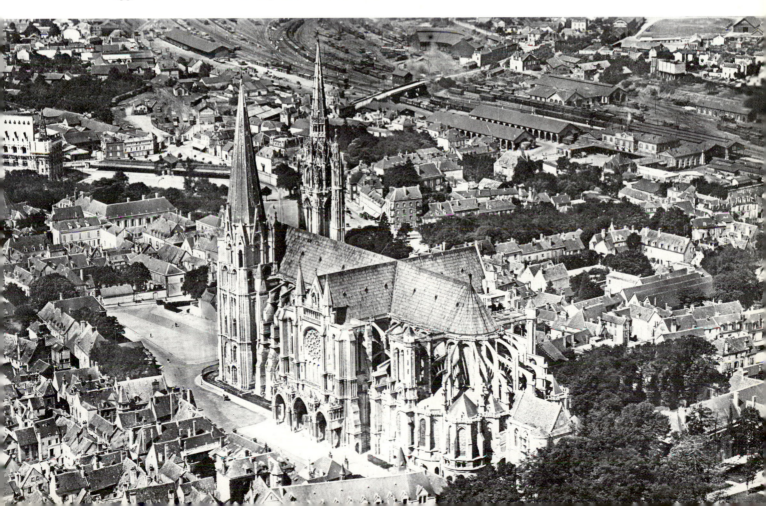

194. BOURGES CATHEDRAL, chevet, 1195–1214 (Ward Archive)

195. BOURGES CATHEDRAL, segment of outer ambulatory with chapel, ca. 1200

in order to leave in the center a more open access to the chapels (Fig. 195), they create a pattern more reminiscent of the ambulatories of the churches of Etampes[9] or of Saint-Remi at Reims than of the systematic zigzagging of the vault arrangement of Notre-Dame. Nevertheless there is a true connection with Notre-Dame, because the ambulatory of Bourges had first been planned differently: the little chapels, which appear suspended against the outer walls of the chevet (Fig. 194), were not part of the original design, and the five segments of the outer ambulatory were not meant to be divided into three bays each as they are now (with a little chapel in the middle) but into two bays only (with a buttress in the middle). This original disposition is still preserved in the crypt, the oriel-like chapels which open at the level of the main church being supported, with a great deal of corbelling, on top of the middle buttress of the twin bays of the crypt wall.[10] And the mode of vaulting which is found in that outer zone of the crypt—and which was to

205

196. BOURGES CATHEDRAL, flying buttresses on S side (Ward Archive)

have been repeated in the choir ambulatory above—is a simple replica of the W pattern of the inner ambulatory of Notre-Dame.[11]

This does not mean that all the twelfth-century forms which were still used at Bourges came from Paris. It has often been suggested that the sexpartite vaults which cover the central vessel of Bourges were one more sign of a close relationship with Notre-Dame; and there is no doubt that these large units of vaulting, which spread over two bays their wide pattern of ribs, proceeding at so much slower a pace than the elevation of the sides, still reflect a turn of mind current in the period when Notre-Dame was designed. But the sexpartite vaults of Bourges have none of the specific features which characterize the Parisian style of sexpartite vaulting;[12] they are in every respect much closer to the sexpartite vaults of Laon or of the west bays of Saint-Remi at Reims; in any case the Parisian touch is lacking. Bourges is simply rather conservative and traditional in the detail of its formal language. It preserves many of the habits or formulas which were in current use in the period of the 1160s and 1170s; and this applies most particularly to the exterior shaping of the building.

From outside, the volumes of Bourges rise in three regular tiers (Fig. 194) covered by sloping roofs, repeating the classic outline of the twelfth-century chevets of, say, Noyon (Fig. 120, p. 125), Saint-Remi, or Notre-Dame as originally built. The great flying buttresses of Bourges were even made to conform to the steep slope of that tiered progression in height, so as not to disturb the silhouette of the building against the sky (Fig. 196). This formula of stepped volumes was normally the expression of an inner structure in superposed floor levels and clearly separated stories: the wide lowest tier corresponding to the ambulatory and chapels, the intermediate tier to a story of tribunes, and the narrow upper tier to the clerestory. The exterior of Bourges follows so exactly this formula that it would be difficult to guess that its inner structure is not that of a tribune church. The designer has clearly been at pains to preserve the peaceful regularity of the almost equal stories of the great tribune churches of the previous generation. The smooth semicircular curve of the chevet at all three levels is one more feature that links the outer appearance of Bourges with the habits of vision of a generation earlier. The novel faceted treatment of the transept chapels of Laon has not touched Bourges: in this respect again it still belongs to an older world.

It preserves even a typical twelfth-century insistence on the horizontal continuity of the zones of windows seen from outside. The intermediate story in particular is treated in the manner of a continuous arcading (Fig. 194), the windows—two per bay—simply forming part of a sequence of four arches, the other two of which, on the right and left, are blind but make a continuous motif with the windows themselves. This arcaded pattern is clearly alien to the spirit of Parisian art (Paris at that time would have left the surfaces of wall undisturbed); but the source of the motif can easily be traced and it leads much further away than Paris. In the cathedral of Arras (Fig. 129, p. 136) the transept (begun probably ca. 1180) had exactly the same rather unusual system of surface patterning in four arches per bay; and this can hardly be a mere coincidence. The only story in the exterior elevation of Bourges that fails to conform to the principle of horizontal continuity is the uppermost zone of windows, the clerestory of the tall central space. There each bay panel becomes autonomous, being entirely filled by the large-scale centralized motif of a composed window in the manner of Chartres. The reason for this may be very simple, for the top story of Bourges was very likely heightened in course of construction;[13] and the original design should therefore be imagined with a clerestory modeled very much after the pattern of the intermediate story: that is, an even sequence of identical arches surmounted by a horizontal zone of wall punctured by a few round holes (which in that top story may have been planned a little bigger and somewhat differently spaced).

If, as seems most likely, Arras was the direct source for that distinctive style of surface treatment, one cannot escape the conclusion that the architect of Bourges must have had an intimate knowledge of the churches of the Northern Group and that he may well have borrowed some other elements from other works of the group. In fact a case could be made for the nave of Notre-Dame-la-Grande at Valenciennes: insofar as the rather inept drawing of Simon Le Boucq can give a proper idea of that interior, the piers in the nave were quite different from those in the choir, since they seem to have been composed of a round core with a number of thin shafts applied against it, which would make them the perfect prototypes for the Bourges piers.[14] When all the possible sources of the style of Bourges are carefully examined, it becomes clear that Bourges cannot be viewed as emanating from one only of the three Gothic milieux of the preceding generation but from all three: it has as many connections with the Southern (Sens, Etampes) as with the Northern group (Arras, Valenciennes) and with the Paris group (Notre-Dame). The background to Bourges is the whole of twelfth-century Gothic, brought together and transfigured.

It is the interior of Bourges (Figs. 197–203) which represents that transfiguration: the deceptively traditional exterior cloaks an interior which astounds by its immense and unobstructed spaciousness. While the triple-tiered mass of the exterior, repeating the silhouette of the great tribune churches, would suggest a compartmented interior structure in which the side volumes, cut up into stories, are screened off from the tall central space, the interior of Bourges instead is emptied of all structural partitioning and opens laterally on all its width (Fig. 198). The shape of that great unified interior is the hollow counterpart of the exterior, the inside of the same shell, with vaults disposed at the three levels marked on the outside by the three zones of roofs, and repeating the regular gradation of the exterior as it widens progressively, from the culminating height of the central vessel to a very tall inner aisle to a low outer aisle.

This kind of interior progression in three stages was not in itself a new idea. Even the existence of some Early Christian prototype cannot be ruled out;[15] and at any rate by the second half of the eleventh century experiments along those lines were multiplying. The unvaulted nave of S. Abbondio at Como (Fig. 41, p. 46) represents the oldest type: begun perhaps in the 1060s, it is impressive by the height of its arcade and the simplicity of its big columns, backed by the depth of double aisles diminishing in height and separated by a second line of smaller columns. The same idea was repeated soon after in the last years of the eleventh century with a completely different intonation in the vaulted structures of Romanesque France: in the choir of Saint-Sever for instance, which was probably barrel vaulted from the start; and more splendidly at Cluny III which stood, until its destruction, as the great Romanesque masterpiece of that staggered pattern of elevation (Fig. 43, p. 47). One hundred feet tall, lit by an augmented number of windows, precociously modern by its pointed arches and vaults but erected on heavy piers which partly blocked the view into the aisles, Cluny may have been one of the models the master of Bourges had

197. BOURGES CATHEDRAL, general interior view, 1195–1255
(Ward Archive)

198. BOURGES CATHEDRAL, diagonal view across nave from S aisle
(Ward Archive)

in mind from the start and meant to emulate and supplant—although he may also have been influenced by some Cistercian examples since that stepped arrangement of the interior space, in a somewhat less ample form, had recently been revived in the new chevet of Clairvaux, which was the starting point for a whole series of similar designs.[16]

What makes Bourges differ from these forerunners is its extreme structural lightness and its general enlargement, especially in the considerable rise of the inner aisle, the height of which is disproportionate to that of the outer aisle. The break is so marked that it is the tall vertical wall of that inner aisle which appears as the true limit of the central volume, making the space of the inner aisle merge into that of the central nave; and the perception of this extraordinary width on two-thirds of the total height[17] is one of the major elements which contribute to the sense of wonder evoked by the interior of Bourges. But that vision of global unity is combined with a vision of extreme multiplicity. Looking straight into the east end, where those long parallel vistas close upon themselves, or from the outer aisle across the width of the nave (Fig. 199), one gets in a flattened perspective the image of a five-storied elevation, even though it remains clear that these five stories operate in two planes and as two distinct sequences. This multiplicity of horizontal zones does not however penetrate the volumes: it is inscribed only on their periphery, flattened against the surface of the thin mantle of stone which wraps around that vast voided space; and what matters here is not so much the number of stories as their insistent repetitiousness, and in particular the recurrence of the same triforium motif in almost identical form at two different heights.

This recurrence, in itself so anomalous, is the clue to the realization that there exists on a colossal scale an interplay between two similar sets of forms. Bourges is in fact composed of two churches in one: two basically identical structures somehow manipulated and distorted to make them fit one into the other. The elevation of the inner aisle is that of a perfectly normal church of average size (Fig. 200), actually taller than Braine and closely related to it in type, except that the heightened triforium story would recall the "tall

199. Bourges Cathedral, full elevation of one choir bay, ca. 1195–1214

triforium" variant of the Flemish borderland.[18] And this lower church, together with the outer aisle which belongs to it, seems to have been enormously widened, as if forced outward, in order to set in the center a second church of the same type (Fig. 201)—but this time forced upward irresistibly, as if raised on stilts to an immense height, where it seems miraculously suspended beneath the dome of the sky. Presenting twice over the same sequence of stories and the identical motif of a triforium of unique design, these two elevations can be isolated and viewed separately as self-sufficient entities. But they are at the same time combined in a single overall pattern, like two voices in a fugue following one another at a measured distance and repeating the same theme on two different registers; and the unity of that contrapuntal structure overrules the sense of duality (Fig. 203). The oscillation between these two contradictory perceptions gives rise to a visual pulsation, a changing

200. BOURGES CATHEDRAL, elevation of "lower church," seen in ambulatory bays, ca. 1200–1208

201. BOURGES CATHEDRAL, "upper church" to W, first six bays, 1195–1214
(Ward Archive)

consciousness of the limits of space as the eye moves from one level to another, which results in an eventual synthesis of the two perceptions and the awareness of a vastness of space simultaneously in height and in width.

With a width of 26.6 meters (87 feet) across its triple central space bounded by the tall aisle walls, and a height of 37.15 meters (122 feet) to the apex of its central vaults, Bourges was indeed in all dimensions the largest building of its age. And what explains the advance of Bourges over its predecessors and made possible its amazing effect of disencumbered space was the logical use of those regular sequences of composite flying buttresses, which block in position the vaults of the inner aisle as well as the high central vaults. The interior partitioning of the side volumes in a high-rise building was no longer necessary; and the only form of extra reinforcement that this tall structure required could be lodged within the fabric of the walls in the form of horizontal belts of arches, 1.20 to 1.35 meters thick (some 4 feet), occupying the full depth of each triforium, binding together longitudinally the parallel files of piers and thus performing a function of stiffening at two levels all around the structure.[19] By imagining a bold structural design which pushed all the stabilizing devices (transverse bracing of the flying buttresses, longitudinal stiffening of the belt of arches) into the upper reaches of the nave elevation, and by making the heightened space of the inner aisle express that distribution of the essential structural elements, the master of Bourges was able to reduce, up to a height of about 20 meters (some 65 feet) the whole substance of the central elevation to nothing but two lines of elongated freestanding uprights—creating one of the most spectacular effects of weightless spaciousness ever achieved. Bourges can be said to mark the climax of that tendency to spatial enlargement combined with maximum lightness which, sixty years before, had been one of the major motive forces in the genesis of Gothic architecture itself and which was already so clearly evident at Saint-Martin-des-Champs in the Paris of the 1130s. But this ideal was now achieved on a much larger scale, with a new kind of complexity and with a refinement in the marshalling of visual effects which would before have been inconceivable.

202. BOURGES CATHEDRAL, N side of choir and nave, showing effect of linear texture

203. BOURGES CATHEDRAL, choir (campaign of 1195–1214), showing staggered extension of the limits of space

204. CHARTRES CATHEDRAL, general interior view 1194–1220, showing simplicity of spatial organization

The use of linear values is particularly subtle at Bourges and it plays an essential part in the visual effects of the building. A tight but light grid of thin lines—shafts, ribs, string courses and moldings, all delicately drawn, not too hard or too dark, rather blond in tonal value—runs over the surface of the whole structure, piers and vaults and arches and wall surfaces alike.[20] They are used here in a most unusual manner, for they are not made to define the component parts of the structure nor to explain how those parts are combined. The effect produced is that of a web of fine vertical lines which covers all forms, passing over the piers as well as over the flat panels of triforium, to unite the whole interior (Fig. 202). The spacing of the thin shafts that surround the piers is almost exactly the same as the spacing of the colonnettes in the triforiums; and this identity in spacing is what gives the impression of an allover texture inherent in the matter out of which the whole building has been fabricated. The corollary to that linear evenness—that is, the absence of a strong bay rhythm—is another factor of great importance at Bourges and one which underlines the very special position of the building. Bourges is a highly elaborate work of art, complex in its interrelationships and handled with superior artistry. But Bourges did not give a new system of organization, an idea which could be used over and over as a standard formula. Its composition is not even in a succession of spatial units which could be analyzed and conceived as self-contained entities: in fact at Bourges there is only one spatial unit, the whole building. So that Bourges is a revelation but not an explanation. It gave a magnificent vision of spatial splendor, but it did not supply a set of simple relations that could lend itself easily to variations in scale and to a certain freedom of reinterpretation.

The New Statement of Chartres

Chartres was in many ways less subtle than Bourges and altogether simpler in its effects; but Chartres offered a much more radical solution to the problems of the day and it had more of a grip on the future. Actually nothing could be simpler than the spatial effect of Chartres. As at Bourges and in all great works of architecture,

205. CHARTRES CATHEDRAL, choir, completed 1220

space is made to play in width and depth as well as in height; but instead of the multiple progression of Bourges, with its vaults at three heights, its three zones of windows and its widening in three stages, the spatial concept at Chartres is based on the elementary contrast between a tall central nave and lower spreading aisles (Fig. 204): the classic basilican pattern, enlarged at Chartres in both height and width. The central nave is 34.45 meters (113 feet) high, a little less than Bourges; but in spite of its great width—for Chartres is very wide at 16.3 meters (53½ feet)—and perhaps because of that width, the vertical movement of the nave becomes even more powerful. Chartres has a magnificent loftiness: when from the nave you look at the great shell of the choir in the distance, you realize that in spite of the width of the building it is the insistence on height that is striking. Is it because, being so wide, so much space is injected into the upward movement? At least what is certain and evident is the vigor of the vertical cadence marked by

221

206. CHARTRES CATHEDRAL, double ambulatory and chapels, ca. 1200–1210

the projection of the piers, which rise uninterrupted to the vault and strongly frame the whole interior space.

Contrasting with this upward movement is the horizontal expansion of the aisles on either side, set at right-angles to the surge of the central space. In the nave single aisles do not give great lateral depth; but in the choir (Fig. 205) there are double aisles continued by a double ambulatory and even by radiating chapels projecting beyond the limit of the buttresses around the whole semi-circle of the chevet, with the result that the horizontal expansion of the aisles becomes very obvious in the eastern half of the building and balances the movement in height of the choir. It is rather difficult

207. CHARTRES CATHEDRAL, double aisles on S side of choir, ca. 1200–1210

now to be immediately conscious of that width and of that continuity of space from right to left because of the early sixteenth-century
choir screen (faced in marble on its inner side in the eighteenth
century), which manages to destroy the interior unity of the choir
of Chartres. But even with this impediment blocking continuity of
vision (Fig. 207), the wide double aisles (especially when they turn
around the east end as a double ambulatory) are spacious enough
to make it possible—once aware of the necessity of such an effort—
to reconstruct mentally what the original effect of Chartres must
have been, when those lateral spaces opened unhindered onto the
central part of the choir and when, across the choir itself, one could

208. CHARTRES CATHEDRAL, vault of "pinched bay" of ambulatory (Ward Archive)

see on the opposite side the equal depth of the double aisles and the even more distant vista of the radiating chapels, projecting beyond the normal limit of the two ambulatories.

The expansion in width is made even more impressive at Chartres, in the curving part of the ambulatory (Fig. 206), by the irregular spacing of the columns, which was made necessary by the disposition of the foundations or rather, by the plan of the Romanesque crypt over which the cathedral was built.[21] The fact may not be evident at first; but the distance between the columns which face the three deeper chapels is much greater than the distance which separates these columns from the neighboring ones on the right and left: between the deep chapels are narrower, pinched bays of ambulatory (Fig. 208). This alternation in the spacing of the ambulatory piers is a subtle solution which makes the space of the chapels seem to penetrate into the ambulatory itself and open it radially toward that expanded periphery. Thus the constraint dictated by the presence of the eleventh-century crypt has been used most imaginatively to enrich with additional directions of movement the spatial pattern of the chevet.

209. BRAINE, SAINT-YVED, bay of N transept, designed ca. 1190

210. CHARTRES CATHEDRAL, bay of N side of nave, designed ca. 1194

But the great novelty of Chartres is the very type of its elevation, this new version of an elevation in three stories. At first sight it does not seem to be so very different from the simplified type of elevation which had been elaborated a generation earlier in the region of Laon[22]—it simply looks very like an enlarged version of the elevation of Saint-Yved at Braine (Fig. 209). However, there is a basic difference between the two buildings and one which changes entirely their expression: the colossal size suddenly taken at Chartres by the upper story of windows (Fig. 210). Instead of being enclosed within the vault as before (at Saint-Yved the sill of the upper windows is still slightly above the level of the capitals from which the vault starts), the clerestory windows at Chartres descend far below the springing line of the ribs and of the whole curvature of the vault.

The small windows of the Braine elevation now become as tall and as wide as the main arcade itself; and as a result the formula of the Braine series, seemingly suited to churches of only moderate size, at Chartres suddenly becomes the point of departure for the achievement of gigantic height. The whole proportions are transformed, for now two equal stories, each of them 14 meters (46 feet) high, are balanced evenly on each side of the narrow horizontal zone of a small triforium placed exactly in the middle of that vertical elevation (Fig. 204). This great enlargement of the upper story carries the evident implication that the central nave must now rise much higher than the lateral volumes—which at Chartres it does, the nave being more than twice as high as the aisles. The outer silhouette of the building consequently becomes quite different from the hunched massing that was unavoidable in twelfth-century structures.[23]

All these changes came from a systematic exploitation of the most radical lines of thought that the flying buttress could suggest. As flying buttresses can by definition be raised to almost any height to perform their function and stabilize the tallest vaults, there was no reason to restrict the height of the central volume: it could be made to rise freely well above the rest of the structure and, as a corollary, that added height was made available for bigger clerestory windows (Fig. 211). But this sudden increase in the size of one of the stories was bound to affect by repercussion the whole design. If the elevation of Chartres is compared with that of Bourges—bearing in mind that both churches are of practically the same height—then one of the most remarkable characteristics of Chartres becomes obvious: the elevation of Chartres is not only simple but colossal, its divisions in height are enormous and few (Fig. 212). While Bourges fills its 37.5 meter (122 foot) elevation with five stories, five horizontal zones staggered in two successive planes (Fig. 199)—, with the result that the divisions are still fairly small and remain on the normal scale of late twelfth-century Gothic—, Chartres for almost the same height (being just 2.7 meters or 9 feet shorter) has three stories only; and it would even be probably more accurate to say two stories and a half, because the triforium is so much smaller than at Bourges. We are so used to the Chartrain proportions that it is difficult for us to come to be fully aware now of their strangeness; but in fact Chartres represented a complete change of scale in Gothic architecture, a sudden enlargement of every component part of the building: arches, windows, piers, bays and stories. Every individual unit became truly colossal in size; and this massive simplification must have appeared brutal and coarse to many, whose eyes were not accustomed to such enlarged forms. It is often said that Gothic is an architecture which always keeps a sense of scale in relation to the human figure; but there is a range of variations in the application of this rule, and in the huge interior of Chartres there are few elements to recall that reference to man. This would appear to have been intentional: Chartres was meant to seem almost out of scale in order to achieve an effect of overwhelming dimensions.

This change of scale becomes perhaps even more striking in the first cathedral in which the Chartres pattern of elevation was repeated a few years later, the cathedral of Soissons, where the choir was ready for use by 1212 and must therefore have been begun before 1200, within five years at most of the opening of the work at Chartres.[24] Soissons is more striking because of the presence, next to that new choir, of the slightly earlier south transept which illustrates the immediately preceding stage in Gothic architecture—the one Chartres was now displacing—and provides a ready comparison of the old scale of stories against the new one (Fig. 213). In that smaller south transept the twelfth-century elevation in four stories, with its multiplicity of divisions, makes a tight grid of small-scale units; while the choir and nave are not only taller by some 9 meters (nearly 30 feet), but also treated in two major stories only, in the manner of Chartres, with just a narrow belt of a triforium to separate them. The height of the main arcade, the height of the upper story of windows, the width of the arches and bays, everything is on a completely different scale when compared with the south transept, which had been completed only ten years before the new choir was designed. But of course this contrast merely represents the intervention of the Chartres formula, with its new concept of structure and its radical change in the size and proportions of all the components of the elevation.

211. CHARTRES CATHEDRAL, nave, S side, ca. 1194–1210, topmost flight of flying buttresses added ca. 1215–1220

212. CHARTRES CATHEDRAL, N transept from choir triforium, ca. 1200–1225 (Ward Archive)

A no less essential feature of the new architectural order as it becomes defined at Chartres is the strong delineation of the bays (Fig. 214). On the side of the supports facing the nave, heavy shafts are applied as part of a new style of pier design, up to the level of the lower zone of capitals; and above that level these heavy shafts are continued, without a real break in their movement, by strongly projecting groups of five shafts which stand out in sharp relief against the flat vertical plane of the bay panels. The vigorous projection of these continuous vertical uprights makes a marked contrast with the thinness and the flat graphic quality of the bay grid in the nave of Notre-Dame (Fig. 131, p. 139), built less than a generation earlier.

213. SOISSONS CATHEDRAL, S transept and easternmost bays of nave, showing difference in scale (Ward Archive)

214. CHARTRES CATHEDRAL, sequence of bays on N side of nave, ca.
1194–1210 (wartime photograph, stained glass removed)

The new architecture is one of vigorous vertical accentuation.
But to what purpose? Was there already at Chartres a sort of mysti-
cism of soaring lines? As a general rule of method, great care must
always be taken not to cast back onto past events the intentions of
more recent generations, by applying to earlier periods of history
the turns of mind which developed only later. If we look at Chartres
without preconceptions, it becomes fairly clear that the strong verticals were part of a context which gave them a very definite signifi-

215. CHARTRES CATHEDRAL, S side of nave, ca. 1194–1210 (Ward Archive)

cance. They jut out as they do to cut incisively into the space of the nave and transept, making immediately perceptible the way in which that interior is composed: a space organized in a succession of large transverse slices, narrow for their height, compressed one behind the other, each defined within the limits of a bay, which by their steady succession finally make up the long vista of a nave. The tall uprights which insistently bar the interior elevation are meant to suggest and indeed impose the vision of an overall formula of spatial organization; and that rhythm of interior partitioning is nothing more than the manifestation in visual terms of the structural pattern of the whole fabric, since at the back of that elevation, behind those strong vertical lines, stand on the outside the powerful vertical members of the buttresses and flying buttresses (Fig. 215), which cut deep into the exterior space itself and do so even more vigorously than the corresponding bay divisions in the interior. Taken

232

together, these huge buttressing screens which slice out the exterior and the strong vertical accentuations which reflect them on the inside, impress on the mind the presence of a colossal system of transverse divisions, a succession of huge transverse vertical planes cutting through the whole width of the building, as a necessary and superhuman pattern of ordered forces.[25] The vaulting of all the main spans in markedly oblong bays (Fig. 216) is merely another application of this overruling principle of organization.[26] Power is the key word at Chartres: power in constructional engineering, power in the carving of space, power too in the whole vocabulary of forms.

Chartres is an architecture of large forms dominated by some colossal motifs. It has inherited from Laon the idea of the huge

216. CHARTRES CATHEDRAL, choir vaults, shortly before 1220 (Ward Archive)

217. Chartres Cathedral, rose window of W façade, ca. 1205–1210

rose window used as the centerpiece for all façades or terminal walls. The west rose at Chartres (Fig. 217), surmounting what was preserved of the twelfth-century porch façade (Fig 90, p. 97), is oldest in type and, apart from the insertion of a large spoked motif, remains very close in design to the north transept rose of Laon (Fig. 186, p. 191), where individually self-sufficient roundels seem to gravitate around a central circular form. In the transepts of Chartres, completed only after 1220,[27] the rose windows change in character: individual forms lose their autonomy and—particularly in the later of the two, the north transept rose (Fig. 227)—become part of an intricate interrelationship set in a network of mullions. But the mark of Laon is still there in the pattern of an outer ring of inverted curves, found twenty years earlier in the west rose of Laon.[28] In these transept façades of Chartres the rose window, standing over a row of

234

218. CHARTRES CATHEDRAL, detail of flying buttress of nave, ca. 1205–1210 (Ward Archive)

five lancets, is the dominant element in a large ensemble of glazed surfaces filling the whole terminal wall above the zone of the porches. This arrangement paved the way for the integration of the rose motif into huge window compositions in the next stage of Gothic development, as in the façade of Saint-Nicaise at Reims.

The motif of the rose-window seems to have had very much of a hold on the imagination of the first architect of Chartres, for it appears also in the flying buttresses of the nave in the form of a fan of spokes, linking the two original levels of superposed quadrant arches and looking like a portion extracted from a rose window (Fig. 218). And the analogy of the rose occurs again, although in a much simplified form and differently handled, in the large composite windows of the clerestory (Fig. 219), which constitute another major motif of the Chartrain vocabulary. In the whole cathedral,

219. CHARTRES CATHEDRAL, E side of S transept

220. CHARTRES CATHEDRAL, cantonné piers of nave, ca. 1194–1205

with the exception only of the hemicycle bays, the clerestory windows are made up of a grouping of three units: two lancets and, above, a very large oculus as wide as the two lancets together. This compositional formula, which associates the divisive principle of the bipartite lancets with the concentrated form of the circle which unifies it from above, was to become the basis for nearly all later Gothic speculations on window composition. That triple grouping had first appeared in a less integrated form—i.e., without a surrounding arch—in the Bishop's Chapel at Noyon (Fig. 221), completed in 1183, and that variant was repeated occasionally, as in the hemicycle of Orbais. But Chartres unified the motif by inscribing it within an arch, and placed the stress decidedly on the rounded form of the upper component of the window. What is most striking at Chartres is the size and complexity of the upper roundel, which is not only cusped but encircled by sixteen quatrefoil satellites, so that it preserves something of a rose composition; and the deep, round-headed arches which frame these windows on the outside (Fig. 215)

221. NOYON, BISHOP'S CHAPEL as before 1914, ca. 1180–1183

222. CHARTRES CATHEDRAL, chevet from NW, ca. 1205–1220 (crypt level 1195–1205)

further underscore the curve of the large upper roundels and demonstrate the predilection of the Chartres master for substantial centralized forms.

Another such form, and no less powerful in its architectural effect, is the new pier type adopted at Chartres and widely followed thereafter for half a century, the *colonne cantonnée* (Fig. 220): a pier with a circular (or octagonal) core but divided into four sections or *cantons* by four big engaged shafts placed on the transverse and longitudinal axes, to act as responds for the vaulting and for the arches of the main arcade.[29] The intrinsic beauty of these piers is that they are a heavy plastic form, rounded, full and sculptural; and at the same time they are also articulated at right angles, facing the cardinal points and thus materializing the two major axes of the building. At Chartres in their massive size they make up another repetitive large-scale motif and give a magnificent impression of weight and solidity. Here again Chartres stands at the opposite pole to the thin lines and the fine and even texture of Bourges.

This aspect of the architecture of Chartres, this taste for large and simple forms, was no doubt the source for the final design adopted in Paris between 1210 and 1215 for the façade of Notre-Dame.[30] There the colossal scale of Chartres becomes even further enlarged (Fig. 223): the doorways range around 15 meters (50 feet) in height and are of a size which ceases to bear any relationship to the human scale; and the upper story of the towers reaches 21 meters (70 feet). Everything in the façade of Notre-Dame has become simple and immense, and this is in the spirit of the new architecture as expressed by Chartres; and so is the sense of weight, which results from the progressive downward thickening of the masses of masonry and from the recession of the planes of the façade, very evident in aerial photographs of Notre-Dame (Fig. 224). But Paris has its own particular vigor which is not that of Chartres; it has its compact tension, its blocklike regularity and the geometry of the cube and square.[31] This was an exaggeration of one of the aspects of Chartres within another artistic context, whereas Chartres itself was treated with an imaginative freedom which embraced a more complex interplay of ideas. Chartres had inherited also that sense

223. Paris, Notre-Dame, W façade, ca. 1200–1250

224. PARIS, NOTRE-DAME, aerial view from SW, showing recessions of façade plane

of mobility of the later parts of Laon, in particular of those astounding transept chapels (Fig. 183, p. 189) which had been the heralds of a new modernity.[32]

It is in the chevet of Chartres (Figs. 222 and 225)—clearly the work of a second master less intent on monumentality—that this new vision of architectural forms is given full expression. But now the effect has become more complex and richer than at Laon with the addition of the open work volume of the flying-buttresses (Fig. 226), which seem to stretch out their grasp to keep a hold on the spreading base. Most remarkable at Chartres in this sense is certainly the existence of the three deep chapels of the chevet pressing beyond the line of the major buttresses as though the interior space, in an effort to expand ever outward, had managed to break

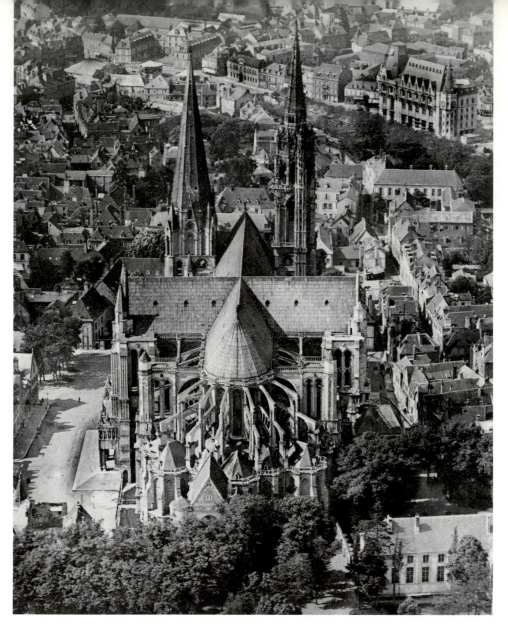

225. CHARTRES CATHEDRAL, aerial view from E, showing chevet composition

226. CHARTRES CATHEDRAL, flying buttresses of chevet, ca. 1210–1220

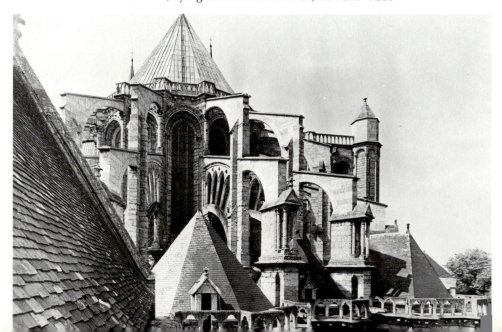

through the restraining cage of the buttresses at three points, in the form of these three chapels bulging between the bars. There is a tremendous spatial dynamism in the shape of the chevet of Chartres, and one which contrasts most markedly with the measured pace of the smoothly rounded chevet of Bourges and with the rigidity of the closed blocks of the façade of Notre-Dame. Chartres has also the kaleidoscopic planes of its faceted chapels and the fan-like movement of its large screens of flying-buttresses, pivoting around the central mass of the chevet; and it is this aspect of Chartres that was to be selected and brought to its climax a little later in the choir of Le Mans.

Presenting as it did so many new ideas—its insistent cadence, its enlarged scale, its weightiness and loftiness, the powerful rise of its central volume, the unprecedented expansion of its chevet seemingly only halted in movement—Chartres opened up a whole new world of architectural expression. Many interpretations of Chartres were possible, some purified, some enriched or lightened, rationalized or mannerized: no building had a more general or a more lasting influence.

227. CHARTRES CATHEDRAL, N transept rose, ca. 1230

228. LE MANS CATHEDRAL, choir, begun ca. 1217, dedicated 1254

CHAPTER VII

After Chartres and Bourges: Diffusion and Changes Between 1200 and 1230

JUST BEFORE 1200, preceding by only a few years the beginning of the new century, Chartres and Bourges had opened for Gothic architects an age of increased power and freedom. In both buildings a most unexpected step forward had been taken, breaking the net of previous architectural conventions and reviving—transformed by the imaginative power of two intensely individual minds —all of the basic urges which had inspired from the start the Gothic quest. What Bourges had brought to life again, in an enlarged and more richly modulated version, was the very first aim of the creators of Gothic, that dream of combined lightness and spaciousness which had guided the first decisive steps of the new architecture and which was to remain to the end one of the major motive forces behind its ever-widening European diffusion; while at Chartres what had been renewed and reaffirmed was rather the concept of Gothic as a method, as a systematic and analytical mode of thought, breaking down problems into their simplest terms in order to solve them and reaching finally a clear and convincing visual formula. Chartres had revealed a new pattern of regularity based on units of an unaccustomed type and size; but the overall vision that emerged was of

245

the same kind as in the earlier forms of Gothic: that of an intelligible and perfectly ordered universe. Whatever their divergences, Bourges and Chartres had much in common in terms of size, of substantiality, of permeability of the limits; and still more basically, both had answered the same need of the time for a reassessment of all values following the sudden revelation of the power of the flying buttress. The impact of these two major creations brought about a reorientation of the Gothic movement and initiated in the leading centers of northern France what must be recognized as a completely new stage in the development of Gothic.

A period of intense architectural production followed, which covered the first three decades of the thirteenth century. It is to this period that the label "High Gothic" tends now to be applied.[1] Other names have been used to describe it: it has been variously called the Classic Phase of Gothic, Gothic at its Climax, the Age of the Great Cathedrals, or quite simply the Architecture of the Early Thirteenth Century. In the preceding chapter it has been referred to as the Second Gothic System or as the Architecture of the Flying Buttress, because these expressions were thought to be more direct and more explicit of the reality of the change that was then taking place. But once the facts and their significance have been defined, it is good to have at one's disposal a more rapid idiom, and High Gothic is a convenient shorthand term. In conformity with present usage the term will be understood here as an element of strict stylistic definition, applying to that stage of Gothic architecture which in the most progressive centers of northern France coincides with the years 1195 to 1230, and to the reflections or equivalents of that architecture in other areas of Europe. But once another spirit begins to alter the nature of the architectural language, then the term High Gothic ceases to apply, and the greatest care should be taken not to extend its use beyond the first manifestations of the shift in values which indicates the emergence of that later version of Gothic which is commonly known as the "Rayonnant Style."[2] Within these limits High Gothic is certainly a most useful label—though any notion of necessary superiority, which might be inferred from the use of the adjective "high", must evidently be avoided at all cost.

That new Gothic architecture of the last years of the twelfth century and of the early part of the thirteenth has often been identified in an overall historical perspective with the rise of the Capetian monarchy, the diffusion of the most recent forms of French Gothic being considered as one of the signs of the growing influence of the French kings in Europe in the course of the thirteenth century; and there is little doubt that from 1200 or 1205, after the death of Richard I of England (1199) and the conquest of Normandy (1204) and even more after the Battle of Bouvines (1214), the prestige of Philip Augustus (1180–1223) reinforced the artistic authority which the new style intrinsically possessed. But it would be misleading to treat that slightly later situation as the explanation for an outburst of creativity that was in fact already under way; for a margin of even a few years makes a great difference in terms of historical meaning. The monarchy in France was not yet triumphant in the years 1194–95 when the artistic breakthrough was made, and it is perhaps worth noting again that major artistic invention tends to precede rather than follow the actuality of power. In 1194 the ambitions of Philip Augustus were evident, he was laying plans for future action and that potential of growth was in the air; but he had not yet gained any decisive advantage and his position was even insecure. Richard the Lion-hearted had just been released from his captivity (on 4 February 1194) and had immediately begun harassing the royal lands. Both Chartres and Bourges were conceived in a moment of uncertainty and in cities that were under threat: around Bourges the province of Berry was being constantly raided by the troops of Richard or of his supporters; and Chartres, that sort of neutral city, half Capetian, half Blois-Champagne in allegiance, would have been the first objective in any offensive starting from nearby Verneuil in Normandy and aimed at the royal domains south of Paris. In this context the undertaking of the building of these two cathedrals cannot really be construed as the reflection of a sudden increase in the power of the monarchy; it was rather a sign of confidence in the future. From 1194 to 1199 the situation continued critical for Philip of France;[3] but ten years later the conjuncture of events was reversed, the threats had evaporated, victories had been won, and the new Gothic style had inherited the glow of that military and political success.

Immediate as was their impact, Bourges and Chartres did not have the effect of instantly wiping out all the tendencies which had prevailed just before. Many of these tendencies preserved for quite a while all their vitality: the wide diffusion of the Braine formulas of plan and elevation, the continued speculations on the skeletal effects of double-wall structure, the temporary secession of the Parisian milieu itself absorbed in its own set of problems, these are indications of the diversity of artistic forces at work in the early part of the thirteenth century. There was, in a number of sectors, a definite resistance to the new trends of High Gothic;[4] and perhaps more generally, after a moment of bewilderment, an incitement was felt to start experimenting again in a variety of directions. But it was all the same Bourges and Chartres that dominated the scene— in rivalry, for these two buildings were so different in the revelation they offered that they were bound to inspire two distinct lines of buildings. Even if they are unequal in numbers, there is a Bourges series and a Chartres series which can be plotted on the map (Fig. 274) and analyzed in the sequence of their development. Of course repetition inevitably alters the nature of things: even the most revolutionary ideas soon turn into established formulas and, losing the intensity of their original meaning, they tend to become at best points of departure for the expression of other intentions, the most individual aspects of a work being the most rarely transmitted.

The Bourges Series

The descendance of Bourges (Fig. 229.A-D) is composed of the choirs of Saint-Martin at Tours (ca. 1210) and of the cathedral of Le Mans (ca. 1217), then the cathedral of Toledo (ca. 1222) in central Spain, and the choir of Coutances Cathedral (ca. 1235 or 1240) in the western part of Normandy.[5] This makes a small series (not surprisingly, Bourges being a rather exacting prototype to follow) and a not very consistent one; for while some of these buildings, especially the choir of Le Mans, were among the most progressive of their time, others, such as Toledo or Coutances (Figs. 230 and 232), were pioneering efforts at transplanting the most modern forms of Gothic architecture in the less receptive and less pre-

229. Reconstructed plans of chevets of the Bourges series

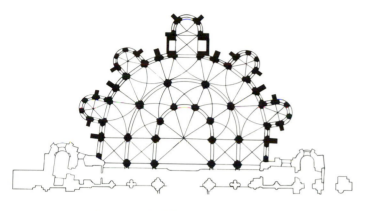

A. Tours, Saint-Martin, ca. 1210–1230

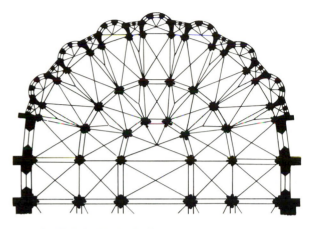

B. Toledo Cathedral, ca. 1222–1247

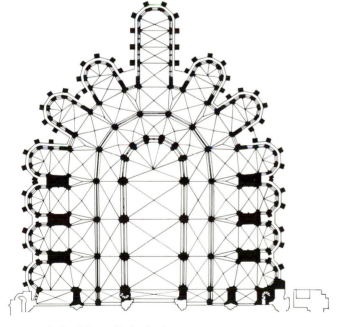

C. Le Mans Cathedral, ca. 1217–1254

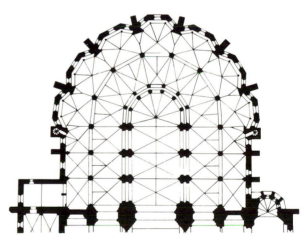

D. Coutances Cathedral, ca. 1235–1255

0   10   20 METRES

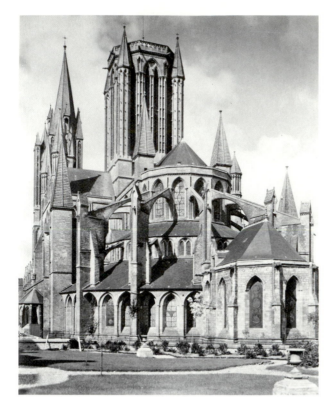

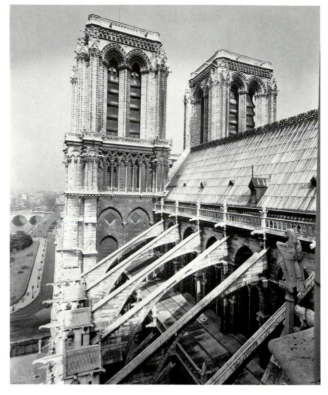

230. COUTANCES CATHEDRAL, chevet, ca.
1235–1255 (Ward Archive)

231. PARIS, NOTRE-DAME, flying buttresses of nave, as
rebuilt ca. 1230 and restored in 19th c. (Ward Archive)

pared soil of distant peripheral areas. Furthermore, both Toledo and Coutances are characterized by a certain degree of stylistic ambiguity due to the revival of elements of design belonging to earlier stages of Gothic, which alter and somewhat complicate the bold pattern of Bourges. These superimpositions of concepts are of interest in that they give some insight into the processes of workshop transmission at a time when long-distance exchanges were multiplying, and into the type of response Gothic architecture evoked in those peripheral centers, where past and present tended to become intermingled as if there were between them no difference in modernity.

What the Coutances master saw irresistibly behind Bourges and had to quote in the plan of his outer ambulatory was the image of the chevet of Saint-Denis (Figs. 233, and 38, p. 39): a fairly natural textbook association since Saint-Denis was historically the source of all later Gothic speculations on the double ambulatory. Toledo (Fig. 23A) on the other hand shows a much more specific selection of ideas: what can be found here, in addition to Bourges and to the flattened widening of mosquelike interiors, is a reflection of one of the direct sources of Bourges, that unusual disposition of small chapels which had first been used in the church of Sainte-Croix at Etampes and which had suggested at Bourges the revised scheme of vaulting adopted for the outer ambulatory when the addition of chapels was decided. It seems therefore evident that when he visited Bourges ca. 1220, the Toledo master was not interested only in the building itself but in the whole collection of workshop records, which must have included drawings of older buildings used as sources, as well as of recent works belonging to the Bourges filiation. Further confirmation of this transmission process is afforded by the treatment of the flying buttresses at the

232. COUTANCES CATHEDRAL, view into choir from N transept (Ward Archive)

233. COUTANCES CATHEDRAL, tall inner and low outer ambulatory (Ward Archive)

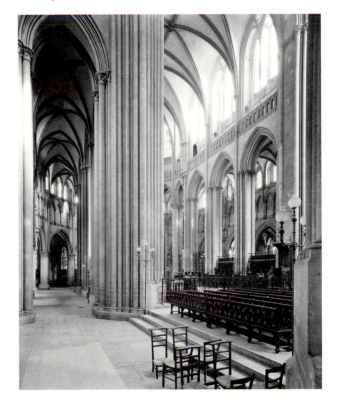

234. TOLEDO CATHEDRAL, two level double ambulatory, ca. 1222–1247

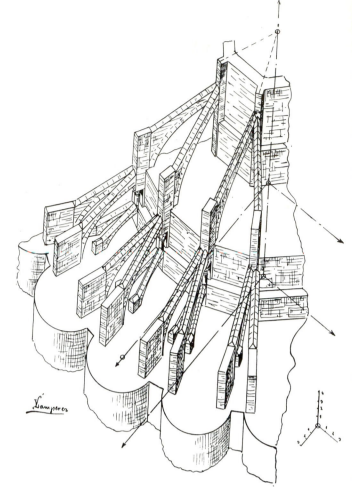

235. TOLEDO CATHEDRAL, diagram of flying buttresses of chevet, by V. Lampérez y Romea

east end of Toledo (Fig. 235): while their V-shaped bifurcations imply some knowledge of the choir of Le Mans (begun in 1217 or very soon after), their tiered arrangement in height seems to have been copied from the original buttressing system of the nave of Notre-Dame, older by some forty years. These superimpositions of designs of different dates, which produce unexpected mixtures of elements coming from two or three different chronological layers, reveal a specifically "peripheral" mode of thinking: as a result of the simultaneous transmission of the heritage of several generations of Gothic inventions, the perspective of history becomes flattened and time loses its normal depth.

In the derivation of Bourges only Tours and Le Mans, the first two representatives of the series, conform to the kind of acute modernity which characterizes the major centers of Gothic art. It is difficult to know exactly every detail of structure of the choir of Saint-Martin at Tours, as the church was destroyed during the Revolution and all we have in the way of documents is some eighteenth-century plans, confirmed by the excavations of the late nineteenth century, and a fifteenth-century miniature by Jean Fouquet which shows the top of the Gothic choir above the city walls.[6] The plan of the chevet of Saint-Martin at Tours was very close indeed to the plan of the chevet of Bourges, having the same number of piers in each row around the hemicycle of the choir and, though the chapels were slightly larger than at Bourges, the same way of spreading them by inserting between them two small bays on either side of a main buttress. The exterior view in the miniature shows only the upper parts of the church (Fig. 236), but it looks as if the choir of

236. TOURS, SAINT-MARTIN, view ca. 1450 from miniature by Jean Fouquet (Paris, Bibl. nat., Ms. fr. 6465, f.223)

Saint-Martin had already had the unconventional feature of colossal flying buttresses spanning the two ambulatories in a single flight, as was done a little later at Coutances and even before Coutances in the nave of Notre-Dame in Paris (Fig. 231), when it was modernized around 1230 with larger windows and a simplified system of buttressing.

The chevet of Le Mans,[7] where the enlargement of the cathedral beyond the old city walls was authorized in 1217, was much more decisive in its innovations and can be taken as a significant indication of the attitudes of mind which had currency among the more advanced Gothic architects in the early years of the thirteenth century. For the clear intention of its designer was to inject into an interior structure of the Bourges type some of the basic elements of Chartres and make the two great models of the 1190s merge into an exceptionally complex composition of volumes, by applying to architecture that principle of *concordantia* (or reconciliation of contradictory authorities) which was one of the rules of scholastic thinking.[8] But since Le Mans placed itself in that ambiguous position, in which it belonged both to the descendence of Bourges and to that of Chartres, before analyzing what resulted from that convergence of sources, it would be useful to get an accurate picture of the geographical distribution of the two series and of their relative importance.

The Chartres Series

On the map (Fig. 274) it becomes obvious that the Bourges type with its particular formula of interior spaciousness remained all the time restricted to the south and southwest margins of the Gothic lands, spreading along that border from Bourges to Tours and Le Mans, and after that moving to frankly colonial centers (the far end of Normandy and even central Spain), as if an invisible barrier prevented it from reaching the Seine Valley or even that old front line of the first Gothic advance represented in the 1140s by Chartres, Etampes and Sens. The Chartres formula, on the other hand, took hold almost at once in some of the major Gothic centers on either side of Paris. It had a local following which covered the whole area of the plains of Beauce, rapidly reaching Bonneval and Blois (nave of Saint-Laumer) to the south, Gallardon and Dourdan in the direction of Paris, with the nave of Saint-Père at Chartres itself (Fig. 188, p. 194) as a particularly fine example of the style. But more remarkable and much more decisive was the almost instantaneous adoption of the tall-clerestoried Chartrain elevation in the Soissons-Reims area, for this meant that the Chartres type became from that moment the recognized new style of the Northern group of Gothic which had proved to be, since the 1160s, the most vital area of Gothic production and initiative. From Soissons Cathedral (Fig. 237), where the new choir was begun even before 1200, and from the neighboring Cistercian site of Longpont, the propagation of the Chartres series can be followed, south to Orbais (Fig. 238) and Troyes, southeast to Reims, north to Saint-Quentin and Cambrai; spreading also soon after that from the Soissons area in a westerly direction to Amiens, Beauvais, and even to Rouen (choir of the cathedral) or Les Andelys in eastern Normandy. The active trading roads which at that time crisscrossed the plains of Picardy and Champagne became the essential network of diffusion of the Chartres formula, once it had been transplanted to that area north and northeast of Paris.

237. SOISSONS CATHEDRAL, N side of nave, built ca. 1210–1225 to design of late 1190s

In the Beauce region close to Chartres, whether at Blois or at Saint-Père at Chartres, what is found is a sense of stability in the proportions and of solidity in the form and size of the piers, reflecting the effect of ponderousness aimed at in the cathedral of Chartres itself. But in the area north of Paris, starting with Soissons and Longpont, the Chartres type of elevation becomes extremely light in its structure, the piers being reduced to a tall column, often with the addition on the nave side of a single shaft, to mark by that vertical accent the division of the bays (as at Soissons Cathedral, Mont-Notre-Dame or Saint-Quentin) and sometimes without any shaft at all. At Longpont, for instance (Fig. 239), the plain round columns with octagonal capitals are simply an elongation of the type of support used in the Braine group just before the Chartrain revolution. Other forms of piers also existed, which again tended to stress the solidity of the structure;[9] and that return to the weightiness of Chartres characterizes in particular the most outstanding

238. ORBAIS, choir from S transept, ca. 1200–1220 (Ward Archive)

239. LONGPONT, ruins of nave, ca. 1210–1227 (Ward Archive)

member of the Chartres series, the cathedral of Reims, designed in 1210 or 1211. Together, Reims and the choir of Le Mans (younger by a few years) can be seen as constituting one of those perfect contrasting pairs of buildings which seem to recur at each of the stages in the development of the Gothic movement: Saint-Denis and Sens in the 1140s, Laon and Notre-Dame in the 1160s, Chartres and Bourges in the mid-1190s; and now, between 1210 and 1220, Reims and Le Mans, which illustrate with particular clarity the two divergent interpretations that could be given to the novelty of Chartres.

LE MANS

The choir of Le Mans (Fig. 228) cannot be treated as a purely Chartrain design since it performs a sort of ideal synthesis between Chartres and Bourges; and in that process of synthesis it was clearly Bourges (Fig. 203, p. 218) that served as the point of departure,

240. LE MANS CATHEDRAL, chevet from SE, ca. 1217–1254

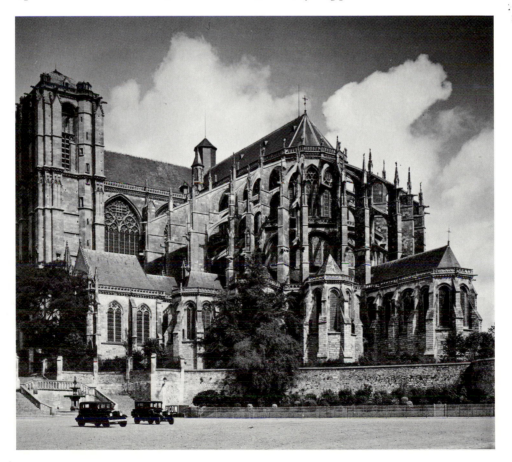

241. LE MANS CATHEDRAL, choir at mid-height, central vessel ca. 1240–1254

giving to the building its inner shape, its formula of progressive heightening and its magnificent amplitude at mid-height. As at Bourges the general effect in the choir of Le Mans is that of two churches in one; and the tall inner ambulatory has a full triforium elevation which, running continuously behind the open arches of the very tall main arcade, acts as the true limit of the enlarged central space (Figs. 241, 242). But if Bourges furnished the essential concept, it has been at Le Mans significantly altered and its expression transformed. While at Bourges the repetition of the same triforium motif in the upper reaches of the main vessel makes for an even enveloping of space in all directions, at Le Mans the central elevation upsets that pattern of regularity, rising in two stories only and thus creating a contrast of scales; and the tight grouping of the piers of the seven-sided hemicycle closes the whole perspective of

258

242. LE MANS CATHEDRAL, inner ambulatory at mid-height, chapels and ambulatories ca. 1227–1240 (Ward Archive)

the interior on an effect of intense verticality (Fig. 228). Balancing this increased movement in height, a new insistence is also given to the horizontal spread of the building, by the outward push of deep chapels which expand beyond the normal limits of the lateral volumes. And it is this intensification of two contrasting extremes, in height and in width, grafted onto what would otherwise be a purely Bourges-like structure, that reveals already in the interior arrangement the intervention of Chartrain concepts.

Does this definition of the interior effect of the choir of Le Mans actually correspond to the original intent of the first designer, or was it achieved only through important revisions made in the course of construction? The question arises because, inside the ambulatory and choir, changes of style and alterations of detail are evident, showing the succession of three different architects over

259

the period of 35 years it took to complete that part of the building. The first architect, who came from the Soissons-Laon area, built only the outer ring of chapels (Fig. 184, p. 189) and the outer ambulatory walls. By 1230, when the elevation of the inner ambulatory (Fig. 243) was raised, supported on columnar piers, the architect had changed: he was a man from Normandy, using the typical mannerisms of style of that province[10] such as the circular abaci, the sharp pointing of the arches of the triforium (which look as if they were laterally compressed), the richly carved decoration of spandrels and tympana in that triforium zone, and the deeply cut moldings which multiply the linear accentuations on arches and ribs (Figs. 294, p. 320; 322, p. 342). The second architect had clearly decided to impose his own touch by a modification of all the details of execution. And when it came to the building of the central part of the choir, the style had changed again and the upper story in particular was built in a variant of Rayonnant Gothic which bears the mark of the Sainte-Chapelle. Were these alterations of detail accompanied by corresponding changes in the design itself? This seems most unlikely, for the first setting-out of the whole periphery of the chevet had established irrevocably the two most important features of the design: the unusual extension of the chapels and the close spacing of a seven-sided hemicycle. Both the horizontal and the vertical stress were fixed from the start; and if any changes were made after that, they could not have been more than relatively minor adjustments.[11]

On the outside the Bourges style of effects is even more systematically discarded, and the Chartrain elements take over. One of the most obvious borrowings from Chartres is the way in which the chapels are made to project beyond the outer line of the flying-buttresses (Fig. 240); but while Chartres had only three such chapels, at Le Mans their number has proliferated to thirteen (seven disposed radially, the others pursued along the straight bays) and they reach out more deeply than ever beyond the wide semicircle of the double ambulatory. The plan expresses in a diagrammatic manner the emphasis placed on the radiating directional pattern in a chevet surrounded by such a multiplicity of

243. Le Mans Cathedral, inner ambulatory, ca. 1230–1240 (Ward Archive)

outward-pointing chapels. Combined with the spaciousness of the two ambulatories, this gave a formula of expansion in plan that surpassed anything conceived until then as possible, marking the climax of the Gothic effort toward maximum extension on the ground.[12] The only other chevet of comparable coverage is the one that Villard de Honnecourt and Pierre de Corbie, one day discussing together *(inter se disputando)*, imagined as an amplified version of the plan of Vaucelles (1216–1235); but that other chevet was never realized, surviving only as a drawing on parchment (Fig. 244) on one of the pages of the sketchbook of Villard de Honnecourt.[13]

Another principle unknown to Bourges, which Le Mans also

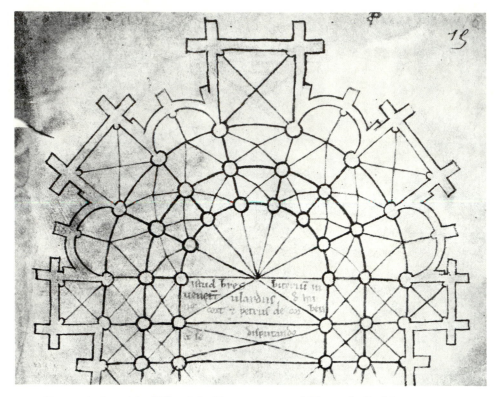

244. Chevet designed by Villard de Honnecourt and Pierre de Corbie
(Paris, Bibl. nat., Ms. fr. 19093, f.15)

borrows from Chartres, is the importance it gives to the organs of
buttressing. In place of the calm silhouette of Bourges (Figs. 192
and 194), where the traditional concept of a chevet in three
graduated tiers had been preserved by reducing the large gesture
of the flying-buttresses and making them cling to the slope of the
volumes, Le Mans substitutes the crowding of a forest of flying-
buttresses (Fig. 246), in a spectacular enrichment of that effect of
vast rotating screens which had first been conceived at the chevet of
Chartres (Fig. 225, p. 242). At Le Mans the flying-buttresses are not
only heightened but multiplied; they are even made to fork in two
in their outer flight all around the curve of the chevet, bifurcating
in the form of a Y, so that the outer pier-buttresses become doubled in number; and being also very tall they make a sort of gigantic
cage around the central volume of the choir, thus changing pro-

245. LE MANS CATHEDRAL, forked flying buttresses of chevet

foundly the silhouette of the building. The idea of using the flying-buttresses to create the skeleton of an open volume which would enter into play with the more substantial masses of the enclosed volumes; the idea of taking advantage of the height of that outlined form to widen the building further on the ground; even the fundamental idea of sketching large arabesques in space and of making complex faceted forms turn in the changing light of day: all this

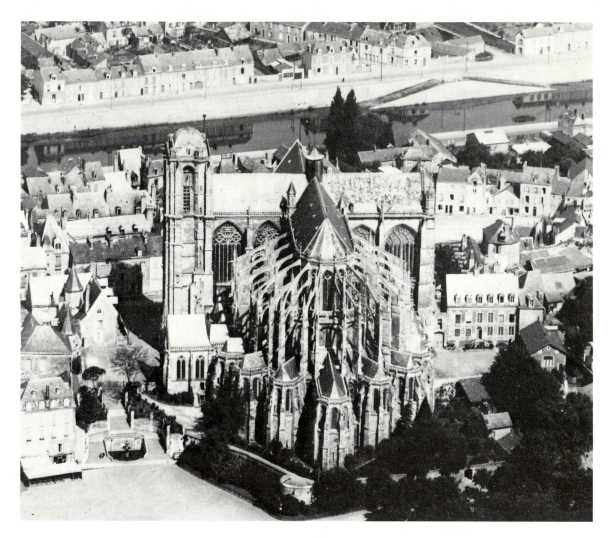

246. Le Mans Cathedral, aerial view of chevet (© I.G.N., Paris)

new mode of vision came directly from Chartres. But at Le Mans the multiplicity of the components and the subtlety of their combinations reveal the workings of a mind particularly sensitive to the sculptural values of architecture.

Forms in openwork and spatial penetrations have become so familiar in the language of contemporary sculpture that there is little difficulty now in visualizing that aspect of early thirteenth-

264

century architecture. Still it is perhaps worth noting that the volumes created by flying buttresses have a shifting and impermanent quality: they vanish at certain angles and at Le Mans, as you walk around the chevet or move from one vantage point to another, the central mass of the choir can be either completely cloaked or else laid bare (Fig. 247), according to the angle at which the buttresses are viewed. This subtle play is part of the sleight of hand with which the designer of Le Mans manipulates the concepts that had originated in the chevet of Chartres; and the composition here is made even more elaborate by the addition of the Bourges element which, acting inside as a principle of spatial widening, happens to work outside as a principle of further complexity. The staggering in height of the two ambulatories creates above the level of the chapels an intermediate step in the vertical rise of the central volume, which appears to emerge from two concentric rings turning at two different heights. And it is the interlocking of these two systems, that of the central core and that of the flying-buttresses and chapels, one concentric and one centrifugal, that gives to the chevet of Le Mans its unique visionary quality (Fig. 246).

247. Le Mans Cathedral, chevet from N, ca. 1217–1254

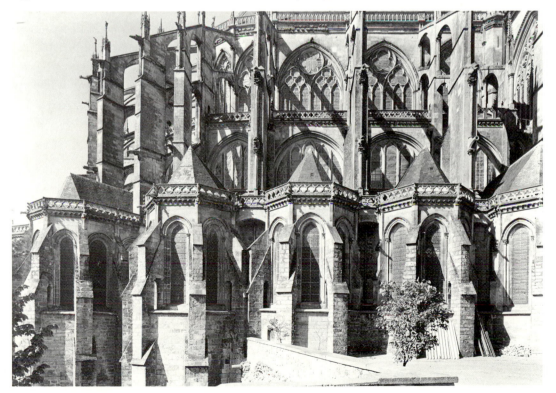

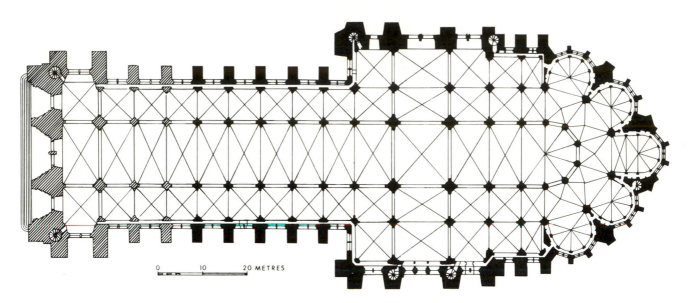

248. REIMS CATHEDRAL, plan (hatching indicates post 1250 work)

REIMS

At the opposite end of that art of extremes and of multiple tensions stands the calm clarified design of Reims Cathedral.[14] The plan itself of Reims (Fig. 248), although still basically cruciform, is singularly compact, as no secondary volumes are allowed to project and even the major articulation of the plan (the projection of the transept in relation to the nave) is reduced to the minimum of one bay. The transept has been aligned on the width of the chevet (Fig. 249) in order to simplify the outline of the plan, and the building appears to be composed of two main blocks only: the long nave, and the eastern ensemble in which an unusually short chevet and the transept are massed together.[15] There is one ambulatory only, as opposed to two at Chartres or Le Mans or in the whole Bourges series, and the radiating chapels—which are five only in number and larger—are kept tightly enclosed within the semicircle of the outer buttresses. Standing on the outskirts, so to speak, of the chevet, these tall buttresses set a sort of ideal limit completely encircling the chapels and restraining their bounds: with the exception of the axial chapel, which was made somewhat deeper and does project a little (giving to the plan of the chevet a slightly pointed shape), the

266

249. REIMS CATHEDRAL, view from SE, showing chevet and aligned transept, 1211–1241

chapels at Reims do not break in any way the alignment of the buttresses. In fact the chapels penetrate into the body of the church and the space, which in a building such as Chartres would have been occupied by a second ambulatory, has at Reims been absorbed by that intrusion of the peripheral chapels and has become partitioned into separate spatial compartments (Fig. 250). From outside Reims defines itself as a compressed composition of volumes held within a strict boundary: instead of spreading at the base, the whole east end rises upward in a single movement, scanned along its semicircular limit by the vertical accents of the buttresses which, topped by tall spirelike pinnacles (one of the most individual motifs of Reims),

250. REIMS CATHEDRAL, ambulatory chapels, ca. 1211–1220

251. REIMS CATHEDRAL, interior, ca. 1211–1280

stand firmly as uprights, straightening the total outline so as to obliterate all consciousness of the slopes of the flying buttresses that come behind.[16]

Inside, Reims is a narrower and slightly taller version of Chartres (Figs. 251, and 204, p. 220). It has the same elevation but with more height given to the main arcade, a change of proportions which lightens the aspect of the upper story. It has the same type of piers, those large *colonnes cantonnées,* particularly smooth and rounded at Reims, of circular core with four engaged columns marking the major axes (Fig. 253). As at Chartres, this type of powerful pier expresses in plastic terms the material strength of the structure, for Reims follows Chartres again in the substantial weightiness of its masses of masonry. The designer of Reims, Jean d'Orbais,[17] even chose to extend the use of the *cantonné* pier to a part of the building where its presence is unexpected, by giving that shape so monumental in itself and the colonnade effect its repetition creates, to the circuit of engaged piers which separate the chapels in the ambulatory. The Champenois passage—then more exactly "Rémois," since it had not yet been used outside Reims— which runs in the thickness of the lateral walls along the aisles and around the chapels at the height of the window sills, also stresses the generous thickness of the structure and the massive solidity of its lower parts.[18] The loftiness of the proportions was increased somewhat while building was in progress: this was discovered by the architect in charge of restorations after the 1914–1918 war. Noticing that there was a change in the curve of the upper vaults of the choir, at about one-third of their height, he was able to draw the curve as originally planned and found that this would have reduced the total height of the building by 1.7m (5′7″).[19] This represented a very significant change in the structure of Reims Cathedral, for it affected the height of the upper walls of the whole building; and since the clerestory windows were built from the start to the greater height, it must have taken place at a fairly early stage in the construction of the upper stories, probably no later than the mid-1220s and certainly well before the interruption in operations due to civil strife in the city between 1233 and 1236; after which it took only five years to complete the whole eastern ensemble of choir and transept, which was put into service in 1241.

Reims is renowned for its invention of bar tracery, which was one of the many refinements that characterize its design. But the major originality of the building lies in the clarity and articulateness of its exterior appearance and, while the basic effect of regularity results largely from the repetition of the same composed window type (two pointed lights and a circle above) at both aisle and clerestory levels, the pinnacles which top the buttresses are another key element in the design. These tall spirelets, each sheltering the winged figure of an angel, are not merely a lovely three-dimensional motif which gives firmness and unity to the upper part of the buttresses, nor is their end simply to accentuate the cadence of the bays: still more important is the horizontal continuity they create all around the building by their succession (Fig. 255); and as the pinnacles themselves correspond exactly in height to the clerestory windows in front of which they are detached, while the solid plinth on which they stand repeats similarly the height occupied inside by the triforium story, these long lines of buttresses rising above the aisle walls and in the same vertical plane erect on the outer face of the structure a replica of its interior elevation (Fig. 253).

That the two systems rigorously coincide and can be integrated into a single pattern is demonstrated by the façades, where these duplicate elevations become superimposed (Fig. 252): at Reims the terminal screens of the façades were conceived as the chosen sites where the principles ruling the organization of the whole structure were explained to the eye. The west façade however does not quite bear this out, because it was altered in its design when it was eventually built with much enlarged portals by Bernard of Soissons in the second half of the thirteenth century; and as the regularity of the north transept façade had been somewhat disarranged as early as 1230 by the addition of two deep-set doorways, it is only at the south end of the transept that the original formula of the Reims façades can be recaptured. The cornice of the aisle walls which bars the whole width of that south façade, marking the height to which the main arcade rises in the interior elevation, defines a large lower story which would normally have been the story of the portals; but here it contains only a sequence of windows (including a group of three tall lancets in the central panel) as this south façade, giving onto the grounds of the archbishop's palace, never had the function of a public entrance. Above that lower story, a narrow zone of arcading, which in the middle encloses a row of circular windows, answers on the façade the interior presence of the triforium (Fig. 254). Then comes the other major story of the structure, that of the great clerestory windows, the value of which as a motif is underlined by the extension of their form to the openings of the towers. But at the same time this upper story is also the story of the pinnacles which, continuing their march across the face of the façade and

252. Reims Cathedral, S transept façade ca. 1211–1241 (early 16th c. gable)

253. Reims Cathedral, S side of nave

254. Reims Cathedral, inner face of S transept façade

marking its vertical divisions, manifest their exact coincidence with the height of the clerestory zone by the way in which they flank on either side the window-like openings of the towers and frame the central motif of the rose window, which here at Reims is inscribed within an ample pointed arch to make it merge into that story of large pointed windows. All these different series of forms, apparently autonomous, fall into line impeccably and an absolute concordance reigns in the divisions of the stories, in the size of all the motifs; for the first time the exterior rigorously reflects the interior

273

and the whole building reveals itself as the unfolding of a unified formula: an image of perfect clarity and harmony.

Reims is best understood from a distance or from the air, when it can be seen entire, like a scale-model of itself (Fig. 255). Then it becomes evident that this vast building was conceived by men[20] who thought above all in terms of condensations and alignments, of equalizations and correspondences. And the design appears more than ever dominated by the motif of the pinnacled buttresses which, through their precision of form and their crystalline density, express within themselves the laws that organize the whole structure. Gothic architecture had never been so limpid, so completely legible and transparent to the mind: the Gothic ideal of self-explanation could hardly be carried further.[21]

The east end is in a way the climax of that spirit of clarification: in absolute contrast with the multiplicity of small forms of the chevet of Le Mans, the chevet of Reims is made up of only a few large-scale units. It seems evident that, while the architect who de-

255. REIMS CATHEDRAL, aerial view

signed Le Mans saw in Chartres—and especially in its east end—a suggestion towards greater mobility and subtlety in the play of volumes, the designers of Reims understood Chartres as an invitation to move even further towards simplification on the grand scale. Yet in spite of that profound difference of tendency, Reims and Le Mans conformed to a common basic principle: in both buildings height was balanced by width, in both the vertical rise however great was conceived not as an end in itself but as one element in a combination of forces which must eventually arrive at an effect of stability and poise. That compensation between divergent movements is what suddenly vanishes around 1220, as can be observed not only in the cathedral of Amiens but also in two other major works of the 1220s, the collegiate church of Saint-Quentin and the cathedral of Beauvais. The 1220s opened a new line of experimentation, this time introducing the element of surprise in the overall proportioning.

AMIENS

Amiens was begun in 1220, under the direction of Robert de Luzarches who completed the nave and west façade by 1236 at the latest;[22] and the nave of Amiens (Fig. 257) is certainly the most magnificent demonstration of the new tendency. It belongs in its general type to the same series as Chartres or Reims, but this type of elevation and of spatial composition becomes now immensely extended in height. A section of the nave of Amiens (Fig. 256) speaks for itself: the total height of the central space under the apex of the vault is 42.3 meters (close to 139 feet)—some 5 meters (17 feet) more than at Reims or Bourges—, and as the nave is only 14.64 meters (48 feet) wide between the walls, this gives a relation of 3:1 between height and width, a coefficient which had never been reached or aimed at before. This time the vertical movement becomes truly overpowering: everything is subordinated to it, and what particularly reinforces its effect is the great height given to the aisles.[23] At Amiens the lower story, up to the string-course which separates it from the triforium above, makes exactly half of the total elevation of the nave. This not only creates an effect of gigan-

256. *A.* AMIENS CATHEDRAL, plan: nave 1220–1236, transept and chevet 1236–1269

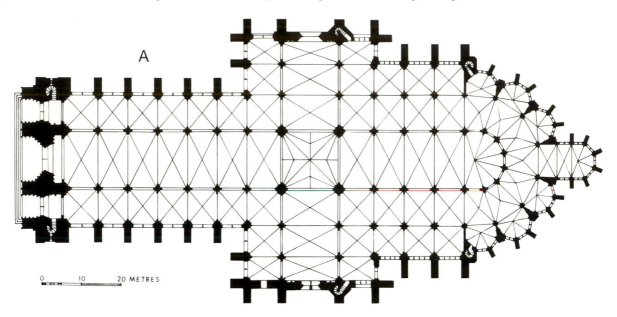

A

0   10   20 METRES

256. *B.-C.* Comparative sections of naves of (B; left) Amiens, begun 1220, and (C; right) Chartres, begun 1194

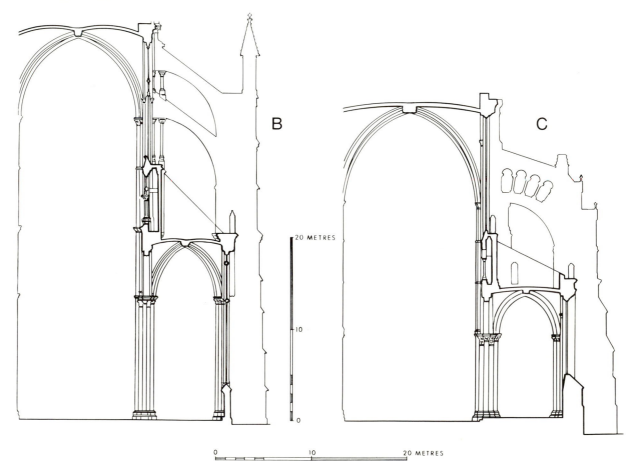

B

C

20 METRES

10

0

0   10   20 METRES

257. AMIENS CATHEDRAL, nave 1220–1236, choir 1236–1269 (Ward Archive)

tic lateral openness which tends to make the aisles merge into the tall space of the nave; this heightening of the aisle story also changes profoundly the expression of the piers. They are still plastic in character, being still of the *cantonné* type, still treated in the round with a neat, four-part articulation, but at the same time they are given such a height and become so slender that one almost forgets the reality of their supporting function. Amiens is actually built very light: while at Chartres and Reims the heads of the clerestory windows were surrounded on the outside by deep arches which stiffened and reinforced the elevation at the very top, no such loads of masonry exist in the upper parts of Amiens, which in this respect belongs to the tradition of lightness of Soissons Cathedral (and of Soissons-influenced buildings such as Longpont or Saint-Quentin). There is no doubt that this general heightening and lightening of the structure produces an exhilarating effect, as if the weight and density of matter were somehow reduced and all the forms of architecture could without danger become less substantial.[24] The interior effect is perfectly consistent; but contradictions appear in great numbers in the façade.

The façade of Amiens (Fig. 258) is at odds with the interior. As opposed to the effect of flatness and of extreme thinness of the interior elevation, the façade is in a variety of planes, in recessions and projections, with cavernous porches, deep set arches, detached galleries, and pinnacles of different sizes. That effect of broken surfaces is further increased by the richness of the decoration: as opposed to the spareness of the interior, where the triforium string-course is the only enrichment, the façade of Amiens is ornate to the point of confusion. Much of the confusion, however, comes from the inherent contradictions of the design. Robert de Luzarches was apparently unwilling to free himself from the accepted formulas of his time; and in the same way as, for the interior structure, he adhered both to the Chartrain elevation and to the use of the *cantonné* pier, he also chose to conform to the principles of composition of the classic Gothic façades. Two sets of rules had become imperative: one, which had only recently been proclaimed at Reims, was that the interior elevation must be expressed on the façade by

258. Amiens Cathedral, W façade, completed by ca. 1236 to cornice above rose (tracery of rose early 16th c.) (Ward Archive)

making the triforium apparent on the outside as a horizontal zone of arcading; and the other, which dated back to the façade of Laon a whole generation earlier,[25] that the composition of a façade should be guided by the two major motifs of the doorways and the rose window. But as these motifs, whatever their size, are fixed forms in which height is dependent on width, at Amiens they were bound to clash with the abnormally narrow proportions of the interior structure. Made fairly small by the narrowness of the nave and necessarily placed right under the vault, the rose was set too high on the façade, while the doorways had to stop short of the colossal height of the aisles; with the result that above and below the triforium zone two gaps were left which had to be filled, by adding a second gallery (the Gallery of Kings) on top of the gallery of the triforium stage and by inserting another half-story of deep triangular windows above the two lateral doorways. The piling up of a multiplicity of differentiated horizontal zones, sometimes overlapping, which unexpectedly characterizes the entrance to the most verticalized of Gothic naves, reflects essentially that unsolved problem of façade composition. The only way of solving it and avoiding the confusion would have been to reject purely and simply all the accepted rules of Gothic west front composition and to anticipate by some ten years the free openness of the façade of Saint-Nicaise at Reims.[26]

Another unusual aspect of the Amiens façade is that it is so thin through. Instead of being a block with square towers solidly based, built over the first bay of the nave aisles, the façade of Amiens is almost a constructional trompe l'oeil, the towers being reduced in depth to a flattened rectangular form and mounted simply over deep arches which overhang the doorways both inside and out.[27] The ground plan shows how compressed a base these towers have been given (Fig. 256). This reduction of bulk and this cantilever construction are in perfect accord with Robert de Luzarches's ideal of minimal weight; but the end of a nave has to be firmly blocked, and in the absence of heavy towers loading them sufficiently at the top the buttresses of the façade have to thicken progressively towards the ground to anchor solidly the west bay of the nave. This bold lightening of the façade structure is therefore the reason why such deep projections were necessary and had to be somehow disguised. It was the logic of structure as well as the logic of proportions and of compositional conventions that imposed upon the designer of Amiens a radical contradiction in terms of visual values between nave and façade.

But whatever the difficulties encountered in the designing of the façade, in the main body of the church all the component parts of the structure are intimately bound together and obey the simple laws of mutual conformity: the aisles equal half the total height of the nave, and the chapels of the chevet are of the same height as the aisles. The stories of Amiens may have been pulled out in height, but they have all followed the movement and there is no disproportion between them. Saint-Quentin and Beauvais are not so simple: they are rather sophisticated in the composition of their volumes, playing on off-balance effects, and they indicate a stage of dissociative, self-contradicting and paradox-prone refinement (a stage which in this form was of short duration) which in many of its methods and modes of thought could be compared to what Mannerism stands for in the history of Renaissance architecture. It is difficult to find another word of common use to express that particular quality.

SAINT-QUENTIN AND BEAUVAIS

In plan and general disposition Saint-Quentin is a most unexpected building (Fig. 259), not so much because of its big west tower, which simply reflects the proximity of the Scheldt basin and of Cambrai in particular,[28] but rather because of the duplication of the transept: east of the main transept, after four straight bays of choir, comes a second narrower transept against which the curved mass of the east end is applied (Fig. 260). The whole of that choir and chevet ensemble was probably begun a little before 1220 but was completed only in 1257.[29] The idea of adding a second transept towards the east to support the composition of the chevet had first appeared at Cluny III in 1088 but had not found much following in France. In England on the other hand that double transept plan was becoming quite popular by the end of the twelfth century,[30] and at Saint-Quentin the great difference of width between the two transepts points actually to some English suggestion. The narrowness of the eastern transept and the sharpness of its roof and gables are among the most striking features of the larger Early Gothic structures of England, such as Lincoln, Salisbury, Worcester or Beverley; but as most of these churches were begun after 1220,[31] the English sources, as far as Saint-Quentin is concerned, narrow themselves down to Lincoln Cathedral (Fig. 261), the oldest of the series (it was started in 1192), which had originally, in addition to its narrow eastern transept, a short polygonal east end with ambulatory and chapels rather analogous to a French chevet termination.[32] There are many obvious differences between Saint-Quentin and Lincoln: Saint-Quentin is much taller, has a richer chevet composition and forms a much more compact ensemble, the transepts being kept within the alignment of the double aisles of the choir section; while Lincoln has single aisles only in all parts of the building and accentuates its articulations by sharply projecting transepts.[33] But in both churches the choir is four bays deep and the proportions of the narrow eastern transept are typical enough to make it most likely that the designer of Saint-Quentin had some contact (if only indirectly) with the Lincoln workshop, which at that time was becoming the most influential of English workshops and had just passed through a period of artistic exchanges with the Continent.[34] As Saint-Quentin

259. SAINT-QUENTIN, reconstructed plan of 13th c. work (mostly ca. 1220–1257), dotted lines indicate parts not completed in 13th c. (W tower late 12th c.)

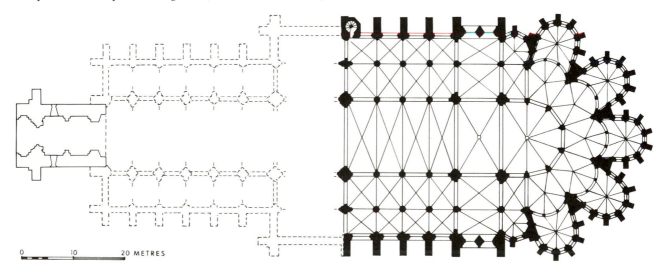

260. SAINT-QUENTIN, aerial view, begun ca. 1220

261. LINCOLN CATHEDRAL, view from SSE, begun 1192, enlarged E end
(Angel Choir) 1256–1280

was then situated on one of the main roads linking England with Champagne and Burgundy, it is not surprising to find there evidence of the transmission and assimilation of an English influence, even though for the last twenty years England had ceased to be a current source of inspiration for Gothic builders.

No less remarkable, at Saint-Quentin, is the general arrangement of the east end (Fig. 264). The five radiating chapels are deep

262. SAINT-QUENTIN, choir ca. 1220–1257, vaults rebuilt later, 15th c. nave

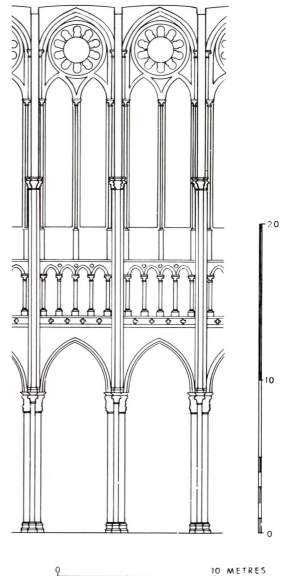

263. SAINT-QUENTIN, elevation of choir, ca. 1220–1257

and seemingly autonomous, each being shaped like a miniature rotunda and separated from the corresponding bay of the ambulatory by an arcade of three stilted arches supported on two thin columns. That screen of arches is clearly derived from the chapels of Saint-Remi at Reims, which had already been imitated in a few buildings;[35] but at Saint-Quentin the impression is quite different because of the great height of the ambulatory, of the scalloped plan of its outer walls, and of the difference in height between ambulatory and chapels. Each bay of ambulatory makes a pronounced curve towards the outside (Fig. 265), rather in the manner of shallow chapels such as those of Soissons Cathedral; and the system of vaulting is actually the same as in the combined ambulatory and chapels of Soissons. This swelling of the ambulatory bays not only orients towards the chapels by creating a centrifugal movement but produces in the ambulatory itself an effect of unusual spaciousness, which is still further enhanced by the fact that the ambulatory is taller than the chapels, so that there is room for a little clerestory stage above the triple entrance to the chapels. From the outside, this difference of height and the insertion of an additional zone of windows give rise to a composition in tiers (Fig. 266) which is closely reminiscent of the chevets of Clairvaux or of Heisterbach. But at Saint-Quentin the play of forms is much richer, since the projecting polygonal shape of the ambulatory bays[36] detaches a second series of chapel-like volumes just above the deeper polygonal forms of the chapels proper.

Another peculiarity of the chevet of Saint-Quentin is the presence of diagonally planted chapels at the contact of the ambulatory with the eastern transepts. This element of design clearly comes from Braine, where two pairs of such chapels flanked the entrance to a simple choir that was without aisles or ambulatory. But here this type of chapel has been adapted to the ambulatory plan, as at Troyes Cathedral and Notre-Dame at Saint-Omer.[37] Vaucelles also made a very similar use of the diagonal planting of chapels to fill the angles between the ambulatory and large rectangular chapels; and at Vaucelles as at Saint-Quentin there was a play on height in the arrangement of the chapels, the large rectangular chapels being

264. SAINT-QUENTIN, hemicycle and ambulatory, ca. 1220–1257

265. SAINT-QUENTIN, entrance to ambulatory chapels (tracery of upper windows 15th c.)

of the same height as the ambulatory, whereas the small rounded chapels huddled in the angles were made shorter so that the apex of their roof reached only to the level of the cornice of the ambulatory walls.[38] At Saint-Quentin there is more evenness in the grouping of volumes since all the radiating chapels are lower than the ambulatory; but the chapels lodged in the angles of the chevet and transept are much taller than the other chapels and rise to the full height of the ambulatory. This juxtaposition of chapels of different heights is so rare in the architecture of the early thirteenth century that it can be considered almost as a signature. The name of Villard de Honnecourt has been suggested for both of these buildings;[39] and, in the case of Saint-Quentin, the presence of Rémois features in the upper parts of the chevet has been adduced as a confirmation of that attribution. But all these assumptions and hypotheses concerning Villard's activity are rather too speculative and Pierre de Corbie could perhaps be an equally likely candidate.

In any case it seems clear that whoever designed Saint-Quentin was not a classicist and that he was attracted by the picturesqueness of complex combinations of faceted volumes repeating themselves at different levels, and by cascade-like effects which recall at the same time the transept chapels of Laon and the chevet of Le Mans. But what is even more typical (and even less classical) at Saint-Quentin is a very special way of playing on proportions. This can already be perceived to some extent in the treatment of the interior space. Whereas at Chartres and Soissons main arcade and clerestory were exactly of the same height and balanced each other on either side of the triforium, and while after that the dominant tendency—as illustrated by Reims and Amiens—was toward a progressive enlargement of the main arcade at the expense of the size of the clerestory, Saint-Quentin was the first building to reverse the trend and make the clerestory taller than the main arcade (Figs. 262, 263), with the resulting effect of an increased verticality of the central space.

On the outside a further element is added, which makes that effect even more evident: the systematic reduction of the height of the radiating chapels. The whole composition of the chevet is aimed at exaggerating the height of the central part of the choir by making it tower above low peripheral masses (Fig. 266). The ambulatory, which from inside seems rather shorter than it should be, appears almost taller than normal when seen from outside, because it rises so markedly above the chapels which surround it. But what is abnormal in that chevet is the squatness of the radiating chapels, which look as if they had been pressed down and flattened against the ground, increasing by contrast the verticality of the high central volume. It has been suggested that the choir of Saint-Quentin was perhaps heightened in the course of construction and that the upper story was not meant at first to have all that height; but it seems most unlikely to have ever been planned much shorter than it is now, precisely because the singular arrangement of the lower stories and the flattened gradation of their volumes imply the deci-

266. SAINT-QUENTIN, chevet and narrow E transept (SE transept rebuilt late 15th c.)

sion to create a marked contrast in height which could be further exploited by deliberate effects of disproportion. If after looking at the chevet one enters the building again and observes the central elevation of the choir so stretched in height, it is difficult to doubt that the intention of the design lay in that method of contrasting two spatial effects one against the other, in order to accentuate their divergent expression and make them more striking each in its own direction.

The choir of Beauvais also was based on the same kind of concerted disproportion. The part of the structure which was built

288

267. Beauvais Cathedral, chevet from S, 1225–1272

first, just after the fire of 1225,[40] and which corresponds to the work of a first master—the chapels and the outer shell of the ambulatory—repeats in its own manner the arrangement of the peripheral volumes of the chevet of Saint-Quentin. But while at Saint-Quentin the duplication of the transept east of the choir isolates the extreme termination of the chevet and limits to that curved ending the novel effect of contrasting volumes, at Beauvais, where no such additional transept exists, that semicircle of dwarf chapels is pursued all along the straight bays of the choir (becoming there in fact a low outer aisle). The continuity of this low tier of volumes right up to the transverse break of the transept creates a sort of base, narrow but uninterrupted, which extends around the whole of the choir structure (Fig. 267), making its overall form much simpler and more unified than at Saint-Quentin.

Many other differences distinguish the two buildings: the chapels at Beauvais have become much less deep and at the same time taller in their general proportions. The plan (Fig. 268) is also more regular and more orthodox than at Saint-Quentin, being related to Chartres in its seven-sided hemicycle and the intended tow-

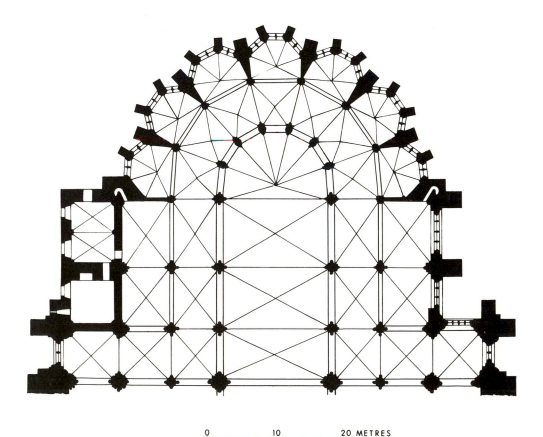

0   10   20 METRES

268. BEAUVAIS CATHEDRAL, plan in 1272 reconstructed

269. BEAUVAIS CATHEDRAL, choir as restored after collapse of 1284 (crossing piers and most of transept 16th c.) (Ward Archive)

ers of its transept façades, or to such typical works of the Chartrain series as the Cistercian choir of Longpont for the type and pattern of the chapels which surround the ambulatory. The connections with Reims are even more striking,[41] extending as they do to the overall silhouette (Fig. 273) raised by the structure as well as to many significant details of style (window types, rounded abaci topping the smaller shafts, *cantonné* shape of the engaged piers which separate the chapels). However, there remains a particularly close relationship between Beauvais and Saint-Quentin: not just a filiation but a community of spirit, as the two buildings follow the same basic and most unusual principle of volume composition.

It is from outside that one can see most clearly how strongly the peripheral zone of the chevet contrasts with the colossal height of the central part of the choir, the sharp projection of the low

270. BEAUVAIS CATHEDRAL, N side of choir as completed in 1272: reconstruction by R. Branner from *Art de France,* II, Hermann, Paris, 1962

271. BEAUVAIS CATHEDRAL, N side of choir, present state following 14th c. repairs: photo R. Branner from *Art de France* II, Hermann, Paris, 1962

lateral volumes stressing the contradiction in size between the lower and upper parts of the structure. But inside the church (Fig. 269) the actual spatial effect is much less evident: one has to walk around the choir for a time and look at it from a variety of angles, to reach a global perception of its shape and of the relative size of its components. At first sight the comparative smallness of the chapels is hardly perceptible because ambulatory and chapels are now almost completely masked behind a tight screen of piers (Fig. 271). This excessive density of supports is due to the structural reinforcements which became necessary after the choir vaults had collapsed in 1284:[42] the number of the piers was then doubled in the three straight bays of the choir, each bay being split into two on its full height and topped by a sexpartite vault in place of the large quadripartite vault which covered it originally. With these additional piers which now block the view, it is difficult to imagine the previous openness of the lateral vistas in the choir of Beauvais when it had its very wide bays.

That original appearance of the interior of Beauvais was reconstructed by Robert Branner in a drawing (Fig. 270) which is the best of demonstrations, for it reveals at a glance what effect the building was meant to achieve. It is evident that it was not only more beautiful in the size and shape of its arches, the spacing of its piers and the vast expanse of its windows: it was also much easier to understand since the spatial continuity between choir and aisles made its interior composition immediately legible. Nothing prevented a direct perception of the difference of scale between the elevation of the outer wall of the ambulatory, which could be seen through the wide arches of the main arcade, and the gigantic elevation of the central space of the choir. The upper half of that central elevation was actually built much later than the rest[43] and in a new style which differs strikingly from the spare neatness of the first Master; but the proportions of these upper stories provide such a perfect counterpart to the treatment of the lower parts of the structure that it appears most unlikely that any basic changes were brought to bear on the design in the later stages of construction. The architect who took over in the course of the 1250s may have

272. BEAUVAIS CATHEDRAL, aerial view showing 13th c. choir and 16th c. transept

adopted a new style of execution, but he seems to have conformed in matters of proportions to the pre-established design.[44]

Here again an aerial photograph sums up with particular clarity the character of the work (Fig. 272). Beauvais remained unfinished, the transept itself being added only in the early sixteenth century, but the silhouette of this tremendously high chevet stands out even more strikingly in that unintended isolation. Beauvais obviously belongs to the same family of chevets as that of Reims Cathedral: a clear vertical rise contained within the perimeter of the tall uprights of the buttresses; and in the middle of that cluster of thin stone piers, all vertical again, rises the towering volume of the central part of this colossal choir, the tallest of all Gothic buildings.[45] At Reims, where it was invented as a principle of formal clarification, that rigorous vertical straightness of outline had been associated with much more stable and quieter proportions. Beauvais represented a remarkable exaggeration of that concept of the re-strained rectangular silhouette: the verticals were multiplied, tight-ened much more closely, drawn out in height (Fig. 273.E); and to this compression and elongation was added the further refinement of the deliberate and insistent contrast between the low peripheral zone of chapels and the towering central volume.

THE END OF A SYSTEM

Beauvais was one more of those intensely personal visions which followed one another in such rapid succession in the wake of Bourges and Chartres. But they all had something in common: whatever the treatment that was given to the flying buttresses, whether they were flattened into huge transverse screens as at Le Mans and Beauvais, or treated more in the round with a suggestion of inner strength and autonomy, as at Reims (where they look rather like a small-scale bridges), in all the buildings of that age the cage of flying but-tresses had a well-defined form and could play on equal terms with the more solid volumes. There is no doubt that the architecture of the years 1195–1230, dominated as it is by the flying-buttress, is an architecture of firm and vigorous framework (Fig. 273 C, D, E). It is never reduced to a mere linear network: its members have sub-stance and weight, they are in all actuality the necessary components of the structure, the instruments of its stability; and they proclaim it. In the same way the façade of Amiens, composed of transverse bridges of masonry built at different heights between projecting vertical buttresses, is again extremely strong and vigorous beneath the ornate surface. The planes of the façade are not reduced to paper-thin screens, as they were to become in Paris thirty years later in the transept façades of Notre-Dame (Figs. 377 and 383). Be-tween the style of the 1220s (nave of Amiens, lower parts of Beauvais, choir and chevet of Saint-Quentin) and the Rayonnant Style of the mid-thirteenth century, between the west front of Amiens and the transept façades of Notre-Dame (the contrast here is of particular clarity), it is evident that what occurred was another major stylistic break, another true stylistic revolution. And it was in the course of the 1230s and in the early 1240s that this third ver-sion of Gothic, this third Gothic system, was created.

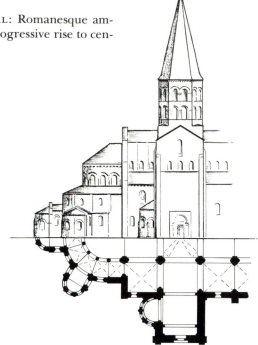

A. PARAY-LE-MONIAL: Romanesque ambulatory formula, progressive rise to central tower

273. Developmental sequence of chevet formulas

0   10   20 METRES

D. LE MANS: High Gothic, maximum expansion formula

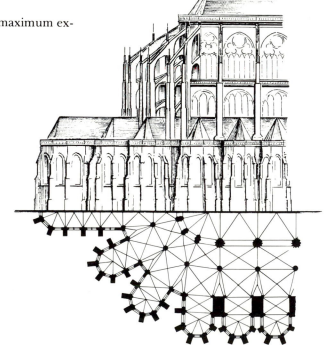

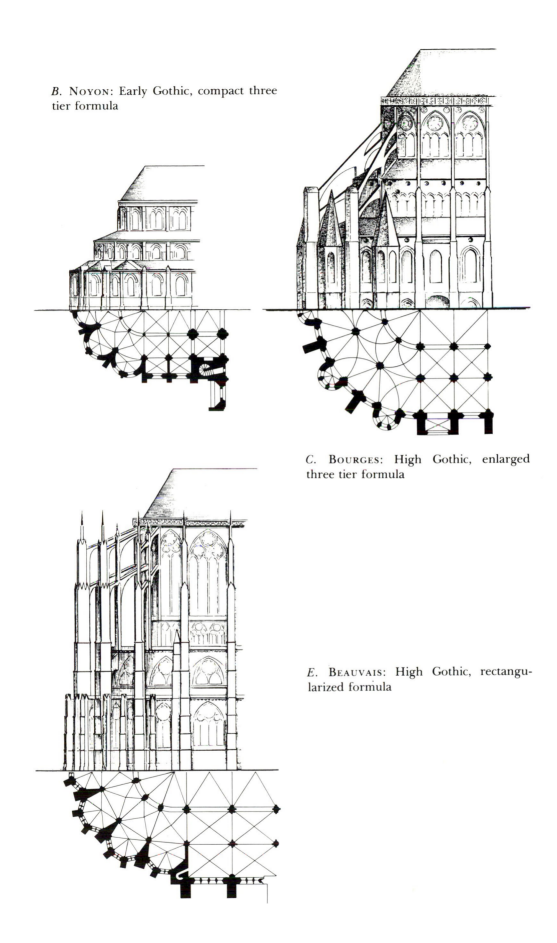

B. Noyon: Early Gothic, compact three tier formula

C. Bourges: High Gothic, enlarged three tier formula

E. Beauvais: High Gothic, rectangularized formula

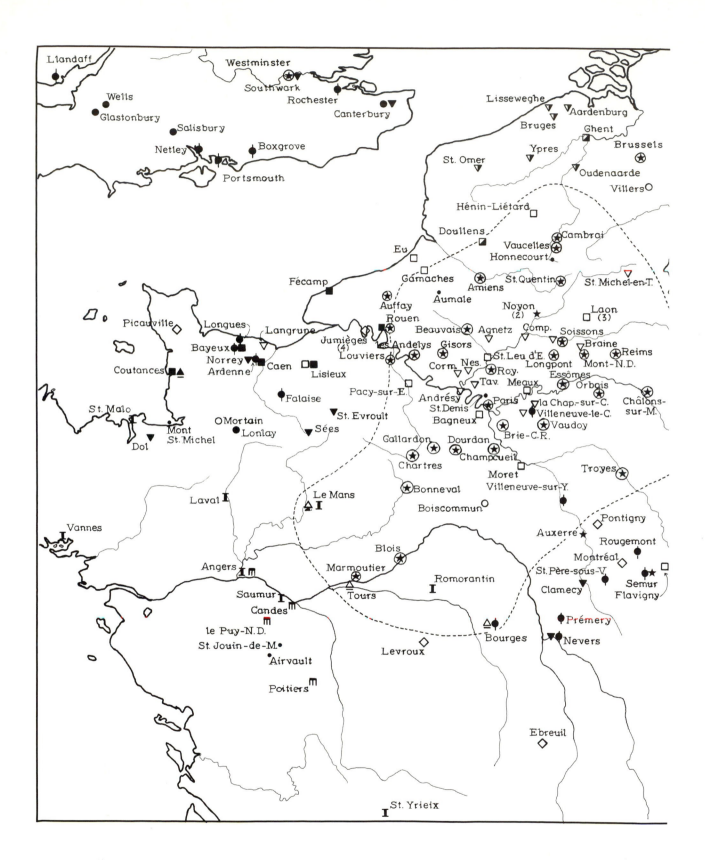

274. MAP: High Gothic Architecture (mid 1190s to mid 1230s) and its relationship with
the surrounding peripheral styles (1180 to 1240s)

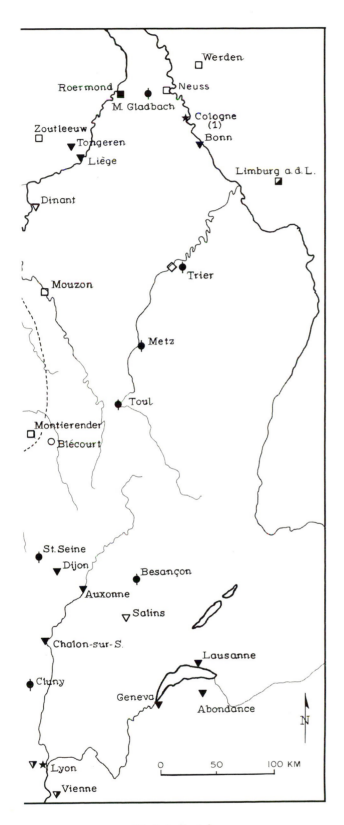

Limits indicated

------- Core area of the High Gothic movement

Footnotes to names

(1) Cologne: St. Gereon   (2) Noyon: façade bay
(3) Laon: eastern extension of choir
(4) Jumièges: Saint-Pierre, S side of nave

LEGEND

Symbols used

☐ Survival of tribune (or tribune-like) elevation, without interior clerestory passage

■ Survival of tribune (or tribune-like) elevation, with interior clerestory passage

◇ Early Cistercian type or related

△ Closely related to north French types

△ Bourges variant of north French type

● Two-story or triforium elevation, with interior clerestory passage

I Aisleless naves

m Hall churches

◉ Powerful effects of space or scale

× Buildings of other periods referred to in Chapter VIII

Limits indicated

- - - - - Core area of the High Gothic movement

Abbreviations

Aux.	Auxerre
Cant.	Canterbury
Cl.	Clamecy
Mont.	Montierender
Oud.	Oudenaarde
Pad.	Paderborn
Puy-N.D.	Puy-Notre-Dame
Ro.	Roermond

St.Leu d'E.	Saint-Leu d'Esserent
St.M.	Saint-Malo
St.O.	Saint-Omer
Sa.	Saumur
Sal.	Salisbury
Sem.	Semur
To.	Tongeren
V.s.Y.	Villeneuve-sur-Yonne
W'min.	Westminster
Worc.	Worcester
Y.	Ypres (Ieper)

For unnamed buildings in France and Belgium, see Fig. 274.

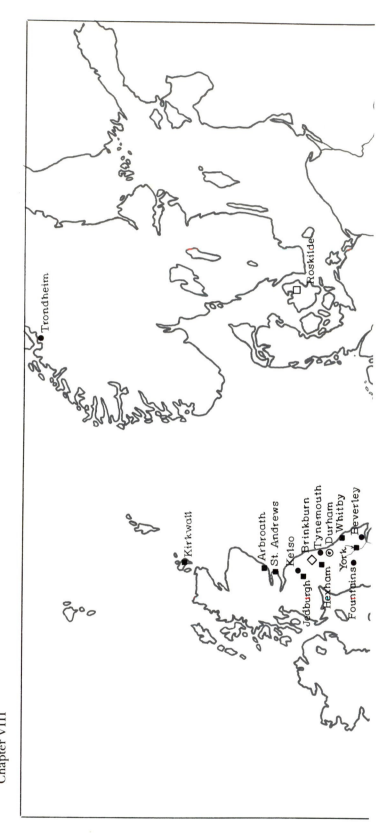

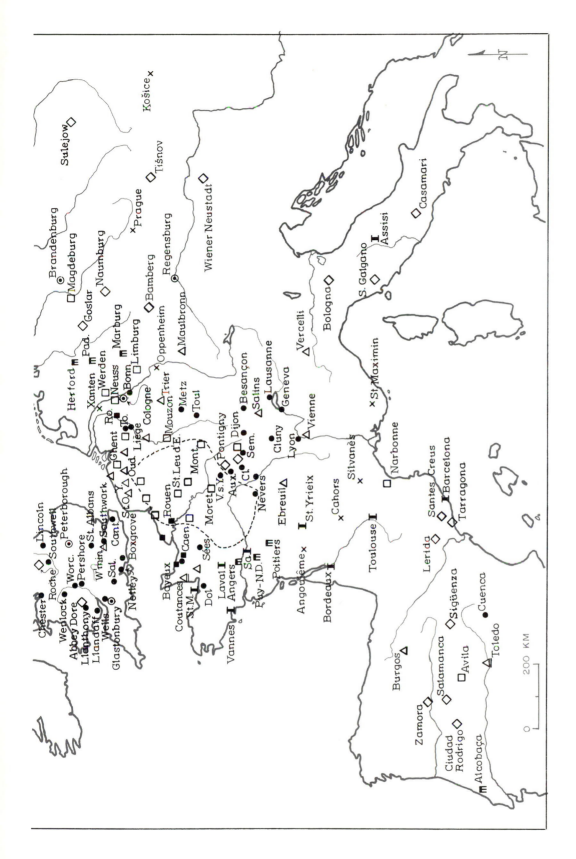

Sulejów

Košice ×

Tišnov

Prague ×

Brandenburg

Magdeburg ⊙

Naumburg

Goslar

Pad.

Regensburg ⊙

Wiener Neustadt

Bamberg

Oppenheim

Maulbronn

Marburg

Limburg

Herford E

Werden E

Xanten

Neuss

Bonn E

Cologne ⊙

Trier

Mouzon

Metz

Toul

Besançon

Salins

Lausanne

Geneva

Vercelli

Bologna

S. Galgano I

Assisi

Casamari

St. Maximin ×

Vienne

Lyon

Narbonne

Silvanès ×

Santes Creus

Barcelona I

Tarragona

Lerida

Sigüenza

Cuenca

Toledo

Burgos

Salamanca

Avila

Zamora

Ciudad Rodrigo

Alcobaça E

Lincoln

Chester

Roche

Southwell ⊙

Pershore

Peterborough ⊙

St. Albans

Worc.

Wenlock

Abbey Dore

Llanthony

Llandaff

Wells

Glastonbury ⊙

Sal.

Southwark

Within

Netley

Boxgrove

Cant.

Ghent

Oud.

Liège

Ro.

To.

Rouen

St. Leu d'E.

Mont.

Pontigny

Dijon

Sem.

Ct.

Aux.

V.s.Y.

Moret

Nevers

Ebreuil E

St. Yrieix I

Cahors ×

Cluny

Bayeux

Coutances

St. M.

Dol

Sées

Caen

Laval I

Angers I

Sa. I E

Puy-N.D. E

Poitiers

Vannes

Angoulême ×

Bordeaux I

Toulouse I

200 KM

0

275. Map: The Peripheral Gothic Milieux (up to mid 13th c.)

276. VILLENEUVE-SUR-YONNE, choir begun ca. 1240–1245

CHAPTER VIII

Divergent Trends in the Early Thirteenth Century

In a study that aims primarily at recapturing the inner vitality of the Gothic movement and at tracking the changes of direction or emphasis which gave such a distinctive curve to its development, attention has naturally had to focus almost exclusively on that northern French milieu in which the new architecture had been created and was kept moving ahead from generation to generation over more than a century, at a rather astounding pace. For what really matters, if one wants to understand how new forms of sensibility come into being in any great movement of art, is the turn things take at the very core of its making. But it would obviously be unrealistic and in the long run misleading to leave the picture of the northern French milieu in artificial isolation, by failing to relate it to the art milieux surrounding it. Certainly, the small cluster of the original Gothic centers stood out at first against the background of a still purely Romanesque landscape;[1] but novelty is not long without a following. Other men in other regions of the Late Romanesque world were themselves searching for new departures and many welcomed the stimulation of the new concepts and new procedures that were coming out of northern France, with the result that by the first decades of the thirteenth century the initial Gothic centers of the Capetian lands were surrounded on all sides by a mosaic of gothicized milieux, in which other Gothic styles were being evolved and in some cases had already reached a high degree of explicitness and originality (Fig. 275, p. 300–301).

In these peripheral areas the Gothic phenomenon was quite different in nature from what it was in its land of origin. For Gothic resulted now from an external stimulus, which means that in every case there was now an interaction of two sets of forces: on the one hand, it was to some definite contact, direct or indirect, with northern French Gothic that all these other styles owed their gothicness (the process of transmission being for the most part easily discernible); while on the other hand it was to the local background of Late Romanesque tendencies that they owed much of their vigor and originality. Each of the regional styles of Gothic reflects a particular combination of circumstances and would ask for an extensive study[2] to define the uniqueness of the situation, the various reactions it brought about, the part played by pure accident, and the process of selection and reinterpretation that occurred in each specific environment. These case histories are all fascinating in themselves, revealing as they do the diversity of cultural traditions and the variability of responses of human sensibility.

But, however essential, such efforts of individual analysis are not enough: these separate styles have also to be situated in relation to the central Gothic movement. Since they all arose through some kind of contact with the architecture of northern France, it is critically important to pinpoint as exactly as possible at what moment—or rather, at what stage in the development of northern French Gothic—that decisive contact took place. For the start of a movement is often determinant, setting a general orientation for the new style, and here marking—to use a somewhat simplified formulation—the point at which it detaches itself from the main Gothic stem. Beyond that crucial period of formation other problems obviously come up: what sets of values did these peripheral styles mean to defend? through what stages did they develop? did they interrelate in any significant manner? and how were they affected by the subsequent pronouncements of northern French Gothic? All these questions need to be answered.[3] But in the perspective of the present study, the first job to be performed is a summary identification of the conditions of formation of these satellite movements and an overall mapping of their relative positions on the time grid of Gothic history.

Autonomous Gothic Developments

As soon as one attempts to make a sorting out of this kind among the regional styles of Gothic, it becomes clear that some of them were related hardly at all, or only in the most general manner, to the architecture of northern France. This is true particularly of the Gothic styles of southern and western France. At the cathedral of Toulouse, which was under construction by 1218,[4] the nave is aisle-

277. Toulouse Cathedral, nave to W, ca. 1205–1235

less and remarkably wide (Fig. 277): with an internal width of just over 19 meters (some 63 feet), it is the widest of early thirteenth century naves; but it is also a work of pure engineering, powerful, logical, absolutely plain, using none of the subtler values of architecture. It could be said that the same spirit had already been at work—but with different constructional methods—at Cahors cathedral and in the early group of domed churches of Aquitaine[5] in the first part of the twelfth century or, a generation later, in the wide barrel vaulted naves of Saint-Pons-de-Thomières and Silvanès;[6] but now that engineering spirit was being applied to the handling of well coursed rib vaults in oblong bays, which by reason of their shape and construction appear definitely Gothic, although in a rather elementary way. Even more remote from the concepts of northern French Gothic were, in the same southern area, the wide unvaulted aisleless naves spanned by a succession of pointed diaphragm arches (Fig. 279): a type which can be illustrated soon after 1250 by the church of Lamourguier at Narbonne.[7] Very plain, utilitarian-looking, but with the particular splendor of their rhythm of arches and their large unencumbered space, these churches have close analogies with the Cistercian dormitories of Poblet or Santes-Creus (Fig. 278) in Catalonia, where the roof is in the same way supported by diaphragm arches. And the sources of this technique of lightweight and spacious construction, far from being northern, were Late Antique or Islamic but gothicized by the thinness of their arches and the repetitiveness of their rhythm of narrow oblong bays: another obvious case of a separately developed formula.

The Gothic architecture of Anjou and Poitou, those western provinces of France which were among the most vital components of the Plantagenet empire, has the same character of an essentially autonomous development based simply, in this case, on the notion of large rib-vaulted units.[8] At Angers Cathedral (Fig. 69, p. 73) and in the whole group that followed, it is quite evident again that the domes of Aquitaine (but this time those of the later series: Angoulême, Saintes, Fontevraud) were instrumental in the transformation of initial Ile-de-France types into that Angevin concept of square self-contained units of vaulting. But this kind of domed rib

278. SANTES-CREUS, dormitory begun 1191

279. NARBONNE, NOTRE-DAME DE LAMOURGUIER, N side of nave, ca. 1250–1270

vault was handled with considerable freedom. Not only was its ribbing soon multiplied by the addition of ridge ribs (as in the choir of Saint-Martin at Angers or the nave of La Couture at Le Mans), but from the 1160s, in units of vaulting somewhat reduced in size, these large Angevin vaults began to be applied to churches of that hall type which since the late eleventh century had become current in both Poitou and the Loire Valley. Poitiers Cathedral (Fig. 71, p. 75) had been the first example of that transfer, and by 1215 or 1220 the hall structures of Anjou reached in the choir of Saint-Serge at Angers (Fig. 280) a new degree of refinement.

Technically the vaults of Saint-Serge are rather strange.[9] Each bay of vaulting is in fact a ribbed ovoid dome mounted on a square plan, rising high in the center and intersected in its lower part by the domes which cover the adjoining bays; and these repetitions of lightweight domes of equal height merging at their bases over slen-

280. ANGERS, SAINT-SERGE, choir, ca. 1215–1220

der piers achieve internally the most striking effect of unified and continuous spaciousness. The stability of this assemblage of vaults is insured on the one hand by a system of heavy loading over the piers, at the meeting points of the different vault units, and on the other hand by heavy surrounding walls which firmly block this clustering of domed vaults; and the presence of these thick outer walls makes the building retain a Romanesque solidity of aspect. In contrast, from within the structure appears extremely light. The piers even look abnormally thin, but—as had already been observed by Rondelet in the eighteenth century—their thinness is explained by the nature of the material used for the construction of the vaults: a light porous local chalk known as *craie tuffeau*. The other element that contributes to that interior effect of lightness is the appearance given to the vaults, in which the ribbing is made to look much thinner than it is in fact, essentially through artifices of molding; for the actual constructional ribs which form the armature of the vault are composed of large stones, much wider than the rib molding that projects on their inner surface and that gives a false impression of frail linearity. The sturdy constructional ribbing even extends in depth through the whole thickness of the vault, so that its vigorous pattern can clearly be read on the extrados of the domes (Fig. 281).

What is Gothic at Saint-Serge of Angers is therefore nothing but features of a purely general nature: the spaciousness of the interior, the lightness of the vaulted structure, the tall slender supports, and the principle of fragmentation. But that principle itself was understood in a very particular way, being applied exclusively to the vaults and according to a rather unusual set of rules. Not only are all the cells of the vault subdivided by the addition of ridge ribs (which makes eight ribs converge on each central keystone), but a further breaking-up process takes place in all the corners of the building, where short sloping penetrations topping the heads of all the windows lead to effects of mannered complexity in the ribbing (Fig. 282). Even more typical of that Angevin tendency to an increased fragmentation of the vault surfaces is the crisscrossing of ribs used a few years later over the naves of Airvault and Saint-Jouin-de-Marnes, on the north margin of Poitou, and

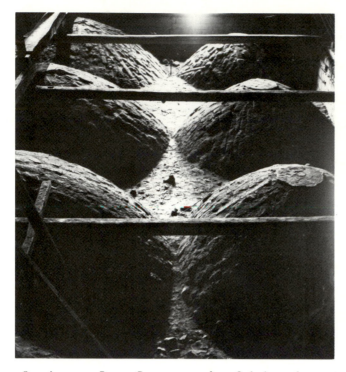

281. ANGERS, SAINT-SERGE, extrados of choir vaults   282. ANGERS, SAINT-SERGE, vault in SE corner of choir

also originally in the church of Toussaint (All Saints) at Angers, now destroyed.[10] Under their regular net-like pattern of ribs, these vaults are of a most unexpected shape, being in fact pointed barrels with short lateral penetrations (Fig. 283) which leave the whole central section of the barrel vault untouched, except for the surface partitioning created by the ribs. These barrel vaults with reduced penetrations, gothicized by the application of a tight net of ribs, belong again to a line of thought completely unrelated to the northern French concept of Gothic. For a century the idea remained of purely local significance. However, it was to enter the major cycle of late Gothic forms through its adoption in a group of buildings in the west of England in the early fourteenth century. Receiving that idea from England in the second half of the century, Germany was to give it an even wider diffusion;[11] but it was only through that detour and in that later age that this form of elaborate

283. AIRVAULT, nave vaults, ca. 1225–1230   284. PONTIGNY, nave, ca. 1160 (Ward Archive)

vaulting network entered the wider stream of international Gothic.

Although these highly individual styles which took shape in southern and western France had been triggered by some precise contacts with the emerging Gothic of the Paris region[12] and could in no way be used to support a theory of simultaneous invention of Gothic in several separate environments, yet they did steer at once a most individual course and were remarkably uninfluenced by the distinctive trends of Ile-de-France architecture. Animated from the start by an autonomous impulse and pursuing a logic of their own, they have to be seen, once launched, not as mere derivations but as other independent Gothic movements; and the same view applies also, outside the confines of France, to the development that was then taking place in northwestern Germany.[13]

Nonetheless, this state of almost complete autonomy was rare; most of the early thirteenth-century styles of Gothic are clearly connected with the northern French movement. These styles simply branch off from the main stream at some point, and in a number of cases this happened right at the beginning of the development of Ile-de-France Gothic. A good example of that precocious branching-off is the first style of Cistercian Gothic,[14] which can be represented by the nave of Pontigny (Fig. 284) in northern Burgundy, built ca. 1160. This rather rudimentary Gothic style, with its simple pattern of bays and intensely mural quality, corresponded well to the form of sensibility favored by the Cistercians and was used by them for a long time: it was still quite common in the early thirteenth century in the whole of the vast area of expansion of the Cistercian order. Viewed in relation to the pattern of development of Gothic architecture, this first Cistercian Gothic appears as a mere continuation of the stylistic stage which had been reached by the early 1140s in the small churches of the area to the immediate northwest of Paris (Vexin, Beauvaisis, southern edges of Picardy): Bury for instance or Airaines (Fig. 33, p. 35) or La Villetertre; which means a very early kind of Gothic, earlier in type and concept than the choir of Saint-Denis and in fact derived from pre-1140 prototypes, such as the earlier parts of Saint-Etienne at Beauvais (Fig. 25, p. 28) (the east bay of the nave and, no doubt, also the original choir). It is very much the same brand of Gothic that is currently found in Germany too, under Cistercian influence, in the early thirteenth century. The nave of Bamberg cathedral (Fig. 285), built in the 1220s, follows a different compositional formula, that of large double bays—a Lombard and Rhenish pattern commonly adopted by the Cistercians in Germany—but otherwise reflects the same principles, the same type of effects and the same stylistic age as the nave of Pontigny.[15]

England also had her first glimpse of the nascent new style through some early forms of Cistercian Gothic.[16] But there the situation became complicated from the outset by the appearance in Yorkshire, at Roche (Fig. 286), by 1170 at the latest, of a more elaborate Cistercian variant in which a blind triforium is inserted above the main arcade. Although the simple two-storied Pontigny type continued in use, sometimes—as at Abbey Dore—sharpened in its element of linearity, it was the more complex pattern of stories sketched out at Roche that was historically significant. Not only did it spread widely in the north of England, where the sequence of its developments can easily be followed, but it also gave the start in the west of England, at the contact of a vital Late Romanesque style, to an early Gothic movement of great originality which in its major works—at Worcester, St. Davids, Wells (Fig. 287) and Glastonbury—showed a remarkable inventiveness in the creation of unexpected rhythms and patterns of elevation.

While Cistercian Gothic detached itself from the Ile-de-France stem right at the start, even before the impact of Suger's choir had yet been felt, another important branching-off must be placed a little later, at the stage of the great tribune churches of the 1160s and 1170s. Around 1215 or 1220, the survival of the type of the trib-

285. BAMBERG CATHEDRAL, nave and W choir, ca. 1219–1237

286. ROCHE ABBEY, ruins of N transept, ca. 1170

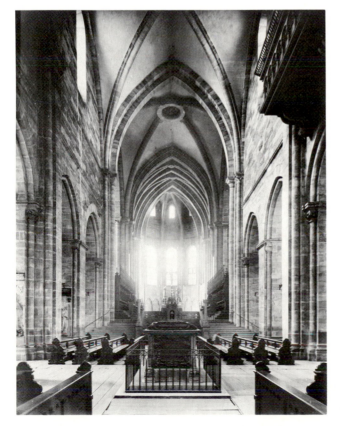

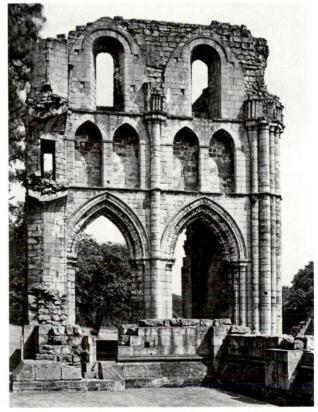

une church was so common—at least for the larger churches—in so many areas of Europe that it can be said to have been for a while one of the basic features of the peripheral Gothic milieux. It reigned in Normandy; in Flanders too, with at Ghent alone the Sint-Niklaaskerk and the destroyed but well-documented main church of Sint-Pietersabdij;[17] it reached to Roskilde in Denmark,[18] to Magdeburg in northern Germany. So general was this fashion for the tribune elevation that it even spread to the Mediterranean sector of Europe, where it is found in southern France in the choir of Saint-Paul-Serge at Narbonne,[19] and as far as Avila in Spain.

A typical example in western Germany is the beautiful little church of Limburg-an-der-Lahn[20] begun, like Bamberg, ca. 1220. Seen in silhouette (Fig. 288), it is fairly evident that, even taking

287. WELLS CATHEDRAL, nave, ca. 1200–1225

288. LIMBURG-AN-DER-LAHN view from NE, ca. 1220–1235

into account all the differences of scale, shaping and proportions, Limburg was meant to emulate Laon with its seven towers. But the forms of the components still follow the precedents of Rhenish Romanesque: typical in this respect are the four-gabled towers of the west façade and the octagonal tower in the center; and no less traditional is the treatment of the wall surfaces, in delicate shallow panels of arches. On the other hand, in spite of this continuing adherence to Rhenish models (and to their north Italian sources), the exterior loggia at clerestory level is likely to reflect once more a stimulus from northern France, from such buildings as the transept of Cambrai, where Van der Meulen's drawing (Fig. 128, p. 135) shows the same two-layer treatment of the wall, with an exterior passage running in front of the windows, under a tall detached portico of three arches of equal height per bay. Inside, Limburg is still

289. LIMBURG-AN-DER-LAHN, view into choir from S. transept, ca. 1220–1235

very much in the late Romanesque style of the Cologne school of the early thirteenth century, like for instance St. Quirin at Neuss. But it has also the four-story elevation (Fig. 289) of the Northern group of French Gothic, in a form which on the whole recalls Laon, although in the end wall of the transepts the linkage established between triforium and clerestory indicates some knowledge of the Reims churches (Saint-Jacques perhaps as much as the west bays of Saint-Remi); while the sexpartite vault again relates to Laon, to the nave of Noyon (as it was then covered) and to a great many other French works of the second half of the twelfth century. Limburg is the ideal case for a study of the interplay of suggestions, borrowings, revivals and reinterpretations.

Normandy too is an area where the tribune type of elevation survived well into the thirteenth century. There had been, in that province, a gap of some sixty years between the Romanesque and Gothic series of tribune churches: in the late Romanesque period, from about 1100, Normandy (as opposed to England) had generally adopted triforium elevations of the Lessay and Boscherville type (Fig. 8, p. 11), the tribune being completely outmoded for a while. But it was revived in the late 1160s, without any doubt in emulation of the great tribune churches of the neighboring Ile-de-France, the rebuilding of the choir of Fécamp after the fire of 1168 being probably the first sign of that revival.[21] However, Normandy did not favor the four-story elevation normally adopted at that time in the Northern French group: at Fécamp and in the series that followed, no triforium appears above the tribune and the wall passage remains situated at the level of the clerestory windows (Fig. 290); which means that the system of heavy wall construction traditional in Normandy since 1067, with its characteristic loading of the structure at the top, was insistently preserved, the bulk of the masses of masonry being only slightly reduced in spite of the Gothic aspect taken by the building. Even though all the arches were now pointed and the moldings sharpened into small-scale profiles, what was still missing was the lightness of truly Gothic structure; and when that lightness was introduced under Ile-de-France suggestion, as happened a little later in the nave of Lisieux Cathedral, it failed to convince the local builders: Fécamp was the formula that stood. It was only a good generation later that the lightweight Ile-de-France mode of construction, which by then had shifted to post-Chartres formulas, became accepted in eastern Normandy, at Petit-Andely for instance or in the choir of Rouen Cathedral. But when the nave of Rouen had been started in its western parts in the 1190s, it was still as a tribune church of the Fécamp type that it had been designed (Fig. 291), more refined in its details but hardly less heavy constructionally.[22]

This thickened variant of the Gothic tribune design—an obvious compromise between the new Gothic forms and the Norman Romanesque tradition—spread rapidly to the whole of Normandy,

290. FÉCAMP, N side of nave, E bays, 1168 to ca. 1210
(Ward Archive)

291. ROUEN CATHEDRAL, nave, begun shortly before 1200

reaching Caen before 1200 and Coutances about 1220. At Caen, the choir of Saint-Etienne[23] was rebuilt in two stages at the extreme end of the twelfth century and in the first years of the thirteenth, to the pattern of a wide three-tiered chevet in the Noyon manner. The central part of the structure seems to date only from ca. 1210 or 1215 and what is remarkable there, in addition to the thickness and weight of the upper story, is the beginning of a play on depth in the treatment of solid surfaces (Fig. 292): the hollowing out of the wall spandrels in sunken rosettes or trilobes was a reflection of the close links which persisted between Normandy and England even after the loss of Normandy by King John in 1204. The next step is marked in the choir of Bayeux Cathedral[24] which cannot have been begun much before 1230. The plan of that east end and the Champenois passage which runs in its outer walls indicate that Reims Cathedral was known to the builder; but the interior elevation (Fig. 294) bears little relation to the Chartres-Reims series. The deep holes dug into the wall, the succession of layers recessed in depth come even closer to the English type of effects than Caen had managed to achieve some fifteen years before; and on the other hand, while this choir of Bayeux has no real tribunes behind the screen of its elevation, the intermediate story remains treated in the manner of a tribune story. It is made to occupy as much height as a tribune, and its groupings of arches, unified in each bay under one large enclosing arch (progressively subdivided into two and four smaller arches) is also derived from the classic type of tribune elevation. Constructionally speaking, that middle story is an authentic triforium with a narrow passage and a wall immediately be-

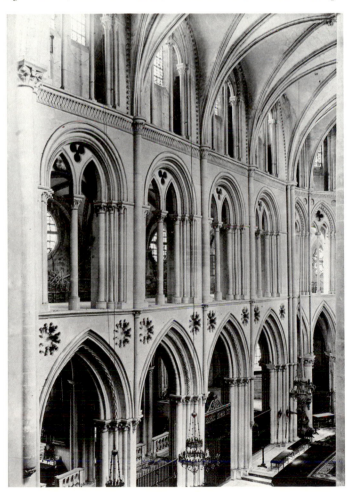

292. CAEN, SAINT-ETIENNE, N side of choir, ca. 1210–1215

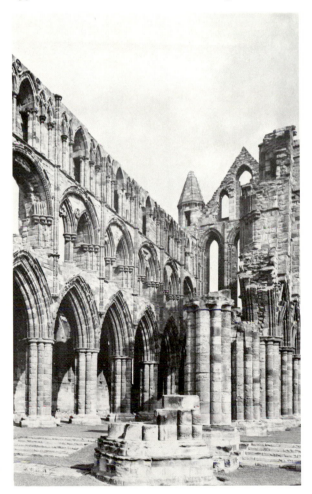

293. WHITBY ABBEY, ruins of choir, begun ca. 1220

294. BAYEUX CATHEDRAL, choir and ambulatory from S transept, begun ca. 1230 (Ward Archive)

hind, and it is all the more remarkable to find such an insistent conformity to the design of a tribune story in what is structurally a triforium.

Stylistic connections with England are obvious in Normandy throughout the first half of the thirteenth century;[25] even the pattern of arches of the pseudo-tribune of Bayeux recalls irresistibly Whitby in Yorkshire (Fig. 293). But this does not mean that the development of Gothic architecture was following the same course in both countries. Not only was the situation in England infinitely more complex, but the type of structure most commonly used in that period (known in England as the Early English period) belonged also to a different lineage. Even in the areas where the tribune survived, its presence was not due to any connection with the French Gothic series;[26] in fact the trend that was to dominate English Gothic was the result of another branching-off, springing from another point on the stem of twelfth-century Gothic. Owing

295. CANTERBURY CATHEDRAL, N side of choir, by William of Sens, 1175–1177

to the enduring impact of a building of exceptional import—the new choir of Canterbury Cathedral (Fig. 295) as designed by William of Sens in 1174–75—the English cathedrals of the early thirteenth century are to a large extent an emanation of the Sens group which, instead of a tribune, used as an intermediate story the shorter sequence of openings of a triforium running in a narrow horizontal zone immediately above the main arcade. The Sens triforium was of the type that pierces the wall right through, opening directly onto the darkness of the aisle roof, and its pattern was one of arches grouped in pairs. This remained the standard type of Gothic elevation in England for the greater part of the thirteenth century. Lincoln Cathedral gives four successive versions of it: in St. Hugh's choir, the main transept, the nave, and even the Angel Choir in the second half of the century. In its east elevation the south transept (Fig. 296), which was built probably between 1215 and 1225, shows the same narrow dark zone of openings as at Sens

296. LINCOLN CATHEDRAL, E side of S transept, ca. 1220

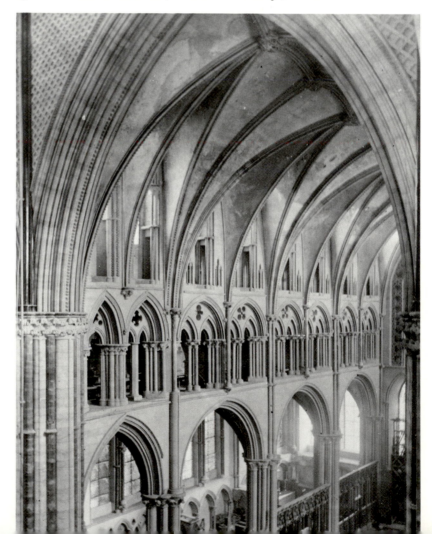

Cathedral but without that other component of the Sens style, the vigorous cadence of the alternating system of piers. The reason for the divergence was that the Sens type had been transmitted to England at Canterbury in an already modified form, with a continuous series of uniform piers instead of the strong iambic beat of Sens or Provins; and that smoothed-out version of the Sens elevation remained the accepted rule in Gothic England.

Together with these survivals of diverse twelfth-century types of elevation, Normandy and England demonstrated in another way their resistance to the new architecture of the early thirteenth century by their definite lack of enthusiasm for the flying buttress. They used it, but they made every effort to reduce its importance and to render it visually as insignificant as possible. At Lincoln for instance the flying buttresses do not rise much above the slope of the aisle roofs (Fig. 299) and they are most efficiently hidden from sight by the tall pinnacles which top the buttresses of the aisle walls.[27] Bayeux uses other methods to achieve similar results with its own characteristic decisiveness. If the east end of Bayeux (Fig. 297) is compared with that of an Ile-de-France building of the early thirteenth century such as Soissons Cathedral (Fig. 298), the juxtaposition of the two works is rather telling. While at Soissons the ensemble of the buttressing system shapes and scans the whole volume of the chevet, at Bayeux the dominant features are rather the continuous sloping roof that covers the ambulatory and chapels and—perhaps even more important—the continuity of the cornice which runs all around the zone of the chapels, passing in front of the buttresses and flying buttresses. The tall vertical line of the usual Gothic buttresses ceases to exist, the actual buttressing members being deliberately hidden on two-thirds of their height so that they hardly affect the appearance of the volumes, which are still treated in a pure twelfth-century manner.[28] No clearer proof could be given of the latent hostility to the new architectural concept and to its whole system of visual effects. At Bayeux that mode of exterior treatment constitutes the equivalent of what can be observed inside the same building, with the persistence of an obstinate tribune effect in what was really a triforium elevation.

297. Bayeux Cathedral, chevet, begun ca. 1230 (Ward Archive)

In the early part of the thirteenth century this refusal of the newest forms of Gothic did not apply only to somewhat provincial or distant areas: it applied also for a while to certain sectors of the Ile-de-France itself. And this can be taken as a sign of the revolutionary nature of the style that had emerged just before 1200 out of the Chartres workshop—the High Gothic style proper—and of the mixed reception it received even in some of the oldest of Gothic centers.

Between 1200 and 1220 Paris and its countryside must have appeared hardly less conservative than Normandy. All around Paris the pattern of the tribune elevation was preserved, and its influence was still perceptible more than thirty years after Chartres had dismissed it from the new Gothic repertory. At Moret (Fig. 300) near Fontainebleau,[29] which belongs to the years 1215–1220, the windows certainly conform to a modern formula, for they are

298. SOISSONS CATHEDRAL, chevet, ca. 1200–1212

299. LINCOLN CATHEDRAL, nave buttresses, ca. 1240

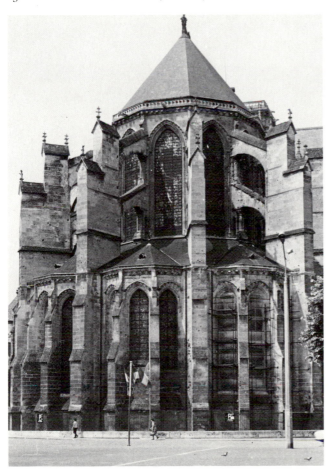

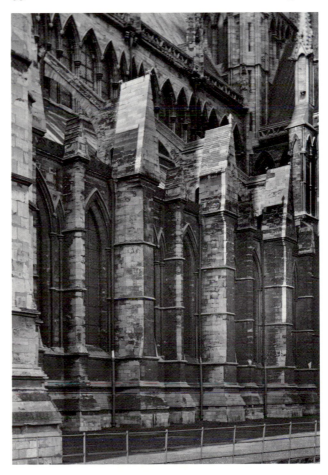

of the composed type as used at Chartres even if smaller; but otherwise the elevation remains of a twelfth-century type with an authentic tribune, and its arrangement in three almost equal stories is still very much in the tradition of the nave of Notre-Dame, or rather—since there is no fourth story—in the tradition of Mantes, which had the same kind of story sequence and the same tribune arches subdivided into three as in the nave of Notre-Dame. On the north side of Paris, the nave of Saint-Leu d'Esserent[30] presents, at about the same date as Moret, a very similar phenomenon (Fig. 301). There also the windows have been designed according to the Chartres model, and so have the piers which are of the *cantonné* type in a shortened version; but the pattern of the elevation is still kept very close to that of the tribune churches. In fact the intermediate story has ceased to be a tribune and has become structurally a triforium, being a shallow passage backed by a wall; but as in the choir of Bayeux (although here in a plainer Ile-de-France style), it is a triforium which aims, through its height and enclosing arch, at preserving the aspect of a tribune story.

300. MORET, choir, ca. 1215–1220

301. SAINT-LEU D'ESSERENT, nave, ca. 1215–1220 (Ward Archive)

A further stage in that movement is found about 1230 in three closely related buildings: the west bays of the nave of Saint-Séverin in Paris, the choir of Brie-Comte-Robert (Fig. 302) (some thirty miles southeast of Paris) and the choir of Cormeilles-en-Vexin (north-west of Paris).[31] All three have the same type of triforium, distinctive in its sequences of twin arches, which relate it to the filiation of Sens. But the height of this triforium story has been so increased as to make it almost as tall as a tribune, so that the characteristic rhythm of the normal triforium elevation, with its pinched horizontality at mid-height, can be seen to have been deliberately avoided in favor of a more regular spacing of the horizontal divisions of the elevation. That conservative taste for a wide grid of stories—which in the Paris area went back at least to the 1160s—seemed to persist almost indefinitely, in spite of the constructional changes that had occurred in the meantime, and was still tenaciously preserved after more than fifty years. But this effort to keep at all

302. BRIE-COMTE-ROBERT, S side of choir, ca. 1230

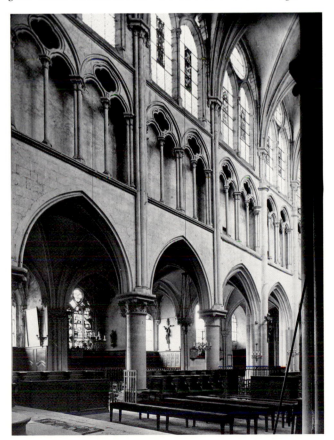

cost the look of a tribune elevation was a somewhat extreme aspect of the state of architecture in the Paris area during the early part of the thirteenth century; for in the same years the Parisian builders were also engaged in another movement, which opened on a different horizon and on another circuit of problems.

BY-PASSING OF THE CHARTRAIN STAGE

The Braine series

In spite of its initial hostility towards all solutions that went against its taste for mural values, the Parisian milieu could not long hold out against the increasing vogue for the new types of triforium elevation, and they soon took a firm foothold in the area. The movement had started even before 1200, gaining momentum as it went, and by the 1220s there were already several groups of such buildings in the vicinity of Paris (Figs. 303 and 304), some around Pontoise (Andrésy, Jouy-le-Moutier, Taverny, Nesles-la-Vallée), some south of the Marne valley (Villeneuve-le-Comte, la Chapelle-sur-Crécy).[32] However, even in that more modernistic series, it was not the more advanced Chartres model that was followed but that earlier variant of it, out of which Chartres itself had evolved and for which the church of Saint-Yved at Braine acts conveniently as the standard-bearer.[33] A comparison between Braine (Fig. 166, p. 173) and Taverny shows clearly that Braine was the model and that its elevation was most carefully copied at Taverny, by repeating the same short triforium and above it the short clerestory which is the specific feature of the series. To Chartres was obviously preferred an earlier and more distant prototype; and what makes the choice historically significant is that Braine provided for the less daring minds of that generation the ideal compromise between the rejection and acceptance of modernity. By its triforium elevation, by the very type and appearance of that triforium, Braine was close enough to Chartres to look simply like a small-scale variant of the Chartres formula. But at the same time it lacked the major novel feature of Chartres, the one that changed the meaning of the whole design and made Chartres so decisive—and for many so disturbing—in its implications: the gigantic clerestory

328

windows, colossal in width as much as in height, which could not exist without the adoption of that most radical of constructional methods, the large-scale use of the flying-buttress.[34] This was the very basis of the Chartres formula, the essence of its modernity; while at Braine the short clerestory still restricting the windows to the area enclosed within the lateral vault cells was the unmistakable mark of the twelfth century and of its old safety rules. Thus, in spite of its more modern appearance, the Taverny series was nevertheless the evidence of a still archaic trend in the Paris area, although less archaic than that which in the same region was responsible for the survival of the tribune story.

This mid-way position, which may be typified by Taverny, did not by any means represent a specifically Parisian phenomenon: it was part of a much larger movement. In fact the Braine formula was having at that time such a widespread success that it may have seemed to be actually outpacing Chartres itself and to be setting the

303. TAVERNY, apse, ca. 1215–1230

304. NESLES-LA-VALLÉE, N side of nave, ca. 1190–1210

tone for the whole generation. A tangible symptom of the growing influence of Braine was the frequent use of its most particular type of plan, characterized by an oblique plantation of the chapels lodged in the angles between transepts and choir (Fig. 305). This unusual mannerism of plan had a remarkable diffusion in the first half of the thirteenth century, overlapping widely the most firmly established stylistic frontiers; for it could be found not only in the vicinity of Meaux and Paris but also and no less commonly in Flanders and as far to the southeast as Dijon or to the east as Trier (Fig. 305.B).[35] Refinements of design such as those of the plan of Braine no doubt have an appeal of their own; but the prestige of Braine, particularly in those marginal areas facing toward the north, east, and southeast, was due to more profound reasons. Braine had become the touchstone for the reactions of all Gothic milieux to the most recent new styles of the day, and the astonishing favor shown to everything connected with Braine must be interpreted historically as the sign of a firm option taken against the newest architectural forms. This was the last major branching-off from the trunk of northern French Gothic; and on that large lateral branch flourished a whole cluster of related styles which in many ways were indeed very close to the most advanced forms of Gothic and often no less vital in their inventiveness, but which could not bring themselves to accept the most radical aspects of the new style of Chartres and for that reason proclaimed as the ideal architectural formula the building that best symbolized the stage immediately preceding Chartres.

This attitude of refusal was at first so widespread and so deeply felt that it succeeded in creating side by side with the new High Gothic style a sort of duplicate Gothic movement which, with a number of variants and a rich diversity in the handling of architectural effects, soon covered a wide zone of countries stretching from Flanders in the north, across Lorraine and Burgundy, to the upper Rhone Valley in the south[36] and, with a further thrust toward the west, reaching as far as Bourges, thus inscribing a full semicircle around the central Ile-de-France nucleus. What survived in all that large peripheral zone was not just the Braine pattern of elevation with its short clerestory in the twelfth-century tradition, but the

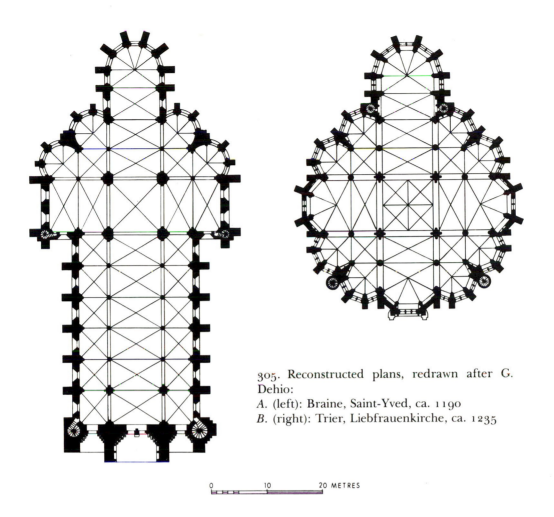

305. Reconstructed plans, redrawn after G. Dehio:
A. (left): Braine, Saint-Yved, ca. 1190
B. (right): Trier, Liebfrauenkirche, ca. 1235

0   10   20 METRES

whole stylistic age of which the formula was part; and that meant in particular[37] the fashion for thin monolithic shafts detached against the masses of solid masonry and, even more typically perhaps, the wall treatment in two layers which resulted from the use of various kinds of wall-passages.

The method which was followed in Flanders, continuing throughout the first half of the thirteenth century, was that of an upper passage opening on the outside at clerestory level in the manner of a very shallow loggia, as had been done around 1180, with a tribune elevation, in the transepts of Cambrai cathedral.[38] The choir of Sint Maarten at Ieper (Ypres) and that of Onze-Lieve-Vrouwekerk van Pamele at Oudenaarde show how this loggia motif was adapted to triforium elevations of the Braine type

331

(Fig. 306): at Ieper in the abrupt vertical silhouette of a plain apse (Fig. 307), at Oudenaarde above the wider expanse of an ambulatory plan (Fig. 308). A little later, in the transept and nave of both churches, the light arcaded screen of the loggia vanished and only a deep arch framing the windows remained in each bay, the outer passage running through the jambs of those deep arches at the height of the window sills.[39] What survived also, together with that Flemish double wall system of the late twelfth century, was a type of window of similar age, the triplet window, particularly prominent as a motif at Oudenaarde but present also at Ieper in the straight bays of the choir; and in both buildings the absence of flying buttresses and the resulting tidiness of the outer volumes remind one of the fact that the refusal of that new means of buttressing was one of the essential elements (perhaps even the essential one) in the rejection of the newest version of French Gothic.

Further east in Belgium and somewhat later in time, at Tongeren (Tongres) near Liège around 1240, Onze-Lieve-Vrouwekerk illustrates another variant of the Braine elevation. While the pro-

306. OUDENAARDE, O.L. VROUWEKERK VAN PAMELE, choir, begun 1235

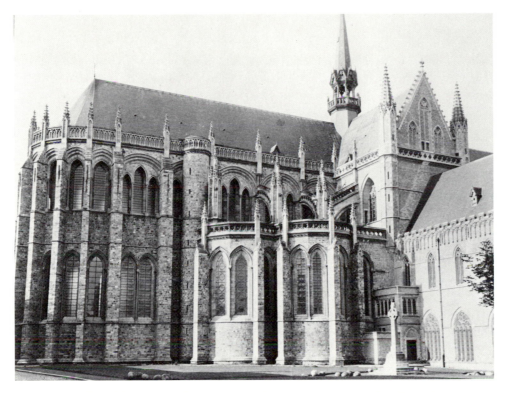

307. IEPER, SINT MAARTEN, chevet from N. begun 1221 (© A.C.L., Bruxelles)

308. OUDENAARDE, O.L. VROUWEKERK VAN PAMELE, view from NE, begun 1235 (© A.C.L., Bruxelles)

portions of the stories are very much the same as in Flanders (Ieper for instance), Tongeren employs another system of passages. The double wall now opens on the inside, not the outside, and the passage which runs along its length becomes an interior clerestory passage in the traditional Norman manner (Fig. 309). But this was not the result of a direct influence from England or Normandy: Tongeren appears rather as one of the symptoms of the expansion to the north of the reinterpretation that Lausanne Cathedral (Fig. 173, p. 178) had given, a generation earlier, of the Braine elevational formula. As has been noted in a previous chapter,[40] there is every reason to believe that the master who came to Lausanne had spent part of his recent career in England, more precisely at Canterbury; and the presence of a clerestory passage at Lausanne Cathedral is one of the signs of direct contacts with the Canterbury

309. Tongeren, O.L. Vrouwekerk, N side of nave, begun 1240 (© A.C.L., Bruxelles)

310. VILLENEUVE-LE-COMTE, choir from S aisle, ca. 1220–1225

workshop, where this particular Gothic variant of the double wall system, characterized by the superposition of interior passages at both triforium and clerestory levels, had been initiated by William the Englishman in 1179. From Lausanne it spread after a while not only toward the north, to Tongeren in east Belgium and Bonn in the Rhine Valley, but also toward the west and north-west across the whole width of Burgundy, to reach almost the heart of Ile-de-France. On the edge of the plains of Brie, only twenty miles east of Paris, the apse of Villeneuve-le-Comte (Fig. 310), built in the 1220s, marks the extreme northwesterly expansion of the Lausanne type of triple arcade (again so very English in character) passing in front of a clerestory passage.

But if ever there was an area where the suggestion of the Lausanne design proved determinant, to the point of bringing about a whole autonomous stylistic development, that was Burgundy itself.[41] Around 1215, at Clamecy in the church of Saint-Martin and at Auxerre in the choir of the cathedral, the double-wall structure acquired a new sharpness of definition; and in their simultaneousness these two buildings also underline an unexpected aspect in the life of that new Burgundian style: the fact that it played constantly on two different keys, using indifferently and in turn two types of elevation. Sometimes, as at Clamecy, the pattern followed was somewhat old fashioned, being that of the Braine type with its short clerestory (Fig. 311); and sometimes, as at Auxerre, it was the bold tall-clerestoried schema of Chartres (Fig. 312). Auxerre even repeated that singularity of the clerestory windows of Chartres, the very large upper oculus.[42]

311. CLAMECY, SAINT-MARTIN, N side of nave, ca. 1215–1230

312. AUXERRE CATHEDRAL, choir, ca. 1215–1233

313. AUXERRE CATHEDRAL, champenois passage in ambulatory and Lady Chapel, ca. 1215–1220

314. AUXERRE CATHEDRAL, upper stories of choir, ca. 1220–1230

Already in progress in 1217, the cathedral of Auxerre seems to have been the main center of elaboration of that new line of Burgundian Gothic, which here took on its recognizable aspect, not only in the hollowing out of the double upper wall but also in the extension of the two-layer treatment to the outer walls of the aisles (Fig. 313). This method of aisle-wall construction, generally known as the Champenois passage, had actually been initiated in northern Champagne, at Reims, in the 1170s in the church of Saint-Remi, being used there only in one chapel, the deep axial Lady Chapel (Fig. 161, p. 169); and it was also at Reims that it was taken up again a generation later in the cathedral, begun in 1210. But in spite of its earlier date, Reims Cathedral, where the lateral walls were built

315. SEMUR-EN-AUXOIS, N side of choir, ca. 1225–1235

316. DIJON, NOTRE-DAME, nave and choir, ca. 1220–1240

with such weightiness, was obviously not the source for Auxerre Cathedral, where the fragility of the perforated aisle wall is much more reminiscent of the axial chapel of Saint-Remi. And in a similar way, harking back to early models, the treatment of the main elevation in the choir of Auxerre (Fig. 314) recalls, translated into an even thinner texture, the double wall effects of the end walls and chapels of the transept of Laon (Fig. 164, p. 171). However, Auxerre was not a mere repeat of the solutions evolved at Noyon, Laon or Reims in the years that just preceded the Chartres revolution: the interest of Auxerre is that it was taking a new step in a direction which, in up-to-date circles, had by then been abandoned. It was the case of an earlier style, kept alive and revitalized, moving

338

forward again after a moment of decline and now offering a whole range of more advanced solutions.

In the 1220s two other buildings duplicated the relationship which had existed between Auxerre and Clamecy some ten years before. At Semur-en-Auxois (Fig. 315) the tall clerestory of the Chartres series was used again, as at Auxerre, with superposed passages, a two-layer structure and an elegant frontage of thin detached shafts; while at Dijon (Fig. 316) the church of Notre-Dame, conforming to the older line of elevations, used once more a short clerestory in the Clamecy manner and even (to be more clearly archaistic) a lantern tower at the crossing and sexpartite vaulting over nave and choir.[43] This second antithetical pair of buildings (Figs. 317, 318) only further stresses the dual play of the new Burgundian style, sometimes favoring a more modern, sometimes a more archaic formula. But in either case the handling remained the same in the unusual delicacy of the two-layer treatment of the walls,

317. DIJON, NOTRE-DAME, chevet, ca. 1220–1230   318. SEMUR-EN-AUXOIS, chevet, ca. 1225–1235

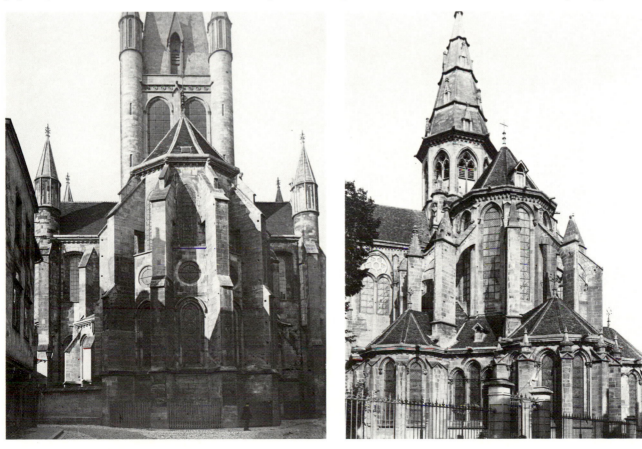

showing that when it came to the sensitive values of architecture, whatever the pattern adopted for the elevation, the thirteenth-century style of Burgundian Gothic was always faithful to the same spirit and that it drew upon the trend of sensibility which, having begun at Noyon in the 1170s and spread by 1180 to Laon and Reims and Soissons, was still in the first stages of its development when it had been stopped short under the impact of Chartres. After a gap of twenty years, the Burgundian masters had felt that it was their mission to give a second chance to that abruptly rejected form of architectural sensibility and to bring it to its full stylistic growth: an aim which was achieved in such refined and firmly articulated structures as that of the upper stories of the nave of Notre-Dame at Dijon (Fig. 319). The elegance of a highly controlled play on depth based on skeletal, on almost filigree-like effects, and on the insertion of layers of space within all the walls between an inner screen and a thin outer membrane: this was what Burgundy proposed to the new generation as a worthy alternative to the flat and plain style of Chartres. And even when an effort was

319. DIJON, NOTRE-DAME, upper stories of nave, ca. 1228–1240

320. LYON CATHEDRAL, N side of nave, begun ca. 1230

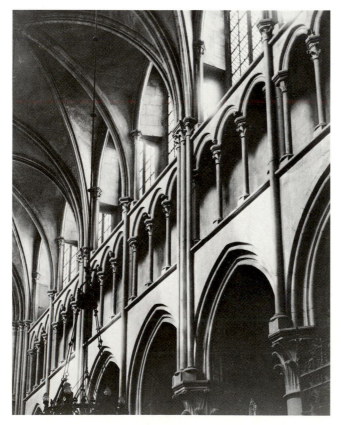

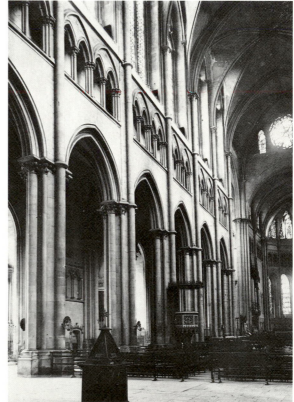

made, as in the nave of Lyon Cathedral (Fig. 320), to emulate the grand scale, the proportions and the powerful accents of the naves of Chartres or Reims, the elevation was still treated in two layers in depth though the fine brittleness of the purest Burgundian style was inevitably lost in the attempt.

A peripheral Gothic movement

Turning away from Burgundy to look further afield and get an overall picture of the tendencies of the time, it becomes clear that this type of open structure with two interior passages running one above the other at both triforium and clerestory height had gained a very widespread popularity by the early 1230s. In most peripheral areas this was the formula that held the expansion of the Chartres style in check, surrounding it on all sides. With the variations of treatment to be expected from region to region, the same type of structure and elevation can be found from Brittany (Dol Cathedral) to the Rhine (Bonn) and from Northumbria (Tynemouth choir) to the edge of the Alps (Vienne, Lyon, Geneva, Lausanne).

The northwest sector, which completes that encirclement of the areas where High Gothic reigned, was less coherent in style than the large eastern semicircle of Braine-influenced countries. Brittany, Normandy and England, although related in many ways, often diverged in their development. The Breton borderlands took an early lead with the nave of Dol Cathedral (Fig. 321), elegant and austere, and for that region so light in structure that a direct contact with Burgundy would seem likely.[44] In Normandy, where the idea of the two superposed passages had been accepted at first only under the guise of a tribune elevation—as in the choirs of Lisieux and Bayeux (Fig. 294)—, the pattern and proportions of a true triforium elevation did not gain favor until after 1230: the nave of Sées Cathedral (Fig. 322), which is one of the early examples, seems to be essentially a work of the mid-1230s.[45] At Sées the triforium is deliberately provincial in the complexity of its design, illustrating the particular style which had been developing in the western part of Normandy since the very first years of the thirteenth century. But Normandy had other buildings of similar constructional type (i.e. provided with the two characteristic interior passages) and

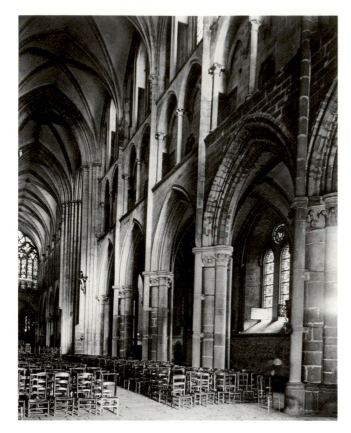

321. Dol Cathedral, S side of nave, ca. 1205–1230

322. Sées Cathedral, nave, ca. 1235–1240 (Ward Archive)

some of them, like Norrey (Fig. 323) near Bayeux, followed much more closely than Sées the pattern of stories and the clear two-layer treatment of Lausanne or Burgundy, in spite of the fact that they remained structurally heavier and less open than Clamecy or Dijon—or, closer at hand, the nave of Dol.

In England also, where experiments on the multiplication of passages perforating the wall structure went back as far as the late eleventh century,[46] various types of triforium elevations with superposed passages had been in use for some time. It was in England that the classic Gothic formula for that kind of elevation had been elaborated under William the Englishman in the east end of Canterbury Cathedral (1179–1184) (Fig. 171, p. 176); and that classic formulation had been preceded and accompanied by a number of

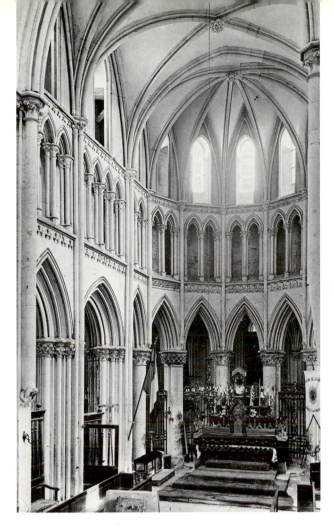

323. NORREY, choir, ca. 1250

somehow related but less fully Gothic variants, as in the west bays of Worcester in western England, the nave of St. Davids in Wales, the western part of the nave of Kelso on the Scottish border and the upper stories of the nave of St. John's, Chester.[47] These earlier attempts explain the diversity of the examples of elevations so structured that can be found in the thirteenth century: the unvaulted choir of Tynemouth (now destroyed) in the far north of the country; Llanthony, Much Wenlock, Worcester choir, all duly vaulted, in the west; in the London area, the west bays of St. Albans nave (where the vaulting originally projected was not carried out in the end). But, within the picture of thirteenth-century architecture, what is perhaps more interesting to note than these spontaneous and essentially autonomous developments is the indication of renewed contacts between England and some of the Continental centers in the course of the 1220s and 1230s. In London, on the south bank of

343

the Thames, the present cathedral of Southwark (Fig. 325) (originally the collegiate church of St. Mary Overie in the diocese of Winchester) has a tall triforium in the manner of Saint-Omer (Fig. 324) and of most Flemish churches, and vertical shafts that rise without interruption from the pavement up to the springers of the vault (a very rare occurrence in England beyond the late twelfth century); and these two characteristic features suffice to prove that England was not out of touch with what was happening on the Continent.[48] In fact Southwark is an English variant, heavier in structure, of the Flemish type of elevation—with perhaps the further addition of a direct link with southern Champagne, where the church of Sainte-Madeleine at Troyes has very similar proportions and a related kind of constructional weightiness.[49] The attention given by the London masters to the forms evolved in those peripheral areas of northern France takes on its full meaning when it is realized that, up to the designing of the new Westminster Abbey in

324. SAINT-OMER, NOTRE-DAME, former cathedral, begun ca. 1205, N side of transept ca. 1225–1250

325. SOUTHWARK CATHEDRAL, S side of choir, ca. 1225–1235

1245,[50] there had been no response in England to the more radical formulas of Chartres-inspired Gothic.

The vitality of this duplicate Gothic movement, which was developing on the periphery of the original core of the Gothic lands, is further confirmed by the fact that when a new elevational formula was adopted in those areas, conforming still to the principle of double-wall construction but simpler in design, it spread again in no time to the same circle of countries and even achieved among them a greater degree of stylistic unification than before. That new formula was a two-story elevation treated in two planes in depth, with a clerestory passage running directly above the main arcade. It appeared in Burgundy around 1230 and its pattern of diffusion matches remarkably that of its parent form, the triforium elevation with two interior passages. The nave of Semur shows clearly the transition from one type to the other (Fig. 326): the triforium, which had been used in the choir and transept, simply vanishes

326. SEMUR-EN-AUXOIS, E bays of nave, showing change in elevation type, ca. 1235

327. BOURGES, SAINT-PIERRE-LE-GUILLARD, S side of choir and of E bays of nave, begun ca. 1220–1225

west of the crossing and one passage only is left, at the foot of the windows, reducing the number of stories from three to two. Burgundy appears to have shared that simplified elevation from the start with the neighboring provinces of Berry and Lorraine. There were many variations on the theme: some remained halfway between the two and three stories, like the cathedral of Besançon; at Cluny, the church of Notre-Dame shows a direct influence of Reims Cathedral in all the details of style (a contact repeated on somewhat different terms at Toul Cathedral); and in the 1240s Villeneuve-sur-Yonne (Fig. 276) was touched in a similar way by the recent Parisian styles.[51] But the most interesting building of the series is the church of Saint-Pierre-le-Guillard at Bourges (Fig. 327). In that small church, which is perhaps earlier than all the examples preserved in Burgundy proper since it was probably begun before 1225, the pattern of vaulting in sexpartite units over single bays and the rhythm of split bays it creates go back, like the double-wall itself, to the stylistic generation of the 1180s and 1190s (Fig. 304, p. 329), the same generation as Braine;[52] and this unusual mode of vaulting is a material sign of the historical continuity which relates those peripheral styles of the first half of the thirteenth century to the lines of experiments that just preceded Chartres.

In Normandy the two-storied treatment is found by 1240 at the latest in the central vessel of the choir of Coutances Cathedral (not in the ambulatory elevation) (Fig. 328); and that entire choir is indeed remarkable by its decorative restraint and for the stimulation it obviously received from sources situated well outside Normandy.[53] Soon after, in the nave of Bayeux Cathedral (which dates from around 1250), the same type of elevation was adopted in circumstances which favored the most radical exploitation of the new formula (Fig. 329): built directly on top of fairly low Romanesque arches, the upper story of windows is extended to colossal dimensions, showing that for those areas which had rejected the orthodox High Gothic forms, this two-story elevation was really the alternative solution to the Chartres type with its great height and very tall windows. The size of the flying buttresses which flank the nave of Bayeux is another sign of the more modernistic approach that

328. COUTANCES CATHEDRAL, view into two-storied choir, ca. 1240–1250 (Ward Archive)

329. BAYEUX CATHEDRAL, N side of nave, ca. 1250 (Ward Archive)

tended to accompany the two-story formula; but as it still belonged to the cycle of double-wall structures, Bayeux continued to exclude the style of surface effects that had prevailed since Chartres in Ile-de-France Gothic.[54]

England was of course part of that movement too: having been since the Norman Conquest a sort of testing ground for all kinds of Romanesque speculations on the play of passages in hollowed-out masonry, it had practiced, since at least 1140, various types of two-story elevations.[55] It is even most likely that England was the source for the first Continental experiments along these lines. After 1200 the English examples become more frequent and tend to get organized into regional sequences: Portsmouth and Boxgrove (Fig. 330) in southern England, Fountains and Southwell choirs in the north, Llandaff and Pershore (Fig. 331) in the west,[56] a screen of arches detached in front of the clerestory giving in all these buildings a strong sense of depth. When the screen disappears, as round 1245 at Netley Abbey (Fig. 332) on Southampton Water,[57] making a wide arched recess, a sort of deep sunken panel in each bay at clerestory level, the analogy becomes so striking with the open wall of the Burgundian series (of Villeneuve-sur-Yonne or Saint-Père-sous-Vézelay) that a conscious imitation of some Continental model seems evident. As in the case of the elevation with superposed passages, a long chain of previous experiments had preceded in England the final alignment on the more decisive Continental variants.

When the maps of diffusion of these two successive types are compared (Figs. 333, 334), it becomes difficult not to conclude that, under what was probably Burgundian leadership—but working on the basis of Anglo-Norman sources—a large movement of dissenting Gothic invention, a sort of other Gothic movement, was truly taking shape more and more consistently in the 1220s, 1230s and 1240s, all the time restricting the expansion of the latest forms of

330. BOXGROVE PRIORY, N side of choir, ca. 1220

331. PERSHORE ABBEY, S bays of choir, ca. 1230

northern French Gothic. It was perhaps not an architecture which could achieve the same prodigies of size as the orthodox Chartres-derived structure; its effects were on the whole of a more delicate nature, and nothing could rival the engineering power of the great northern French school of Gothic. But in the field of sensitivity to the play of forms in space and to the qualities of matter, in the handling of effects of light, in the treatment in depth of the wall

332. NETLEY ABBEY, ruins of S transept, begun 1244

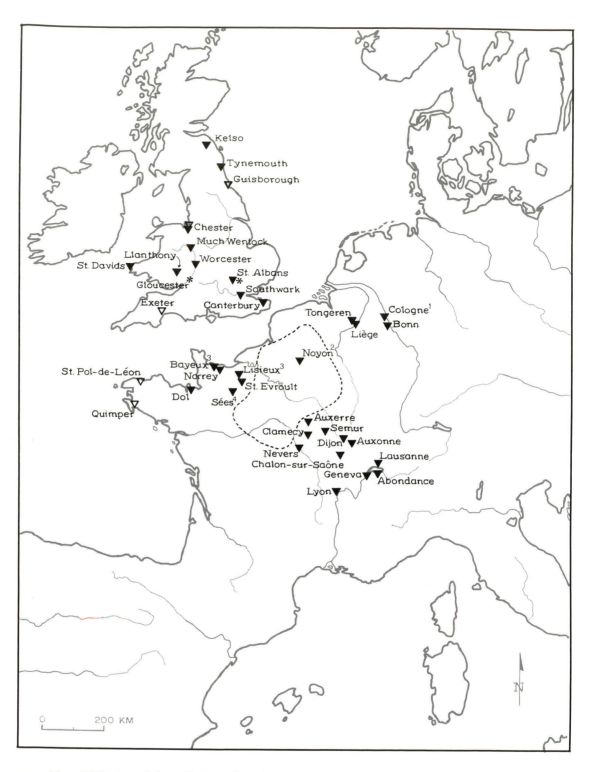

333. Map: Diffusion of the triforium elevation with two superposed interior passages

LEGEND

Symbols used

* Romanesque antecedents
▼ Gothic triforium elevations with two interior passages, up to ca. 1255
▽ Later 13th-century examples, ca. 1255–1300

Limits indicated

------- Core area of the Gothic movement in the first half of the 13th century

Footnotes to names

(1) Cologne: St. Gereon   (2) Noyon: façade bay
(3) Bayeux and Lisieux: choir   (4) Sées: nave

334. MAP: Diffusion of the two story elevation with interior clerestory passage

LEGEND

Symbols used

*   Romanesque antecedents

●   Gothic two-story elevations with clerestory
passage, up to ca. 1255

◇   Later 13th c. examples, ca. 1255–1300

Limits indicated

- - - - - -   Core area of the Gothic movement in the
first half of the 13 c.

Footnotes to names

(1) Southwark: transept   (2) Trier and
Villeneuve-le-Comte: apse   (3) Bayeux: nave

Abbreviations

Béton-B.	Béton-Bazoches
St. Père-s-V.	Saint-Père-sous-Vézelay
V.-le-C.	Villeneuve-le-Comte
V.-s-Y.	Villeneuve-sur-Yonne

limits through the insertion of a cushioning of space within the walls themselves to accentuate the diaphanous nature of Gothic structure, this duplicate Gothic movement had a poetic quality which accounts for its success.

An evolutionary view such as has been taken in this chapter, intent on identifying successive waves of diffusion and on interweaving relationships between a multiplicity of different developments, has the inherent danger that it tends to stress the element of conformity to norms—changing as they may be—and to disregard the exceptional as too divergent, when in fact it may con-

335. PETERBOROUGH CATHEDRAL, W façade, ca. 1205–1235

336. REGENSBURG, ST. ULRICH, interior, ca. 1220–1240

353

tain some of the most significant products of those more distant milieux. If the architecture of Gothic Ile-de-France put in circulation one after the other a number of new patterns to be followed and experimented with, there was present also in the example of its unprecedented achievements a power to liberate which acted on some gifted minds to produce works of a kind unknown in French Gothic, yet unimaginable without the stimulus of its revelations. It was the miraculous quality first proclaimed in Suger's choir, then so many times renewed, that touched off such visionary designs as the grand rise of the Glastonbury elevation, layer slipping upon layer; the three gigantic gulfs of the Peterborough façade (Fig. 335); the heavenward ascension of the decagon of St. Gereon's at Cologne; or the disencumbered inner squareness of St. Ulrich's in Regensburg (Fig. 336): all more unexpected in their concept and less reducible to Ile-de-France criteria than, say, the analytical refinements of the Burgundian churches of the 1220s and 1230s. The High Gothic stage coexisted all along its course with those other versions of Gothic, so different in kind: it was an age of simultaneous realms. But this state of things was not to last very long and a radical change took place when another poetry in stone began to develop in northern France. Its rapid success was to efface most of the regional styles, although the double-wall effects did not vanish,[58] remaining as a permanent addition to the vocabulary of Gothic forms; but they were to be no more than a possible alternative within the new unifying style of the coming age.

337. PARIS, NOTRE-DAME, rose window of S transept façade, ca. 1262–1267

CHAPTER IX

A Third Gothic System: The Rayonnant Style

A STYLISTIC mutation of considerable importance took place in northern French Gothic around the 1230s, when what is conventionally called the Rayonnant Style made its appearance. The French word *rayonnant* means radiating and the name was chosen to describe the gigantic radiating compositions of the rose windows, which at that time became both larger and more complex in their divisions. These rose windows were considered such a striking feature (Fig. 337) by the archaeologists of the first half of the nineteenth century that they made it the symbol of the style and, once coined, the term has remained as an evocative and acceptable approximation. But that pattern of radiation around a center was actually restricted to the rose windows, which were used only in the end walls of buildings,[1] and it might be better to have at hand a more exact and more generally applicable term, if one could be found. Should one speak of an Age of Tracery or of a Mullion Style? Such terms would cover more of the characteristics of Gothic art of that period. But whatever the label, the change that took place then was of great importance because it turned out to be the source or the point of departure for all the later forms of Gothic architecture.[2]

This change was different in nature from the one that had taken place around 1195 at Bourges and Chartres because what had then made the break, in the last years of the twelfth century,

357

had been a constructional invention, the flying buttress, which had compelled architects to elaborate new forms and imagine new ways of composing their buildings. But this time the new style was not called into being by any significant addition to the elements of the architectural organism; it was no more than a change of tone, of expression; it was a new treatment applying to already existing forms, and the new Gothic continued to be based in all its essentials on the Chartres type of structure and elevation. This does not mean that the change should be minimized by labeling it simply a new fashion and seeing in it only its modish character, for this transformation in taste put into motion a cycle of development which lasted for three centuries. It corresponded in fact to a profound shift in artistic sensibility and one which affected all the fields of art. Architecture then became more than ever linear, thinned out to the point of being almost without substance; and it was that very insubstantiality that was so widely enjoyed as a revelation of modernity, aided in its attainment by a new treatment of the stained glass which filled the vast expanses of openwork of the Rayonnant windows.[3]

How this movement got under way and through what stages it won general acceptance are questions on which much research has been done lately,[4] and many essential points have now been clarified or presented in a new light. The second quarter of the thirteenth century happens to be the time when documentary information becomes on the whole a little more extensive, when in particular the names of the most important architects appear increasingly often. Architects began to be so highly considered that their names were set down in documents, even in inscriptions, and that they were soon the object of social jealousies. A sermon by a Dominican, Nicolas de Biard, dated 1261, is typical of these new feelings, which reflect the changed position of the great architects. He complains for instance that "the masters of the masons, holding in their hands measuring rod and gloves, say to the others: 'Cut the stone in this fashion' and they do not labor; yet they receive greater pay. . . ."[5] One of these famous architects was Hugues Libergier of Reims, who built the church of Saint-Nicaise and died in 1263. His tomb has been preserved, a full-size slab of fine draftsmanship;[6] and it shows him wearing cape and gloves and holding the long rod which was one of the insignia of his profession (Fig. 338). He is obviously very far from being a workman: he belongs to that new professional class of architects which had been developing since the end of the twelfth century. As a result of being better informed, we do not have to use so often terms such as "master of Chartres" or "master of Bourges:" there is no need for instance to use at all the term "master of Amiens," for we know that the first architect was Robert de Luzarches, and the second Thomas de Cormont, followed by his son Renaud. And we can say without hesitation that Robert de Luzarches, Hugues Libergier, and a little later the Parisian masters, Jean de Chelles and Pierre de Montreuil, were among the creators and protagonists of the new style. It is of course a great satisfaction to be able to name these men, but many others are still anonymous;

338. REIMS CATHEDRAL, tomb of Hugues Libergier, architect of Saint-Nicaise, died 1263

339. AMIENS CATHEDRAL, S side of nave from triforium of transept, 1220–1235

and even when the names are available many essential problems remain unsolved, since on the whole nothing is known about their formation or—even more important—about their early works and, faced with so much guesswork, historians still have to proceed in the same tentative manner as before.

FIRST SIGNS OF A NEW APPROACH

What were the first centers of the new style and in what order were the new features adopted? At first it was a slow shift, and this occupied the decade of the 1220s. The first building in which a new principle appeared was the nave of Amiens Cathedral (Fig. 339), begun in 1220 by Robert de Luzarches and completed in 1235.[7] At Amiens the Chartres type of elevation with its vast clerestory windows (Fig. 212, p. 229) was stretched in height to a remarkable extent; and it is probably at Amiens that first appeared that idea of record-breaking heights which took possession of northern French builders for nearly a generation, replacing the previous tendency of architects to compensate height by increased width (as had still been done at Bourges, Chartres, Reims and Le Mans). But of more lasting influence even than this change in proportions was the new treatment given to surfaces, particularly in the upper stories of the nave. For the first time a system of progressive subdivision into subordinated series appeared in the windows. The Chartres window form was distinctive but essentially simple, being composed of two lancets topped by a large-lobed oculus, a sort of diminutive rose window. But now, starting at Amiens, this form began to proliferate: each lancet was treated in its turn as a full window on a smaller scale, again subdivided into two and topped by a smaller rose (Fig. 340). This converted each window into a kind of screen-work of thin stone mullions, a complex four-unit composition, rigorously designed: what is called a tracery. And from then on the linear art of tracing within each bay unit lacelike panels of glass and mullions became as important in the work of architects as the proper drawing of a ground plan or the proportioning of stories on the scale of a whole elevation.[8]

This was a new line of stylistic elaboration leading to an increasing refinement in the vocabulary of architectural forms. But in the nave of Amiens the linear treatment affected only the upper half of the building: the main arcade was still supported on piers of the *cantonné* type treated plastically, with a round core which was perceived as a volume—although a very elongated one. Above that, the triforium is linked up with the clerestory windows by the continuity of a central mullion, but it still has substance; and so have the groupings of shafts of the upper piers which rise all the way through triforium and clerestory, preserving a minimal degree of voluminousness which enables them to act as plastic accents framing the tracery panels of the upper windows. These windows are themselves the only element of the elevation that has become absolutely flat and linear; but their effect of cobweb texture, pulled tight in height pursued lengthwise, tends to transmit itself to the whole grid of the elevation—and that all the more strikingly because this flattened treatment of the upper part of the structure accords so well with the particular spatial distortion of the nave of Amiens, which also seems to have been stretched and flattened in an exaggerated vertical elongation. Here was the first decisive breaking up of the large forms and clear bay rhythm of the Chartres elevation. This does not mean that a basic continuity did not exist between Chartres and Amiens: the general elevational pattern remained unchanged, and the principle of subdivision applied to the windows had already been stated in its simplest form at Chartres. But one can feel at Amiens that change of emphasis which marks the beginning of a new style. The vigorous plasticity of Chartres has largely disappeared, and the invasion of brittle, lacelike patterns effaces that sense of a world of large and heavy forms which had been typical of the early years of the century. Bourges had bypassed that ponderousness and used a light touch in the handling of linear values;[9] but at Bourges the thin linearity evenly cloaked all surfaces, including those of the piers (Fig. 202, p. 217), while at Amiens it became organized into neatly framed and logically ordered panels, keeping the cadence of the bay rhythm. Amiens did not really derive from Bourges: it was the result of a mutation within the Chartrain framework.

The style of Amiens nave was particularly influential; but there were also other ways of rejecting the substantial in architecture and,

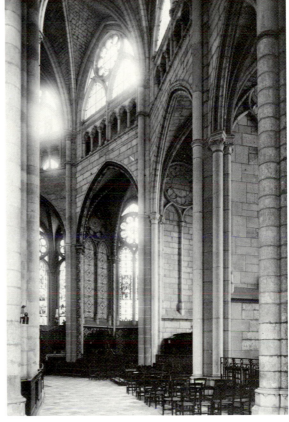

340. AMIENS CATHEDRAL, clerestory window of nave, 1220–1235 (Ward Archive)

341. BEAUVAIS CATHEDRAL, ambulatory and radiating chapels, ca. 1225–1235

whatever direction they took, all such avant-garde attempts prepared in some way the formation of the new style. The early work of the choir of Beauvais Cathedral, which was begun in 1225,[10] cannot properly be described as Rayonnant or even proto-Rayonnant in character, for it has none of the spiderwork texture of Amiens. But it shows another kind of reaction against weighty forms (Fig. 341). The piers between the chapels become of very small section and look even more slender through the use made of monolithic shafts, one of which runs right up to the vault; and the arches which open onto the chapels are reduced to such a sharp thinness as to be structurally unbelievable. That effort toward the immaterial is no less important as a symptom than the more striking network effect

363

of the Amiens clerestory, and it may throw some light on what was being done in other centers of northern France in the later 1220s. As that first work at Beauvais has definite stylistic connections with Reims,[11] it may well reflect what was then being discussed at Reims among the younger men of the team, who no doubt were sometimes glad to escape the tyranny of a fifteen-year-old design. In the absence of that other offshoot of Reims, the choir of Cambrai (of which only the exterior aspect is known), the ambulatory and chapels of Beauvais become a document of particular interest on the state of the Reims milieu in the years that preceded the designing of Saint-Nicaise in 1231.

Amiens, for its part, may yield some information on that other unknown quantity of the 1220s, the more advanced tendencies of

342. ROYAUMONT ABBEY, NE corner of N transept, 1228–1236

343. ROYAUMONT ABBEY, detail

Parisian art, for it demonstrates through the use of some very particular details a clear relationship with the latest stage of the work at Notre-Dame: that is, the middle stories of the façade and the west bays of the nave.[12] This connection is not surprising since Robert de Luzarches, the first architect of Amiens, came from a village close to Paris and must have received some of his training there. But Amiens reveals a much wider background in which Soissons, Reims and Chartres are more important components than Paris: it is evident that Robert de Luzarches had gone far beyond any localized attachment. Advanced Parisian taste in the early 1220s was probably more accurately reflected in works like Royaumont, light in structure, faithful to columnar piers and still using a somewhat heightened triforium (Figs. 342, 343): a Parisianized version of Longpont, but clearly in advance of all other work in the refined, tracery-like treatment of the triforium arcade.[13] This last feature alone had the quality of an anticipation, proving that the Paris milieu was participating in the efforts toward a stylistic breakthrough, although it was perhaps not enough in itself to announce the leading role that Paris was to take in the movement very soon after.

In the early 1230s, when the new trends define themselves with full clarity, Reims and Paris come into prominence as the two main points of crystallization: Reims with Saint-Nicaise, Paris with the new Saint-Denis, both begun in 1231. The northern centers remain active, too: Amiens continues to develop its own precocious brand of linearity; and Cambrai, by terminating its upper stories in a bolder style, adds its contribution to the repertory of Rayonnant forms. To the southeast of Paris another center has also emerged: Troyes, the capital of the counts of Champagne, which may have even preceded both Reims and Paris by a year or two in the production of the first fully Rayonnant work. Stretching on the map (Fig. 384) in two long lines, from Picardy to Paris and from the Scheldt Valley to southern Champagne, these very first manifestations of the Rayonnant almost repeat the pattern of distribution of the Gothic centers of the twelfth century (Fig. 113, p. 114); and this phenomenon of geographical continuity, reverting even to the closer concentration of sixty years before, certainly indicates that the new style was in the genuine line of descent of the original Gothic movement. It grew out of the same land and out of the same tradition.

THE SAINT-DENIS STYLE

It was at Saint-Denis, in the general rebuilding started in 1231 under Abbot Eudes Clément (Fig. 344), that the increased linearization of elevations, which had first made its appearance at Amiens as a sort of counterpoint to a still firmly defined constructional framework, became the exclusive aim of the design and was carried to its most radical conclusions. The new Saint-Denis thus became the paragon of the new style; and the king's prestige, which stood behind everything connected with Saint-Denis, made it even more clearly the model to be followed. But the history of that rebuilding

344. SAINT-DENIS, nave and choir as rebuilt between 1231 and 1281 (Ward Archive)

345. SAINT-DENIS, N side of choir and first bays of N transept, showing changes of design in main arcade between 1231 and ca. 1235

346. GONESSE, nave, ca. 1235 (Ward Archive)

still raises a few difficult problems, of which one concerns the evidence of early changes in the project (Fig. 345). Work was at first started, in 1231, on a rather old-fashioned design and in a no less old-fashioned style, closely related to that of the nave of Gonesse (a few miles north of Saint-Denis) (Fig. 346) and of other Parisian works of the late 1220s. In the lower story of the hemicycle and eastern bays of the choir of Saint-Denis, which were remodeled first, the piers were still of the columnar type accented only by applied triple shafts facing toward the central space; the main arcade was composed of arches built in a single order; and the triforium as it was then planned is likely to have been also fairly simple in design.[14] It was only after a few years of work that the

368

style changed abruptly in the main arcade of the two west bays of the choir, passing to the use of compound piers strongly marked on all their faces, of arches built in two orders and of a simpler and more decisive handling of moldings: all signs of the emergence of a new style, the one we call Rayonnant. Even then, for perhaps another two years, minor adjustments continued to be made which affected the size of the piers, by reducing the number of their shafts from fourteen to twelve, and which altered still less perceptibly the height of the stories, the level of the base of the triforium being raised three consecutive times by a few inches (Fig. 345). These repeated alterations give the impression of some hurried improvisation following a change of architect in the early stages of the operation of rebuilding.

Even if the relative sequence of work is for this reason fairly easy to establish, the exact dating of each part is much more difficult to fix and it is furthermore bound up with the problem of the identity of the architect to whom the concept of the new Saint-Denis—which was to be so influential—should be attributed. The only extant document giving the name of an architect is a charter of 1247 in which Pierre de Montreuil, "architect from Saint-Denis," appears as the purchaser of a quarry a few miles upstream from Paris, no doubt to supply stone for the work that was going on in the abbey church. It has long been considered that this charter supplied the name of the author of the new design. But the date of 1247 is here too late to be conclusive, for a close analysis of the building, of the changes of detail which can be followed from east to west and from north to south in the choir bays, the transept and the east bays of the nave (then part of the liturgical choir), in conjunction with a careful comparison with other Parisian or Court-related works, leads to the conclusion that the new design is likely to have been adopted at Saint-Denis not later than 1235. A gap of some twelve years would then be left unfilled between that critical moment and the first mention of the presence of Pierre de Montreuil.[15] And to make the situation even more disturbing, it has been pointed out that there is a profound contrast between the hard, clear-cut style of the new work at Saint-Denis (Fig. 347) and

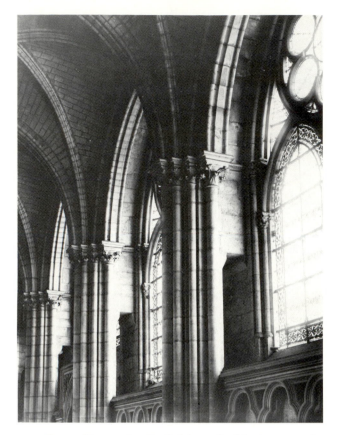

347. SAINT-DENIS, detail of aisle wall with champenois passage, after 1235

348. PARIS, SAINT-GERMAIN-DES-PRÉS, remains of Lady Chapel, begun ca. 1245

the refined manner apparent in what is known with certainty to have been Pierre de Montreuil's work of the mid-1240s: i.e., the pieces that remain from the Lady Chapel of Saint-Germain-des-Prés,[16] today assembled in the garden on the north side of the church (Fig. 348).

From all these observations, the hypothesis has been forcefully advanced that the Saint-Denis style could not have been the creation of Pierre de Montreuil but that it should be attributed to some other, slightly earlier, Parisian master, the same who had redesigned a few years before the upper stories of the choir of Troyes cathedral (Fig. 349) (following their destruction by a hurricane in 1227) and who was on that showing called to Saint-Denis.[17] As no new work in this well-characterized style was begun after 1240, that nameless "Saint-Denis master" could be supposed to have died around that time; in which case Pierre de Montreuil could have taken over the unfinished work and executed it according to the original design, with only a few changes of detail,[18] while simultaneously carrying out at Saint-Germain-des-Prés and in the furnishing of the chapels at Saint-Denis works that reflected his own manner and his own turn of sensibility. A controversial point in this theory is the assumed anteriority of the work at Troyes Cathedral in relation to the first appearance of the new style at Saint-Denis: Troyes might as easily represent a first reflection of stylistic transformations then in process at Saint-Denis. Still, the basic hypothesis of an unknown "Saint-Denis master" remains altogether more convincing than the extraordinary changes of style that would otherwise have to be postulated in the development of Pierre de

349. TROYES CATHEDRAL, choir from ambulatory, aisle story ca. 1208–1220, upper stories rebuilt from ca. 1235

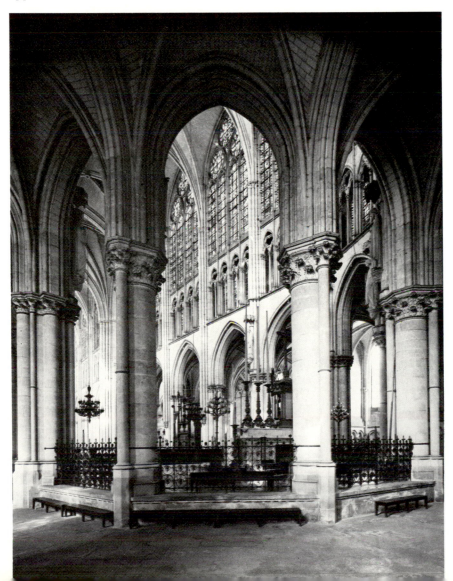

350. SAINT-DENIS, drawing by E. Viollet-le-Duc, showing linkage of triforium and clerestory by means of continuous mullions, and principle of subdivision in tracery composition.

Montreuil's artistic personality to make it possible to attribute to him that new design of Saint-Denis alongside his other, firmly documented works. Whatever the case, the Saint-Denis style has to be recognized as a remarkable and decisive moment in the history of Gothic architecture. Bearing the stamp of Auxerre and Reims (Saint-Remi and Cathedral) as well as of Amiens and Paris, it was a brilliant and vital synthesis which initiated a new vision of the play of forms in space and, putting an end to its hesitations, gave again to the Paris milieu, after a long eclipse, a position of leadership.

The major innovations at both Troyes and Saint-Denis were concerned with the treatment of the triforium and the piers. If, as seems possible, it preceded Saint-Denis by a few years, the choir of Troyes may have been the first building in which the triforium became absorbed into the clerestory, the wall at the back of the triforium passage being pierced with windows on all its height, while in front the mullions of the clerestory windows were carried right down to the base of the triforium (Fig. 350). This linkage of triforium and clerestory by means of continuous shafting was a fairly old idea which had made its appearance around 1170 in two buildings of the Northern Gothic group, Arras Cathedral and the choir of Saint-Remi (Fig. 141, p. 147) at Reims. Thereafter the feature had been preserved in the Reims area:[19] at Châlons-sur-Marne in the late twelfth century, at Orbais abbey in the early thirteenth century, and even in the east end of Reims Cathedral itself, where there is a clear change of rhythm between the straight bays of the choir, conceived in the pure Chartres manner, and the hemicycle, in which the central mullion of the clerestory windows descends into the triforium. This same treatment, with linkage by means of an extended central mullion, was repeated in the nave of Amiens (Fig. 339), begun in 1220, and at Reims once more in the nave of Saint-Nicaise, designed by Hugues Libergier in 1231.[20] If Troyes and Saint-Denis are placed in this context, it becomes evident that they look back to the first examples of the type: the small scale of the triforium arches and their multiplicity recall the Saint-Remi formula (also used more recently at Orbais and Essômes) rather than the looser linkage of Amiens.

373

But what is new at Troyes and Saint-Denis and has far-reaching consequences is the glazing of the back wall of the triforium,[21] which turns that intermediate story into an annex of the clerestory. Being composed of two layers in openwork, the triforium still preserves its own particular range of effects: the glazed surface is recessed by the width of the passage, while the plane of the upper windows is continued in the open screenwork of the front arcading of the triforium (Fig. 345). But with the stained glass which fills its outer windows, repeating the same colors and the same muted lighting as above it, the triforium acts now as a sort of *predella* for the larger panels of the clerestory windows, differing from them only by the richer linearity of its double pattern of mullions. Because of this downward extension of the window treatment the lean-to roof,

351. SAINT-DENIS, slab roof above S aisle of nave

352. SAINT-DENIS, main arcade and piers on N side of nave

which used to cover the aisles at the back of the triforium, had to disappear and some other—and less natural—solution be devised, such as a flat terrace of slabs, with a minimal incline (Fig. 351) so that it did not intrude on the base of the triforium windows; or a series of separate little roofs shaped like pyramids, one over each bay of the aisles, requiring an elaborate system of guttering. The idea of glazing the triforium revealed itself, through these practical implications, as a rather paradoxical refinement.

At the same time the new treatment given to the piers (Fig. 352) brought about in the lower part of the elevation a very similar change of emphasis: the compound pier with its multiplied linear accents replaced the simpler and more plastic types of piers of the early thirteenth century. Troyes is in this respect less typical than Saint-Denis, for the original structure, of which the whole lower story was preserved, already used piers of complex shape which could readily be incorporated into the analytical detailing of the new style. But at Saint-Denis the change was dramatic and, from the moment the new master took over, the columnar piers of his predecessor gave place to compound piers (Fig. 345) divided into a multiplicity of thin shafts, each shaft answering an order of arches or a particular rib of vaulting.[22] Having lost its former sculptural value, the pier now could be read only in terms of lines and integrated itself into the same play of clearly legible divisions as the upper stories: in fact the new treatment that guided the design of both triforium and pier had the effect of extending to the whole elevation the subtle linear language first invented at Amiens for the clerestory windows.

In this new architecture conceived entirely as filigree work, all forms become almost indefinitely repetitive; but they are organized in a whole hierarchy of different levels of reasoning. Of the twelve shafts of the piers, the three which face the nave are there to frame the bays and delineate them: they go right up to the vault, follow the curve of the vault itself and, after exchanging their two lateral strands with the adjoining bays in the neat criss-cross pattern of the ribbing, come down on the other side. The scale is that of the whole nave, of its full size in height and width. The next groups of three

353. SAINT-DENIS, N side of nave: change in size of cusped circles in tracery indicates pre and post 1241 work

shafts on either side of the pier belong to the subordinate, half-size level of the main arcade, the two orders of which command that triple articulation in the pier; while the other three shafts, on the aisle side, correspond to the triple groupings of ribs of the aisle vaults. The arches of the main arcade give in turn the size and shape of the large window panels which, with their annexed segments of triforium, fill the upper half of the elevation; and it is in these vast panels of tracery, drawn with the greatest geometrical rigor, that the system reaches its clearest formulation (Fig. 353). The windows are exclusively composed of series of similar forms progressively subdivided in increasing numbers and decreasing sizes: one big window arch per bay, two major divisions, a further splitting into four lancets, making within the window story alone when a few bays are seen in succession, three running sequences on three different scales, enclosed one within the other as three successive levels in a logical progression. And as the triforium, now treated as part of the window itself, works on an even smaller scale and encloses two of its arches within the smallest unit of the window, this further splitting into twos adds a fourth step to the progression.

This pattern of subordination working on homologous forms repeating themselves in multiple series set on a succession of logically related scales has been defined by Panofsky[23] as the basic law of the Rayonnant style; and he has shown that it conforms in its mechanism to the method of exposition of Scholasticism. It reflects the same mental structuring as a logical argument of the time and reveals an intensely rationalistic approach to the play on forms. Extreme linearization had provided the means for these extremes of systematization. In purely optical terms it could be added that the new architecture tended everywhere to cancel out depth and often played on almost infinitesimal recessions. With the voluminous now dismissed from the range of architectural values, surfaces had become more than ever flattened. Just enough relief was preserved to make the linear systems perceptible.

The new style of architectural expression had been conceived essentially for the interior of churches, where it achieved the miraculous effect of a fragile insubstantiality: a modernized version

377

of the concept of the Heavenly Jerusalem. But the exterior preserved a much plainer aspect: at Saint-Denis buttresses and flying buttresses have a workmanlike look and the north transept façade (Fig. 356), apart from the large square of tracery which encloses the rose window, is made up mostly of plain solid surfaces. This contrast between interior and exterior treatment can best be judged from the third (and last) work in the Saint-Denis style: the chapel of the château of Saint-Germain-en-Laye (Figs. 354, 355), which was probably finished in 1238.[24] Seen from outside, it gives an image of firmness and stability. The linear panels of the windows are mounted in a vigorous constructional framework: strong buttresses of rectangular section, a solid horizontal base, and a projecting cornice to neatly outline the volume at the top. The windows themselves are larger than ever, for they have absorbed the spandrels of solid wall which normally remain unpierced on either side of the window heads. This has been made possible by the adoption of a wall structure in two lightly built layers in the Burgundian manner, which detaches the window from the curve of the vault with the

354. SAINT-GERMAIN-EN-LAYE, chapel, ca. 1238

355. SAINT-GERMAIN-EN-LAYE, S side of chapel

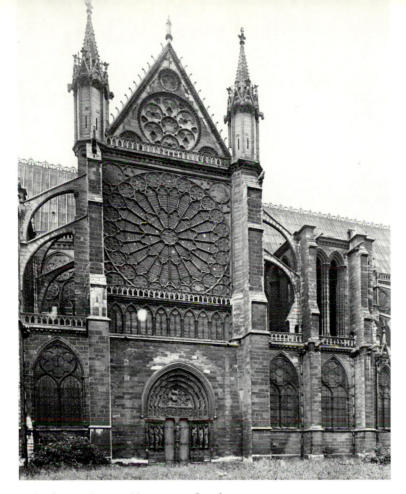

356. SAINT-DENIS, N transept façade, ca. 1235–1240

result that the whole rectangular panel defined by the buttresses and cornice can be pierced and filled with tracery. But that ultimate extension of the voids, far from increasing the effect of visual fragility, in fact reduces it, because the rectangularity of the windows emphasizes the clarity of the design and the balance so resolutely maintained on the exterior between structural framework and linear lacework.

That outer stability was an essential component of the style of the Saint-Denis architect, and it had its equivalent in the proportions he gave to the interiors he designed. His art was not one of exaggerated loftiness, of vertiginous vertical heights (Fig. 344): in this he ceased to follow the lead of Amiens, his works demonstrating even a marked reaction against that kind of technical extravagance. The transept façades of Saint-Denis (Fig. 356) are a clear manifestation of the taste of their designer for a balanced relation-

379

ship between height and width: conforming to the rule which had been set at Reims, these façades are made to reflect in their outer divisions the stories of the interior elevation. The lower zone of wall with its single doorway corresponds to the main arcade and aisles, above which the triforium, seen in transparency, appears on the façade as a band of openwork passing just below the rose window. As for the rose itself, the square in which it is inscribed is drawn on the basis of the height of the clerestory in the nave elevation (Fig. 357): which means that it was the size of the clerestory that commanded the width of the nave,[25] and in an age of large windows the adoption of such a formula led to wider interiors. In both dimensions and proportions Saint-Denis stood for a return to moderation and harmony, and the reasonableness of the overall shape of the building and of its interior space was clearly meant to counterbalance the dreamlike fragility of its interior surfaces.

357. SAINT-DENIS, N transept

This element of classicism was absent from the other variant of the new style that was developing in the same years at Reims and in the centers of the north, particularly Cambrai. The façade of the abbey church of Saint-Nicaise at Reims (Fig. 358) was a striking illustration of a tendency to break away from the accepted formulas and create more open, lighter and even looser combinations of forms. In its elements and in the way they were assembled, it contrasted as markedly with its immediate local predecessors, the façades of the transepts at Reims Cathedral, as with its Parisian contemporaries, the transept façades of Saint-Denis. The whole church has long since disappeared, but its façade is well known from pre-Revolutionary engravings. Construction had begun in 1231 and, as the nave was built first, the general design of the façade is likely to go back to the start of work.[26]

Its architect, Hugues Libergier, had obviously decided to do the opposite of what was then being done around him. Rejecting the ponderousness of the façades of Reims Cathedral, the tightness of their formal construction and the rationality of their divisions, he desired an architecture devoid of such rigor and freed from the obligation of a strict correspondence between the stories of the façade and those of the interior elevation. The design of Saint-Nicaise would even seem to have been established on the principle of a manifest discordance between façade and nave. Colossal portals conceived on the scale of the interior space were abandoned in favor of fairly small doors conceived rather on the scale of man, with the result that, far from filling the whole height of the aisles, the doorways at Saint-Nicaise were so small in size that a full-scale window had to be added above them to attain the level of the aisle vaults. What had been done tentatively at Amiens was now given the force of a law: the new feeling was clearly that aisles should no longer end to the west in a blind wall, that there was no special virtue in large doorways occupying the full height of a major story, and that entrances should now be reduced in size to leave room for the light of a window above.

In the central part of the façade, this new concept was even

358. REIMS, SAINT-NICAISE, begun 1231, 17th c. engraving

359. STRASBOURG CATHEDRAL, view showing rood screen of ca. 1255, from 17th c. engraving (Strasbourg, Musée de l'Oeuvre Notre-Dame)

more disruptive of the accepted modes of composition. No horizontal division remained, no gallery zone passing at the foot of the rose-window at triforium level to make a link between the two sides of the nave. Even the height of the main arcade ceased to be readable at first sight, for above the low doorway zone the single form of a gigantic arch, entirely glazed, rose in one vertical sweep to the apex of the nave, like an open cut revealing the void of the interior space behind; and the screening tracery that filled that huge west opening was patterned on the model of a normal composed window into which the rose had been integrated as an upper oculus, enormously enlarged. It was that element of openness and of complete freedom in the organization of the general design that gave a modernistic quality to the façade of Saint-Nicaise: dismissing the principle proclaimed twenty years before at Reims Cathedral, it was a controversial but liberating design, which made even the façades of the transept of Saint-Denis seem uninventive in their conformity. This opening of the façade from top to almost bottom by means of a gigantic window overriding all three stories of the interior elevation can be compared only to the type of simplified east end, pierced on all its height by a single enlarged window, which was becoming popular at that time in the vicinity of Paris: at Andrésy and Saint-Maur-des-Fossés for instance or, a few years later, at Cambronne-les-Clermont. The current type of window at Saint-Nicaise (two trefoil-headed lights with quatrefoil above) being also of a form used commonly in Parisian buildings of the 1220s,[27] it seems likely that Hugues Libergier, either directly or through Amiens, was in close contact with the Paris milieu at the stage which immediately preceded the activity of the Saint-Denis master and that he borrowed from the Paris of the 1220s some of the most characteristic of his motifs.

The other major novelty in the façade of Saint-Nicaise was the new concept of the portal story treated as a running sequence of small gabled arches, passing in front of solids and hollows alike without taking too much account of the actual construction behind. In the middle section of the façade the triple porch which leads to the central doorway occupies, in addition to the central bay, two more half-bays of the gabled arcade, the other half of these two flanking bays being filled by the buttresses of the towers; and while the next gabled arches on either side are hollowed out into porches opening onto the aisle doors, the very last ones, again filled with solid masonry, are applied as a pure *trompe l'oeil* against the large terminal buttresses of the façade. The autonomy of the linear pattern of that elegant gabled arcade is thus patently admitted: the inner law of the motif constantly overrules the reality of the structure, the gabled porches looking like a rich band of ornament, merely applied; and this divorce between form and structure further increases the overall impression of fragility created by the lightness and openness of the whole building. In its original bright polychromy, this zone of delicate porches must have looked like some temporary decoration such as were mounted in and around the cathedral at the coronations of the kings of France.

An element of playfulness and pageantry seems to have had some part in the elaboration of this unusual kind of façade; but there must have been also some new intention of religious symbolism. While the classic two-tower façades were based on a city gate concept, the church entrance being seen as representing the gates to the Heavenly Jerusalem,[28] Saint-Nicaise would seem to have been meant to evoke another kind of symbolic transposition, that of an announcement of the Holy of Holies, of the inner sanctuary contained within the church, through the projecting onto the façade of a choir-screen motif. The porches of Saint-Nicaise have been compared with the roodscreen of Strasbourg Cathedral (Fig. 359), a work of Rémois design but one which is dated to the 1250s and hence clearly too late to have been the prototype for Hugues Libergier's porches. What other screen was instrumental in the genesis of the design of Saint-Nicaise? Perhaps that of Chartres, on which sculptors were working by 1230, or some other one of similar type and age.[29] The gable motif itself had first appeared in Early Christian times as a theme reserved to the choir entrance, in churches of central Italy and the Adriatic area;[30] and the multiplication of the gable form on choir screens can be traced back in northwestern Europe to at least the second half of the twelfth cen-

384

tury.[31] The tendency of the new generation of the 1230s to a more intimate tone of piety—and perhaps some additional influence of the cult of the Eucharist—would explain the shift which took place at Saint-Nicaise from city-gate to choir-screen symbolism in the concept of the church façade.

Another element as well seems to have been present in the background of the design: Cistercian churches were commonly preceded by low arcaded porches, looking rather like one side of a cloister. But at Longpont[32] this low continuous arcade had already been divided by the tall buttresses of the façade into groupings of wide and narrow bays, in a manner which announced the rhythm of openings of the porches of Saint-Nicaise (Fig. 360). Longpont does not appear to have had gables over its porches, which seem to have terminated horizontally; but it was upon the cadence of spacing of the porches of Longpont that Hugues Libergier applied his choir-screen motif, so that it truly seems as if a sight of these small size Cistercian porches had been necessary to touch off the imagination of the designer and give him the idea of transposing forms of that scale onto a façade.

360. LONGPONT, ruins of W façade, ca. 1210–1227

The multiplication of the gable motif, begun as a way of emphasizing the doorway zone on a façade, was soon extended to the whole building. This important new step was taken around 1240. Unfortunately the building in which gables were probably used for the first time to top on the outside the clerestory windows, breaking by their zigzag the line of the roof base, the choir of the old cathedral of Cambrai (Fig. 128, p. 135), is again a building of which nothing remains. It was pulled down at the time of the Revolution and is known only through two seventeenth-century records: a drawing by Van der Meulen in the Musée des Gobelins and a model of the town of Cambrai, now destroyed but of which a few photographs are preserved.[33] The choir of Cambrai seems to have been started in the late 1220s, the aisles and chapels being completed by 1239. But in that lower story no gables were used: what might appear on the drawing to be gables was actually—the model made it plain—sloping terminations of the roofs themselves and, like them, slated. It was only in the last stage of the work, between 1239 and 1251, when the upper stories of the choir were built, that the gable appeared as an accompaniment to the windows.[34] As there were close stylistic links between Cambrai choir and Reims Cathedral, a contact with Saint-Nicaise would seem quite likely; and Cambrai in turn must have been the source for the next two major examples of the use of gables in the early 1240s: the choir of Tournai Cathedral and the Sainte-Chapelle.

At Tournai gables are everywhere: their sharp point accents the windows of the choir aisles and chapels, as well as the clerestory windows which tower above that lower zone of the chevet (Fig. 361). It would be excessive to describe the choir of Tournai as a mere emanation of the Cambrai workshop: while in its plan the choir of Cambrai was something of an enlarged copy of the choir of Reims Cathedral and used the same generous masses of masonry, Tournai refers to another model, that of Soissons Cathedral, in the type of its choir plan with shallow chapels and in its lightness of structure.[35] But when it comes to the use of gables and the resulting general sharpness of forms there is no doubt that Tournai, forty miles downstream on the same River Scheldt, was part of the same movement as Cambrai, simply presenting another variant of its modalities of application.

Begun in 1243, the choir of Tournai followed Cambrai by only a few years and may reasonably be regarded as an accentuation of the tendencies which had been developing at Cambrai Cathedral, where there had been a considerable lightening of the structural substance between the construction of the ground story and that of the upper parts of the chevet. In the choir of Tournai all forms take an air of extreme lightness, of near-weightlessness. The outside is all sharpness and angularity: thin pinnacles rising like spikes; acute-angled gables with apex chopping into the horizontal line of cornice and balustrade; and a hard but brittle quality in the outlining of all the volumes. Inside (Fig. 362), although the formal vocabulary is quite different, the impression of refined leanness is no less remarkable: in the spandrels of the main arcade, roundels in shallow relief treated as mere surface adornment suggest through their flatness an insubstantial structure; while the triforium is not only very thin in its shafts and arches but perforated by all sorts

361. TOURNAI CATHEDRAL, chevet, begun 1243

362. TOURNAI CATHEDRAL, choir

of holes stamped out of parchment-like surfaces, suggesting again an architecture entirely devoid of substance. Tournai defines a Rayonnant style which formulates itself in thin fretwork shapes rather than in the filigree work of Saint-Denis. That kind of effect was already taking form at Saint-Nicaise, and the upper stories of the choir of Cambrai were probably the actual link between the two works.

It was also in all likelihood from these northern sources that the Sainte-Chapelle (Fig. 363) derived its gables. Begun before 1244, the Sainte-Chapelle was dedicated in 1248.[36] Apart from the gables which surmount all the upper windows and which are most likely to have come from Cambrai, the Sainte-Chapelle is very closely related to Amiens, particularly to the lower story of the chevet, which was built between 1235 and 1247 under the direction of Robert de Luzarches's successor, Thomas de Cormont. The chapels of Amiens, which were begun at least six years before the Sainte-Chapelle, have buttresses treated in exactly the same man-

363. PARIS, SAINTE-CHAPELLE, S side, ca. 1242–1248

ner, with the same sheer vertical rise and the same succession of horizontal dripmolds (Fig. 365). The tracery patterns of the windows are also in many cases identical.[37]

This close relationship with Amiens applies equally to both of the stories of which the Sainte-Chapelle is composed. In the lower chapel (Fig. 366) the wide triangular windows, although more complex in design, can be considered as enlarged and more evolved versions of the simpler triangular windows that had been used at Amiens at the end of the aisles (Fig. 367), immediately above the lateral porches of the façade. In the same way the star-shaped plan of the abaci over the columns in the lower chapel is clearly derived from the type of capitals used at Amiens in the upper parts of the nave;[38] while the restrained but decided roundness and plasticity of the engaged piers in the upper chapel (Fig. 364) also recall most strikingly the treatment of the shafts which rise to the vaults in the nave of Amiens.

The impression of extraordinary lightness produced inside is

364. Paris, Sainte-Chapelle, upper chapel, ca. 1242–1248

365. Amiens Cathedral, chevet chapels, ca. 1236–1245

366. PARIS, SAINTE-CHAPELLE, lower chapel, ca. 1242–1245

367. AMIENS CATHEDRAL, S aisle of nave looking W, 1220–1236

well balanced on the outside by the strength and projection of the buttresses which carry at the top, instead of the horizontal of a cornice, the pointed gables of the window heads. Less dry in its substance than Tournai choir or Saint-Nicaise, less systematic than the new Saint-Denis in its effects of weightlessness, the Sainte-Chapelle is characterized by a great boldness of design combined with a rather soft touch in the modulation of architectural forms: a combination which had been from the start the hallmark of the Amiens workshop. Except for the novelty of the gables, in most of its essentials the style of the Sainte-Chapelle went back to the 1220s.

That tendency to work out a certain degree of compromise and re-establish links with the preceding decades was perhaps the dominant trend of the 1240s. Although the type of elevation of Saint-Denis, with its openwork treatment of the triforium, was now adopted as the standard solution, the general handling of forms became less radical, being tempered by reminiscences of the past. This can be perceived even in the very special case of Strasbourg Cathedral. The nave of Strasbourg (Fig. 368), which must have been begun in the early or mid-1240s (the three east bays were completed by 1261) is very close in style to Saint-Denis and to the choir of Troyes.[39] But the subtle shift of emphasis which took place at Strasbourg, the desire for separateness and clarity expressed in the greater width of the nave, in the stronger accentuation of the bays and in the lack of actual linkage between triforium and clerestory (Fig. 369), did not stem from some continuation of the previous stages of French Gothic: it reflected rather the persistence in the Rhineland of the strong classical feeling which had for centuries accompanied the Imperial idea. That classicized version of Saint-Denis would not have been quite possible in the old Gothic lands. In those purely French areas the most conservative design of the 1240s was the choir of Tours Cathedral, begun either in 1241 or very close to that date.[40] There the outline of the volumes of the east end (Fig. 370), with the compact grouping of the chapels tightly enclosed within the semicircle of vertically rising buttresses, is directly derived from the chevet of Reims; and inside the building the use of the *cantonné* pier and of a triforium reminiscent of Royaumont

368. STRASBOURG CATHEDRAL, nave, E bays ca. 1245–1255, rest of nave ca. 1255–1275

369. STRASBOURG CATHEDRAL, N side of nave from S aisle

370. TOURS CATHEDRAL, chevet, begun ca. 1241 (Ward Archive)

again evokes the habits of earlier years and tends to smooth over the recent stylistic break.

This sense of continuity from the 1220s to the 1240s is no less perceptible in the great romantic undertakings of that generation: the colossal structures of Metz, Beauvais or Cologne cathedrals. Moderation may have been the keyword for some of the early Rayonnant works, for Saint-Denis, Strasbourg or Tours; but the taste for the gigantic, which had been initiated at Amiens in 1220, continued to inspire some of the major works of the 1240s. Metz equalled Amiens in height, while Cologne and Beauvais rose even higher, reaching the limits of the technically feasible. At Metz, where the *cantonné* pier is again in evidence,[41] the enormous disproportion between fairly low aisles and an immensely tall nave rising between huge traceried windows (Fig. 371) marks a distinct return to the dramatic effects of contrast which had first found expression about thirty years before in the east end of Saint-Quentin.

An even more obvious example of that continuation of the spatial speculations of the 1220s is provided by the cathedral of

371. METZ CATHEDRAL, nave, begun 1257 (Ward Archive)

372. BEAUVAIS CATHEDRAL, triforium of hemicycle bays, ca. 1250–1255

Beauvais, where the choir begun in 1225[42] was built only halfway up (i.e., to the base of the triforium story) by the time the building operations slowed down in the early 1240s (Fig. 269, p. 291). The redesigning that took place around 1247 or 1250 and which gave its purely Rayonnant character to the upper part of the elevation does not however seem to have affected, at least significantly, the proportions of the original design. But what was certainly changed was the style of execution: all the members of the structure were refined in their profiles and the triforium followed the most advanced formula of the new style, being treated in two layers of tracery and glazed on all its height (Fig. 372). The extreme elegance of these upper stories, as redesigned after 1247, can still be observed in the hemicycle bays, which were not touched by the collapse of the choir vaults in 1284 and so escaped the rebuilding and reinforcements to which the straight bays had to be subjected before the vaults could be put up again. When it had been first completed in 1272 and for some twelve years until the catastrophe of 1284, that vertiginous version of the Saint-Denis style had briefly brought

373. COLOGNE CATHEDRAL, choir 1248–1322, 19th c. nave

374. COLOGNE CATHEDRAL, chevet, lower story 1248–1268, upper parts ca. 1270–1320

together into a most daring combination the gigantism of the 1220s and the insubstantiality of the 1240s. Patched up after the disaster, it remained at 48.2 meters (just over 158 feet) the colossus of Gothic height.

But Beauvais could in a way be considered atypical, for it was after all a design of the mid 1220s simply retouched and brought up-to-date; on the other hand the next tallest of Gothic structures, the choir of Cologne Cathedral,[43] carried none of that ambiguity of meaning. Begun in 1248, it was a brand new design of the 1240s— even if it did take a long time to complete, being vaulted only ca. 1305 (Figs. 373 and 374). With a height of 43.5 meters (not quite 143 feet), it was less tall than Beauvais but passed Amiens by 1.20 meters (4 feet); and this continued attraction of colossal height is all the more interesting to note because Cologne was perhaps the purest emanation of the Parisian milieu of the later 1240s. Its relationship with the style of the Sainte-Chapelle is particularly striking: piers and groups of shafts are treated in both buildings with the same restrained but somewhat unctuous plasticity, suggesting very much the same kind of sensibility in the approach to light effects and architectural modeling. Cologne is indeed very close to being simply the cathedral-sized version of the Sainte-Chapelle.[44] Both succeeded in bringing together the towering ambitions of the Amiens generation and the incisive analytical elegance that had inspired the first creators of Rayonnant Gothic in the 1230s.

TOWARD A NEW BRITTLENESS

After that lapse of some ten years, during which architects had been interested rather in bridging the gap with the twenties by having the new style absorb some of the ideals of High Gothic, in the 1250s the movement forward was resumed and reached a dual climax at the chevet of Amiens Cathedral and on the transept façades of Notre-Dame in Paris. At Amiens the contrast is remarkable between the early work of the nave (1220–1235), or even between the chapel story of the east end (1235–1249), and the upper parts of the chevet (Fig. 375), which were built to a new design from about 1254 or 1255 and completed in 1269.[45] Up to the mid-1250s,

375. AMIENS CATHEDRAL, chevet, lower story ca. 1236–1245, upper parts ca. 1254–1269 (Ward Archive)

both nave and choir chapels had preserved a great firmness of outline with the same abrupt vertical buttresses, simple in shape, and the same vigorous horizontal cornice to terminate clearly the volumes. But in the upper half of the choir nothing of this firmness remains. There is no more cornice, and the upper termination of the building is treated in an even more broken and flimsy style than the upper parts of the choir of Tournai: the gables have become so insubstantial that they look rather like cut-outs in plywood.

The buttresses also now make up a sort of forest in which general directions are difficult to discern, and when looked at closely they are seen to be broken up into a multiplicity of smaller units. While in their lower part these buttresses were simple and rectangular in section, their shape changes halfway up and becomes a complicated multiform assemblage. Small-scale pinnacles are superposed in stories, seeming to pivot on their bases and face in all directions, with the topmost one set on the diagonal. Whole sequences

397

of forms are deployed in a play of astounding mobility. Everything seems to be in the process of breaking up and multiplying: even the flying buttresses are visually self-contradictory in that their insistent vertical perforations are in conflict with the long sloping curve of their arches and with the radial placement of the voussoirs that compose them. The high buttressing piers change in plan from cruciform in the straight bays of the choir to Y-shaped in the semicircular part of the chevet; and the obtuse angles so produced again contradict the general sweep of the volumes. It is this combination of multiplied and systematically discordant details that gives to the chevet of Amiens its bushy, spiky aspect: a bunching together of innumerable small-scale forms, all of them finishing in sharp little points—and not just weightless but shooting upward with a sort of inner vitality. It is not surprising that the choir of Cologne was soon revised in its design to achieve in its upper parts the same kind of effect.[46]

This was one of the novel styles of the 1250s, but not the only

376. AMIENS CATHEDRAL, upper parts of chevet, ca. 1250–1269

377. PARIS, NOTRE-DAME, N transept façade, begun shortly before 1250

one. In Paris that new taste for sharpness and complexity was being given another interpretation—less concerned with mobility in space but no less subtle and elaborate—in the transept façades of Notre-Dame.[47] The north transept façade (Fig. 377) was built by Jean de Chelles and must have been completed by 1259. Its general composition is clearly derived from the north transept façade of Saint-Denis (Fig. 356), of which it renders a taller and enriched variant: it has the same type of rose window within a square framing, the same transparent triforium zone; and even the novel features of the lower part of the façade can be taken as confirming that Saint-Denis relationship. The succession of thin flat planes applied one upon the other recalls the flatness and the faint recessions of the interior elevation of Saint-Denis; and the principle of families of similar forms operating on different scales finds within the portal zone a new mode of application. Blind gables on either side of the doorway dominate groupings of smaller gables (Figs. 378, 379), which themselves surmount niches within which statues originally stood. This

378. PARIS, NOTRE-DAME, gables flanking N transept doorway

379. PARIS, NOTRE-DAME, portal zone of N transept façade, ca. 1250

whole effect of progression, with subordinate forms framed within larger versions of themselves, was just an extension of the system which had been first defined in the mullion compositions of windows. In another respect it is interesting also to compare that design of thin pinnacles and gables used by Jean de Chelles at Notre-Dame with its direct forerunners. From the façade of Laon to that of Amiens and to the north transept of Notre-Dame, the same vocabulary can be followed, losing progressively in material presence: gabled porches and pinnacles which at Laon had been used with full three-dimensionality (Fig. 187, p. 192), and which at Amiens, although somewhat reduced in depth, were still voluminous and weighty (Fig. 258, p. 279), have at Notre-Dame become flattened, telescoped almost, against the façade wall; and what had been conceived in terms of volumes, having lost all substance, has become in the 1250s a purely linear motif.

The façade of the south transept (Fig. 383) is somewhat later, being a work of the 1260s. Begun in 1259 by Jean de Chelles, who died very soon after, it was built essentially by Pierre de Montreuil, who had probably completed it by the time of his death in 1267. In the hands of this new master the design of Jean de Chelles' façade takes on a slightly different character. There is less insistence on subordination: the large gables cease to contain groups of smaller gables. The sculptural decoration has become a little richer and the planar recessions more simplified.[48] If anything, the treatment is even flatter than on the north façade, giving the impression of a thin sheet of pale metal delicately embossed.

Terms of metalwork come irresistibly to mind in the description of Rayonnant works, and the term "shrine treatment" is commonly used in connection with some of the major edifices in which the style was first defined. This applied specifically to the Sainte-Chapelle, which was intended as the most sacred of reliquaries and was indeed conceived, in a certain sense, as a shrine with its rich surface turned outside in.[49] But the shrine comparison should be handled with great caution, for its reference is far more to the decorative element than to truly architectural forms. It was the enameling of shrines and the richness of their carved decoration

380. EVREUX, SAINT-TAURIN, Shrine of Saint Taurin,
completed by 1255

that were imitated inside the Sainte-Chapelle. But the shape of the
building or even of its arcadings did not reflect metalwork prototypes: rather, the process worked the other way round, and the
shrines which ca. 1250 took on the appearance of Rayonnant chapels,
the shrine of Saint Taurin at Evreux for instance (Fig. 380), were
conceived in imitation of architecture.[50] The only major work of
architectural composition that was truly treated in a shrinelike spirit
in its relief and modeling was the glorious west façade of Reims
Cathedral (Fig. 381), as designed most probably in the mid-1250s
by the new master, Bernard de Soissons.[51] But this remained an
unique exception based on a compromise, unlikely ever to be re-

401

381. REIMS CATHEDRAL, W façade, begun ca. 1254–1255 (Gallery of Kings and towers built only in 14th and 15th c.)

382. WELLS CATHEDRAL, detail of W façade, begun ca. 1225

peated, between the substantial forms of High Gothic and the sharp refinements of a rising modernity.

The actual influence of metalwork on architectural forms was probably more current in England than in France. At Wells Cathedral (Fig. 382) the façade, designed in the mid-1220s, some five or six years before that of Saint-Nicaise, truly transferred into stone some of the techniques of the minor arts and some characteristic elements of their formal vocabulary.[52] Earlier indications of this process of transfer had for some time been evident in a number of

403

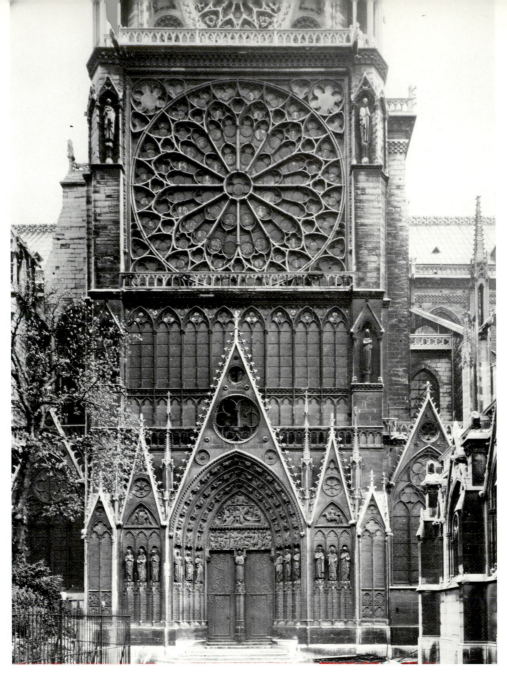

383. PARIS, NOTRE-DAME, S transept façade, 1258–1267

English centers, and there is every likelihood that its first manifestations went back to some great Romanesque work such as the lost façade of Bury St. Edmunds of the 1130s and 1140s.[53] In northern France on the other hand and in Paris particularly, the stylistic development that led to Rayonnant Gothic was the product of a very different line of thinking, dominated by that predilection for flatness which was one of the oldest constructional traditions of the area. It was still the old Parisian ideal of extreme thinness, of taut light walls, which had expressed itself in such works as Saint-Pierre-de-Montmartre (Fig. 35, p. 37) in the 1140s and again and even more strikingly, at Mantes (Fig. 147, p. 153) or Champeaux in the last decades of the twelfth century. In the great screens of tracery of the 1230s (Fig. 345), in the flat façade planes of the 1250s (Fig. 377), that same quality continued to be present. It was now treated differently, in a sharp linear idiom that resulted from newly developed technical means: among them especially, an increased refinement in stonecutting and a new precision in architectural draughtsmanship.[54] These advances explain how the Parisian feeling for the hardness of stone discovered at this time a whole range of analogies with the hardness of metal.[55] But it was in stone that the new forms were first conceived, and in the minds of masons and stonecutters who prided themselves on their skill in the handling of their material. So the situation should not be oversimplified. In its apparent fragility and brittleness, in its love of small-scale forms, the Rayonnant can perhaps be viewed as situated midway between church and shrine. But even allowing for that ambivalence of effect and that suggestion of metallic tension, the new style was still above all a renewed version of the thin stone architecture of the Paris of the later twelfth century; and a Parisian dryness remained as its mark of origin (Figs. 379, 383).

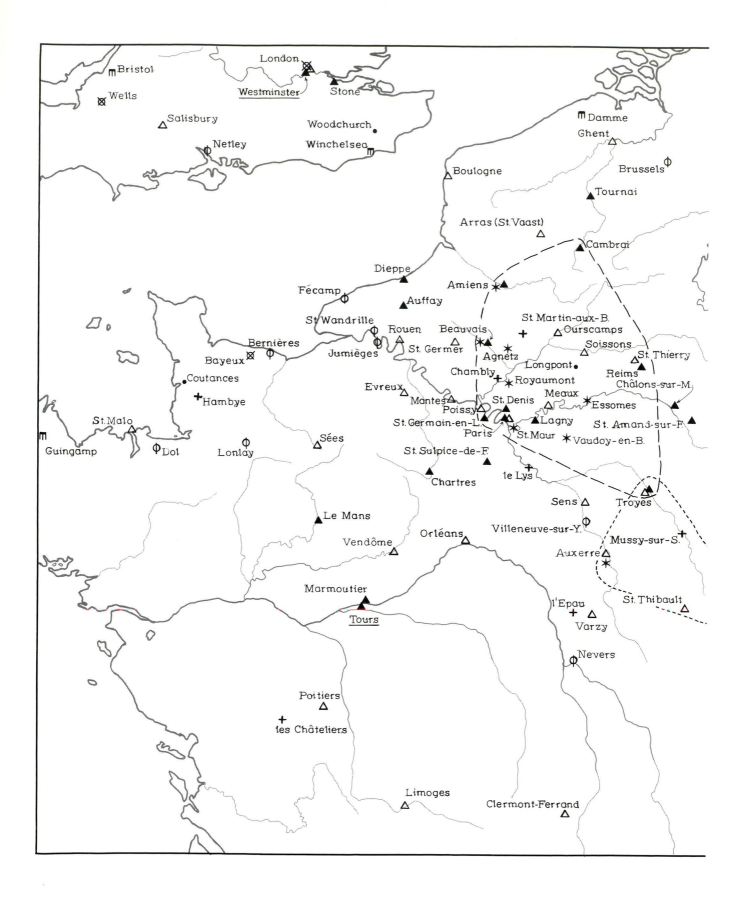

Bristol

London

Wells

Westminster   Stone

Salisbury

Woodchurch

Netley

Winchelsea

Damme

Ghent

Brussels

Boulogne

Tournai

Arras (St. Vaast)

Cambrai

Dieppe

Amiens

Fécamp

Auffay

St. Martin-aux-B.

St. Wandrille

Beauvais

Ourscamps

Soissons

Rouen

St. Germer

St. Thierry

Bernières

Jumièges

Agnetz

Longpont

Reims

Bayeux

Chambly

Royaumont

Châlons-sur-M.

Coutances

Evreux

Meaux

Essomes

Hambye

Mantes

St. Denis

St. Amand-sur-F.

Poissy

Lagny

St. Malo

St. Germain-en-L.

Vaudoy-en-B.

Guingamp   Dol

Lonlay

Paris   St. Maur

Sées

St. Sulpice-de-F.

le Lys

Chartres

Sens   Troyes

Le Mans

Villeneuve-sur-Y.

Mussy-sur-S.

Vendôme

Orléans

Auxerre

Marmoutier

l'Epau

St. Thibault

Tours

Varzy

Nevers

Poitiers

les Châteliers

Limoges

Clermont-Ferrand

384. Map: The Rayonnant Style (ca. 1230–1300)

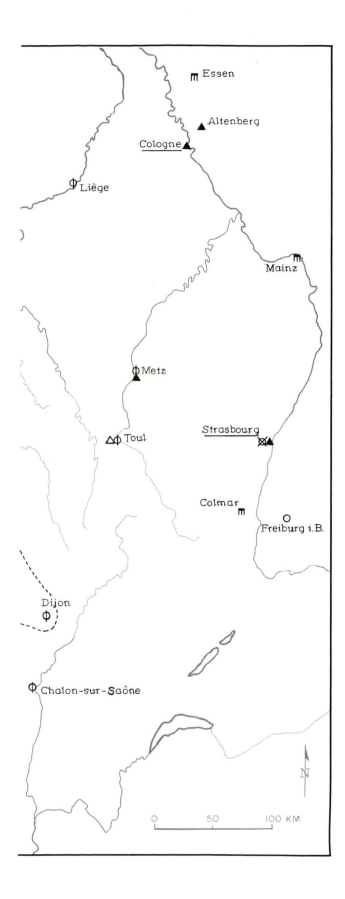

Essen

Altenberg

Cologne

Liège

Mainz

Metz

Toul

Strasbourg

Colmar

Freiburg i.B.

Dijon

Chalon-sur-Saône

N

| 0 | 50 | 100 KM |

LEGEND

Symbols used

△   Buildings in the north French style, or closely related

Ⅰ   Aisleless naves

Ⅲ   Hall churches

◉   Other types of late 13th-century spaciousness

⊗   Buildings in the new linear styles of the late 13th century

Name references

IN ENGLAND
Northampton: Eleanor Cross at Hardingstone
Hereford: north transept of cathedral
Wells: Chapter House

London: choir of Old St. Paul's
Westminster:
  Chapter House and transept façades of Westminster Abbey
  St. Stephen's Chapel in the old Palace of Westminster

IN SOUTHERN FRANCE AND CATALONIA
Toulouse:
  choir of the cathedral
  Cordeliers and Jacobins
Narbonne:
  cathedral
  Lamourguier
Barcelona:
  cathedral
  churches of the Dominicans and Franciscans

Abbreviations

Beau.	Beauvais
Carc.	Carcassonne
Clermont -F.	Clermont-Ferrand
Châ.	Châlons-sur-Marne
Cham.	Chambly
Fra.	Frankfurt
Freiburg i.Br.	Freiburg-im-Breisgau
Po.	Poissy
R.	Rouen
St.B. de C.	Saint-Bertrand-de-Comminges
St.G.	Saint-Germer
St.W.	Saint-Wandrille
W'min.	Westminster

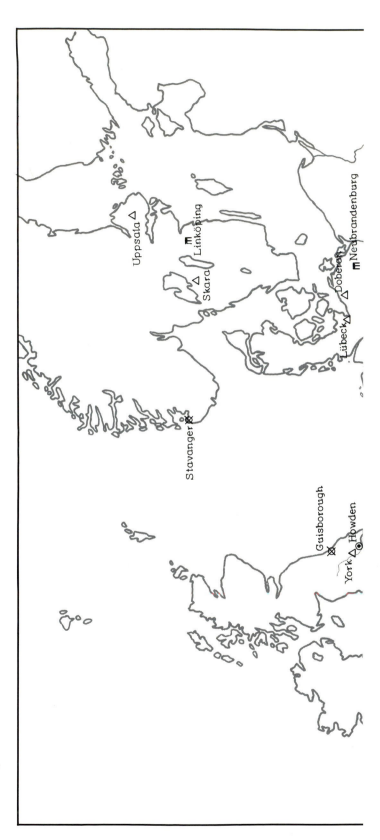

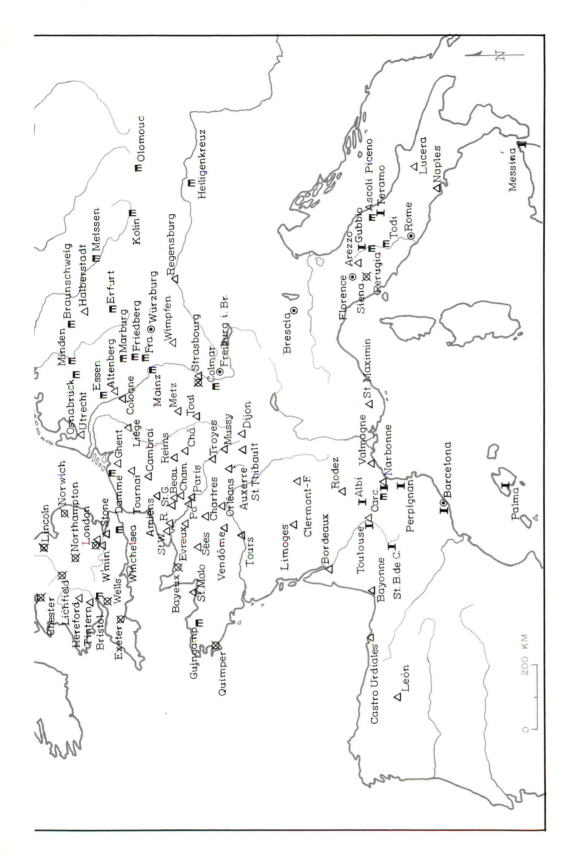

385. MAP: Gothic Europe in the second half of the 13th century

Chester
L.Lincoln
Norwich
Lichfield
Hereford
Northampton
Tintern
London
Bristol
Stone
W.min.
Exeter
Wells
Winchelsea
Damme
Ghent
Tournai
Cambrai
Liège
Osnabrück
Utrecht
Minden
Braunschweig
Halberstadt
Meissen
Essen
Altenberg
Cologne
Marburg
Friedberg
Fra. Würzburg
Kolin
Regensburg
Wimpfen
Strasbourg
Colmar
Freiburg i. Br.
Heiligenkreuz
Olomouc
Erfurt
Mainz
Metz
Toul
Reims
St.G.
Cha.
Troyes
Mussy
Dijon
Amiens
R.
Beau.
Paris
Chartres
St.Thibault
St.W.
Evreux
Po.
Orléans
Auxerre
Bayeux
St.Malo
Sées
Vendôme
Tours
Guingamp
Quimper
Limoges
Clermont-F.
Rodez
Bordeaux
Brescia
St.Maximin
Valmagne
Narbonne
Albi
Carc.
Perpignan
Barcelona
Toulouse
Bayonne
St.B.de C.
Castro Urdiales
León
Palma
Florence
Arezzo
Siena
Gubbio
Perugia
Ascoli Piceno
Todi
Rome
Teramo
Lucera
Naples
Messina

0   200 KM

386. CLERMONT-FERRAND CATHEDRAL, choir, ca. 1250–1286

CHAPTER X

Late Thirteenth Century Architecture

THE NEW architecture which had taken shape in the 1230s and 1240s, apparently so fragile, had a more decisive impact than all the preceding forms of Gothic. What High Gothic in all its splendor had not been able to achieve, the artistic conquest of Europe, was performed in no time by the Rayonnant. It has often been suggested that the new style owed its widespread acceptance to the power of the French monarchy, by now predominant. The new Saint-Denis and the Sainte-Chapelle had established Rayonnant Gothic as the court style of the Capetian kings, and there is no denying that the prestige and renown of Louis IX—the future Saint Louis—were bound to help in the diffusion of the forms of taste which were associated with his name.

But the Rayonnant had in itself all the qualities to assure immediate success. Being essentially an art of surface treatment rather than one of new spatial or constructional concepts, it was more easily accessible than the earlier forms of French Gothic and could even superimpose itself upon a variety of pre-existing traditions. Furthermore, its vocabulary was of enormous attractiveness. Much of its charm came from the fineness of the shapes it drew in space and their effects of unreality: this resulted mostly at first from the filigree tracery of stone mullions, multiplied in orderly series of progressive subdivisions (Fig. 353, p. 376), suggesting a pattern of

411

387. PARIS, NOTRE-
DAME, Porte Rouge (on
N side of choir), ca. 1270

389. PSALTER OF SAINT LOUIS, ca. 1260, Cain and Abel
sacrificing (Paris, Bibl. nat., Ms. lat. 10525, f. lv)

388. STRASBOURG CATHEDRAL, arcaded plinth
in clerestory window of nave, ca. 1270–1275

pure logic. In the third quarter of the century, while this tracery was extending its field in blind patterns to the tympana of doorways[1] and more and more to all remaining surfaces of solid walls, another element was beginning to take an increasing part in the development of the Rayonnant vocabulary: a play on transpositions of scale which made the same forms range with equal validity from the colossal to the minute and tended to blur all perception of actual size. The most all-pervasive motif in that line of speculation was the gabled arch between pinnacled supports—a kind of abbreviation for a full-scale building—which had first been used to monumentalize doorways, like those of the transept façades of Notre-Dame (Figs. 377 and 379, p. 398f). Reduced in size, it could be applied to smaller doors, such as the Porte Rouge at Notre-Dame (Fig. 387), to the facing of wall panels or even buttresses; or, inside the building, to the decoration of choir screens and the framing of effigies on tombs.[2] Becoming more and more miniaturized (Fig. 388) and more calligraphic in its handling, it soon covered altars, stalls, shrines and reliquaries, the plinths of statues on doorway jambs,[3] the panels of stained glass in window lights, the bindings of missals, the leaves of ivory triptychs, the illuminated pages of manuscripts (Fig. 389).[4]

This versatility of form and this ready transferability from technique to technique must have given to the designers a wonderful sense of freedom, for architectural framings began to proliferate into elaborate canopied superstructures; and it was perhaps in stained glass that this tendency manifested itself most clearly. At Strasbourg the movement can be followed in successive stages: from the earliest north aisle windows, probably of the late 1250s (Figs. 390, 391), to the major series of the clerestory windows, datable in the early to mid-1270s (Fig. 392), the painted canopies rose progressively into turreted multigabled spirelike compositions in two or three tiers, accompanied by tiny pinnacles and flying buttresses, creating a dreamworld of architectural fantasies which was to spread after 1300 to all the workshops of Europe.[5] A style which could stretch at will from the most logical and orderly to such extremes of fancy was bound to capture the imagination of an age which took a special delight as much in the subtle as in the incredible.

413

390. STRASBOURG CATHEDRAL, sequence of windows in N aisle of nave, ca. 1255–1270

391. STRASBOURG CATHEDRAL, detail from window in N aisle of nave, ca. 1255–1260

392. STRASBOURG CATHEDRAL, detail from window in S clerestory of nave, ca. 1270–1275

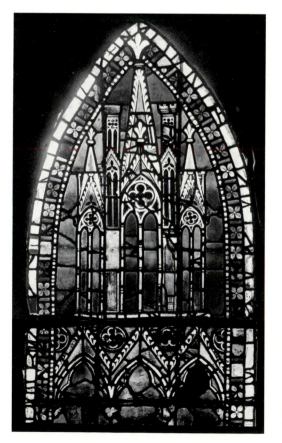

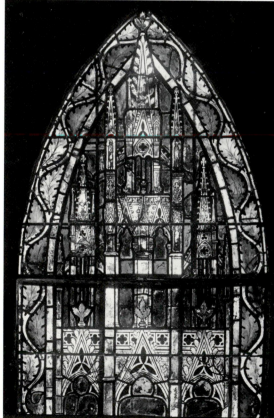

The range of possible adaptations of the new style, its lightness of touch and its modernistic appeal explain why it swept so rapidly across Europe. In all directions the barriers collapsed and the Rayonnant repertory was everywhere adopted. This movement of diffusion can be traced all over Europe. Toward the south it jumped straight to the Pyrenées and even beyond: the choir of Bayonne Cathedral, in the extreme southwest of France, was begun in 1258 in a rather sedate version of this latest style.[6] But Spain was already outdoing Gascony: at León, that old capital of Romanesque days, the cathedral, on which work was started soon after 1255, was built in the purest Rayonnant (Fig. 393), all mullions in the upper

393. LEÓN CATHEDRAL, view into choir from S transept, begun soon after 1255

stories, with colossal traceried windows and a glazed triforium. The design can even be identified as coming from Champagne, from a typical mannerism which detaches a very narrow lancet on each side of the bay both in the triforium and in the clerestory, and makes the whole of the central panel recede slightly in relation to these lateral lancets.[7]

In central France and in the Languedoc area directly south of it, the movement which started a few years later was dominated for more than thirty years by the personality of Jean des Champs, an artist who doubtless came from northern France and who seems to have had close connections both with Amiens and with the Parisian milieu. His name appears for the first time at the cathedral of Clermont-Ferrand (Fig. 386), built to his plans and under his direction by the early 1250s.[8] He completed the whole peripheral part of the chevet, i.e. the chapels, ambulatory and the eastern termination of the central space of the choir. But he left the completion of the choir further west and the building of the transepts and nave to his son Pierre des Champs, while he himself was more and more concerned with new large-scale undertakings, all started in the early 1270s, at Limoges, Toulouse, Rodez and, dearest to his heart and most important of all, the cathedral of Saint-Just in the old city of Narbonne (Figs. 419, 420) where he died in 1295. A consistent de-

394. VALMAGNE, main arcade of choir, late 1260s

velopment of his style can be followed from his earlier to his later works; but at Clermont-Ferrand he was already propounding a calm and somewhat austere version of the Rayonnant style, rejecting in particular the openwork treatment of the triforium in order to restore to the elevation a stabilizing zone of darkness. The Cistercian church of Valmagne (Fig. 394) near Béziers, in the coastal plain of Languedoc, appears closely related to the work of Jean des Champs and seems to date from about the same time as the east end of Clermont-Ferrand. Preceding Narbonne Cathedral by a few years, it is another early example of the diffusion of the Rayonnant style in the South.[9]

In all the provincial or peripheral Gothic milieux the same story repeats itself; everywhere the new style breaks down almost at once the stylistic resistance which until then had been opposed to the propagation of the most advanced forms of northern French Gothic. In Normandy for instance, Rayonnant at its purest and

395. ROUEN CATHEDRAL, N transept façade (Portail des Libraires), begun 1281 (Ward Archive)

396. BAYEUX CATHEDRAL, S transept façade, ca. 1260–1280 (Ward Archive)

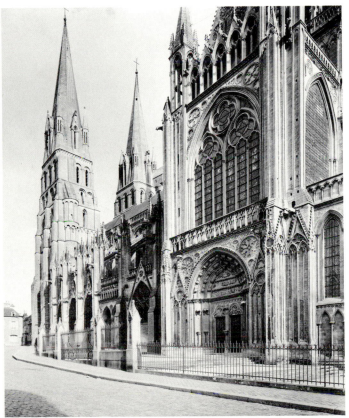

397. WESTMINSTER ABBEY, Chapter House window, ca. 1245–1253

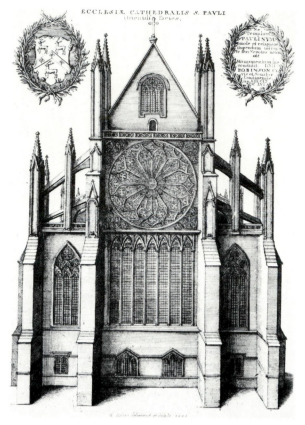

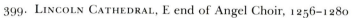

398. LONDON, OLD ST. PAUL'S CATHEDRAL, E end, ca. 1270–1280, engraving by W. Hollar

399. LINCOLN CATHEDRAL, E end of Angel Choir, 1256–1280

with the excitement of the most extreme novelty is found in the choir of Evreux Cathedral, begun in the 1260s, in that of Sées (Fig. 410) of a few years later; and after 1280 in an even more spectacular fashion in the elaborate openwork façades of the transept of Rouen Cathedral (Fig. 395), which were the most unprovincial of works and expressed better than any Ile-de-France building the typical trends of the final years of the thirteenth century.[10] But in the same span of time, at Bayeux Cathedral, both in the designing of the transept ends (Fig. 396) and in the remodeling of the west front, the new stylistic vocabulary was used with a considerable degree of freedom and in much less orthodox combinations. The presence of contrasting variants juxtaposed within the same province is a sign of the duality which was to characterize Rayonnant architecture in many of the more recently converted areas.

In England, the new French style made its appearance during the first campaign of rebuilding at Westminster Abbey, between 1245 and 1259,[11] in the large traceried windows of the Chapter House (Fig. 397), copied from the nave chapels of Notre-Dame, and in the complex mullioned compositions of the rose windows of the transept façades, patterned after those of Saint-Denis or Notre-Dame. But within a few decades the divergences of interpretation became even wider than in Normandy. While the east end of Old St. Paul's in London (Fig. 398), glazed on all its height, was in the most orthodox French Rayonnant style with its rose window inscribed in a square and its tall straight pinnacles, at Lincoln the east end (Fig. 399) took a more unexpected line, by selecting the single theme of the large traceried window and freely orchestrating it on a number of scales and levels. And at the end of the century, a very similar contrast opposes the nave of York Minster and the choir of Exeter Cathedral. With its strongly accentuated bays, York is once more a perfect image of regular Rayonnant design (Fig. 400) and one which can be related with some identifiable models on the Continent, notably Jean des Champs' choir of Clermont-Ferrand Cathedral. But Exeter on the other hand uses Rayonnant forms as a basis for inventive experimentations of a new kind (Fig. 401): on texture effects, on recessions in depth, and on tight linear grids in which are combined the two systems of the French multi-mullioned window and the English multi-ribbed tierceron vault.[12]

Though it was the same movement that swept over all the countries of Europe, the significance of that new style and the terms in which it spoke to those who received it varied profoundly from region to region, according to the conditions which had locally prevailed before its adoption. In all the areas which had rejected the boldness of forms of High Gothic, such large motifs as the composed window of Chartres became acceptable only in the filigree-like version now made possible by the technique of Rayonnant tracery. So that in addition to its own stylistic message, which was essentially one of refinement, the Rayonnant style often brought with it the first revelation of the power of the large synthetic forms which in northern France had been in common use for quite a while.

400. YORK MINSTER, view into nave from N transept, ca. 1291–1320

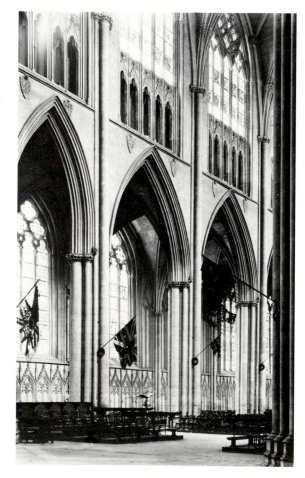

401. EXETER CATHEDRAL, N side of presbytery and choir, ca. 1288–1310

In those countries that had resisted the previous advances of Ile-de-France Gothic, architecture in the mid-thirteenth century made a sudden jump of fifty years, passing directly from the Braine stage of the 1180s or 1190s (Fig. 166, p. 173) to the Saint-Denis stage of the 1230s and 1240s (Fig. 353, p. 376); and this meant a very deep change of outlook. But whatever mental readjustments had to be made, the new architecture was adopted everywhere; and that general conversion to the new modernity was the basis for the wide international unity of taste which characterizes the later part of the thirteenth century. In art as in literary feeling, all the nations of the western world now shared a common culture and reacted similarly to the same novel inflections of sensibility.

With that sudden abolition of frontiers distance ceased to be a measure of the degree of stylistic purity: Spain at León Cathedral was closer in form and spirit to the new northern French production than was nearby Normandy. And the country which in those days proved most up to date and most faithful in its reception of the Rayonnant style was indubitably Germany. The rich trading cities along the Rhine were first to mirror, and almost instantly, what was happening in Paris, Picardy or Champagne. The nave of Strasbourg (Fig. 368, 369, p. 392f) had opened the movement by the mid-1240s at the latest, by giving a close but in some ways very personal replica of the type of elevation of the choir of Troyes. The choir of Cologne (Fig. 373, p. 395) followed soon after, in 1248, in a style related at the same time to Beauvais, Amiens, the Sainte-Chapelle and Notre-Dame. Although further away geographically, Cologne preceded Metz and seemed closer to the sources of the style.[13] Then came Utrecht, very slowly built, and the transept of Wimpfen, and in 1277 the final design for the west front of Strasbourg Cathedral.[14] At Cologne, when work reached the upper stories of the choir (Fig. 374, p. 395) about 1270 under Master Arnold,[15] the contact with the Amiens workshop was renewed—but this time with the latest of its styles, that of the upper parts of the chevet (Fig. 375, p. 397), designed around 1255. In this last stage both Cologne and Amiens practiced the same breaking up of forms, with sharp zigzagging gables and spiky clusters of buttresses. The style is more florid at Cologne where some details, such

403. Troyes, Saint-Urbain, view from SE, 1262-ca. 1270 (Ward Archive)

402. Regensburg Cathedral, choir from S, ca. 1275-1325

404. Troyes, Saint-Urbain, general interior view, 1262-ca. 1270 (Ward Archive)

as the tri-radial motif inscribed in the heads of the gables, reveal in addition a relationship with the workshop of the Strasbourg façade (Fig. 407). But the richness of that late thirteenth-century work at Cologne should not be seen as a symptom of a general change of tone, for further inland, on the Danube and in Saxony, the cathedral of Regensburg (Fig. 402)[16] and that of Meissen in its eastern parts went on handling the Rayonnant repertory with a precision and incisiveness which placed them on the same stylistic level as the most recent works of Troyes or Paris. That French idiom was spoken also and with no less purity as far to the northeast as Uppsala[17] and to the southeast as Cyprus:[18] its extension practically coincided now with the limits of Latin Christendom.

But while this remarkable artistic propagation was going on, the style itself had not halted in its own movement. So the central question remains: what new orientations were now emerging? what new antinomies were to stimulate efforts of invention in the coming years?

THE NEW DIRECTIONS

A Brittle Linear Style

In northern France the thin dry style, the crisp style of the Paris workshops of the 1250s, became more brittle than ever in works such as the church of Saint-Urbain at Troyes (Figs. 403, 404), which was clearly conceived as a paragon of modernity, commissioned by a pope, Urban IV, who was a native of Troyes, and built in its early stages with astonishing rapidity. Begun in 1262, within four years the choir was completed and the transept must have been finished shortly before 1270.[19] Inside, the elevation is simplified by the complete disappearance of the triforium, which had ceased to be functionally necessary since it had for some thirty years generally been treated as a mere extension of the clerestory zone. Even so, that reduction of the interior to two stories was the sign of a bold and unconventional approach, also evident in the insistent accentuation of the moldings of the main arcade. In the skeletal structure of the apse the simplification of the story pattern leads to a junction of the two zones of windows (Fig. 405), creating the effect

423

of a veritable glass cage rising in one movement from the solid plinth right up to the vault. In actuality the windows are not continuous, for the lower zone is treated in two layers, with the glazed surface recessed by the depth of an interior wall passage;[20] and a thin dividing line marks that change in structure, at the height of the string course which in the rest of the building separates the two stories of the elevation. The mullions being thinner than ever, the feeling is now properly that of a filigree of stone; and in the lower story dissimilar tracery patterns are superimposed in subtly discordant layers, as in the windows of the lateral chapels or in the lower part of the apse. But what really defines the style of Saint-Urbain is its exterior, and above all the unique type of the detached gables which

405. TROYES, SAINT-URBAIN, S side of choir and apse, 1262–1266

surmount its upper windows, crowning the walls on all sides. Around the apse and at the transept ends, which specially catch the eye, these tall gables and their spandrels are mounted in openwork, like large pieces of tracery posed in front of the solid structure; and this treatment in two clearly detached layers recalls the methods used in Burgundian architecture some thirty years before (Fig. 319, p. 340),[21] but now with the lacelike quality and effects of fragility which were in the nature of Rayonnant Gothic.

The climax of that tendency was reached a decade later at Strasbourg Cathedral, in the west façade (Figs. 406, 407) built from 1277 and to which the name of Master Erwin is attached.[22] Here the whole façade is given that openwork treatment in two planes

406. STRASBOURG CATHEDRAL, W façade, begun 1277 (tall N spire and block between original towers late 14th c. additions)

407. STRASBOURG CATHEDRAL, detail of W façade, design of 1277 revised ca. 1298

which at Saint-Urbain was used in certain locations only. Perhaps the most striking feature of the design is the screen of tall, string-like shafts which pass in front of the windows in the middle zone of the façade and which have often been compared to the strings of a harp. In fact, these immense shafts of the window story were not part of the project as originally set out in 1277: they were the result of an alteration made by Master Erwin in the course of construction, probably following the fire of 1298, which had stopped work on the façade for a time. But the large gabled windows planned in 1277 would also have been detached in openwork in front of the façade plane, as is the framing of the rose window; and the string effect that was finally adopted was simply a new and more open variant of the mode of treatment which had already been applied to the whole of the portal story. That redesigned middle zone was probably more or less complete by the time of Erwin's death in 1318.

Another modality of this new kind of two-layer treatment is found in the two-bay vestibule which leads from the ambulatory to the Lady Chapel at Saint-Germer-de-Fly (Fig. 408), west of Beauvais. The Lady Chapel itself dates from the late 1250s[23] and the vestibule would seem to have been built at most some ten years later. On either side the windows are recessed behind the sharp outline of a framing arch. Actually this arch is a cusped wall rib, detached in front of the windows rather in the manner of the Saint-Denis aisles (Fig. 347, p. 370) and of other such Champenois passages, a feature which always creates that double-layer effect. But in the vestibule of the Saint-Germer chapel there is no wall passage, no solid dado zone to support it, and the whole bay panel, wall and window from vault to pavement, recedes behind the projecting wall rib and the corresponding responds. And here another interesting element of handwriting also appears: the mullions of the windows, instead of stopping at the height of the sills, are carried down on the wall face to pavement level. The downward extension of mullions from the clerestory into the triforium had been one of the guiding principles of Rayonnant design ever since the 1230s, and the idea went back to much earlier attempts toward story merging. But the lower part of the structure had at first remained untouched by such linear speculations, and in the aisles or chapels the dado zone, even when it was decorated by a blind arcading, had preserved its autonomy. It was only after a while that the base of the walls became incorporated into the pattern of verticals of the windows, to achieve an effect of complete linear unification.

The first signs of this supremacy of the mullion can be spotted in Paris as early as the mid-1240s: in the last three chapels on the north side of the nave of Notre-Dame (Fig. 409), almost certainly built by Jean de Chelles,[24] and in that famous work of Pierre de Montreuil, the Lady Chapel of Saint-Germain-des-Prés (Fig. 348), begun in 1245, the reassembled remnants of which are sufficiently explicit.[25] But another twenty years were needed for this new idea to take firm hold, as it did in the later 1260s, when it became suddenly diffused in a scattering of buildings which all seem to have had some connections with court circles. More or less contemporaneous with the Saint-Germer vestibule and applying the same principle of vertical continuity were: in Normandy, the choir of Sées Cathedral, begun in all probability a little before 1270; in Languedoc, the choir of Saint-Nazaire at Carcassonne (Fig. 434), designed in or

408. SAINT-GERMER, vestibule leading to Lady Chapel, ca. 1270

409. PARIS, NOTRE-DAME, dado in a chapel on N side of nave, ca. 1245–1250

410. Sées Cathedral, view into ambulatory and choir, ca. 1270–1280

411. Sées Cathedral, N side of choir (Ward Archive)

just after 1269; and a little later, in Burgundy, the chevet of Saint-Germain at Auxerre (Fig. 422), begun in 1277.[26] The choir of Sées is a particularly good example of the new trend, as the same tight pattern of verticals covers all the interior surfaces of the building—the lateral walls of the ambulatory and radiating chapels as well as the central elevation (Fig. 410)—placing an overriding insistence on the continuity of the linear grid. In the main elevation (Fig. 411), pursuing the mullions of the clerestory windows, these omnipresent verticals not only intersect the tracery patterns of the triforium

428

story; they even pass through the hitherto intangible base line of the triforium into the spandrels of the main arcade, ending only at the contact of the gables which at Sées top the arches of the choir arcade.[27] And at this arcade level the subtle interweaving of carved crockets and linear mullions, originally supplemented by a whole array of little statues inserted between the striations of the spandrels of wall, establishes a tone of extreme refinement. In that choir of Sées as, in a freer and more dramatic way, on the façade of Strasbourg (Fig. 407), the rhythmical patterning of surfaces was reaching a new degree of systematic accentuation.[28]

A Simplified Severe Style

But this was not the only important tendency of the time: even before 1250 a reaction had already begun in the opposite direction, toward austerity and simplification, with a return to plain wall surfaces and generally to a more severe treatment of architecture. This would seem to suggest a sudden upsurge of Cistercian influence, for there is no doubt that for over one hundred years, since the days of Saint Bernard, in architecture as in all things, the Cistercians had been the protagonists of an ideal of ascetic restraint (Fig. 284, p. 311). Even if they had become less strict in practice and had since the end of the twelfth century given to some of their major churches a cathedral splendor (e.g. Longpont or Royaumont), their original message had not lost its call. But the new monastic style which came into prominence in the middle years of the thirteenth century was not due entirely to the Cistercians: other orders seem to have played a no less active part in its elaboration, among them the Augustinians, a widespread order of Regular Canons generally of reformist leanings, who tended to translate in less radical terms the precepts of Cistercian taste.

One of the earliest and most beautiful examples of that emerging tendency is the church of Saint-Martin-aux-Bois (Figs. 412, 413), an Augustinian foundation, on the southern edge of the plains of Picardy.[29] The structure, incomplete as it remained, was certainly finished by the early 1260s when the stained glass was being mounted in the windows of the apse; but it had been begun long before that,

429

probably in the later 1240s, and in its refined spareness it stands as something of a retort to the luxury of the Sainte-Chapelle. Most striking is the mural quality of its tall interior elevation (Fig. 414), a quality which is stressed by the little quatrefoils stamped out of its very thin walls at the level which would normally be occupied by a triforium. Related in their very shape to the type of small-size openings used in the lower parts of the towers of Notre-Dame (Fig. 231, p. 250), these quatrefoil perforations are very much in the line of the Parisian style of the later twelfth century, which used the motif of the oculus (Fig. 144, p. 150) to set off the same mural values.[30] The smooth continuity of these flat wall surfaces, here combined with a powerful vertical movement both in the proportions of the

412. Saint-Martin-aux-Bois, E end, begun ca. 1245–1250

413. SAINT-MARTIN-AUX-BOIS, choir

414. SAINT-MARTIN-AUX-BOIS, N elevation

volumes and in the shape and height of the windows, provided a particularly interesting alternative to the linear openwork of the orthodox Rayonnant style. But this did not preclude an unusual vigor in some of its linear accents: in the immensely tall windows of the apse, the crosswise mullions which halfway up intersect those endless lancets, are perhaps the first true transoms to occur in a pattern of Gothic tracery.[31]

A completely different variant of the same ideal of austerity is found in Normandy at about the same time in the ruined abbey church of Hambye (Fig. 415),[32] a monastery of the Order of Tiron, close in spirit to the Cistercians. The choir of Hambye, conceived as a simplified version of that of nearby Coutances Cathedral, has the

431

same compositional structure with vaults at three levels—although in its plan it has obviously been influenced also by the Cistercian formula of ambulatory chevets, in which a succession of rectangular chapels is built as a continuous semicircular volume around the east end of the church.[33] Here again, in the interior elevation small holes piercing in each bay a zone of plain solid wall (Fig. 416) replace the usual triforium or the upper passages of Normandy; and the wall structure becomes at the same time thinner,[34] as if whatever the local context there was some irresistible logic of the mural working necessarily toward the creation of like effects.

Another element that intervened powerfully in the development of that austere tendency in mid-thirteenth century architecture was the influence of the mode of building adopted by the new

415. Hambye Abbey, E end, ca. 1240–1260 (chapel zone earlier)

416. HAMBYE ABBEY, choir, ca. 1240–1260

Mendicant Orders, otherwise known as the Friars,[35] which were by
then reaching the peak of their spectacular propagation. For it appears that the earliest churches of the Friars were, as a rule, either
reduced to the elementary simplicity of purely utilitarian structures
or modeled on the simplest of Cistercian types.[36] Actually the evo-
lution of the style of Jean des Champs, who worked in an area deeply
penetrated by the influence of the new religious orders, must have
owed more to this general environment of Mendicant architecture
than to any links he may have had at one time with the Cistercians.

433

At Clermont-Ferrand by the 1250s, in his first identifiable work (Fig. 386), Jean des Champs appeared essentially as a man recently arrived from northern France: his use of gables in the triforium recalls the choir of Amiens or that, now vanished, of Saint-Thierry near Reims;[37] and his favorite patterns of tracery repeat those of the clerestory of Beauvais, the Lady Chapel of Saint-Germer or, closer to Paris, the choir of Chambly (Fig. 418). But there was already, at Clermont Cathedral, a remarkable and unorthodox feature: a narrow margin of wall on either side of the clerestory windows and carried down into the triforium zone—which has the effect of binding together triforium and windows in each bay panel, while at the same time creating a pause at each pier, interrupting the rhythmical procession of the bays. The presence of this strip of wall contradicted the principle, established since Chartres and Bourges, that a Gothic structure should be reduced to piers, vaults and openings, and that the windows should of necessity fill the whole space between consecutive piers. In advanced

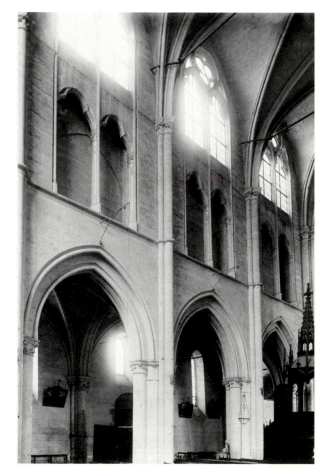

417. AGNETZ, N side of nave, ca. 1245

Gothic design surfaces of solid wall had from that moment ceased to exist; but they had persisted in other circles, and not only in Cistercian[38] or related workshops, for margins of wall are also found in many works of the Paris region, specially in the area between Paris and Beauvais, where Agnetz (Fig. 417) as early as the 1240s had given a first clear figuration of the formula, and where Chambly (Fig. 418) around 1260 applied the same principle with great refinement to a simpler, two-story elevation. Whatever significance these analogies may have had in connection with the early training of Jean des Champs, what is certain is that the margins of wall were to remain one of the constant features of his later style, as it appears for instance at the cathedral of Narbonne, begun in 1272.

Narbonne Cathedral is a gigantic building, as tall as Amiens; but as it was left unfinished and presents only a huge choir without nave, it looks rather like a southern Beauvais (Fig. 419). Both inside and outside the simplicity of Jean des Champs' late style is striking. The exterior is more compact than it would be in a Rayonnant

418. CHAMBLY, general interior view, begun ca. 1260

419. NARBONNE CATHEDRAL, view from SE, begun 1272

420. NARBONNE CATHE-
DRAL, choir

work of northern France: with its three groups of turreted buttresses rising above the chapels and linked by battlemented bridges, it has a touch of the military, most apt in one of the cities from which the crusade had been fought earlier in the century against the Cathars. The interior is even more remarkable (Fig. 420), for here the tight Rayonnant gridwork has almost vanished and the surfaces have become bare with simply a few thin lines drawn on them in places, sparingly: a single engaged shaft of small section rises up to meet the vaults. A most unexpected restraint marks the whole design and this colossal barren style, which was to be repeated at Limoges begun just a year later,[39] shows clearly how far Jean des Champs had moved away from the Rayonnant of the 1250s after some ten years in central and southern France, where his taste for simplicity and austerity had found exceptionally favorable soil.

THE NORTHERN EDGES OF BURGUNDY

During the last quarter of the thirteenth century northern French Gothic went on renewing itself with its accustomed vitality; but the most active centers of invention seem to have moved to the southeastern edges of the old Gothic lands, to an area which straddled the north of Burgundy and the extreme south of Champagne, in the triangle Troyes-Auxerre-Dijon, where the most imaginative works of that generation were to be produced, again oscillating between the richly linear and the austere. At Auxerre the new choir of the abbey church of Saint-Germain (Fig. 421), begun in 1277, bears the mark of its time and place. Along the outer walls can be recognized that common motif of the 1270s, the unbroken pattern of verticals linking wall arcade and window tracery (Fig. 422); and, in the vestibule which leads into the large octagonal axial chapel,[40] the extraordinary lightness of the supports shows what modern use could be made of the skeletal forms of earlier Burgundian Gothic.[41] But a novel feature appears, which sets the seal on these effects of linearity: the piers are now treated as the mere continuation of the arch moldings, extended downward without the distinguishing break of a capital. This fusion of elements had happened a few

437

years before, in an almost incidental manner, in the south porch of Saint-Urbain at Troyes and, in Paris, in arcadings on the south façade of the transept of Notre-Dame.[42] But at Auxerre in the choir of Saint-Germain the adoption of the continuous order becomes a principle consistently applied: in the responds of the axial chapel, in the thin columns which divide its entrance bay and, most spectacularly, in the main arcade of the choir, where the same uninterrupted moldings go up one pier, continue through the arch and descend on the face of the next pier, abolishing all distinction between pier and arch (Fig. 421).

This tendency to a reduced distinctness of forms was to become one of the common characteristics of Late Gothic. A shift was taking place in the way architecture was understood; and on this specific point, where a symptom of change can be so clearly perceived, it is interesting to note the likelihood of a suggestion from

421. AUXERRE, SAINT-GERMAIN, choir, begun 1277

422. AUXERRE, SAINT-GERMAIN, entrance to Lady Chapel (Ward Archive)

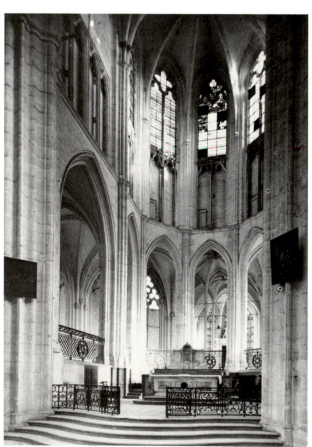

outside. For England had led the way in the adoption of the continuous order:[43] from about 1200 it had been used in English Cistercian buildings, at Fountains in the vast cellars of the west range, at Valle Crucis; and the first example of a nave with a continuously treated arcade was probably that of Llanthony (Fig. 423) near Hereford, a work of about 1210, Augustinian but closely related in concept and style with the Cistercian architecture of western England.[44] Some ten years later the vestibule to the chapter house (Fig. 425) of Chester abbey (the present cathedral) in the repetition of its roll-molded arches had given a strong accentuation to the theme. Were these English experiments known on the Continent? In Normandy without any doubt, as proved by the nave of Saint-Pierre at Jumièges (Fig. 424). But could the same be said of the major Gothic centers of northern France? Since the opening of the Westminster workshop in 1245, exchanges of masons between England and Ile-de-France had increased notably, and by 1260 some specifically English inventions were being adopted by northern French masters, as for instance the tierceron vault which was used

423. LLANTHONY PRIORY, nave, ca. 1205–1210

424. JUMIÈGES, SAINT-PIERRE, S side of nave, ca. 1230–1240

first—it would seem—at the crossing of Amiens cathedral (Fig. 426) and soon imitated at Chambly (Fig. 418) and Saint-Riquier.[45] In southern Champagne at that time contacts with England could be expected for in 1274, with the agreement of the king of France, Blanche of Artois, widow of the last count of Champagne, married the second son of Henry III of England, Edmund "Crouchback", Earl of Lancaster. And for ten years Crouchback took part discreetly in the governance of the county of Champagne, coming repeatedly to Troyes from England or Gascony.

Another remarkable case of the use of the continuous order on the largest scale, and again with overtones of Englishness, is the church of Mussy-sur-Seine (Fig. 427) on the very border between Champagne and Burgundy. Built right at the end of the century, it seems to have been the work of an architect from Troyes, named Geoffroy, who was resident in Mussy in 1297.[46] What would indicate some fresh contact with England, much more than the two-story elevation with passages—which was then as current in nearby Burgundy and Lorraine as in England or Normandy[47]—is the

425. CHESTER CATHEDRAL, vestibule to Chapter House, ca. 1215–1220

426. AMIENS CATHEDRAL, tierceron vault over crossing, ca. 1265

427. MUSSY-SUR-SEINE, begun ca. 1295

widely chamfered profiles, so conspicuous in the main arcade but also used in many other arches throughout the building. Being combined here with the principle of the continuous order, the slanting surfaces of these large chamfers extend down the full length of the piers, giving them an unusual prismatic form, unadorned except for the very thin shaft applied against them on both nave and aisle side.

The chamfered profile in arches was definitely a feature of English origin. First used in a main arcade by the Cistercian builders of Yorkshire (in the naves of Fountains [Fig. 428] and Kirkstall), it had become current by 1200 in all parts of England, spreading to Normandy in the 1230s but never becoming as universally popular there as in England.[48] From the early years of the thirteenth century the chamfering of arches had sometimes been associated in England with the continuous order, as at Llanthony (Fig. 423).[49] But as a rule in England and Normandy these arches of chamfered

441

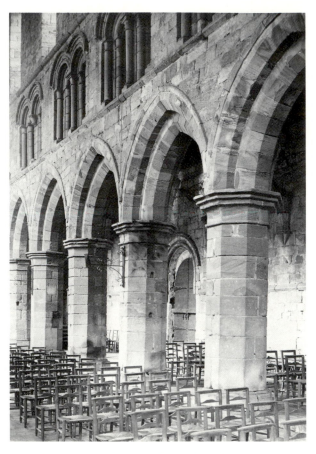

428. FOUNTAINS ABBEY, N arcade of nave, ca. 1135–1147

429. BRINKBURN PRIORY, N arcade of nave, begun ca. 1190–1200

section—like main arcade arches generally—had been built in two orders, with a clear separation between the two chamfers (Fig. 429); whereas at Mussy the arches are sheared off to a single broad chamfer of striking effect. These borrowed forms were being used here in a new and distinctively French manner, as part of a mode of surface treatment which even exceeds the spareness of Narbonne (Fig. 420). The austerity of the smooth flat planes, which at Mussy define the simplified forms of the structure, is relieved only by an overlay of thin lines: wall shafts, vault ribs and string courses, all reduced to the same thin cordlike section, drawn with the neatness of a diagram over the starkness of the underlying surfaces. So remarkable is that purity of effect that even without the enigma of its English affinities,[50] Mussy would stand out as a building of exceptional interest, for it shows that a most original style of bareness was present also in southern Champagne at the end of the thirteenth century; and it offers a telling contrast with the other major building of that area, the choir of Saint-Thibault-en-Auxois.

Situated 85 km (53 miles) to the south of Mussy-sur-Seine, Saint-Thibault (Fig. 430) was a priory church which was rebuilt in slow stages from ca. 1250, beginning with the north transept. The choir is attributed to the years around 1290, at least on two-thirds of its height (Fig. 431), clerestory and vaults having been added a little later and to a slightly altered design.[51] While at Mussy the formulation of style is at its most sparing, Saint-Thibault gives a display of the most insistent and regular of linear gridworks. With

430. SAINT-THIBAULT, view from NE, ca. 1290–1320

431. SAINT-THIBAULT, choir, ca. 1290–1320

the paneling of all its surfaces, with the multiplicity of its vertical shafts which run uninterrupted from clerestory to pavement, intersecting arches and cornices, cutting through quatrefoils and cusped circles, this amazing choir imposes a vision of tense vertical linearity which, although it did not have much following in France, happened to exercise an almost immediate attraction in England and—in a reversal of the movement of influence which had effected Auxerre and Mussy—set the London masters on the course

444

that led them to the elaboration of the Perpendicular style. For, going far beyond the kind of effects achieved in the vestibule of Saint-Germer, the choir and transept of Carcassonne or even the choir of Sées, Saint-Thibault was suggesting a new system of overall treatment of voids and solids alike, which was to reach its climax some forty years later in the tall cagelike casing of mullions of the choir of Gloucester Cathedral (Fig. 432).[52] Extreme severity on the one hand, linear abundance on the other, Mussy-sur-Seine and Saint-Thibault manifested in full clarity, in those final years of the thirteenth century, a contrast of expression which was to dominate the whole of the Late Middle Ages. More than a conflict of rationality versus fantasy, as had been the case in the early stages of the Rayonnant style, it was now rather an opposition between two tonalities of feeling, both arising out of the same belief in the power of affective values. Gothic architects had just discovered that the treatment of surfaces could be loaded with a new emotional content, and overinsistence or impoverishment were contrasting means of intensifying its expressiveness. In that sense these two buildings marked the opening of a new Gothic era.

EMERGENCE OF A NEW GOTHIC WORLD

At that same moment a change of even greater consequence was in the making. All over Europe new formulas of spaciousness were appearing in those peripheral countries which had until then taken no leading part in the development of Gothic architecture, but which were now demonstrating a sudden vitality. The phenomenon was complex in its sources. In many of those outlying areas—in western France, in southern France, in northwestern Germany—experiments had been made in Late Romanesque times tending to the achievement of enlarged interior space. These novel lines of development had lost much of their immediate relevance with the spread of Gothic forms, becoming incorporated into those regional variants of Gothic to which we have applied the name of peripheral styles; and although they preserved a potential for renewal, they had not managed to compete in attractiveness and authority with the formulas evolved in the northern part of France.

445

But after 1250 the situation became progressively reversed. This was due in part to the diffusion of northern French Gothic itself in its most modern, Rayonnant form, which injected some of its daring and inventiveness into those peripheral milieux. But the most decisive factor seems to have been everywhere the influence of the Mendicants, who by then were all over Europe (and even on their way to China), and whose aims were altering the very purposes of religious building. Born out of the revulsion and distress felt at the destructiveness of heresies—whether Waldensian or Albigensian—and of the repression they called forth, the new orders sent their members out on a missionary task, to live in poverty among the people in the growing towns, dependent on their alms and intent on calling forth in them, through the feeling and vividness of their preaching, a more personal form of devotion and a more spiritual attitude in everyday life. Being little concerned with liturgical splendor, the Mendicants had no need in their simplified services for the expanse of the chevet; it was now the nave of the church that had to be big, to hold the crowds they attracted, and unobstructed, to allow the voice of the preacher to carry everywhere. This concept of the preaching nave was purely functional and bore no specific structural implications. It could accommodate itself to a variety of architectural types: wide single or double naves, or any kind of enlarged triple-aisled arrangement, whether vaulted or unvaulted. Detached from any set form and leaving the widest freedom of choice, it was as a call for spaciousness as such that the program of Mendicant churches became a potent new force in the history of medieval architecture.

The area where this new convergence of elements can be most clearly observed is the Languedocian sector of southern France, in full growth after the upheavals that had accompanied the Albigensian Crusade and then closely linked with Aragonese Catalonia, on the other side of the Pyrenees. In this ensemble of countries, around the three centers of Toulouse, Narbonne and Barcelona, from the middle years of the thirteenth century a movement of active experimentation built up, which proved particularly inventive in its handling of architectural space. Even works executed in

446

the most orthodox Rayonnant style, such as the east end and transepts of Saint-Nazaire at Carcassonne, designed around 1270,[53] showed a striking combination of the Court Style of northern France with the new pervasive spaciousness of the South. While the exterior (Fig. 433), all tall mullioned windows and narrow buttresses, has a Sainte-Chapelle look, the interior (Fig. 434) is an unexpected variant of a hall space: a hall-transept structure, in which each transept is duplicated to the east on all its height by a continuous series of inter-communicating chapels, built as narrow double aisles and merging completely into the space of the transept.

That cohabitation in the same design of two stylistic systems of different origin was not a frequent occurrence, and the operative forces of the new movement were situated elsewhere. In the architectural production of the South, the tone was set in the second half of the thirteenth century less by the buildings that mirrored the fashions of northern France (such as Saint-Nazaire or the cathedrals of Jean des Champs) than by the simpler and more austere churches of the Mendicant Orders, which were multiplying in

432. GLOUCESTER CATHEDRAL,
N side of choir, begun 1337

433. CARCASSONNE, SAINT-NAZAIRE, begun ca. 1269

434. CARCASSONNE, SAINT-NAZAIRE, S transept with intercommunicating chapels, ca. 1269–1325

number as the century advanced and which were grounded in the indigenous building traditions. Wide aisleless naves had a long history in the south of France, where they had enjoyed a particular popularity in Late Romanesque days; and the nave of Toulouse Cathedral (Fig. 277, p. 305) in the first years of the thirteenth century had given a first and rather ponderous Gothic version of these simple spacious structures. In the hands of the Mendicants, who had to keep costs down and for that reason favored the lightest construction possible, new versions of the aisleless nave began to develop. Often they adopted the convenient and effective device of large pointed diaphragm arches carrying a simplified timber roof, reduced to its rafters. By the 1240s the Dominicans already were using this method of cheap construction over the nave of their church at Perpignan; and it quickly became widely diffused along the Mediterranean coast of Languedoc, as well as in Majorca and

448

Catalonia. These unvaulted Mendicant churches must have directly influenced the final design of the Benedictine priory-church of Lamourguier at Narbonne,[54] which as the only building of the type surviving in its original state, furnishes unique evidence of the spatial splendor that could be achieved by these simplest of means (Fig. 279, p. 307).

Within the same years the Mendicant Orders were also producing a modernized version of the vaulted aisleless nave, more elaborate in type than the nave of Toulouse Cathedral. This new formula, which seems to have appeared first at Barcelona in the church of the Dominicans, Santa Catalina,[55] begun about 1247, consisted in tall, rib-vaulted structures in which lateral chapels lodged between the buttresses opened onto the nave in a series of arches, giving very much the look of an aisled nave. The adoption of Rayonnant features—thin shafts and moldings, traceried windows—contributed to create a general impression of lightness and discreet elegance. The formula spread widely in the following decades and became enlarged to a very great size in the tall brick structures of the Mendicant churches of Toulouse, the Cordeliers and Jacobins, in the last quarter of the century.[56] In the church of the Cordeliers (Franciscans), destroyed in the late nineteenth century (Fig. 435), the vast single nave had acquired a considerable verticality, marked by the great height of its three-light Rayonnant windows dominating a zone of low chapels; and on the outside, deep arches bridging the space between the buttress heads (Fig. 436) gave that firm definition of volumes which can still be admired in the church of the Jacobins (Dominicans). Even taller than the Cordeliers, the Jacobin church is also more spacious, being structured as a huge double nave (Fig. 437), the vaults of which are supported centrally on a line of extremely tall columns (almost 21 m, or some 68 feet high) set so far apart that the unity of space remains unbroken.

What best summarizes this powerful new movement of architecture which swept through Languedoc and Catalonia is the dual climax represented by the antithetic designs of the cathedrals of Albi and Barcelona. Albi was begun in 1282 by a Dominican bishop, Bernard de Castanet, who was head of the Inquisition in

449

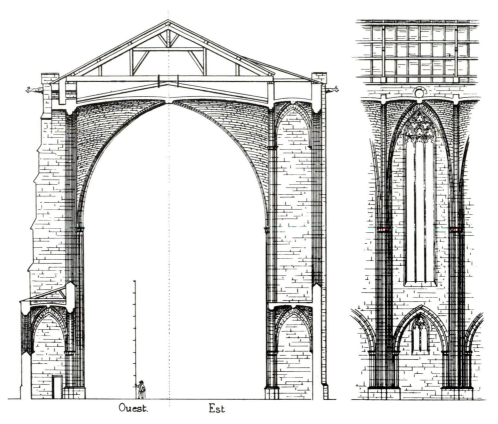

Ouest. Est

435. TOULOUSE, old church of the Cordeliers (now destroyed), ca. 1268–1305, section and elevation by T. King

436. TOULOUSE, church of the Jacobins, E half ca. 1275–1292

Languedoc. Supreme expression of the huge Languedocian aisle-less nave, it carries further than ever the principle of unification (Fig. 438), for the chapels which surround the whole building are made to reach the full height of the nave, merging with it into a single volume within and without. Inside (Fig. 439), the transverse walls which separate the chapels slice the inner space almost as dramatically as the diaphragm arches of Lamourguier; while on the outside, rising in one sheer block of red brick, the cathedral has the aspect of a fortress, down to the detail of the splayed footing of its turretlike buttresses.[58] At Barcelona the cathedral has none of that unified compactness and plays on spatial splendor according to a much more complex set of rules.[59] Laid out on a northern French type of plan derived from the cathedrals of Jean des Champs, the building mounts in a tiered arrangement of inner volumes based on the model of Bourges, but transformed in its proportions to fit it to the new feeling of widened Southern spaciousness (Fig. 440). With its immensely heightened aisles which force the upper stories right against the vault, reducing the clerestory in particular to truly dwarfish proportions, the vaults of ambulatory and choir seem to float far above the dimly lit space of that great diffused interior. As

437. TOULOUSE, JACOBINS, mostly 1275–1292; W bays later, heightening walls of earlier structure

438. ALBI CATHEDRAL, view from SE, begun 1282

Barcelona Cathedral was begun in 1298, it is clear that even before the end of the thirteenth century the new architecture of the South, by then firmly established on both sides of the Pyrenées, had reached the full range of its many modes of expression.[60]

A very similar conjunction of forces was at work in Germany, for it had had, like southern France, its own native line of early spatial experiments. In the last quarter of the twelfth century Westphalia in northwestern Germany had received from northern Italy one of the Late Romanesque formulas of spaciousness: that of the groin-vaulted hall church with its central space usually divided into large square bays. This formula had taken root around Münster and Dortmund shortly before Gothic reached the area.[61]

452

Changed and modernized in its appearance by the progressive diffusion of Gothic forms and of the Gothic handling of details, the north German hall church had diversified its range of effects in the 1220s and 1230s through contacts with Angevin Gothic, before turning to the Gothic of northern France for an even more up to date look. But the High Gothic format of narrow bays, as followed in the nave of Marburg-an-der-Lahn for instance, by tightening the sequence of the piers, tended to screen off the aisles from the central nave. It was only the impact of the Rayonnant that returned the hall church to its search for maximum spaciousness, for the adoption of the amplified form of the traceried window imposed a wide spacing of the piers, which resulted in complete lateral openness. The nave of Minden Cathedral (Fig. 441) in the 1270s shows the degree of spatial clarity that was being arrived at through this assimilation of the most recent variant of French Gothic into the pre-existing scheme of the hall church. By then structures of the Westphalian type had spread well beyond the limits of their prov-

439. ALBI CATHEDRAL, begun 1282

440. BARCELONA CATHEDRAL, begun 1298

ince of origin;[62] and their rapid acceptance throughout Germany was indicative of the swing in taste which was then in many countries prompting efforts toward increased interior spaciousness.

But the strength of this autonomous movement must not make us underestimate the importance of the part played in Germany by the Mendicants in the late thirteenth century. The stage became set for the development of Late Gothic only when the Mendicant builders brought in from the southern parts of Europe their techniques of unvaulted lightweight construction, their sense of freely flowing space, and the fluid merging of tall arches into smooth round piers.[63] While they sometimes built hall churches of a much lightened, unvaulted variety—which was to culminate at Colmar in the 1320s in the church of the Dominicans[64] in an effect of almost total dematerialization—they had also imported from Italy by the 1270s or 1280s[65] their spatialized version of the two-story basilican nave with enlarged arcade and reduced clerestory, which was to take a most striking form just after 1300 in the nave of the Franciscan church at Freiburg-im-Breisgau (Fig. 442). And this heightened and loosened airiness introduced into German architecture a potential for spatial liberation that was not present in the poised stability of the native kind of hall church.

441. MINDEN CATHEDRAL, hall nave, begun ca. 1270

That Italy could now supply models of modernity was also a new phenomenon; for it was only well after the middle of the thirteenth century, following the assimilation of several different waves of Gothic and under the pressure of the vast program of building made necessary by the growing number of Mendicant communities, that the realization had come to Italian builders that the new modes of constructional lightness held all kinds of untapped possibilities. The importance of this movement and its vitality are demonstrated in particular, toward the end of the century, by the churches which were being built by the Mendicant Orders in central Italy, from the Abruzzi to Tuscany.[66] Sometimes they used the form of the wide aisleless and continuous nave, unvaulted as at Siena, or cut by diaphragm arches as at Teramo in the Abruzzi; more often they turned to one or other of the hall-church types, either timber covered and almost barnlike as at Ascoli Piceno, or entirely vaulted on widely spaced piers as in the Franciscan church of S. Fortunato at Todi, which gave in the 1290s an image of perfectly unified and unencumbered space.

442. FREIBURG-IM-BREISGAU, church of the Franciscans, nave from N aisle, ca. 1310

Most of Tuscany was penetrated by these formulas, but Florence followed a somewhat different line.⁶⁷ Its great Mendicant churches were conceived on the basis of the Cistercian schema of two-storied naves, enlarged from within and offering in the simplicity of their compositional pattern the Gothic version of that Florentine clarity which had found its first expression, two hundred years before, in the impeccable precision of structure and decoration of the cathedral baptistery and of the façade and nave of S. Miniato. Begun around 1279, the Dominican church of S. Maria Novella (Fig. 443) has so transformed the type of the Cistercian nave by the widening of the bays and by the size given to the main arcade (which now eats up two-thirds of the total nave height) as to achieve an inner openness almost equal to that of hall churches. Soon diffused by the Mendicants all over Europe, this new version of the basilican elevation with tall arcade and small clerestory was to become, with a few variants of design,⁶⁸ one of the major architectural formulas of the Late Gothic age. The substance of walls and piers is so reduced in that large airy nave of S. Maria Novella that they seem to have lost all weight and to serve simply to define and enclose space. Its paper-thin quality gives to the main arcade a close analogy of effect (though hardly of size) with the nave arches of Saint-Pierre-de-Montmartre (Fig. 35), in which Gothic at the very start had stated its claim to the conquest of space through an extreme structural thinness. Some fifteen years later in the huge Franciscan church of S. Croce (Fig. 444), begun in 1294, Arnolfo di Cambio was to carry even further this process of enlargement and simplification. Dropping the very notion of vaulting and aiming at the vast emptiness of Constantinian naves, but in a spare Gothic idiom, he achieved through an unusual economy of means an overwhelming spatial presence. In the calm rhythm of its wide bays, drawn lightly but on a grand scale, in the serenity of the great rectangular form of its central nave, set off by the theatricality of a multipartitioned east end, S. Croce is pure colossal clear-cut space: an exceptional and most personal vision, but one of the most telling formulations of the new outlook of the time.

Even in England, where space had been so long held within the

443. FLORENCE, S. MARIA NOVELLA (Dominicans), begun ca. 1279

444. FLORENCE, S. CROCE (Franciscans), begun 1294

stiff structure of the Norman double wall, variously gothicized (Fig. 445), the end of the thirteenth century was the moment when tendencies toward the opening up of space became suddenly manifest; and here once more the main agents of change seem to have been the Mendicants. None of their churches of the thirteenth century has survived. But on the evidence of later buildings of theirs,[69] such as the mid-fourteenth century Austin Friars of London (which stood until 1940) or the fifteenth-century Blackfriars of Norwich (still in existence as St. Andrew's Hall), and on the further evidence of the new kind of large-scale parish churches[70] built for the new towns in the late thirteenth century or in the fourteenth and clearly modelled on early Friars' churches, it can be deduced with certainty that the Mendicants had brought to England before the end of the thirteenth century two major types of structures, both lightweight, thin walled, wide and unvaulted. One was the hall type, which seems to have been dominant in London and southern England; and the other, more common in the Midlands and northern England, was that same Southern type of two-story elevation with tall arcades which was being imported at the same moment into southern Germany. In England this second type appears in a variant characterized by the use of two clerestory windows per bay;[71] and proof that this particular formula existed as early as the last quarter of the thirteenth century is supplied by the nave of the collegiate church of Howden,[72] to the south of York (Fig. 446), which was under construction by 1290 at the latest and in which the duplication of the windows and the great enlargement of the arcade story indicate the direct imitation of a Mendicant prototype, probably one of the Friars' churches of York.

Another building of that turn of the century which marks the break away from the traditional approach of earlier English Gothic, answering the call for spaciousness in a most sophisticated manner, is the choir of Bristol Cathedral.[73] This large vaulted hall choir (Fig. 447) reveals in every part the hand of a master: in the merging movement of arches, vaults and piers; in the wealth of patterns which put a distinctive stamp on each component of the structure; and in the multiplicity of unexpected features that are incorporated into the design, both in matters of building engineering and in the art of marshalling visual effects. Behind the strong personality of a great artist can be recognized close affinities with certain trends of London court art, as in the lierne pattern of the main vault, as well as a surprising familiarity with Continental works, and not in the usual northern French line but rather from western France: the hall church concept itself perhaps, drawing on Poitiers Cathedral (Fig. 71, p. 75); the system of passages running, as at Poitiers, at the base of the aisle windows; the purely Angevin type of the aisle vaults, which are actually ribbed barrels with short penetrations in the Airvault manner (Fig. 283, p. 311), but turned at right angles to the axis of the church—as had also been done in Late Romanesque buildings in west and southwest France.[74] Whether this highly individual vision of hall space was actually suggested by the lightweight hall structures then being built in southern England by the Friars or was an autonomous inspiration arising in the mind of an architect who had through his training acquired a very wide

445. SALISBURY CATHEDRAL, choir, begun 1220

446. HOWDEN, N side of nave, ca. 1290–1310

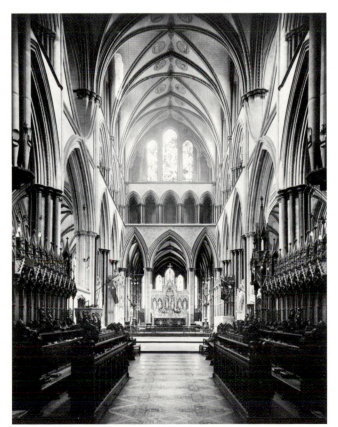

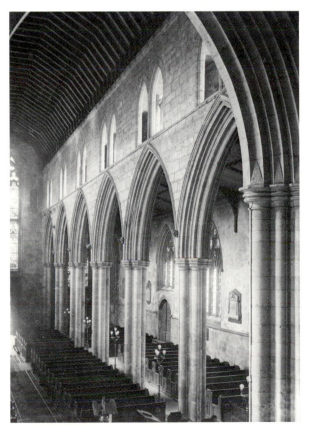

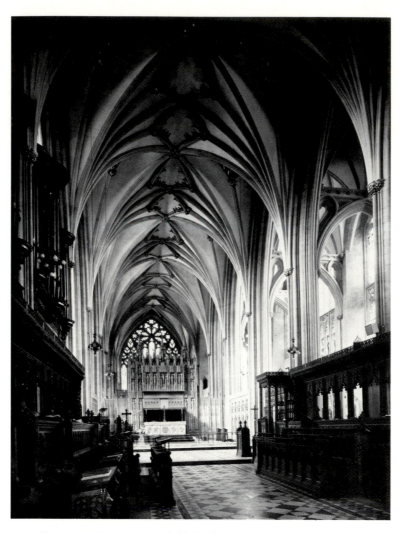

447. Bristol Cathedral, hall choir, ca. 1298–1330

range of references,[75] either way the choir of Bristol must be viewed as another significant indication of the active interest taken in spatial speculations by the new generation of architects who were then coming to the fore in England.

So it was that throughout western Europe—in southern France, Spain and Italy as in Germany and England or, for that matter, Flanders[76]—an urge for spaciousness was felt in the late years of the thirteenth century as overwhelmingly as it had been felt in the concentrated limits of Parisian Ile-de-France at the time of Saint-Martin-des-Champs and of Suger's Saint-Denis, when it had brought into being Gothic itself a century and a half before. But this time the situation was reversed: alone in western Europe, northern France and those areas still under the spell of its immediate influence were left untouched by the tide of renewal. There is even clear evidence that Rayonnant orthodoxy stiffened more and more in the northern half of France under the centralizing rule of Philippe-le-Bel (1285–1314). Close to the monarchy, the architecture of the end of the thirteenth century can be typified by a new royal foundation, the priory church (now destroyed) of Saint-Louis at Poissy (Fig. 448), begun in 1298,[77] an academic codification of early Rayonnant forms which even in the 1260s would have appeared unprogressive. There was not more novelty in the newly rising choir of Orléans,[78] last of the great cathedral founda-

448. POISSY, destroyed abbey church of Saint-Louis, begun 1298, drawing by R. de Cotte (Paris, Bibl. nat.)

tions of northern France; and to the southeast of Paris, where Mussy and Saint-Thibault were giving such convincing signs of renewal, these two avant-garde buildings remained isolated and without descent, as Burgundy settled into the calm conventionality of the nave of Saint-Bénigne (Fig. 449) at Dijon.[79] The power of invention that had driven forward the masters of northern France and given them for so long their position of pre-eminence had arrived at a point where it suddenly failed, and the first era of Gothic came to an end.

But by then history had already taken a new turn: artistic initiative was passing to other lands and a new architectural world was emerging, that of Late Gothic. Capturing space by other means and less intent on structuring it, the builders of this new age were also to handle differently the linear element intrinsic to Gothic, making it flow in streams or weaving it into intricate nettings. And if it was from the south through the Mendicants that the feeling for space had been renewed, it was conversely from the north, from England, that the new networks came: these were the two sources

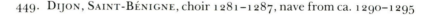

449. DIJON, SAINT-BÉNIGNE, choir 1281–1287, nave from ca. 1290–1295

of Late Gothic architecture.[80] The English sense of pattern, which had been so notable in architecture since the mid-twelfth century and which went far back into the Saxon past, reached in the first forty years of the fourteenth century a climax of freedom and fantasy which was to have a powerful impact on the Continent. But in a less open and fluid form than was to become the fashion by 1320,[81] that new way of playing with lines and multiplying them for their own sake as much as for their ability to insinuate themselves around space and enclose it, was already fully defined in the Chapter House of York and the presbytery of Exeter (Fig. 401) in the late 1280s or, just after 1300, in the chapter house of Wells. Clearly these final years of the thirteenth century were a time of decisive reappraisal, when new approaches were being tried out to give to architecture a new subtlety and a new forcefulness: the feeling must have been abroad that Gothic was starting afresh. A new cycle of radical experiments was building up, similar in its impetus to the one which in the 1130s had launched the original Gothic movement, inspired by the same discovery of the beauty of extreme spaciousness and of extreme lightness, and soon equipped in its turn with the tool of a new linearity.

What was happening in an almost accidental manner in that rapid gathering of new forces was in fact nothing less than a relaunching of the Gothic movement; and the new sets of problems which then appeared, oriented by a new sensibility, were to exercize the inventiveness of builders all over Europe for the next two hundred years. That new age was to be more affective than analytical, more concerned with merging forms and movements than with explaining them in terms of clearly ordained units, more intent than before on effects of totality. And the cycle of Late Gothic was also to proceed at a cadence other than that of the earlier age, conditioned by other structures of thought and feeling: it was not going to repeat that quick succession of systematic reassessments which had propelled northern French Gothic along its course through the twelfth and thirteenth centuries.

Notes

1. The choir of Soissons was ready for use in 1212, which means that it must have been started ca. 1200 at the latest. See Chapter VI above, p. 227.

2. See H. Focillon, *The Art of the West in the Middle Ages,* 2nd ed., London and New York, 1969, I, 55, n.2. No rib-vaulted building of northern Italy can be dated before 1090. The Italian rib vaults are technically very different from the rib vaults of the English series, being always domed and the shafts which receive the diagonal ribs being in general diagonally set. It seems therefore out of the question that one of the series could be derived from the other: they must have developed separately under the stimulus of some common source of inspiration. But in Normandy, from ca. 1120, some buildings such as the chapter house of Jumièges or the excavated Romanesque choir of Evreux, give the impression that the contact has been established between the two series: see my article "Diagonality and Centrality in Early Rib-Vaulted Architectures," *Gesta*, XV, 1976, 15–25.

3. On this vexed question, see the convincing remarks of E. Gall, in *Zeitschrift für Kunstgeschichte*, XVIII, 1955, 86.

4. J. Bilson, "The Beginnings of Gothic Architecture," *Journal of the Royal Institute of British Architects,* 3rd series, VI, Nov. 1898–Oct. 1899, 259–319; *id.*, "Durham Cathedral: The Chronology of its Vaults," *Archaeological Journal,* LXXIX, 1922, 101–160. See also my article: "Le projet premier de Durham: Voûtement partiel ou voûtement total?," *Urbanisme et architecture, études écrites et publiées en l'honneur de Pierre Lavedan*, Paris, 1954, 41–49, in which I draw attention to the importance of the non-

Norman elements in the stylistic make-up of Durham. These elements are actually of two kinds, some being of Saxon or "Overlap" origin, while the others are of a more exotic nature and seem to point to Spanish sources.

5. See: J. Fossey, *Monographie de la cathédrale d'Evreux*, Evreux, 1898, 20–24; G. Bonnenfant, *La cathédrale d'Evreux*, Paris, 1925, 9–13 and 28–32.

6. This dating results from a reinterpretation of the evidence presented in Y. M. Froidevaux, "L'abbatiale de Lessay," *Les monuments historiques de la France*, 1958, 139–149, which remains the most penetrating study so far written on Lessay. The style of the building being incompatible with a date earlier than 1100, all the mentions which occur in documents of the eleventh century must refer to an older church built at the time of the foundation of the monastery (between 1056 and 1064).

7. G. Lanfry, "La salle capitulaire romane de l'abbaye de Jumièges," *Bulletin monumental*, XCIII, 1934, 323–340.

8. The first western examples of that Islamic series are the large rib vaults of the great mosque of Cordova, dating from the time of al-Hakam II, 961–965. The two little mosques of Toledo (i.e. Bib Mardom, better known as the church of El Cristo de la Luz, and las Tornerías) are a little later, being of the last years of the tenth century; and the very small scale of their vaults makes the ribbing there essentially ornamental. See M. Gómez-Moreno, *El arte árabe español hasta los Almohades. Arte mozárabe* (Ars Hispaniae, 3), Madrid, 1951, 110–140 and 201–212. At the origins of this series must certainly be placed Mesopotamian or Syrian prototypes, which would also explain the eleventh and twelfth century rib vaults of Armenia.

9. Intersecting ribs were also applied by Romanesque builders to vaults of the dome or cloister-vault types; e.g. at the north tower of Bayeux Cathedral (perhaps ca. 1077), in the ruined Tour Charlemagne at Tours (the north transept tower of Saint-Martin, probably not earlier than ca. 1120), and in the towers of Cormery and Loches. This series is likely to relate with earlier Mozarabic examples, such as San Millán de la Cogolla (Logroño).

10. On these arches of brick incorporated into the concrete of Roman vaults, see: A. Choisy, *L'art de bâtir chez les Romains*, Paris, 1873, 74–80, pl.VII–IX; G. T. Rivoira, *Architettura romana*, Milan, 1921, 178–184, 204, 249–253, 286–287; G. Lugli, *La tecnica edilizia romana*, Rome, 1957, I, 684–686; A. Boëthius and J. B. Ward Perkins, *Etruscan and*

more, 1970, 510–511.

11. The sharpest criticism of Viollet-le-Duc's theory was given in P. Abraham, *Viollet-le-Duc et le rationalisme médiéval*, Paris, 1934; but the postulates on which that criticism was based, concerning the functioning of masonry vaults, have themselves been largely invalidated in recent years by the application of modern methods of structural analysis. For a more up to date evaluation of the behavior of Gothic vaults, see: J. Heyman, "On the Rubber Vaults of the Middle Ages, and Other Matters," *Gazette des Beaux-Arts*, LXXI, 1968, 177–188; R. Mark, "Structural Analysis of Gothic Cathedrals," *Scientific American*, CCXXVII (5), Nov. 1972, 90–99; R. Mark, J. F. Abel and K. O'Neill, "Photo-elastic and Finite-element Analysis of a Quadripartite Vault," *Experimental Mechanics*, XIII, 1973, 322–329; K. D. Alexander, R. Mark, and J. F. Abel, "The Structural Behavior of Medieval Ribbed Vaulting," *Journal of the Society of Architectural Historians*, XXXVI, 1977, 241–251.

12. J. Fitchen, *The Construction of Gothic Cathedrals. A Study of Medieval Vault Erection*, Oxford, 1961, has thrown a new light on these questions. They appear now to have been of decisive importance in the elaboration of the Gothic methods of vaulting.

13. The early examples are reviewed in K. A. C. Creswell, *A Short Account of Early Muslim Architecture*, Harmondsworth and Baltimore, 1958, 102–104. A very slight pointing had appeared in a Syrian church of the second half of the sixth century, Qasr Ibn Wardan, and it was also in Syria that this arch form was revived in the first years of the eighth century (Great Mosque of Damascus, audience hall of Qusayr ᶜAmra, between 705 and 715); the pointing became more marked and this form spread to Mesopotamia and Persia in the second half of the eighth century, then to Egypt and Tunisia in the ninth. The pointed arch was probably a schematisation of the parabolic curve used by Sassanian builders since the early third century for the construction without centering of domes and barrel vaults (e.g. the huge *iwan* of the Tāq-i-Kisrā at Ctesiphon).

14. Recent expositions of the Montecassino hypothesis can be found in: K. J. Conant, "The Pointed Arch—Orient to Occident," *Palaeologia*, VII, 1959, 269–70; J. H. Harvey, "The Origins of Gothic Architecture: Some Further Thoughts," *Antiquaries Journal*, XLVIII, 1968, 87–99 (particularly 89–90); K. J. Conant and H. M. Willard, "Early Examples of the Pointed Arch and Vault in Romanesque Architecture," *Viator*, II, 1971,

203–210. The redating of the porch of S. Angelo in Formis is the result of a study of the frescoes which decorate it: on the façade wall were found two layers of painting, the more recent one (which corresponds to the present pointed vaults of the porch) clearly dating from the late twelfth century, while the earlier one (the original late eleventh century scheme of decoration) had been made for a porch with round-headed vaults and arches. See P. Anker and K. Berg, "The Narthex of S. Angelo in Formis," *Acta Archaeologica*, (Copenhagen), XXIX, 1958, 95–110. The possibility of a direct Sicilian transmission of the pointed arch to Burgundy has been suggested by W. Krönig, *The Cathedral of Monreale*, Palermo, 1965, 165 and 276, n. 120. In the two oldest Sicilian churches of Norman date, the cathedral of Mazara (founded between 1086 and 1093) and the cathedral of Catania (begun between 1086 and 1090 as the abbey church of S. Agata), the apses are decorated on the outside by tall blind pointed arches, purely Islamic in character, which are considered in both cases to belong to the original late eleventh century structure. The original state of the nave of these two churches is not known, since they were rebuilt in the twelfth century following an earthquake; but it is most likely that these early naves were characterized already by pointed arcades of the type commonly found in twelfth-century Sicily (e.g. Messina or Cefalù around 1130).

15. The thorough analysis made by Francis Salet of the masonry and of all details of construction in the south transept of Cluny has revealed that the first pointed arches (the entrance arches to the chapels) are not connected with the earliest type of masonry, but belong to a second stage, which followed very soon after and can be dated in the early 1090s. The final design of Cluny corresponds to a third stage in the work of the south transept and should be dated later in the 1090s. See F. Salet, "Cluny III," *Bulletin monumental*, CXXVI, 1968, 235–292, particularly 264 (on the chapel arches). This chronology is at variance with that given by K. J. Conant, *Cluny: Les églises et la maison du chef d'ordre*, Cambridge, Mass., 1968.

16. See the figures given by P. Abraham, *Viollet-le-Duc et le rationalisme médiéval*, Paris, 1934, 14. The slightly more pointed "third point" arch of the thirteenth century achieves a reduction of 25 percent.

17. Reading Abbey may have been the source for the earliest pointed arches in England, if Stukeley's reconstruction of a pointed barrel over the chapter house can be trusted. In 1128 the first Cistercian mission came to England and Waverley (founded in that year) may have

been another point of diffusion of Burgundian methods of construction. And, of course, Durham may also have had direct contacts with Cluny.

18. On the destroyed church of Notre-Dame at Soissons, in addition to Tavernier's engravings in the *Voyage Pittoresque de la France . . .*, Paris, vol. VIII, 1792, see P. Héliot, "Les églises de l'abbaye Notre-Dame à Soissons et l'architecture romane dans le nord de la France capétienne," *Revue belge d'archéologie et d'histoire de l'art*, XXXVII, 1968, 49–88. Tavernier's wash drawing gives the impression that the original stone vault of the choir and apse may have been later replaced by a wooden one; but the change-over from a three-storied nave to a two-storied east end indicates that the choir was intended from the start to be barrel vaulted. The precocious appearance of the pointed arch in the Soissons-Compiège area is probably due to the proximity of early Cistercian foundations: Igny (1126), Ourscamp (1129), Longpont (1132).

19. See L. E. Deladreue and Mathon, "Histoire de l'abbaye royale de Saint-Lucien (ordre de Saint Benoît)," *Mémoires de la Société académique d'archéologie, sciences et arts du département de l'Oise*, VIII (1871–73), 257–385 and 541–704. The lithograph, entitled "Première vue des ruines de l'église de l'abbaye de Saint-Lucien près Beauvais," is inserted between 256 and 257; it was made in 1864 after a drawing by Augustin Van den Berghe.

20. See: E. Gall, *Niederrheinische und normännische Architektur im Zeitalter der Frühgotik*, I, Berlin, 1915; J. Bony, "La technique normande du mur épais à l'époque romane," *Bulletin monumental*, XCVIII, 1939, 153–188: an old study which needs to be updated on a number of points (no clerestory passage existed in the Romanesque nave of Coutances; Cerisy-la-Forêt cannot be earlier than the 1080s; on the question of origins, see note 22 below).

21. This refers to the classic type of Gothic triforium, characterized by a passage running in the thickness of the wall: the type which starts at Laon in the 1160s and becomes the rule, from the mid-1190s, in French Gothic architecture. A more detailed explanation of the different types of triforium used in Early Gothic buildings can be found in Chap. III, n. 20, p. 480. First used by Gervase of Canterbury in his description of Canterbury cathedral (written in the 1180s), the term "triforium" is a latinization of the Old French word *trifoire*, which may be a contraction of the Latin *transforatum*, meaning "pierced right through" (or "in openwork"). In modern terminology, triforium signifies a zone of small openings (or, at the extreme, a blind arcading) inserted in an interior elevation below

the clerestory stage and corresponding on the exterior to a zone of roof.

22. The origins of the thick-wall system was a problem I had not investigated in my article of 1939 (see note 20 above). When I later researched it, I soon found that this method of heavy but open construction went back to Late Antique prototypes, such as the octagon of S. Aquilino in Milan (part of the S. Lorenzo complex) and had been revived in Italy (baptistery of Florence, begun in 1059) shortly before the appearance of thick-wall construction in Normandy. The same conclusions were reached independently by P. Héliot, "Les antécédents et les débuts des coursières anglo-normandes et rhénanes," *Cahiers de civilisation médiévale,* II, 1959, 429–443. On the crucial problem of the Florence baptistery and its sources, see W. W. Horn, "Das Florentiner Baptisterium," *Mitteilungen des kunsthistorischen Institutes in Florenz,* V, 1937–1940, 100–151; reprinted in W. Horn, *Die Fassade von Saint-Gilles. Das Florentiner Baptisterium,* Berkeley, 1974. It seems to me most likely that the Florentine revival had been preceded, perhaps some twenty years before, by a first revival in the region of Milan; and this would explain the scattered experiments found in Trier, Bernay or Jumièges from ca. 1050, as well as the northern Italian series of double-shell apses of the early twelfth century.

23. After that date two different variants of the double-wall structure were used, one at Soissons (choir of the old abbey church of Notre-Dame), another at Tournai (nave of the cathedral).

24. For the original choir of Saint-Etienne at Beauvais, see the plan published by J. P. Paquet, "Les tracés directeurs des plans de quelques édifices du Domaine Royal au Moyen-Age," *Les Monuments Historiques de la France,* 1963, 71. On Romsey, see *The Victoria History of Hampshire,* IV, 1911, 460–468 (plan fac. 460); and on the whole problem raised, see M. F. Hearn, "The Rectangular Ambulatory in English Mediaeval Architecture," *Journal of the Society of Architectural Historians,* XXX, 1971, 187–208.

25. This new English version of the geometric style is particularly well represented ca. 1140 in the Oise valley (e.g. Villers-Saint-Paul) and in the Vexin Français, i.e., the little district situated just north of the Seine between Pontoise and the border of Normandy.

26. Burgundian pointed arch and Anglo-Norman vaulting met in England, probably for the first time, when the nave of Durham was vaulted; they met again in Cistercian churches such as Kirkstall Abbey in Yorkshire and a little later in the nave of Malmesbuy in Wiltshire. All that resulted was a pointed rib-vaulted version of current Romanesque.

27. Rib-vaulting was simply the most convenient method of vaulting for the time; hence the pioneering rôle it played in the countries of northern Europe which had preserved until a late date the practice of timber covering.

28. The naves of Jumièges (1052–1067) and Mont-Saint-Michel (1063 ff.) represent in Normandy the climax of that early Romanesque constructional system. Even though in Normandy itself it was soon to be replaced in all major buildings by the new technique of hollow-wall construction, throughout the rest of northern France thin-wall construction remained supreme. A good example of that technical conservatism in the immediate vicinity of Paris is the nave of Deuil, probably no earlier than the 1120s, in which the type of the mid-eleventh century nave of Saint-Germain-des-Prés was repeated almost unchanged.

29. This strengthening of the piers became particularly accentuated in a number of buildings of the 1150s and 1160s. Following the experiment in maximum reinforcement which had been made at Sens (and a little later at Senlis) on the basis of an alternating system of piers, powerful groupings of five shafts in vigorous projection were adopted for all piers in the nave of Cambrai Cathedral (destroyed at the time of the French Revolution), in the church (also destroyed) of Saint-Evremond at Creil, at Courmelles and Coulonges to the south of Soissons, and in the nave of Saint-Germer, followed around 1170 by Chars in the Vexin and le Bourg-Dun near Dieppe. This mode of pier reinforcement, with the strong emphasis it places on the bay rhythm, persisted in the sector to the north-west of Paris into the thirteenth century, as is shown by the nave of Rouen Cathedral.

30. E. Lefèvre-Pontalis, "Les campagnes de construction de Notre-Dame d'Etampes," *Bulletin monumental*, LXXIII (1909), 5–31, attributed that nave to the period ca. 1130–1135; in "Etampes. Eglise Notre-Dame," *Congrès archéologique de France*, LXXXII (Paris), 1919, 6–29, he had become a little less specific and simply stated that the nave was standing by 1140. He based his dating on the style of the capitals, which relate clearly with the earliest types used at Saint-Martin-des-Champs. Nothing has invalidated that reasoning. A date in the mid-1130s is further supported by the fact that the capitals of Etampes nave appear to antedate those of the north tower of Chartres cathedral, themselves generally dated between 1134 and 1145. The present vaults of the nave are a modern rebuilding, but the upper capitals, which are original, show that the nave had always been planned with a type of groin-vaults similar to that of the

471

aisles, with the same wide pointed formerets and transverse arches. This method of groin vaulting indicates without any doubt direct contacts with Burgundy, specifically with the beginnings of the Avallon group. But the lightness of the structure, of the piers in particular, is a feature unknown in Burgundy. That was a properly Ile-de-France element, which differentiated clearly the production of the Paris region not only from that of Normandy but from that of Burgundy too. It must be noted that the large clerestory windows which now light the nave represent a mid-nineteenth century alteration.

31. See S. McK. Crosby, *L'abbaye royale de Saint-Denis,* Paris, 1953, 24–56.

32. A rich plastic style, characterized by the use of heavy soffit rolls, had been developing in England since about 1120, particularly in Hampshire: choir of Romsey, nave of Christchurch. Its influence had soon been felt in Normandy.

33. The nave of the destroyed cathedral of Cambrai should be added to this list: an excellent drawing by Van der Meulen leaves little doubt in this respect (see Fig. 128).

34. The idea seems to have come from England and Normandy: quadrant arches had been built under the lateral roofs in the nave of Durham cathedral (tribune story, ca. 1125) and at La Trinité at Caen (remodeled and vaulted ca. 1145). But it is very difficult to know whether these arches were meant to prop up the walls or were conceived simply as supports for the roofs, as was the case at Norwich. The functional intention may have developed only in the Ile-de-France context of technical urgency.

35. On this point, see Chap. V, p. 183 and n. 24, p. 493.

36. From the geographical distribution of the earliest examples, it seems evident that the exterior flying buttress was a Parisian invention, and it is likely to have been used first in the nave of Notre-Dame, begun between 1175 and 1180. See Chap. V, pp. 179–186.

Notes: Chapter II (pp. 45–76)

1. See K. J. Conant, "The Third Church at Cluny," *Medieval Studies in Memory of A. Kingsley Porter,* Cambridge, Mass., 1939, II, 327–357; *id., Cluny, Les églises et la maison du chef d'ordre,* Cambridge, Mass., 1968.

2. The height of the main arcade was even greater originally, since the pavement of the narthex was 1.80 meters (nearly six feet) lower: see

S. McK. Crosby, *L'abbaye royale de Saint-Denis,* Paris, 1953, 41.

3. See E. Lefèvre-Pontalis, "Eglise de Saint-Martin-des-Champs à Paris," *Congrès archéologique de France,* LXXXII (Paris), 1919, 106–126; J. Ache, "Le prieuré royal de Saint-Martin-des-Champs, ses rapports avec l'Angleterre et les débuts de l'architecture gothique," *Centre international d'Etudes Romanes, Bulletin trimestriel,* 1963:1, 5–15.

4. The layout of the outer walls and outer piers indicates clearly that a different type of hemicycle had been planned at first: the central part of the choir was meant to have a circuit of eleven bays, instead of seven. The design was probably altered when the old apse of the eleventh century, which had been preserved during the first stage of the works, was pulled down in the second stage of the rebuilding. In view of its more advanced style, this second stage cannot be placed before 1140 or 1145.

5. The destroyed abbey church of Saint-Lucien at Beauvais has often been added to this list, on the basis of a somewhat tentative reconstruction by Ernst Gall; but recent excavations, incompletely published, have proved that Saint-Lucien had originally one chapel only, in the axis of the church. The other examples of continuous chapels, such as Déols or Avénières, are later than 1140.

6. On Cluny II, see K. J. Conant, "Les églises de Cluny à l'époque de Saint Odon et de Saint Odilon," *A Cluny, Congrès scientifique, fêtes et cérémonies liturgiques en l'honneur des saints abbés Odon et Odilon, 9–11 juillet 1949,* Dijon, 1950, 37–43; *id.,* "Medieval Academy Excavations at Cluny, VIII. Final Stages of the Project," *Speculum* XXIX, 1954, 5–9.

7. E. Fels, "Saint-Sever-sur-l'Adour," *Congrès archéologique de France,* CII (Bordeaux-Bayonne), 1939, 345–364, remains of basic value but has to be corrected in its dating of the different parts of the structure, following more recent investigations, see: J. Lauffray, "Les chevets-martyria de Saint-Sever-sur-l'Adour et de Sorde-l'Abbaye (Landes)," *Cahiers archéologiques,* XVI, 1966, 107–119; J. Cabanot, "Les premières étapes de la construction de l'abbatiale de Saint-Sever au XIe siècle," *Bulletin de la Société de Borda,* XCII, 1968, 307–320.

8. On Fontgombault, see L. Demenais, "L'église abbatiale de Fontgombault (Indre)," *Bulletin monumental,* LXXX, 1921, 91–117. On Saint-Laumer (or Lomer), see F. Lesueur, "L'église abbatiale Saint-Lomer de Blois," *Bulletin monumental,* LXXXII, 1923, 36–65. Begun in 1138, the choir of Saint-Laumer was built very slowly in several campaigns and completed only in 1186. At the level of the ambulatory and chapels the construction appears to date mostly from the 1150s and early 1160s.

473

9. E. Panofsky, *Abbot Suger on the Abbey Church of St. Denis and its Art Treasures,* Princeton, 1946, 100–101, lines 18–21.

10. On Saint-Denis, the reliable work remains S. McK. Crosby, *L'abbaye royale de Saint-Denis,* Paris, 1953. J. Formigé, *L'abbaye royale de Saint-Denis. Recherches nouvelles,* Paris, 1960, adds some new elements of information resulting from further excavating but his reconstructions are often too hypothetical to be trusted. Excellent plans of the east end of Saint-Denis, analysing its geometric construction, are found in S. McK. Crosby, "Crypt and Choir Plans at Saint-Denis," *Gesta,* V, 1966, 4–8.

11. This was the interpretation of E. Viollet-le-Duc, *Dictionnaire raisonné de l'architecture française du XIe au XVIe siècle,* Paris, VII, 1864, 162 (s.v. "Pilier"); still repeated in M. Aubert, *Notre-Dame de Paris, sa place dans l'histoire de l'architecture du XIIe au XIVe siècle,* Paris, 2nd ed., 1929, 74–75. A confusion between pre-Romanesque and Romanesque is the source of that misinterpretation.

12. E. Panofsky, *Abbot Suger . . . ,* 90–93 and 213: Suger even thought of having marble columns shipped from Rome to meet these requirements.

13. To S. Costanza should be added, in the early Christian period, the baptistery of Nocera near Naples, as well as a number of basilicas in North Africa, for instance at Tigzirt, ca. 450. A few scattered examples appear at the beginning of the Romanesque period, e.g., the choir of S. Pere de Roda in Catalonia, dedicated in 1022. In the twelfth century, shortly before its adoption at Sens, the twin column was revived independently at Jerusalem (hemicycle of the choir of the St. Sepulcher, dedicated in 1149) and at Trani in southern Italy. Under the influence of Sens, this type of pier became quite popular in the early Gothic period: between 1150 and 1210 its use can be traced to more than twenty buildings.

14. In comparison, the width of the central space at Saint-Denis is about 10.30 meters (not quite 34 feet).

15. Originally an abbey church, Saint-Père-en-Vallée has become now a parish church and its name has been changed to Saint-Pierre. Begun by Abbot Foucher, elected in 1150 or 1151, the new choir seems to have been completed by ca. 1175: see P. Héliot and G. Jouven, "L'église Saint-Pierre de Chartres et l'architecture du moyen âge," *Bulletin archéologique du Comité des travaux historiques et scientifiques,* new ser., VI, 1970, 117–177.

16. On Avranches, see R. Branner, *La cathédrale de Bourges et sa place dans l'architecture gothique,* Paris-Bourges, 1962, 165.

17. F. Salet, "La cathédrale de Sens et sa place dans l'histoire de l'architecture médiévale," *Comptes-rendus de l'Académie des inscriptions et belles-lettres,* 1955, 182–187.

18. Henri le Sanglier (archbishop of Sens from 1122), who is given as the initiator of the rebuilding of the cathedral, died in 1142 and was succeeded by Hugues de Toucy (1142–1168). On the two designs of Sens, see R. Branner, *Burgundian Gothic Architecture,* London, 1960, 180–182; and K. W. Severens, "The Early Campaign at Sens, 1140–1145," *Journal of the Society of Architectural Historians,* XXIX, 1970, 97–107.

19. That colossal width already characterized the Romanesque cathedral of Chartres, built by Bishop Fulbert after the fire of 1020. It is impossible to know whether the plan of the Romanesque cathedral of Chartres or the first design of Sens were in any way connected with Roman models. At any rate, excavations have uncovered in Rome the foundations of four large ambulatory basilicas without transept and remarkably spacious, all dating from the fourth century: see R. Krautheimer, "Mensa-Coemeterium-Martyrium," *Cahiers archéologiques,* XI, 1960, 15–40; *id., Early Christian and Byzantine Architecture* (Pelican History of Art), Harmondsworth and Baltimore, 1965, 31–32.

20. On the buildings of western France, see A. Mussat, *Le style gothique de l'ouest de la France (XIIe–XIIIe siècles),* Paris, 1963. Concerning Saint-Loup-de-Naud, on the basis of a donation made to the priory in 1167, the west bays of the church have sometimes been dated as late as ca. 1170: e.g. F. Salet, "Saint-Loup-de-Naud," *Bulletin monumental,* XCII, 1933, 129–169; but the donation does not seem to have been related with the start of that campaign of construction which, on the evidence of style, would seem to be datable in the 1150s.

21. Sens was conceived on a much larger scale than the choir of Saint-Denis: while at Saint-Denis the double aisles of the choir make a width of 7.30 meters (some 24 feet) at their widest, at Sens the single aisle alone is 6.70 meters (22 feet) wide. As for the height of the ambulatory, while at Saint-Denis it ranges around 7.60 meters (25 feet), at Sens it is 12.10 meters (40 feet)

22. The rebuilding of the cathedral of Angers was started by Bishop Normand de Doué, 1149–1153; see J. Bilson, "Les voûtes de la nef de la cathédrale d'Angers," *Congrès archéologique de France,* LXXVII (Angers-Saumur), 1910, II, 203–223. The nave of Angers is made up of three square bays 15.45 meters wide (50′ 8″).

23. The term *Hallenkirchen* or "hall-churches" refers to a type of

structure in which the aisles are nearly (and sometimes exactly) of the same height as the central nave. In the Romanesque period the churches of Poitou conformed generally to that type (e.g. Saint-Savin, Chauvigny, Parthenay, Lusignan, Montierneuf and Notre-Dame-la-Grande at Poitiers, etc.), but its use was widespread also in northern Spain, in southern and central France, and in northern and central Italy. The German series (essentially in Westphalia) seems to have been dependent at first on Italian models.

24. E. Panofsky, *Abbot Suger . . .* , 100–101, lines 5–6.

Notes: Chapter III (pp. 79–111)

1. On the thirteenth century work at Saint-Denis, see S. McK. Crosby, *L'abbaye royale de Saint-Denis,* Paris, 1953, 57–65; and more recently R. Branner, *St Louis and the Court Style in Gothic Architecture,* London, 1965, 39–55; see also Chapter IX, pp. 366–380.

2. See R. Krautheimer, *Early Christian and Byzantine Architecture,* (Pelican History of Art), Harmondsworth and Baltimore, 1965: pl. 65B (Tebessa, mid-fourth century), pl. 65A (Tigzirt, ca. 450); pl. 85 (Alahan Manastiri, late fifth/early sixth century), pl. 46 (R'safah, Saint-Sergius, before 520), pl. 111A (Grado cathedral, 571–579); Ruwêha "cathedral" (Syria, early sixth century) is not illustrated but is described on 113–115.

3. See W. W. Horn, "On the Origins of the Medieval Bay System," *Journal of the Society of Architectural Historians,* XVII:2, 1958, 2–23: note in particular fig. 8 reproducing P. J. Tholen's reconstruction of the Carolingian timber church of Breberen near Aachen; for a full study, see W. W. Horn and E. Born, *The Plan of St. Gall, A Study of the Architecture and Economy of, and Life in a Paradigmatic Carolingian Monastery,* 3 vols., Berkeley and Los Angeles, 1979. But the slowness of the development of methods of prefabrication in carpentry work has been underlined by J. T. Smith, "The Early Development of Timber Buildings: the Passing Brace and Reversed Assembly," *Archaeological Journal,* CXXXI, 1974, 238–263, specially 238–239.

4. For an up-to-date plan and a bibliography, see J. Hubert, *L'architecture religieuse du haut moyen âge en France,* Paris, 1952, No. 26–27.

5. At Vicenza the first Romanesque structure revealed by the excavations had vertical pilasters applied against square piers; it was built after—and perhaps quite a while after—the last Hungarian invasions of the mid-tenth century: see B. Forlati-Tamaro, F. Forlati and F. Barbieri, *Il*

duomo di Vicenza, Vicenza, 1956. Shallow pilasters rising from the capitals of the columns had been used earlier in that same area at Grado, in the cathedral of S. Eufemia and in the church of S. Maria delle Grazie, which both date from the late sixth century: see G. Brusin and P. L. Zovatto, *Monumenti paleocristiani di Aquileia e Grado*, Udine, 1957.

6. In England the architecture of the East Anglian group, which had produced since the 1080s a long list of illustrious buildings, pursued its old elevational formula right into the second half of the twelfth century (naves of Castle Acre and Peterborough for instance); and in Scotland and northern England Gothic architecture itself went on using for quite a while that same kind of unvaulted structure, with the lack of connection it implies between the two sides of the nave. In the extreme north of France, in the old county of Flanders, the nave of Lillers indicates a similar survival of that older type of bay rhythm into the middle years of the twelfth century.

7. The nature of the scars left in the nave walls excludes any other hypothesis. The diaphragm arch had spread from Italy to Lower Lorraine ca. 1040.

8. Barrel vaults with transverse arches appear in Catalonia at Sant Vicens de Cardona, ca. 1030; but the heightened vaulting of the nave must be placed only in the second half of the eleventh century, which makes it more or less contemporaneous with the naves of S. Pere de Roda, Quarante and Saint-Guilhem-le-Désert. In Burgundy, the upper story of the narthex of Tournus, ca. 1030–1035, established a model which was followed soon after at Chapaize and at Cluny II, when the originally timber-covered nave of the second half of the tenth century was vaulted late in the abbacy of Odilo (d.1049). Under the influence of Cluny this type of vaulting was repeated in the 1040s and 1050s in a number of buildings in Burgundy and the neighboring areas (e.g. Romainmôtier and Payerne in Switzerland, or Ris in Auvergne). Bay divided, barrel vaulted naves were also known in Italy, as proved by the remaining example of the church of S. Maria at Portonovo, near Ancona (ca. 1040). Many more structures of that type are likely to have existed in northern Italy before the destructive earthquakes of the late eleventh and early twelfth centuries. The aisleless nave of Balocco, near Vercelli, is one of the few witnesses which happen to have survived.

9. The structural formula of the Pilgrimage Road Churches seems to have been initiated at Limoges, in the now destroyed abbey church of Saint-Martial, in the late 1060s, a few years after the arrival of abbot

Adhémar in 1063; the church was dedicated in 1095. The type of the Pilgrimage Road Church was the result of a synthesis of the two early series of bay-divided structures of northern and southern Romanesque. In that process of synthesis, the vaulting of the central space led to the disappearance of the clerestory. But there exists also a variant of the same design, built on a small scale and with clerestory windows: the church of Saint-Etienne at Nevers (begun in 1083), in which the nave retains under the barrel vault the complete grid of stories of the unvaulted tribune churches of northern France.

10. For a reconstruction of the original state of Saint-Etienne at Caen see G. Bouet, "Analyse architecturale de l'abbaye de Saint-Etienne de Caen," *Bulletin monumental,* XXXI, 1865, 417–479; see also J. Bony, "La technique normande du mur épais à l'époque romane," *Bulletin monumental,* XCVIII, 1939, 153–188.

11. See S. McK. Crosby, *L'abbaye royale de Saint-Denis,* Paris, 1953, 40–41; *id.,* "Abbot Suger's St. Denis. The New Gothic," *Studies in Western Art, Acts of the Twentieth International Congress of the History of Art, New York, 1961,* Princeton, 1963, I, 86; and id., "The Inside of St. Denis's West Facade," *Gedenkschrift Ernst Gall,* Munich and Berlin, 1965, 59–68.

12. On this method of self-explanation of the design and on its analogy with the Scholastic method of *manifestatio* refer to the fundamental study of E. Panofsky, *Gothic Architecture and Scholasticism,* Latrobe, 1951 (new ed., Cleveland-New York, Meridian Books, 1957), particularly 27–35 and 58–60.

13. For the essential geometrical data concerning the east end of Saint-Denis and its designing, see S. McK. Crosby, "Crypt and Choir Plans at Saint-Denis," *Gesta,* V, 1966, 4–8. An indication, which may be of great importance for a proper understanding of the genesis of Gothic, can be found in G. Beaujouan, *L'interdépendance entre la science scholastique et les techniques utilitaires (XIIe, XIIIe et XIVe siècles),* Paris, 1957 (Conférences du Palais de la Découverte, ser. D, 46): it is in the writings of Hugh of Saint-Victor—i.e. between ca. 1125 and 1141—that, for the first time in intellectual history, the art of the architect is listed as a science among the branches of geometry (as a subdivision of *Geometria practica,* which includes all forms of engineering). That such a mention appears at that date under the pen of a Parisian philosopher is no doubt significant and suggests that a new degree of geometrical elaboration was developing around the 1130s in the architectural workshops with which Hugh of Saint-Victor was acquainted.

478

14. On this surface patterning in English Romanesque architecture, see G. F. Webb, *Architecture in Britain. The Middle Ages* (Pelican History of Art), Harmondsworth-Baltimore, 1956, particularly 37–39 and 47–48.

15. S. McK. Crosby, "New Excavations in the Abbey Church of St. Denis," *Gazette des Beaux-Arts,* ser. 6, XXVI, 1944, 115–126; *id.,* "Fouilles exécutées récemment dans la basilique de Saint-Denis," *Bulletin monumental,* CV 1947, 167–181; *id., L'abbaye royale de Saint-Denis,* Paris, 1953, 49–50 and 68–69 (plan).

16. The only point that can be made with certainty concerning the upper stories is that Saint-Denis could not have had tribunes: the columns which separate the two ambulatories of the choir are too weak to have ever supported the load of a tribune wall, let alone the additional load of tribune vaults; and the upper surface of the ambulatory vaults does not show any trace of ever having supported any superstructure: see S. McK. Crosby, *L'abbaye royale de Saint-Denis,* 46. This deprives the "tentative approximation" of an elevation given in the 1946 edition of Panofsky's Abbot Suger (figure on 221) of any possible validity. The sexpartite vault suggested on that drawing must also be rejected, since such vaulting was still unknown in the Ile-de-France at that date: it made its appearance for the first time outside Normandy at Sens in the redesigning of the mid-1140s; and the choirs built with wide straight bays in imitation of Saint-Denis, as those of Noyon and Saint-Germain-des-Prés, are covered with oblong quadripartite vaults, as was certainly the choir of Saint-Denis itself. Crosby suggests for the upper elevation a triforium in the manner of Sens; but in view of the greater height of the lateral roofs which at Saint-Denis had to cover the width of double aisles (not of a single aisle as at Sens), that triforium story is likely to have been taller than at Sens. See the new drawing in Panofsky's *Abbot Suger,* 2nd ed., 1979, 239.

17. The descendence of Saint-Denis is therefore probably more complex than has been generally imagined. It cannot be restricted to the buildings which reflect more or less exactly the design of the choir, i.e. the choirs of Noyon, Saint-Germain-des-Prés and, when it was still standing, Saint-Martin at Pontoise; the design of the nave of Saint-Denis, which must have been known to some architects, seems also to have exerted some influence. It should be noted that at Saint-Denis the difference in height between nave and choir (3.18 m, i.e. just over 10'5″) is exactly equal to the height of the monolithic shafts of the columns of Suger's choir: which means that the piers of the new nave had most probably been designed as two such monoliths, one on top of the other, with a band

at their junction (an enlarged version of the type of intermediate support used in the openings of the upper chapels of the narthex: see S. McK. Crosby, *L'abbaye royale de Saint-Denis,* pl. 54–55). If this reconstruction is right, then it was from the projected Saint-Denis nave that the second master of Arras Cathedral, around 1170, borrowed both the idea of its tall two-tiered piers and the principle of unusually narrow bays, which gave its uniqueness of aspect to that vanished structure (see P. Héliot, "Les oeuvres capitales du gothique français primitif et l'influence de l'architecture anglaise," *Wallraf-Richartz Jahrbuch,* XX, 1958, 98–99; also R. Branner, *Burgundian Gothic Architecture,* London, 1960, 32–33). The rebuilding of the choir of Canterbury cathedral by William of Sens and William the Englishman, between 1175 and 1184, would appear also as another reflection of the twelfth century design of Saint-Denis.

18. See M. Aubert, "Le portail royal et la façade occidentale de la cathédrale de Chartres. Essai sur la date de leur exécution," *Bulletin monumental,* C, 1941, 177–218; E. Fels, "Die Grabung an der Fassade der Kathedrale von Chartres," *Kunstchronik,* VIII, 1955, 149–151; W. Sauerländer, *Gothic Sculpture in France 1140–1270,* London, 1972, 383–386. It was at the start of the rebuilding of the West front of Chartres in 1145 that men of all conditions decided to help the work by harnessing themselves to the carts loaded with stones and beams which had to be drawn up the hill from the banks of the river Eure, thereby initiating that brief craze of dramatized devotion that has been called the "cult of the carts:" see V. Mortet and P. Deschamps, *Recueil de textes relatifs à l'histoire de l'architecture et à la condition des architectes en France au moyen âge,* Paris, II, 1929, 63–67; P. Frankl, *The Gothic, Literary Sources and Interpretations through Eight Centuries,* Princeton, 1960, 22–23 and 207–210; T. G. Frisch, *Gothic Art 1140–c.1450,* Englewood Cliffs, 1971, 23–26.

19. On the dating of Sens Cathedral, see Chapter II, pp. 66–68.

20. The nave of Mont-Saint-Michel was begun in 1063; English examples of that triforium pattern are the transept (and originally also the choir) of St. Albans abbey church, begun in 1077, and the nave of Gloucester, built after the fire of 1122. It must be noted that at Sens the arches of the triforium cut right through the wall and originally gave onto the dark roof space over the aisle vaults (as in the nave of Mont-Saint-Michel): the wall which can now be seen behind the triforium arcade is a modern addition, put in to mitigate the draftiness of the cathedral. Triforiums of the wall-passage type appear in Gothic architecture only some twenty years later. The existence of two successive types of triforium in Gothic architecture—a first type in which the arches pierce the wall struc-

ture right through as at Sens (type which could be reduced to a smaller number of openings, as in the nave of Le Mans, or even to a mere blind arcading, as in the choir of Noyon); and a second type beginning at Laon in the mid-1160s, in which a shallow passage runs between an open arcading and a wall close behind it—is an important point to remember. These two types should not be confused, for the switch from the first type to the second corresponds to a very significant change in the constructional methods of Gothic architecture.

21. Should this superimposition of rhythmical patterns be related with the development of polyphony in which the School of Notre-Dame seems to have taken the lead as early as ca. 1140? The names of Léonin and Pérotin, precentors of Notre-Dame in the second half of the twelfth century, are well-known; but precentor Albert was mentioned already in the *Codex Calixtinus* (written ca. 1140) as the author of the earliest three-voice composition that can be identified. Musical and architectural progress would seem to have advanced together in the Paris milieu, and they may well have interacted. See J. Chailley, *Histoire musicale du moyen âge,* 2nd ed., Paris, 1969, 151–167.

22. That diffusion of the tribune elevation in northern France and western Belgium between 1090 and 1140 or 1145 can be summarized in the following list: Saint-Lucien at Beauvais, Saint-Corneille at Compiègne, Notre-Dame at Soissons, Sint Donaas (Saint-Donatien) at Bruges (all destroyed), nave of Saint-Vincent at Soignies, nave of Tournai cathedral.

23. See C. Givelet, *Le Mont Notre-Dame. Histoire et description,* 2nd ed., Limé, 1893; E. Lefèvre-Pontalis, "Eglise du Mont Notre-Dame," *Congrès archéologique de France,* LXXVIII (Reims), 1911, I, 250–258; a corrected plan can be found in R. Branner, *Le cathédrale de Bourges et sa place dans l'architecture gothique,* Paris-Bourges, 1962, 166–167.

24. On Noyon, refer to the monograph by C. Seymour Jr., *Notre-Dame of Noyon in the Twelfth Century. A Study in the Early Development of Gothic Architecture,* New Haven, 1939; new ed., New York, 1968.

25. Essen was totally rebuilt between 1039 and 1058, under Abbess Theophano: W. Zimmermann, *Das Münster zu Essen* (Die Kunstdenkmäler des Rheinlands, 3), Essen, 1956; A. Verbeek, "Die ottonische Bautengruppe um Essen und Werden und die viergeschossige Wandgliederung," *Karolingische und ottonische Kunst: Werden, Wesen, Wirkung* (Forschungen zur Kunstgeschichte und christlichen Archäologie, 3), Wiesbaden, 1957, 150–158.

26. Corrections have now to be made to my old article: "Tewkesbury

481

et Pershore, deux élévations à quatre étages de la fin du XIe siècle," *Bulletin monumental*, XCVI, 1937, 281–290 and 503–504. Pershore, which is actually a little later than I had originally suggested, does not seem to have ever had in its transept a full four-story elevation, the clerestory having been sacrificed to allow for a barrel vault: a truncation analogous to what is found in the Pilgrimage Road Basilicas. At Tewkesbury on the other hand a full four-story elevation seems to have existed at least in some parts of the east end for there are, on the outside, clear indications of the blocking of two windows high up in the east walls of the transepts. The crucial fact, at both Tewkesbury and Pershore, is the presence of a triforium (and even one of the wall-passage type) immediately above the arches of the tribune story. Even when the clerestory is dispensed with, this superposition of two intermediate stories suffices to keep these buildings in the direct line of origins of the Gothic series of four-story elevations. As Tewkesbury seems to have been the work of a Lotharingian architect familiar with the architecture of the Rhineland as well as of Burgundy, Essen is likely to have been the actual source of the four-story elevation in the eastern parts of Tewkesbury: see my article on "La chapelle épiscopale de Hereford et les apports lorrains en Angleterre après la conquête," *Actes du XIXe congrès international d'histoire de l'art, Paris, 8–13 septembre 1958*, Paris, 1959, 36–43.

27. Luc Devliegher, "Het koor van de romaanse Sint-Donaaskerk te Brugge," *Bulletin de la Commission royale des Monuments et des Sites*, XIV, 1963, 309–327; see also Broeder Firmin (de Smidt), *De romaanse kerkelijke bouwkunst in West-Vlaanderen*, Ghent, 1940, 17–38.

28. On this whole question, see the important article by Robert Branner, "Gothic Architecture 1160–1180 and its Romanesque Sources," *Studies in Western Art, Acts of the Twentieth International Congress of the History of Art*, Princeton, 1963, I, 92–104.

29. Pierre Héliot, "La nef et le clocher de l'ancienne cathédrale de Cambrai," *Wallraf-Richartz Jahrbuch*, XVIII, 1956, 91–110. Interesting remarks on the nave of Cambrai are also found in R. Branner, "The Transept of Cambrai Cathedral," *Gedenkschrift Ernst Gall*, Berlin-Munich, 1965, 69–86, particularly 74.

30. The adoption of the four-story elevation at Noyon seems to correspond to the "second phase of construction," which began between 1155 and 1160: see C. Seymour, Jr., *Notre-Dame of Noyon*, 55. Saint-Germer also is now dated in the late 1150s, on the evidence of the moulding profiles and of the carved decoration of the choir: see A. Lapeyre, *Des*

31. On Laon, in addition to E. Lambert, "La cathédrale de Laon," *Gazette des Beaux-Arts,* ser. 5, XVI, 1926, 361–384, and to H. Adenauer, *Die Kathedrale von Laon,* Düsseldorf, 1934, see now W. W. Clark and R. King, *Laon Cathedral,* London, in press.

Notes: Chapter IV (pp. 117–155*)*

1. This revival of interest in Saint-Denis began with the first excavations of S. McK. Crosby in 1938; and the work that gave the new orientation to Sugerian scholarship was E. Panofsky, *Abbot Suger on the Abbey Church of Saint-Denis and its Art Treasures,* Princeton, 1946: on the philosophy of the Pseudo-Areopagite and its relevance to Saint-Denis, see particularly 18–24, 37 and 101.

2. The influence of the "historical moment" on the design of Saint-Denis is stressed by O. von Simson, *The Gothic Cathedral, The Origins of Gothic Architecture and the Medieval Concept of Order,* New York, 1956, 58–90. For a proper evaluation of the political situation, in addition to A. Luchaire, *Louis VI-le-Gros, annales de sa vie et de son règne,* Paris, 1890, see: M. Pacaut, *Louis VII et son royaume,* Paris, 1964; and A. Grabois, "De la trêve de Dieu à la paix du roi. Etude sur les transformations du mouvement de la paix au XIIe siècle," *Mélanges offerts à René Crozet,* Poitiers, 1966, II, 585–596.

3. The significance of these geographical changes must not be misconstrued. There was no regression in the movement of civilization which had started around Paris 15 or 20 years before. The tone of civilization was not changed and the spirit of *courtoisie* initiated under Aquitanian influence in the first years of the reign of Louis VII went on developing as well as the new trends of art. This atmosphere of ease and lightheartedness has been well perceived and defined by R. W. Southern, *Medieval Humanism and Other Studies,* New York, 1970, 135–157. The diminution of power of the Capetian monarchy did not reduce its appeal or its popular support: it seems even to have drawn more closely into the Capetian orbit the powerful houses of Champagne and Flanders, whose counts became after 1150 the king's closest advisers. Leading the same style of life, protecting the same writers, they must have also favored the same artistic circles. Far from receding, Gothic began to spread beyond the limits of the purely Capetian lands. The less exclusive predominance of

Paris had probably given Gothic a chance to diffuse more widely.

4. On Saint-Père at Chartres, see P. Héliot and G. Jouven, "L'église Saint-Pierre de Chartres et l'architecture du moyen âge," *Bulletin archéologique du Comité des travaux historiques et scientifiques,* new ser., VI, 1970, 117-177; on Saint-Quiriace at Provins, G. de Maillé, *Provins. Les monuments religieux,* Paris, 1939, I, 45-173; on Saint-Etienne at Troyes, R. Branner, *Burgundian Gothic Architecture,* London, 1960, 186-188; on Voulton, F. Salet, "Voulton," *Bulletin monumental,* CII, 1943-1944, 91-115.

5. In addition to the early examples of Sens, Saint-Loup-de-Naud, and Saint-Père at Chartres, this principle of alternating types of piers was used at Provins (Saint-Quiriace), Troyes (Saint-Etienne), Corbeil (Notre-Dame), Vermenton, and Voulton. It was also adopted in the Cistercian churches of this area: Barbeau (begun 1156), Preuilly (begun ca. 1170) and Jouy (begun ca. 1190). It must be noted that the Saint-Loup-de-Naud variant, characterized by the use of large quadripartite vaults in the Lombard manner over the double bay units, was repeated at Corbeil, Vermenton and even in the west bays of Voulton; this kept alive the connection with Le Mans (nave of the cathedral) and Avénières mentioned above (see Chapter II, p. 70). In the choir of Saint-Martin at Etampes, the alternation of large and small piers is used simply to create a rhythm and has no structural necessity.

6. The triforium of the Sens type, opening directly onto the aisle roof, is found at Provins, Corbeil, Saint-Martin at Etampes, Saint-Eusèbe at Auxerre, and a little later in the choir of Vézelay.

7. One of the few signs of influences derived from other Gothic centers was the occasional adoption of the Parisian form of expanded chevets: Saint-Denis and Saint-Germain-des-Prés were obviously the source not only for the choir of Vézelay, begun ca. 1180, but also for the Cistercian adaptation of the large Gothic east ends first elaborated at Clairvaux (1154-1174) and repeated after a while at Pontigny (ca. 1186-1210).

8. Until fairly recently a very early date was generally attributed to Saint-Germer (also called Saint-Germer-de-Fly): the construction of the choir and transept was considered to have been begun ca. 1135 and completed by 1150 at the latest. This early dating will still be found in some of the most recent and authoritative handbooks; but on the basis of a closer analysis of the profiles, the sculpture and the style of decoration it has now been recognized that the building cannot have been started before the mid-1150s.

9. See P. Héliot, "Les anciennes cathédrales d'Arras," *Bulletin de la Commission Royale des Monuments et des Sites,* IV, 1953, 7–109.

10. The first examples of quadrant arches under a side roof are found in non-vaulted buildings: Norwich cathedral, begun in 1096; and in Normandy, Cerisy-la-Forêt, north side of the choir, also ca. 1100. Obviously these arches were not conceived as devices of buttressing: they should probably be described as quadrant-shaped diaphragm arches intended to help support the sloping roof of the tribunes. Even in the nave of Durham cathedral, which was built as an entirely vaulted structure between ca. 1115 and 1133, the quadrant arches under the tribune roof seem unlikely to indicate a buttressing intention. But that intention may already have been present some 20 years later in two rib-vaulted buildings of Normandy: the nave of the church of la Trinité at Caen (rebuilt in its upper parts in the 1140s or early 50s) and the choir of Saint-Gabriel near Bayeux (slightly later). As Saint-Germer is situated only a few miles away from the border of Normandy, its builder must have taken the idea from some Norman prototype. Another building of ca. 1160 in which quadrant arches of a kind were used under the aisle roofs is the nave of Pontigny.

11. The cathedral of Cambrai, like so many major churches in the north of France, was destroyed at the end of the eighteenth century, as a consequence of the French Revolution. See the most recent studies, by P. Héliot, "La nef et le clocher de l'ancienne cathédrale de Cambrai," *Wallraf-Richartz Jahrbuch,* XVIII, 1956, 91–110; and R. Branner, "The Transept of Cambrai Cathedral," *Gedenkschrift Ernst Gall,* Munich and Berlin, 1965, 69–86. A full monograph of Cambrai Cathedral has just been completed by J. Thiébaut and its publication can be expected shortly.

12. Mantes was begun ca. 1170: see J. Bony, "La collégiale de Mantes," *Congrès archéologique de France,* CIV (Paris-Mantes), 1946, 163–220. Another example of the type is Gonesse, begun ca. 1185.

13. Hermopolis, near Cairo, is a fifth century example: see R. Krautheimer, *Early Christian and Byzantine Architecture* (Pelican History of Art), Harmondsworth and Baltimore, 1965, 87–89.

14. See L. Serbat, "Quelques églises anciennement détruites du nord de la France," *Bulletin monumental,* LXXXVIII, 1929, 365–435.

15. On Noyon, see C. Seymour Jr., *Notre-Dame of Noyon in the Twelfth Century,* New Haven, 1939. The transept was begun ca. 1170. Two Cistercian churches of ca. 1200, Chaâlis (Oise), and Quincy (Yonne), adopted a variant of the trefoil plan, reflecting with some delay the popularity of

this type of design: see M. Aubert, *L'architecture cistercienne en France,* Paris, 1943, I, 210–212.

16. At Tournai Cathedral the style and the methods of construction reveal direct connections with northern Italy; and when it comes to the composition of the transept the prototype is undoubtedly the fifth century church of S. Lorenzo in Milan: see the reconstruction of the original aspect of S. Lorenzo in P. Verzone, *L'architettura religiosa dell'alto medioevo nell'Italia settentrionale,* Milan, 1942, 179.

17. The importance of Saint-Lucien was discovered by Ernst Gall, "Die Abteikirche Saint-Lucien bei Beauvais," *Wiener Jahrbuch für Kunstgeschichte,* IV (1926), 59–71. But because of the recent excavations (1960–62) it is now possible to give an amended reconstruction of the building. The plan published in Marcel Aubert, "A propos de l'église abbatiale de Saint-Lucien de Beauvais," *Gedenkschrift Ernst Gall,* Munich and Berlin, 1965, 51–58, is not absolutely complete since it does not show the horseshoe-shaped chapel which was applied against the east side of the north transept (on a slightly oblique axis, as it opened onto the first curving bay of the transept ambulatory). The trefoil plan of St. Maria-im-Kapitol at Cologne, a mid-eleventh century work, was certainly one of the sources which had some influence on the design of Saint-Lucien.

18. First revived on the banks of the Loire river in the last years of the tenth century at Orléans cathedral and a little later at Saint-Martin at Tours, whence it spread to Reims and beyond, the cruciform plan with aisled transepts became particularly widespread after 1065, when it was adopted first in the so-called "Pilgrimage Road Churches" (Saint-Martial at Limoges, Santiago de Compostela, Saint-Sernin at Toulouse, etc.) and then from 1079 in a series of great English churches (Winchester, Ely, Old St. Paul's Cathedral in London, etc.). Pisa Cathedral (officially founded in 1063, but perhaps not begun until 1089) represents another autonomous revival more closely related to Early Christian prototypes such as the fifth century church of St. John at Ephesus.

19. On the chronology of construction at Notre-Dame, see: M. Aubert, *Notre-Dame de Paris, sa place dans l'histoire de l'architecture du XIIe au XIVe siècle,* Paris, 2nd ed., 1929; R. Branner, "Paris and the Origins of Rayonnant Architecture Down to 1240," *Art Bulletin,* XLIV, 1962, 39–51; B. Mahieu, "La naissance de Notre-Dame de Paris," *Bulletin de la Société de l'histoire de Paris et de l'Ile-de-France,* XCI, 1964, 34–36; J. Thirion, "Les plus anciennes sculptures de Notre-Dame de Paris," *Académie des inscriptions et belles-lettres, Comptes-rendus des séances,* 1970, 85–112.

20. On Laon Cathedral, see Chapter III, note 31, p. 483.

21. The choir of Notre-Dame is 33 metres (108') high. From the dimensions given in old descriptions, the choir of Arras must have been almost exactly the same height; and the nave of Cambrai seems to have been a little taller, at 18 toises (i.e., almost exactly 35 metres or 115'). These were the three tallest buildings of their time. The height of the nave of Laon is only 24 metres (79').

22. Multiple towers had been used already, in a slightly different manner, at Saint-Trond (soon after 1085) and had also been planned at one point (a little before 1100) at Winchester cathedral: see L. F. Génicot, "L'oeuvre architecturale d'Adélard II de Saint-Trond et ses antécédents," *Revue belge d'archéologie et d'histoire de l'art*, XXXIX, 1970, 3–91; and for Winchester, R. Willis, "The Architectural History of Winchester Cathedral," *Proceedings of the Annual Meeting of the Archaeological Institute of Great Britain and Ireland at Winchester, September 1845*, London, 1846, I, 25–28. The system of dating followed here for Tournai cathedral is, with some minor corrections, the one first formulated by C. Seymour, Jr., *Notre-Dame of Noyon in the Twelfth Century*, New Haven, 1939, 124, note 16, and which is now commonly accepted: nave begun soon after the synod of 1135 (probably in the early 1140s); transepts begun ca. 1150–1160 (perhaps rather ca. 1160). The "late chronology" advocated by Fr. Mémoire-Marie (J. Cornet), "La chronologie de la cathédrale de Tournai," *Annales du XXXIIIe Congrès de la Fédération archéologique et historique de Belgique*, Tournai, 1951, III, 544–554, and more recently by V. Scaff, *La sculpture romane de la cathédrale Notre-Dame de Tournai*, Tournai, 1971, placing after 1171 the totality of the transept and the two upper stories of the nave, seems excessive in the use it makes of the dedication date of 1171: the style of the lower stories of the transept would be consistent with a date in the early or mid 1160s.

23. This is what has been described as the Gothic principle of *Diaphanie* by Hans Jantzen, "Über den gotischen Kirchenraum," *Freiburger Wissenschaftliche Gesellschaft*, XV, 1928; reprinted in *Über den gotischen Kirchenraum und andere Aufsätze*, Berlin, 1951, 7–20; French translation under the title "Structure interne de l'église gothique," *Information d'Histoire de l'Art*, XVII, 1972, 103–112.

24. See J. Bony, "La technique normande du mur épais à l'époque romane," *Bulletin monumental*, XCVIII, 1939, 178–183.

25. On the use of English sources in the Northern Gothic group after ca. 1160, see R. Branner, "Gothic Architecture 1160–1180 and its

Romanesque Sources," *Studies in Western Art, Acts of the Twentieth International Congress of the History of Art,* Princeton, 1963, I, 92–104; also J. Bony, "The Façade of Bury St. Edmunds: an Additional Note," *ibid.,* 105–107.

26. See A. Prache, *Saint-Remi de Reims. L'oeuvre de Pierre de Celle et sa place dans l'architecture gothique* (Bibliothèque de la Société française d'archéologie, 8), Geneva, 1978. On the more complex, but eventually related, church of Notre-Dame-en-Vaux at Châlons-sur-Marne, see A. Prache, "Notre-Dame-en-Vaux de Châlons-sur-Marne. Campagnes de construction," *Mémoires de la Société d'agriculture, commerce, sciences et arts du département de la Marne,* LXXXI, 1966, 29–92.

27. Another building of the greatest refinement was the choir of the cathedral of Arras, as redesigned by its second architect, probably soon after 1170: see my remarks as quoted by P. Héliot, "Les oeuvres capitales du gothique français primitif et l'influence de l'architecture anglaise," *Wallraf-Richartz Jahrbuch,* XX, 1958, 98–99. The great height of the central space, the lightness of its very tall supports made up of twin monolithic columns of blue Tournai marble, the narrowness of the bays and the linear play of the triplet-like arrangement of the clerestory into which the triforium arcading was enmeshed, must have produced the effect of an almost weightless structure; and the many concealed irregularities which characterize the design indicate a "Manneristic" turn of mind. R. Branner, *Burgundian Gothic Architecture,* London, 1960, 32–34, has shown the influence exerted by the unusual mode of vaulting of the choir of Arras upon the final design of the choir of Vézelay.

28. On Champeaux, see J. Messelet, "La collégiale Saint-Martin de Champeaux," *Bulletin monumental,* LXXXIV, 1925, 253–282. On Mantes, see note 12 above, p. 485.

29. This orientation of the Parisian milieu crystallized rather suddenly in the mid-1160s under the influence of the great architect who conceived the design of Notre-Dame (ca. 1163). Just before that, Paris seems to have been strongly influenced by Sens, as indicated by the choir of Saint-Germain-des-Prés, dedicated in 1163 (type of elevation copied from Sens, while plan and type of pier are derived from Saint-Denis), and even more clearly by the choir of Saint-Julien-le-Pauvre, of ca. 1165 (alternating supports, sexpartite vault, wide proportions): a continuation of the trend which had started at Senlis ten years earlier. However in the same years Saint-Germer (begun ca. 1155–1160) was already to some extent preparing the stage for Notre-Dame, by treating the additional story above the tribunes not as a triforium but as an essentially mural zone—

although at Saint-Germer the wall was not made so very thin and still possessed a rich plasticity inherited from the late Romanesque style of the area.

Notes: Chapter V (pp. 157–193)

1. On the origins of this technique of construction, see J. Bony, "Origines des piles gothiques anglaises à fûts en délit," *Gedenkschrift Ernst Gall*, Munich and Berlin, 1965, 95–122. At Saint-Denis these thin detached shafts had first been used, but in a less structurally significant manner, a bit before 1140 in the upper chapel of the narthex, where the hand of the master of the choir can already be recognized.

2. M. Aubert, *Notre-Dame de Paris, sa place dans l'histoire de l'architecture du XIIe au XIVe siècle*, Paris, 1920; 2nd ed., 1929, 40–42. Definite proof that the nave of Notre-Dame must have been begun before 1178, and that by that date some at least of the capitals of the large columns of the nave were already carved and ready to be mounted, is afforded by the fact that at Canterbury one of the piers erected in 1178 has a capital which is an obvious copy of the type of composition and style of foliage characteristic of the big capitals of the nave of Notre-Dame: see J. Bony, "French Influences on the Origins of English Gothic Architecture," *Journal of the Warburg and Courtauld Institutes*, XII, 1949, 8.

3. On the work of the years 1175–1184 at Canterbury Cathedral, in addition to my article just mentioned (*Journal of the Warburg and Courtauld Institutes*, XII, 1949, 1–15), see R. Willis, *The Architectural History of Canterbury Cathedral*, London, 1845, which remains the fundamental monograph.

4. In the nave of Tournai, there are four detached blue-stone shafts on the diagonals of the main arcade piers (which are of the compound type), four again but on the main axes around the piers of the tribune story (which are of the *cantonné* type with an octagonal core), and one short little shaft on each of the wide pilasters which support the arches of the triforium.

5. See L. Serbat, "L'église Notre-Dame-la-Grande à Valenciennes," *Revue de l'art chrétien*, LII, 1903, 366–383; and *id.*, "Quelques églises anciennement détruites du nord de la France," *Bulletin monumental*, LXXXVIII, 1929, 365–435.

6. Apart from England, where marble shafts were universally accepted from the late twelfth to the early fourteenth century (the Lady Chapel at Ely being the last major example), that style of architectural

polychromy was particularly popular in Flanders (including Saint-Omer) and Hainault, with more scattered examples in most of present-day Belgium; also in the Rhineland, where it characterizes the school of Cologne of the late twelfth and early thirteenth centuries; and it is found also at Trier and in a few Burgundian buildings such as the east end of Vézelay and the cathedral of Besançon: see R. Branner, *Burgundian Gothic Architecture,* London, 1960, 33-34.

7. In spite of their comparative thinness, these monolithic shafts cannot be viewed only as creating linear accents: their tubular roundness gives them an intrinsic plastic value which could be compared to that of the column-statues of the Portail Royal of Chartres for instance. Like the column-statues, these monolithic shafts are applied against, and almost completely detached from, the supports they underline plastically. They belong to the same world of autonomous plastic forms, added with a certain freedom on the surface of a structure to express its inner functions in terms of thin but still substantial volumes, rather than to the abstract sharpness of angular moldings.

8. This plate was first published in the *Journal of the Warburg and Courtauld Institutes,* in my article mentioned in Note 2 above.

9. See Chapter IV, pp. 145-146.

10. On the problems raised by that treatment of the walls in the transept of Noyon, see C. Seymour, Jr., *Notre-Dame of Noyon in the Twelfth Century,* New Haven, 1939, 127-133.

11. These north Italian sources have been stressed by R. Branner, "Gothic Architecture 1160-1180 . . . ," *Studies in Western Art, Acts of the Twentieth International Congress of the History of Art,* Princeton, 1963, I, 96-97; on the persistence of these influences in the thirteenth century, see also R. Branner, "St. Leonardus at Zoutleeuw and the Rhein Valley in the Early Thirteenth Century," *Bulletin de la Commission royale des monuments et des sites,* XIV, 1963, 257-268.

12. The wall passage which originally ran at the level of the window sills at Westminster Hall (ca. 1097-1100), above a surface of blank wall, is the only possible forerunner of the Champenois passage. Westminster Hall was divided into three aisles of equal height by two rows of timber posts. No other example of a domestic hall with wall passages has survived; but there must have been one somewhere in the north of England, since otherwise it seems rather difficult to explain the low level passage of the originally aisleless nave of Ripon (which in addition had a clerestory), and the simpler wall passages of the chancels of Nun Monkton and Cold-

ingham: see G. F. Webb, *Architecture in Britain, The Middle Ages* (Pelican
History of Art), Harmondsworth and Baltimore, 1956, 66–67, 84, and pl.
74A. ...
Notes, pp. 169–72

ingham: see G. F. Webb, *Architecture in Britain, The Middle Ages* (Pelican
History of Art), Harmondsworth and Baltimore, 1956, 66–67, 84, and pl.
74A. This native tradition gave rise in England to a series of quasi-
Champenois passages, which seems to have developed at first indepen-
dently of any French contacts: east end of Tynemouth, retrochoir of
Winchester Cathedral, choir and retrochoir of Worcester Cathedral, etc.

13. The next examples in France were Reims Cathedral (designed in
1210) and Auxerre Cathedral (begun ca. 1217), both of which were very
influential in the thirteenth century. However, the little story of trefoil-
headed windows, which was added by William of Sens on top of the aisle
walls of the Romanesque structure in the choir of Canterbury Cathedral
(1175–1177), includes a longitudinal passage running at the level of that
second row of windows; and although it is placed at a much higher level
than usual, this passage should probably be considered as a mere variant
of the arrangement followed a few years earlier in the Lady Chapel of
Saint-Remi at Reims.

14. See J. Summerson, *Heavenly Mansions and Other Essays on Architecture*, London, 1949, 1–28.

15. At Laon and Mantes the inside of the tower bases opens onto the
nave only from the level of the tribune floor; a similar treatment of the
interior of the façade block is found also a little later in the ruined church
of Saint-Thomas at Crépy-en-Valois. In another type of hollowed-out
façade that horizontal partitioning disappears and the interior of the towers opens on all its height onto the nave: e.g. at Saint-Germer, Noyon,
or Mont-Notre-Dame; on the origins of this other series, see J. Bony,
"The Façade of Bury St. Edmunds," *Studies in Western Art, Acts of the Twentieth International Congress of the History of Art*, Princeton, 1963, I, 105–107.

16. See P. Héliot, "L'abbatiale de Saint-Michel-en-Thiérache, modèle
de Saint-Yved à Braine, et l'architecture gothique des XIIe et XIIIe siècles," *Bulletin de la Commission Royale des Monuments et des Sites*, new series,
II, 1972, 15–43; on the general position of the Braine series in the context of late twelfth century architecture, see also J. Bony, "The Resistance
to Chartres in Early Thirteenth Century Architecture," *Journal of the
British Archaeological Association*, 3rd series, XX–XXI, 1957–8, 35–52. The
dating of Braine remains somewhat uncertain: the church was dedicated
in 1216; a considerable gift of money had been made to the monastery in
1179; but the new church was probably not begun at once: on the basis of
style, it seems to have been started only ca. 1190 or soon after that date.
Another problem which remains to be solved is that of the origins of the

plan of Braine (or of Saint-Michel-en-Thiérache): the diagonal plantation of the chapels is quite abnormal in a plan of the basilican type; it would be normal only in cruciform octagons such as the martyrium described by Gregory of Nyssa or the great church at Qalat-Siman. The little angular chapels inserted between the lobes of the trefoil at S. Maria im Kapitol in Cologne suggest that a contamination could have taken place between cruciform octagon and trefoil plan, leading—in a non-trefoil version— to the one chapel formula of Saint-Quentin at Tournai, as the first step toward the more elaborate layout of Saint-Michel-en-Thiérache and Braine. If that ideal developmental sequence corresponds to historical reality, the elaboration of the Braine type of plan would be likely to have taken place in the Rhenish-Netherlandish area, as the location of the earliest examples of that type of plan (Saint-Michel-en-Thiérache, Saint-Quentin at Tournai) would in itself suggest. Trizay in Charente-Maritime would seem to be, like Saint-Quenin at Vaison, an offshoot of the cruciform octagon stage of that development; but it so happens that the cruciform octagons of the 1030s excavated in Germany (Krukenburg near Helmarshausen, Busdorfkirche at Paderborn) have no chapels on their oblique sides.

17. See E. Lambert, "L'ancienne abbaye de Saint-Vincent de Laon," *Comptes-rendus de l'Académie des inscriptions et belles-lettres*, 1939, 124–138.

18. In my article on "The Resistance to Chartres in Early Thirteenth Century Architecture," *Journal of the British Archaeological Association*, 3rd, ser., XX–XXI, 1957–1958, 45, note 2, I suggested that the choir of the destroyed church of Saint-Amé at Douai might have been the prototype for the upper parts of the choir of Lyon cathedral. This supposition must now be dismissed, as it has since been proved that the choir of Saint-Amé was rebuilt in the sixteenth century: see P. Héliot, "Trois monuments disparus de la Flandre wallonne: l'abbatiale d'Anchin et les collégiales Saint-Pierre et Saint-Amé de Douai," *Revue belge d'archéologie et d'histoire de l'art*, XXVII, 1959, 129–173.

19. On Lausanne, see: E. Bach, L. Blondel and A. Bovy, *La cathédrale de Lausanne* (Kunstdenkmäler der Schweiz, 16), Basel, 1944; M. Grandjean, "La construction de la cathédrale de Lausanne (fin XIIe–début XIIIe siècles): notes sur la chronologie et les maîtres d'oeuvre," *Genava*, new ser., XI 1963, 261–287; *id.*, "La cathédrale actuelle: sa construction, ses architectes, son architecture," in J.-C. Biaudet et al, *La Cathédrale de Lausanne*, Berne, 1975, 45–174. Another variant of this type of elevation is illustrated by the little church of Nesles-la-Vallée near Paris (ca. 1190–

1200); but an earlier prototype situated somewhere in the Laon-Soissons sector is suggested by the early diffusion of this variant and of the peculiarity of vaulting upon which it is based, to Brabant, England, even as far as Wales, and in the other direction, to Burgundy and Switzerland. The split-bay system which characterizes that group complicates again the simplified pattern of Braine, but this time by multiplying its divisions in length, not in height. Each single bay of the lower story, spanned by one arch in the main arcade, splits up into two bays above, from the level of the triforium, and is covered by a compressed sexpartite vault, the intermediate rib of which falls on a short vertical shaft right above the apex of the wide arch of the main arcade. This unexpected syncopation of the piers in the lower story (which means that each alternate vault-springer is suspended over the void) gives a manneristic irrationality to the whole pattern of bays. It is worth noting that the nave of Geneva cathedral was planned at first for such a system of vaulting. Lyon, Geneva and Lausanne, the three cathedrals of the upper Rhône valley, gave a perfect sampling of the possible variations on the main theme of the new triforium elevations.

20. See Chapter IV, p. 128. On the date of the earliest external flying-buttresses, the best study is still E. Lefèvre-Pontalis, "L'origine des arcs-boutants," *Congrès archéologique de France,* LXXXII (Paris), 1919, 367–396.

21. The flying buttress was adopted at Mantes when the lower story was already built, i.e. ca. 1180–85; but the present aspect of the flying buttresses is untypical, as they were altered in their upper parts soon after the middle of the thirteenth century.

22. This figure has been kindly supplied to me by Dr. Robert Mark of the School of Engineering and Applied Science of Princeton University. It results from his recent study of the vaults of Bourges, made in association with K. Alexander.

23. The nave of the abbey church of Cluny was given ca. 1200 the reinforcement of a full system of flying buttresses modeled on that pattern, which was repeated, in a more elaborate form, at Toledo Cathedral as late as the 1220s. I am pleased to learn that W. W. Clark has come independently to conclusions practically identical with mine.

24. This evaluation of an angle of 30 degrees was given by V. Sabouret, "Les voûtes d'arêtes nervurées," *Le Génie Civil,* XCII, 1928, 205–209; and it was repeated in P. Abraham, *Viollet-le-Duc et le rationalisme médiéval,* Paris, 1934, 9–10. Robert Mark has pointed out to me that this angle corresponds more or less to the height of the rubble fill used by

Gothic builders to reinforce the haunches of the vault. At the beginning of the nineteenth century an evaluation in the order of 45 degrees had been given by J. B. Rondelet, *Traité théorique et pratique de l'art de bâtir,* Paris, 1802–1817; 7th ed., 6 vols., 1864–1867, pl. 193, fig. 11. On the experiments made in the nineteenth century to test the collapse mechanism of masonry vaults, see J. Heyman, "On the Rubber Vaults of the Middle Ages and Other Matters," *Gazette des Beaux-arts,* LXXI, 1968, 181.

25. See J. Bony, "La collégiale de Mantes," *Congrès archéologique de France,* CIV (Paris-Mantes), 1946, 196–197.

26. See above, pp. 169–172.

27. See C. Seymour, Jr., *Notre-Dame of Noyon in the Twelfth Century,* New Haven, 1939, 129–131.

28. At Senlis the spire was added only in the thirteenth century; it belongs to another age. The first rose windows were small and placed high up on the façade, as at Saint-Denis and at Senlis, where the central opening of the west front was just a large window. The enlargement of the rose window to monumental size seems to have taken place at first at transept ends: e.g. the north transept of Saint-Etienne at Beauvais, ca. 1150.

29. For the formulation of this basic law of Gothic architecture, see E. Panofsky, *Gothic Architecture and Scholasticism,* Latrobe, 1951, which is the deepest analysis ever given of Gothic modes of thought as they manifest themselves in the forms of architecture.

Notes: Chapter VI (pp. 195–243)

1. On Chartres cathedral, the most useful studies are: E. Lefèvre-Pontalis, "Les architectes et la construction des cathédrales de Chartres," *Mémoires de la Société nationale des Antiquaires de France,* LXIV, 1905, 69–136; L. Grodecki, "Chronologie de la cathédrale de Chartres," *Bulletin monumental,* CXVI, 1958, 91–119; Y. Delaporte, "Remarques sur la chronologie de la cathédrale de Chartres," *Bulletin de la Société archéologique d'Eure-et-Loir,* XXI, 1959, 299–320. On the much debated question of the sequence of operations following the fire of 1194, it seems that the old Romanesque choir was somehow repaired, that the construction of the platform that was to support the expanded east end and transepts was immediately begun, giving the overall layout of the whole site: the exact position of the new crossing clearly had to be fixed before the actual building of any part could be initiated. But while that preparatory work was going on, the first part to be raised above pavement level was un-

doubtedly the eastern half of the nave (as proved by Y. Delaporte in 1959). The western half of the nave came next, after it had been decided to preserve the twelfth century façade; then the choir and transepts, built to an altered design. The choir was completed by 1221, when the choir stalls were assembled; the completion of the transepts followed.

2. On Bourges cathedral the basic work is R. Branner, *La cathédrale de Bourges et sa place dans l'architecture gothique,* Paris and Bourges, 1962; reviewed in *Art Bulletin,* XLVII, 1965, 521–525.

3. The importance of that counterthrust has sometimes been unduly exaggerated, see in particular P. Abraham, *Viollet-le-Duc et le rationalisme médiéval,* Paris, 1934, 82–92.

4. On the basis of the one example for which the calculations have been made, the choir of Cologne Cathedral, analyzed by Robert Mark, it can be said that even at their moment of maximum power (i.e. just after the wooden centering of the vaults had been removed, when the slow-setting medieval mortars had not yet fully hardened and some slippage was therefore possible) twin batteries of flying buttresses must rarely have developed a counter-force of a greater magnitude than one quarter of the horizontal thrust concentrated by the vaults at the head of each pier; and after the mortars had hardened the value of that counter-thrust fell to a much smaller percentage (in the order of 5 percent of the vault thrust). The methods of photomechanical model analysis applied by R. Mark to the study of Gothic construction are of the utmost interest for they give the means of testing and calculating what had remained until very recently purely hypothetical. See for instance, R. Mark and R. A. Prentke, "Model Analysis of Gothic Structure," *Journal of the Society of Architectural Historians,* XXVII, 1968, 44–48; R. Mark and R. S. Jonash, "Wind Loading on Gothic Structure," *ibid.,* XXIX, 1970, 222–230; R. Mark, "The Structural Analysis of Gothic Cathedrals," *Scientific American,* CCXXVII, 1972, 90–99; R. Mark, J. F. Abel and K. O'Neill, "Photoelastic and Finite-element Analysis of a Quadripartite Vault," *Experimental Mechanics,* XIII, 1973, 322–329; K. D. Alexander, R. Mark and J. F. Abel, "The Structural Behavior of Medieval Ribbed Vaulting," *Journal of the Society of Architectural Historians,* XXXVI, 1977, 241–251.

5. See M. Wolfe and R. Mark, "Gothic Cathedral Buttressing: The Experiment at Bourges and Its Influence," *Journal of the Society of Architectural Historians,* XXXIII, 1974, 17–26. Chartres is very heavily built and the safety margin allowed was very wide. Bourges is lightly built by comparison: its architect had an exceptional understanding of the behavior of

masonry. But it was through other qualities that Chartres imposed itself as a model.

6. Early thirteenth century examples are: the Gothic choir of Saint-Martin at Tours (destroyed); the choirs of the cathedrals of Le Mans, Coutances and Toledo; and the plan drawn by Villard de Honnecourt on Folio 15 of his sketch book (see Chapter VII, pp. 261–262). It was only in the late fifteenth century and in the sixteenth that the double ambulatory was revived, as in the Parisian churches of Saint-Séverin, Saint-Nicolas-des Champs and Saint-Eustache.

7. On the cosmic value of a structure facing in all four cardinal points, see A. C. L. Brown, *The Origin of the Grail Legend*, Cambridge, Mass., 1943, 149, 346 and 368–370.

8. Chartres was planned at first with a lantern tower over the crossing but no towers at the transept ends: see Y. Delaporte, "Remarques sur la chronologie de la cathédrale de Chartres," *Bulletin de la Société archéologique d'Eure-et-Loir*, XXI, 1959, 305–307 and 317. That a lantern was intended is proved by an anomaly in the upper part of the western piers of the crossing (no capital to receive the diagonal ribs of the crossing vault); and as this anomaly does not exist in the eastern crossing piers, it is evident that when the choir was built the idea of a lantern tower had been abandoned—which shows incidentally that the nave was built before the choir. It was in that second stage that it was decided to build towers at the transept ends and that the overall pattern of eight peripheral towers was adopted. This complicated, but incontrovertible sequence of changes of intention alters one's conception of the way in which the influence of Laon was felt at Chartres.

9. The church of Saint-Martin at Etampes is still standing, but the destroyed church of Sainte-Croix was no less typical and seems to have influenced Toledo: see R. Branner, *La cathédrale de Bourges et sa place dans l'architecture gothique*, Paris and Bourges, 1962, 166–167.

10. See R. Branner, *La cathédrale de Bourges et sa place dans l'architecture gothique*, Paris and Bourges, 1962, 32, fig. 9, for a reconstruction of the original plan of the ambulatory; 38–42, on the addition of the chapels, which also included the little rectangular chapels flanking the last straight bay of the choir; 107–121, for a detailed analysis of the crypt.

11. The ambulatory of the round church of the Temple in Paris, which was somewhat earlier than Notre-Dame, had the same pattern of vaulting: see E. Viollet-le-Duc, *Dictionnaire raisonné de l'architecture française du XIe au XVIe siècle*, Paris, IX, 1868, 14–17. But where Bourges is

concerned, Notre-Dame is by far the more likely source.

12. The most remarkable characteristic of Parisian sexpartite vaults (beginning with the choir of Notre-Dame and that of Saint-Julien-le-Pauvre nearby) is the unusual curve given to the intermediate transverse ribs, which are stilted and hardly pointed if at all at their apex; the main transverse ribs are also generally less pointed than in the other groups of sexpartite vaults of the twelfth century, and a rectangular profile with two edge-rolls is used for all the ribs.

13. See R. Branner, *La cathédrale de Bourges* . . . , 52–53.

14. It even looks as if the piers of the nave of Valenciennes had been treated in a "colossal order," i.e., had been made to rise directly from the ground to the arches of the tribune story, the main arcade being de-emphasized and slightly recessed in relation to the plane of the upper stories. If that were true, the very tall piers of the nave of Bourges would have been prefigured to some extent in the nave of Valenciennes—which on the other hand would appear related in its "colossal order" with such English buildings as the nave of Romsey, Oxford Cathedral or Glastonbury Abbey.

15. The great five-aisled basilicas of the Constantinian age often had an inner aisle somewhat taller than the outer one; but originally there was no direct lighting of the tall inner aisle and the same slanting roof covered both aisles: see R. Krautheimer, *Early Christian and Byzantine Architecture* (Pelican History of Art), Harmondsworth and Baltimore, 1966, 25–26, 32–36 and 63; the zone of windows which appears in the seventeenth-century view of the Lateran basilica (*ibid.*, pl. 3) was the result of medieval alterations.

16. See R. Branner, "Encore Bourges," *Journal of the Society of Architectural Historians,* XXV, 1966, 299–301. Cîteaux gave another version of that staggered structure, this time adapted to a rectangular plan; but the closest imitation of Clairvaux is at Heisterbach (begun in 1202). The reduced height of the intermediate story, treated like an insertive zone of small windows, had appeared previously in the raised ambulatories of the chevets of Cluny III and Paray-le-Monial. The later Gothic chevets of Saint-Quentin and Beauvais Cathedral should be viewed as part of the Clairvaux derivation.

17. The distance between these two elevation planes is 26.6m (a little over 87 feet).

18. The tall triforium is particularly in evidence in Flanders, e.g. Notre-Dame at Saint-Omer or Onze Lieve Vrouwekerk at Bruges; but it

is also found in the late twelfth-century choir of La Madeleine at Troyes: see R. Branner, *Burgundian Gothic Architecture*, London, 1960, 34-35 and 188. The tall triforium is not usually accompanied by a system of relieving arches such as that used at Bourges—but at Bourges these arches reflect a structural reality: see below, note 19.

19. The existence of these deep, "viaduct-like" arches and the part they play in the stability of the fabric were first revealed by R. Branner, *La cathédrale de Bourges et sa place dans l'architecture gothique*, Paris and Bourges, 1962, 80-85 and 162-163. The relieving arches, which in each bay enclose the stretch of arcading of the triforium, mark exactly the position occupied in depth by these heavy, incorporated, longitudinal arches, which directly cover the triforium passage. Branner has noted differences between the two series of reinforcing longitudinal arches, the lower ones (triforium of the inner aisle) being thicker by some six inches (15 cm), while the upper ones are not only thinner but are surmounted by an exterior passage (this difference in treatment was due to the partial redesigning of ca. 1205-1210, and originally they were certainly meant to be like the lower ones). Above these zones of thick arches the structure becomes unusually thin.

20. The type of the Bourges piers, particularly the thinness of the shafts and their placing, suggests a prototype in which the shafts would have been *en délit* and simply applied against the cylindrical core. The thinness of the shafts recalls the piers of the east crossing at Canterbury Cathedral. This is why the idea of a possible contact with Valenciennes is so tempting.

21. It has been suggested that a five-sided hemicycle had been planned at first, instead of the seven-sided hemicycle that was actually built: see J. van der Meulen, "Histoire de la construction de la cathédrale Notre-Dame de Chartres après 1194," *Bulletin de la Société archéologique d'Eure-et-Loir*, XXIII (1965), 99. But this hypothesis fails to explain all the facts of the situation. It is true that the chevet of Chartres was built to a modified design, but the alterations which took place were more in the nature of adjustments than of a radical change of pattern for the whole layout.

22. On the series leading to Braine, see Chapter V, pp. 172-175.

23. This abrupt rise of the central vessel contrasting with the wide base of aisles and chapels defines the properly Chartrain concept of the organization of volumes, as opposed to the Bourges idea of a progressive build-up of height both inside and outside.

24. See C. F. Barnes, Jr., "The Cathedral of Chartres and the Architect of Soissons," *Journal of the Society of Architectural Historians,* XXII, 1963, 63–74.

25. This overall pattern is rather in the nature of a scientific hypothesis, expressing as it does both the laws of matter (transverse direction of the vault thrusts, transverse buttressing to absorb them) and a mental need for the ordering of space and proportions. Chartres seems to have been the very source of the notion of a "functional" architecture (in the sense of an architecture expressing visually the structural functions of its parts); and the way in which Chartres influenced both the turn of mind of thirteenth century architects and the architectural speculations of eighteenth and nineteenth century theorists would be worth investigating.

26. It is often said that the sexpartite vault preceded the oblong vault, but this is erroneous: the oblong vaults of Durham and Lessay preceded the first sexpartite vaults ever built, i.e. those of the Caen group (beginning with the nave of Saint-Etienne); and there is not the slightest doubt that the choir of Saint-Denis must have had oblong vaults, like its imitators, the choirs of Noyon Cathedral, of Saint-Germain-des-Prés in Paris, and of the destroyed church of Saint-Martin at Pontoise. In that first Gothic generation, Sens alone used the sexpartite vault; and even in the period when sexpartite vaulting became very popular (between ca. 1155 and 1195), the oblong vault remained equally common: e.g. Cambrai nave, Saint-Germer, Arras Cathedral, the choir of Saint-Remi at Reims, Notre-Dame-la-Grande at Valenciennes, Saint-Vincent at Laon, Saint-Michel-en-Thiérache, Saint-Yved at Braine, etc.

27. The transept façades of Chartres had been planned at first without towers and with only one doorway; they were redesigned when the final plans for the choir were established, probably ca. 1205, but their design was altered again when it was decided to add projecting porches in front of the doorways. These porches and the upper stories of the terminal bays of the transepts do not seem to have been built until after the choir had been completed in 1221.

28. The pattern of the west rose of Laon Cathedral was copied at the other end of the building a few years later, when a very long rectangular choir (begun ca. 1205) replaced the short original one. The first design of Chartres already showed close connections with the Laon group (perhaps more Saint-Vincent at Laon and Saint-Yved at Braine than the cathedral itself); the second design—which involved the planning of three pairs of

499

peripheral towers, the use of exterior passages around the chapels and, soon after, the addition of porches to the transept façades—reinforced these links even further: all the picturesqueness of Laon Cathedral was revived in that second design.

29. The *cantonné* type had been used occasionally in the Romanesque period: at Santiago de Compostela for instance or, less systematically, in the choir of Peterborough Cathedral; a common variant found in the Loire area (e.g. crossing piers of Vendôme and Loudun) and in Normandy (e.g. nave of Sainte-Marguerite-sur-Mer, crossing of Dives) involved the addition of rectangular pilasters between the engaged shafts and the round core of the pier. In the presbytery of Canterbury Cathedral one pair of piers (dated 1178) has four thin marble shafts placed on the axes of an octagonal column. But Canterbury was not a prototype for Chartres, where the combination of the columnar type of pier with a cruciform articulation has an entirely different character. Such combinations of forms were probably being reinvented constantly.

30. W. Sauerländer, in "Die kunstgeschichtliche Stellung der Westportale von Notre-Dame in Paris," *Marburger Jahrbuch für Kunstwissenschaft*, XVII, 1959, 1–56, has shown that the façade of Notre-Dame was first started, ca. 1200, to a design derived from that of Sens Cathedral: the central doorway would have been a little narrower than it is now and distinctly shorter, owing to the much less pointed curve of the archivolts (and also to the lesser width of the door). It was only ca. 1215 that the final design was adopted, with its taller stories and its considerably enlarged portals. The thickness of the lower part of the façade wall was even increased when the portals had already been built to half their height, as revealed by the unusual method of corbeling at the springers of the outer archivolts.

31. The façade of Notre-Dame is a rigorous composition seen three-dimensionally and established on a modular basis: it was designed to look like an assemblage of eight large blocks, identical in size and piled up in three layers. These modular units are 14 meters (46 feet) square in horizontal section and make in height a cube and a half, being 21 meters (69 feet) tall. The main mass of the façade, not counting the detached upper story of the towers, is made up of six of these units assembled into a colossal square 42 meters (138 feet) high and 42 meters wide. Two more such units make the towers, with a void of the same volume to separate them. Actually, the façade does not quite conform to this ideal pattern: the south tower had to be reduced in width by about one meter because

the bishop's palace came too close on that side; the upper gallery or *galerie à jour* (i.e. in openwork) was probably made one meter taller than had been planned originally. Such adjustments would explain the actual dimensions, which are: width of the façade (exclusive of the buttresses which project on the lateral faces of the towers), 41 meters (135 feet); height to the top of the upper gallery, 43 meters (141 feet); total height to the top of the towers, 63 meters (207 feet). It is important to note that the interior structure of that façade (vaulted rooms inside the towers, nave vault between the towers) does not coincide with the horizontal divisions of the exterior: the rooms inside the towers are only some 14 meters (about 46 feet) high, which makes them noticeably shorter than the portals; and the two rooms one above the other come up to only two-thirds of the height of the panels with large composite windows which flank the central rose. The composition of this façade reveals itself, when analyzed closely, as a grand act of rationalization, expressing the will to present a vision of perfect volumetric order.

32. See above, Chapter V, pp. 186–191.

Notes: Chapter VII (pp. 245–295)

1. e.g.: R. Branner, *Gothic Architecture,* New York, 1961, 28 ("The High Gothic Phase"); H. Jantzen, *High Gothic. The Classic Cathedrals of Chartres, Reims, Amiens,* London and New York, 1962 (translation of *Kunst der Gotik,* Hamburg, 1957); W. S. Stoddard, *Art and Architecture in Medieval France,* New York, 1972, 165 ("Part III. High Gothic of the Early Thirteenth Century").

2. This note of caution is necessary in view of the labeling which is found in P. Frankl, *Gothic Architecture* (Pelican History of Art), Harmondsworth and Baltimore, 1962, 79: "Chapter 3. The High Gothic Style, 1194–1300." This pooling under the name of "High Gothic" of two distinct phases in the development of Gothic architecture simply continues a mode of classification which was current in nineteenth century German archaeology and made the single label *Hochgotik* cover the whole span of time from the end of Early Gothic to the beginning of Late Gothic, then commonly fixed around 1350. On the need to differentiate the "Rayonnant Style" as an independent stage in the history of Gothic, see Chapter IX, p. 357ff.

3. On the state of Berry between 1194 and 1199, see A. Cartellieri, *Philipp II. August, König von Frankreich,* III, Leipzig, 1910, 109–110 and

145–146. The complex elements of political propaganda involved in the rebuilding of Chartres cathedral have been analyzed by O. von Simson, *The Gothic Cathedral,* London, 1956, 173–182.

4. On this movement which, widely diffused at first, was progressively pushed to the edges of the area of Gothic leadership, becoming more and more "peripheral" in character (without however losing its potential of invention), see Chap. VIII p. 303ff: see also J. Bony, "The Resistance to Chartres in Early Thirteenth Century Architecture," *Journal of the British Archaeological Association,* 3rd ser., XX–XXI, 1957–58, 35–52.

5. On this question generally, see R. Branner, *La cathédrale de Bourges et sa place dans l'architecture gothique,* Paris and Bourges, 1962, 170–190; *id.,* "The Movements of Gothic Architects between France and Spain in the Early Thirteenth Century," *Actes du XIXᵉ Congrès International d'Histoire de l'Art, Paris 8–13 Septembre 1958,* Paris, 1959, 44–48. On Coutances, the chronology proposed by A. Mussat, "La cathédrale Notre-Dame de Coutances," *Congrès archéologique de France,* CXXIV (Cotentin-Avranchin), 1966, 9–50, tends to be a little too early.

6. E. Lambert, *Etudes médiévales,* Toulouse and Paris, 1956–57, IV, 18, fig. 20.

7. See F. Salet, "La cathédrale du Mans," *Congrès archéologique de France,* CXIX (Maine), 1961, 18–58; also A. Mussat, *Le style gothique de l'ouest de la France,* Paris, 1963, 121–133. But Mussat's hypothesis of a first project for the choir of Le Mans is unconvincing, for it does not stand up to the test of a graphic reconstruction.

8. See E. Panofsky, *Gothic Architecture and Scholasticism,* Latrobe, 1951, 64.

9. The lower part of the choir of Troyes, built between 1208 and 1225, but rebuilt in its upper parts after the hurricane of 1227, is an example of that heavier version, using compound piers in the straight bays, and in that sense related to the nave of Saint-Père at Chartres. See R. Branner, "Les débuts de la cathédrale de Troyes," *Bulletin monumental,* CXVIII, 1960, 111–122.

10. The style of the inner ambulatory at Le Mans is related to that of the choir of Bayeux Cathedral, ca. 1230, of the nave of Sées, ca. 1235, and of the choir of Norrey, ca. 1240.

11. The only element of some importance which does not seem to have been part of the original design is the reduction of the central elevation to only two stories. But if, as seems likely, a triforium of some kind had been planned at first for these upper parts of the building, there is

every probability that what had been conceived was a small triforium of the Chartres type, already placing the emphasis on the heightening of the clerestory; and the total height of the choir certainly remained unaffected.

12. Le Mans being on a smaller scale than Chartres in all its parts, the reach of the radiating chapels of Le Mans from the center of the hemicycle is no greater than that of the three deep chapels of Chartres; if its formula had been applied on the same scale as Chartres, Le Mans would have broken all records for coverage on the ground. It is only in the straight bays of the choir that Le Mans, having chapels along these bays, exceeds Chartres in total interior width.

13. Folio 15 of Villard's manuscript: see H. R. Hahnloser, *Villard de Honnecourt, Kritische Gesamtausgabe des Bauhüttenbuches ms. fr* 19093 *der Pariser Nationalbibliothek,* Vienna, 1935; 2nd ed., Graz, 1972, 69–72 and pl. 29. This design looks in fact rather theoretical, very much the product of an academic *disputatio.*

14. On Reims, some of the most important recent studies are by R. Branner: "Historical Aspects of the Reconstruction of Reims cathedral, 1210–1241," *Speculum,* XXXVI, 1961, 23–37; "The North Transept and the First West Façades of Reims Cathedral," *Zeitschrift für Kunstgeschichte,* XXIV, 1961, 220–241; "The Labyrinth of Reims Cathedral," *Journal of the Society of Architectural Historians,* XXI, 1962, 18–25. To these must be added: F. Salet, "Le premier colloque international de la Société française d'archéologie (Reims, ler-2 juin 1965). Chronologie de la cathédrale," *Bulletin monumental,* CXXV, 1967, 347–394; and J.-P. Ravaux, "Les campagnes de construction de la cathédrale de Reims au XIIIe siècle," *Bulletin monumental,* CXXXVII, 1979, 7–66.

15. The shortness of the east end of Reims and its merging with the transept into a single compositional unit seem to have been dictated by the ceremonial of the Sacre, which must have been one of the basic requirements with which the design of Reims cathedral had to comply. Of all the major Gothic cathedrals of northern France, Reims is the only one in which the liturgical choir (i.e. the space occupied by the choristers and by the stalls of the canons) was not placed east of the crossing, continuous with the sanctuary, but was placed west of it, as in early Romanesque days; and it is no doubt significant that Westminster Abbey, which was rebuilt thirty-five years later to suit the requirements of an almost identical coronation ceremony, presents the same particularity of plan. The English coronations, which have preserved with few changes the ceremonial of the thirteenth century, explain why the transept had to be placed

in that position close to the altar: for the throne of the new king could then be raised in the center of the crossing and the ceremonies of enthronement and homage, which followed the crowning, take place in full view of the large assistance assembled on either side in the transepts.

16. On the constructional function of the pinnacle and the efficacity of its placement on the outer edge of the buttresses, see: R. Mark & R. A. Prentke, "Model Analysis of Gothic Structure," *Journal of the Society of Architectural Historians,* XXVII, 1968, 44–48; and R. Mark & R. S. Jonash, "Wind Loading on a Gothic Structure," *ibid.,* XXIX, 1970, 222–230.

17. On Jean d'Orbais, see R. Branner, "Jean d'Orbais and the Cathedral of Reims," *Art Bulletin,* XLIII, 1961, 131–133.

18. On the sources of the Champenois passage: Chap. V, pp 168–169. An outer passage at the same height and without any thickening of the structure (which constitutes the essential difference between these two systems of low passages) is found in the choir and chevet of Chartres cathedral, at the apse of Vétheuil near Mantes, in the whole chevet of Le Mans, and also a little later at Marburg-an-der-Lahn, Saint-Germain-en-Laye, Saint-Amand-sur-Fion, the cathedral of Tours, and that of León in Spain.

19. See H. Deneux, "Des modifications apportées à la cathédrale de Reims au cours de sa construction du XIIIe au XVe siècle," *Bulletin monumental,* CVI, 1948, 121–140, particularly 127, fig. 6. In the old design, with an elevation shorter by about 1.7m (5′7″), the triforium and clerestory combined would have equalled the height of the main arcade story, anticipating the Amiens formula. As Villard de Honnecourt's drawing of the Reims elevation shows precisely that system of proportions (and not the present one), one would be tempted to place Villard's first visit to Reims somewhat earlier than it is generally thought to have occurred.

20. A plural seems to be required, because it is quite possible that Jean le Loup should be credited with the invention of one of the most remarkable features of the design of Reims: the pinnacles of the buttresses. If it could be proved that the drawing given by Villard de Honnecourt on Fol. 32v of his sketchbook (pl. 64 of the Hahnloser edition) truly represents the flying buttresses of the choir of Reims as designed by Jean d'Orbais, the motif of the pinnacles would certainly have to be attributed to Jean le Loup, who would then be shown to have been as much of a classicist as Jean d'Orbais himself. The plan of the chevet of Reims is enough to mark Jean d'Orbais as the first leader of that tendency to rationalization and purism. It is thus possible that the workshop of Reims

Cathedral, as a result of the prestige of Jean d'Orbais, became the center of a classicizing school of Gothic and that the successive masters went on perfecting the original design by further inventions, carried on along the same lines and in the same spirit. But this is only a likely hypothesis.

21. See E. Panofsky, *Gothic Architecture and Scholasticism,* Latrobe, 1951, 43–44.

22. On Amiens, see G. Durand, *Monographie de l'église cathédrale Notre-Dame d'Amiens,* Amiens, 2 vols., 1901–1903; R. Branner, *St Louis and the Court Style,* London, 1965, particularly 24–28 and 138–140; D. Kimpel and R. Suckale, "Die Skulpturenwerkstatt der Vierge Dorée am Honoratusportal der Kathedrale von Amiens," *Zeitschrift für Kunstgeschichte,* XXXVI, 1973, 217–265; and, suggesting an altered chronology, A. Erlande-Brandenburg, "Le septième colloque international de la Société française d'archéologie (ler et 2 octobre 1974). La façade de la cathédrale d'Amiens," *Bulletin monumental,* CXXXV, 1977, 253–293. P. Frankl, "A French Gothic Cathedral: Amiens," *Art in America,* XXXV, 1947, 294–299 gives of Amiens Cathedral an interpretation which is completely at variance with mine, but which is interesting in itself as an extreme case of systematic thinking.

23. The aisles at Amiens are 19m (62′4″) tall, which means that their height surpasses that of the central nave of Saint-Yved at Braine (18.3m or 60′) and approaches that of the naves of Wells Cathedral and Beverley Minster (20.4m or 67′).

24. On the novel treatment of the upper stories of the elevation of the nave of Amiens, see Chapter IX, pp. 361–362. A. Erlande-Brandenburg, in the article mentioned above, suggests that this change of treatment may have been the result of a revision of design in course of construction.

25. See Chapter V, pp. 191–193.

26. On the façade of Saint-Nicaise, designed by Hugues Libergier and begun in 1231, see Chapter IX, pp. 381–385.

27. The upper story of the towers is much later than the rest of the façade and does not conform to the original plan. The north tower was completed in 1410. As planned the towers could never have been very tall, since they have so little depth; but they might have been meant to carry two stone spires of which the lateral stair-turrets would appear to give a scaled-down version.

28. There are many other groups of one tower façades, but Saint-Quentin is related in type to a group which covers Hainault, Brabant,

and Flanders. Eleventh-century prototypes can be found at Lobbes and Soignies; in the twelfth century, from 1138, a west porch-tower was added to the old church of Sint Baafs (Saint-Bavon) at Ghent, destroyed in the sixteenth century; Saint-Pierre at Ypres and Dudzeele are actually later than Cambrai. The west tower at the cathedral of Cambrai was built after the fire of 1148 and completed ca. 1180: see P. Héliot, "La nef et le clocher de l'ancienne cathédrale de Cambrai," *Wallraf-Richartz Jahrbuch,* XVIII, 1956, 91–110.

29. A chaplaincy, which seems to have been always located in the chapel of the southeastern transept, was founded in 1220. This might mean that by 1220 that chapel was nearing completion, which would place the beginning of the work some five or perhaps ten years before: but chaplaincies were sometimes founded well before a chapel was ready to receive them, although such foundations normally indicate that work has been started on some enlargement of the fabric. At any rate work proceeded at a slow pace: gifts to the fabric are recorded in 1228 and an elevation of relics (a fund-raising operation) in 1229. A long time elapsed before a second chaplaincy was founded, in the axial chapel, in 1254 (thirty-four years after the first one); and the solemn translation of all the relics into the new choir, in the presence of King Louis IX, took place only in 1257. The west tower had been built in an older style at the end of the twelfth century, before the enlargement of the east end had been decided. See P. Héliot, "Chronologie de la basilique de Saint-Quentin," *Bulletin monumental,* CXVII, 1959, 7–50; *id., La basilique de Saint-Quentin et l'architecture du moyen âge,* Paris, 1967.

30. In France the double transept of Cluny III was repeated only at Souvigny. In England the Cluniac priory of Lewes also copied the mother church of the order, but that plan was not adopted before the second quarter of the twelfth century. On the other hand, a second transept had been added to the plan of Canterbury Cathedral in Ernulf's enlarged choir, begun soon after 1096; and Roger's new choir at York Minster, ca. 1170–80, seems to have had some kind of an eastern transept. But the great popularity of the double transept started in England with the Gothic rebuilding of the choir of Canterbury Cathedral by William of Sens (1175–78), who revived and further monumentalized the articulations of the Romanesque choir. It is on the basis of the Gothic choir of Canterbury that the architect of Lincoln developed his more formalized two-transept lay-out, in which the two transepts are sharply differentiated.

31. Salisbury Cathedral was begun in 1220, the new choir of Worces-

ter cathedral in 1224, Beverley Minster about 1225. The east transept of Rochester, freely repeated from Canterbury Cathedral, is much less narrow than in the Lincoln-derived series.

32. On the plan of the east end of Lincoln in the late twelfth century, see E. Venables, "On the Foundations of the East End of St. Hugh's Choir of Lincoln," *Archaeological Journal*, XLIV, 1887, 194–202; A. W. Clapham, *English Romanesque Architecture After the Conquest*, Oxford, 1934, 89–90; or the plan published in the *Archaeological Journal*, CIII, 1946, pl. XI, fac. 103. The present rectangular east end (Angel Choir) is an enlargement of the second half of the thirteenth century (1256–1280).

33. The non-projecting transepts of Saint-Quentin are both two bays deep (the depth of the double aisles of the choir). At Lincoln the smaller east transept is three bays deep, projecting by two bays, and the main transept is four bays deep and projects by three bays.

34. That contacts with the Continent were renewed at Lincoln, ca. 1215, is proved by the return to sexpartite vaulting, by the split-bay elevation of the main transept (related to Nesles-la-Vallée, Geneva nave, etc.) and by the design of the north rose-window (known as the "Dean's Eye").

35. The triple entrance arch is found in the late twelfth century in the chapel of the south transept of Soissons and in the ambulatory chapels of Notre-Dame-en-Vaux at Châlons-sur-Marne. In the early thirteenth century, in addition to the chapels of Saint-Quentin, the Lady Chapel of Auxerre Cathedral should also be mentioned.

36. While the curve of the ambulatory bays is rounded on the inside, it takes a faceted polygonal shape on the outside.

37. Troyes Cathedral, begun in 1208, initiated that series; Saint-Omer also must be slightly earlier than Saint-Quentin. Later examples are: Saint-Nicaise at Reims (begun in 1231, now destroyed), Saint-Pierre at Lagny (mid-thirteenth century, partly preserved), and the church of St. Mary (ca. 1250, now destroyed) in the abbey of Sint-Pieter (Blandinium) at Ghent.

38. This can be seen on a seventeenth-century bird's eye view of the abbey reproduced in M. Aubert, *L'architecture cistercienne en France*, Paris, 1943, I, 129. The choir of Vaucelles was built between 1216 and 1235, the year when it was dedicated. It was an enlargement of the church built between 1190 and 1216. On Vaucelles generally, in addition to C. Nicq-Doutreligne, "L'abbaye de Vaucelles (Nord)," *Bulletin monumental*, LXXVIII, 1914, 316–328, see the recent articles by F. Baron, "Histoire architecturale de l'abbaye de Vaucelles," *Citeaux in de Nederlanden*, IX,

1958, 276–285, and "Les églises de Vaucelles," *ibid.,* XI, 1960, 196–208.

39. This attribution was first made by P. Bénard, "Recherches sur la patrie et les travaux de Villard de Honnecourt," *Travaux de la Société académique . . . de Saint-Quentin,* 3rd ser., VI, 1864–1866, 260–280; it has been accepted by H. R. Hahnloser, *Villard de Honnecourt: Kritische Gesamtausgabe . . . ,* Vienna, 1935; 2nd ed., Graz, 1972, 234–237; but it has recently been seriously questioned by C. F. Barnes, Jr.

40. For the chronology of Beauvais, see R. Branner, "Le maître de la cathédrale de Beauvais," *Art de France,* II, 1962, 77–92. Much new information can be expected from the full-scale monograph of Beauvais Cathedral now being prepared by Stephen Murray.

41. I tend to subscribe to R. Branner's opinion that the first master of Beauvais came from the Reims workshop where he worked probably up to 1225, when he was called to Beauvais. He was obviously dissatisfied with the rather heavy, classicizing tendency of the design of Reims cathedral and adopted the new sophistication first proclaimed at Saint-Quentin ca. 1215. The original design of Beauvais would then demonstrate the impact Saint-Quentin had on one of the most brilliant younger members of the Reims team.

42. On this disaster, see M. Wolfe and R. Mark, "The Collapse of the Beauvais Vaults in 1284," *Speculum,* LI, 1976, 462–476: an essential study, which disproves the explanation given by Viollet-le-Duc and shows that the collapse was due to the excessive overhang of the intermediate piers of the buttressing system. Wind buffeting must have progressively produced cracks in the danger area of one of those pier-buttresses (i.e. just above the level of the ambulatory vaults), and once a hinge was created there, the process of collapse started, spreading inevitably to the upper structure of the whole of the straight bays.

43. R. Branner, *St Louis and the Court Style,* London, 1965, 95, suggests that the upper stories, triforium and clerestory, may not have been started until about 1255. The choir was finished in 1272, but remained standing in its original state for only twelve years.

44. It has sometimes been suggested that the height of Beauvais Cathedral was increased in the course of construction. Some slight changes in the dimensions of the upper stories may have been adopted in the final redesigning of the 1250s. But the effect of disproportion, which was intended from the start, as proved by the systematic reduction of the height of the chapels, implies that Beauvais—like Saint-Quentin—was always meant to have an exceptionally tall clerestory and a total height at least

equal to that of Amiens. In a discussion of the spatial concept of Beauvais, the analogy with Bourges must not be carried too far: the elevation of the ambulatory at Beauvais is a dwarf elevation, where the triforium is as if telescoped into the windows, while Bourges is characterized by the perfect normality and completeness of each of its duplicated elevations. These differences are so basic and they affect so profoundly the spatial expression of the two interiors that it seems difficult to establish a close affinity between the buildings.

45. The full interior height of the choir of Beauvais is 48.2m (a little over 158′); Cologne is shorter by 4.7m (not quite 15½′), Amiens by 5.9m (almost 19½′).

Notes: Chapter VIII (pp. 303–354)

1. The exchanges between these late Romanesque milieux and the Gothic centers of northern France have been described in R. Branner, "Gothic Architecture 1160–1180 and Its Romanesque Sources," *Studies in Western Art, Acts of the XXth International Congress of the History of Art,* Princeton, 1963, I, 92–104.

2. This has been done in all countries and often in the most remarkable manner:

FOR BELGIUM & HOLLAND—S. Leurs, *Geschiedenis van de Vlaamse Kunst,* Antwerp, 1937; S. Brigode, *Les églises gothiques de Belgique,* Brussels, 1944; R. M. Lemaire, *Les origines du style gothique en Brabant,* III, Antwerp, 1949; M. D. Ozinga, *De gothische kerkelijke bouwkunst,* Amsterdam, 1953; S. J. F. Andreae & E. H. Ter Kuile, *Duizend jaar bouwen in Nederland,* I, Amsterdam, 1957;

FOR ENGLAND—T. S. R. Boase, *English Art 1100–1216,* Oxford, 1953; G. F. Webb, *Architecture in Britain: The Middle Ages,* Harmondsworth & Baltimore, 1956; P. Brieger, *English Art 1216–1307,* Oxford, 1957; P. Kidson & P. Murray, *A History of English Architecture,* London, 1962;

FOR GERMANY—G. Dehio, *Geschichte der deutschen Kunst,* 4th ed., Berlin & Leipzig, 1930; E. Gall, *Dome und Klosterkirchen am Rhein,* Munich, 1956;

FOR ITALY—W. Gross, *Die abendländische Architektur um 1300,* Stuttgart, 1948; R. Wagner-Rieger, "Die italienische Baukunst zu Beginn der Gotik," *Publikationen des österreichischen Kulturinstituts in Rom* (Abteilung für historische Studien, 1. Abhandlungen, 2), 2 vols., Graz & Cologne, 1957;

FOR SPAIN—E. Lambert, *L'art gothique en Espagne aux XIIe et XIIIe siècles,* Paris, 1931; L. Torres Balbás, *Arquitectura gotica,* (Ars Hispaniae, 7), Madrid, 1952;

FOR SWITZERLAND—J. Gantner, *Kunstgeschichte der Schweiz,* II. *Die gotische Kunst,* Frauenfeld, 1947; J. Vallery-Radot, "Introduction à l'histoire des églises de la Suisse romande des origines au milieu du XIIIe siècle," *Congrès archéologique de France,* CX (Suisse romande), 1952, 9–39;

On the various provinces of France, see principally:

BURGUNDY—R. Branner, *Burgundian Gothic Architecture,* London, 1960;

NORMANDY—G. Huard, *L'art en Normandie,* Paris, 1928; D. Jalabert, *L'art normand au moyen âge,* Paris, 1930;

WEST OF FRANCE—A. Mussat, *Le style gothique de l'ouest de la France (XIIe–XIIIe siècles),* Paris, 1963;

SOUTH OF FRANCE—R. Rey, *L'art gothique dans le Midi de la France,* Paris, 1934; M. Durliat, *L'art dans le royaume de Majorque,* Toulouse, 1962; *id.,* "L'architecture gothique méridionale au XIIIe siècle," *Ecole Antique de Nîmes, Bulletin annuel,* new ser., VIII–IX, 1973–1974, 63–132.

3. I raised these questions quite some time ago in "The Resistance to Chartres in Early Thirteenth Century Architecture," *Journal of the British Archaeological Association,* 3rd ser., XX–XXI, 1957–1958, 35–52.

4. See M. Durliat, "L'architecture gothique méridionale au XIIIe siècle," (see note 2 above), 82–88.

5. R. Rey, *La cathédrale de Cahors et les origines de l'architecture à coupoles d'Aquitaine,* Paris, 1925.

6. A. Anglès, "L'abbaye de Silvanès," *Bulletin monumental,* LXXII, 1908, 41–60; *id.,* "La date de l'église de Silvanès," *Bulletin monumental,* LXXIII, 1909, 319; M. Aubert, *L'architecture cistercienne en France,* Paris, 1943, I, 167–8. The church of Silvanès was begun between 1151 and 1164; the nave is 14.17 m (46′6″) wide, for a height of 18.58 m (61′).

7. See J. Thirion, "L'ancienne église de Lamourguier à Narbonne," *Congrès archéologique de France,* CXII (Roussillon), 1954, 433–445. The nave alone, on a length of six bays, shows three successive designs: the last of them, which gave the building its present appearance, must be placed in the third quarter of the thirteenth century; the choir and last bay of nave were added in a fourth campaign, ca. 1300. On the use of the diaphragm arch, see: C. Martinell, "Les monastères cisterciens de Poblet et de Santes Creus," *Congrès archéologique de France,* CXVII (Catalogne), 1959, 98–128; L. Torres Balbas, "Naves cubiertas con armadura de madera

sobre arcos perpiaños a partir del siglo XIII," *Archivo Español de Arte*, XXXIII, 1960, 19–43. A similar method was used at Fontfroide near Narbonne, in the dormitory of the *conversi*.

8. On the development of Gothic in the west of France, the basic study is A. Mussat, *Le style gothique de l'ouest de la France (XIIe–XIIIe siècles)*, Paris, 1963; the beginnings of the movement are well analyzed in J. Bilson, "Les voûtes de la nef de la cathédrale d'Angers," *Congrès archéologique de France*, LXXVII (Angers-Saumur), 1910, II, 203–223; and in M. Aubert, "Les plus anciennes croisées d'ogives, leur rôle dans la construction," *Bulletin monumental*, XCIII, 1934, 37–67.

Should the Aquitanian sources of the design of Angers Cathedral be viewed as reflecting the new orientation given to the Angevin state by Henry of Anjou's marriage with Eleanor of Aquitaine? If so, the start of the work would have to be placed in 1152, rather than in 1149 or 1150.

9. The vaults of Saint-Serge are analyzed by A. Mussat, *Le style gothique de l'ouest de la France*, 223–232; see also the drawings by J. Trouvelot in M. Aubert's article cited in the preceding note, *Bulletin monumental*, 1934, 61.

10. Other examples of that unusual type of rib-vaults are: Cheviré-le-Rouge, Fougeré, la Boissière (Maine-et-Loire), and Saint-Germain-sur-Vienne (Indre-et-Loire). They all seem to belong to the second quarter of the thirteenth century.

11. The English series begins with the aisle vaults of the choir of Bristol, probably designed in 1298 (there, the ribbed Angevin barrels are used as transverse barrels); then come the vaults of Tewkesbury nave, ca. 1320–1325, followed in the 1330s by the chancel of Urchfont (Wilts.), the choir of Wells, the nave and choir of Ottery St. Mary (Devon), the choir of Gloucester; and somewhat later by the nave of Winchester cathedral, begun in 1371. In the Empire, first examples are the choir of Prague cathedral, vaulted by Peter Parler between 1376 and 1385; and the choir of the church of S. Martin at Landshut, by Hans Stethaimer, built between 1392 and 1407.

12. In the case of Anjou, the stimulus came, via Le Mans (nave of the cathedral), from the Chartres workshop of the 1140s; and behind that first line of contact can be perceived a retransmission of more distant suggestions emanating from as far as southern Picardy (Airaines) or eastern Normandy (Montivilliers). In the twelfth century churches of Saumur and Angers, the frequent appearance of a three-roll profile in vault ribs can be regarded as one of the material signs of the importance

of these initial contacts.—In the Languedoc area, where the impact occurred only later, at the beginning of the thirteenth century, it was the Gothic concept of lightness and the oblong bay pattern that were the determinant factors, when combined with the bold spatial formulas which had developed in southern France in the late Romanesque period.

13. On that autonomous German line of development, that of the hall-churches of Westphalia, see Chapter X, pp. 452–453.

14. On Cistercian architecture generally, see: H. Rose, *Die Baukunst der Zisterzienser,* Munich, 1916; M. Aubert, *L'architecture cistercienne en France,* Paris, 2 vols., 1943; H. P. Eydoux, *L'architecture des églises cisterciennes d'Allemagne,* Paris, 1952; H. Hahn, *Die frühe Kirchenbau der Zisterzienser,* Berlin, 1957 (Frankfurter Forschungen zur Architekturgeschichte, 1); F. Bucher, *Notre-Dame de Bonmont,* Bern, 1957 (Berner Schriften zur Kunst, 7); J. A. Schmoll, "Zisterzienser-Romanik. Kritische Gedanken zur jüngsten Literatur," *Formositas Romanica,* Frauenfeld, 1958, 151–180; and two useful repertories: A. Dimier, *Recueil de plans d'églises cisterciennes,* Grignan and Paris, 2 vols., 1949; and F. van der Meer, *Atlas de l'ordre cistercien,* Paris and Brussels, 1965. Italian Cistercian architecture has now been fully analyzed by R. Wagner-Rieger, *Die italienische Baukunst zu Beginn der Gotik,* Graz and Cologne, 2 vols., 1956–7 (Publikationen des oesterreichischen Kulturinstituts in Rom, Abteilung für historische Studien, Abhandlungen, 2); and by L. Fraccaro de Longhi, *L'architettura delle chiese cisterciensi italiane,* Milan, 1958.—On Pontigny, see R. Branner, *Burgundian Gothic Architecture,* London, 1960, 16–17 and 163. Among the many variations on the Pontigny type can be mentioned: in the twelfth century, Santes-Creus (Catalonia), Orval (Belgium); in the early thirteenth century, Casamari (central Italy), Sulejow abbey (Poland).

This Gothicization of Cistercian architecture had been preceded by a complex Romanesque development comprising two main movements: on the one hand, in the northern sectors of Europe is found an unvaulted and non bay-divided first Cistercian architecture, which can be represented in France by the naves of Clermont near Laval, Boquen, and Melleray; in England by the Rievaulx-Fountains-Buildwas-Kirkstall series (with Furness nave as a variant); in Ireland by Jerpoint; in Germany by Marienthal, Heilsbronn, Amelunxborn, Maulbronn. On the other hand, in the more southerly regions where vaulting was the rule, a sequence of development can be followed from Bonmont (Switzerland), which has no bay articulation at all, to l'Escale-Dieu (Hautes-Pyrénées), where the bay articulation affects only the vault story, then to Fontenay, Fontfroide, le Thoronet, Obazine, Flaran, etc., where the bay articulation bars the whole elevation, and finally to the groin-vaulted type of Pontigny transept, les Vaux-de-Cernay, or Fossanova, in which the very shape of the vault units stresses the autonomy of each bay. The adoption of the rib vault with its sharp linear accentuation (at Clairvaux in 1153, at Pontigny nave ca. 1160) can be viewed as the fifth stage in this progressive development toward increasingly rhythmical articulations.

15. A similar stage (with some interesting variations) is represented in Spain by the cathedrals of Zamora, Salamanca, Ciudad Rodrigo, Tarragona, Lerida and Sigüenza: see E. Lambert, *L'art gothique en Espagne aux XIIe et XIIIe siècles,* Paris, 1931. In the kingdom of Germany, the double-bay formula illustrated by Bamberg was used also at Goslar (Neuwerkskirche), at Naumburg Cathedral, at Rouffach in Alsace, etc.

16. On English Cistercian architecture, the basic work remains John Bilson, "The Architecture of the Cistercians, with Special Reference to some of their Earlier Churches in England," *Archaeological Journal,* LXVI, 1909, 185–280. On early English Gothic, see the works listed in n. 2.

17. On the churches of Ghent: P. Deruelle, *De Sint-Pietersabdij te Gent,* Ghent, 1933; P. Verhaegen, "L'église Saint-Nicolas de Gand," *Bulletin monumental,* XCVI, 1937, 133–189; *id., Les églises de Gand* (Ars Belgica, 7–8), Brussels, 2 vols., 1938; E. Dhanens, *Sint-Niklaaskerk, Gent* (Inventaris van het Kunstpatrimonium van Oostvlaanderen, 3), Ghent, 1960.

18. C. M. Smidt, *Roskilde Domkirkes Middelalderlige Bygningshistorie,* Copenhagen, 1949; E. Moltke and E. Moeller, *Roskilde Domkirke* (Danmarks Kirker, 3:3), Copenhagen, 1951; P. Héliot, "La cathédrale de Roskilde et l'influence de l'architecture française en Danemark vers 1150–1220," *Bulletin monumental,* CXXII, 1964, 233–260.

19. R. Rey, "La collégiale Saint-Paul de Narbonne," *Congrès archéologique de France,* CXII (Roussillon), 1954, 476–485.

20. E. Gall, "Sankt-Georg in Limburg-an-der-Lahn und die nordfranzösische Frühgotik," *Festschrift für Adolf Goldschmidt,* Leipzig, 1923, 7–24; R. Branner, "Sint-Leonardus at Zoutleeuw and the Rhein Valley in the Early Thirteenth Century," *Bulletin de la Commission Royale des Monuments et des Sites,* XIV, 1963, 259–268.

21. See: J. Vallery-Radot, "Fécamp. Eglise abbatiale," *Congrès archéologique de France,* LXXXIX (Rouen), 1926, 405–458; *id., L'église de la Trinité de Fécamp,* Paris, 1928. The Fécamp series can be described as follows: Fécamp east bays, Fécamp west bays, Rouen cathedral nave, Eu, choir of Saint-Etienne at Caen (all with vaulted tribunes), Coutances nave

(built probably after the fire of 1218, with non-vaulted tribunes later blocked).

22. It is difficult to reconstruct exactly the original design of the nave of Rouen Cathedral, for it was changed considerably in the course of construction (tribune floor done away with, clerestory heightened by several meters to bring the vaults to the same height as in the new choir) and further remodelled in its upper stories in the fourteenth century. With a shorter clerestory the elevation would have had much more normal proportions. See G. Lanfry, *La cathédrale après la Conquête de la Normandie et jusqu'à l'occupation anglaise,* Rouen, 1960.

23. On the two stages in the construction of the east end and choir of Saint-Etienne at Caen, see E. Lambert, "Caen roman et gothique," *Bulletin de la Société des Antiquaires de Normandie,* XLIII, 1935, 46–54. But Lambert's reconstruction of the actual sequence of operations must now be revised in the light of Eric Carlson's discoveries: see E. G. Carlson, "Excavations at Saint-Etienne, Caen (1969)," *Gesta,* X:1, 1971, 23–30. Lambert postulated at Saint-Etienne a deep Romanesque choir, the same length as the present Gothic choir. Carlson having proved that the Romanesque choir was much shorter (only two bays deep), another explanation must be found for the anomalies of the hemicycle piers. Now it would seem that a much more Ile-de-France building was planned in the first stage, most probably a thin-wall structure supported on columnar piers as in the nave of Lisieux; and when the piers were thickened in the second stage of the work, that was done because the plans had been changed in favor of a more Norman kind of structure, thicker, richer in its decoration, and provided with the traditional clerestory passages.

24. The choir of Bayeux is later than the east end of Lisieux, which was remodeled after the fire of 1226. At Bayeux the Romanesque transept (and most likely the choir also) was still in existence in 1228. The rebuilding was begun only after 1228. See J. Vallery-Radot, *La cathédrale de Bayeux,* Paris, 2nd ed., 1958.

25. A strong current of English influences had begun in Normandy in the first years of the twelfth century, and had continued to the end of the Romanesque period. But it had ceased to be felt after about 1170, when Ile-de-France Gothic had replaced English Romanesque as the major source of extraneous artistic inspiration. It is therefore somewhat puzzling to find that English influences were suddenly revived in the early thirteenth century, at a time when England did not play a particularly vital rôle in the development of the new art forms. As this revival

coincides with the conquest of Normandy by Philip Augustus, it is reasonable to construe that attempt at Englishness as a sign of hostility against the French conquerors. —For the elevation of Whitby choir, see F. Bond, *Gothic Architecture in England,* London, 1905, 114. The pattern of the intermediate story at Bayeux choir does not recall only Whitby but also the transepts of York Minster and the westernmost bay of the choir of Rievaulx.

26. The revival of the tribune elevation (in fact as pseudo-tribunes in the Romsey manner) which occurred in the north of England at the end of the twelfth century and in the first decades of the thirteenth was linked to a late Romanesque movement, neo-classical in tendency, which had begun in Scotland in the 1160s, with St. Andrews Cathedral as one of its earliest exponents, and which was based on a conscious imitation of the pattern of regularity of the great East Anglian churches of the late eleventh and early twelfth centuries (such as Norwich, Ely, Castle Acre or Peterborough). That movement veered to Gothic at the end of the twelfth century. Jedburgh in Scotland, in England Hexham (Northumberland), Whitby (North Yorkshire) and Lanercost (Cumbria) illustrate that second, early Gothic stage. None of these buildings was vaulted and the constructional type remained essentially Romanesque, with a mere gothicization of surface treatment. The persistent vogue of that tribune pattern in the northern areas of England explains the elevation of the transepts of York cathedral and, in the second half of the thirteenth century, such belated examples as St. Mary's at York and the north elevation of Bridlington nave.

27. Flying buttresses of a rather elementary form had been used at Canterbury by William the Englishman as early as 1184 (they are contemporaneous with the building of the clerestory of the Trinity Chapel). Three buildings in Sussex have bold flying buttresses of early date which are closely related with French models of the late twelfth century: the choir of Chichester cathedral, remodelled between 1186 and 1199, and the choirs of New Shoreham and Boxgrove Priory, of the first years of the thirteenth century. But on the whole Early English architecture tended either to reduce the prominence of the flying buttress, as at Lincoln and Beverley, or to do away with it altogether, as at Salisbury Cathedral (begun in 1220) or in the choir and Lady Chapel of Worcester (begun in 1224). It was only in 1245 that Westminster Abbey introduced into England the high-rise buttressing of thirteenth century French churches, together with the Chartrain type of interior elevation.

28. A general hostility to the flying buttress can be observed in nearly all peripheral styles of Gothic: in Flanders, Denmark and Germany, as well as in the Mediterranean countries and in most of the provincial milieux of France. Changes of visual habits, especially when they affect the definition of architectural volumes, always meet with considerable resistance.

29. See A. Bray, "Moret-sur-Loing," *Bulletin monumental,* LXXXVIII, 1929, 437–449.

30. On the nave of Saint-Leu d'Esserent, see R. Branner, *St Louis and the Court Style,* London, 1965, 35 and 38. A similar treatment of the triforium story is found at Pacy-sur-Eure (Eure) and at Hénin-Liétard (Pas-de-Calais).

31. On this group, see R. Branner, "Paris and the Origins of Rayonnant Gothic Architecture down to 1240," *Art Bulletin,* XLIV, 1962, 43 and note 21. Related forms of triforium elevation are found at Boiscommun (Loiret), in the choir of Cambronne (Oise), the transept of Saint-Quiriace at Provins (Seine-et-Marne) and the nave of Gonesse (Val d'Oise).

32. E. Lefèvre-Pontalis, "Eglise de Taverny," *Congrès archéologique de France,* LXXXII, 1919 (Paris), 50–69.

33. On the church of Saint-Yved at Braine, see above, Chap. V, pp. 172–175; see also my article "The Resistance to Chartres in Early Thirteenth Century Architecture," *Journal of the British Archaeological Association,* 3rd series, XX–XXI, 1957–58, 35–52.

34. See Chapter VI, pp. 220–239.

35. The series includes: around Paris, Herblay, Marly-la-Ville, Ferrières-en-Brie, La Chapelle-sur-Crécy, Villeneuve-le-Comte; to the north of Paris, the old church of Saint-Martin at Aumale, Mons-en-Laonnois, Saint-Michel-en-Thiérache, Chaudardes and Braine itself; east and south-east of Paris, the destroyed Sainte-Chapelle of Dijon and Saint-Gengoult at Toul; in the south of France, Saint-Maximin (Var); in Belgium, Saint-Quentin at Tournai, Sint Maarten at Ieper, Lisseweghe; in Germany, the Liebfrauenkirche at Trier, S. Victor at Xanten, Oppenheim, and a number of late Gothic examples such as Ahrweiler, Osterburg and Münstermaifeld; the church of St. Elizabeth at Košice in Czechoslovakia is probably no earlier than 1380.

Diagonally planted chapels were also used occasionally in ambulatory plans: e.g., in a roughly chronological order beginning ca. 1205, in Troyes Cathedral, Notre-Dame at Saint-Omer, Saint-Quentin, the destroyed churches of St. Peter and St. Mary at Ghent (in the old monastery of Blandinium), Vaucelles, the ideal plan given by Villard de Honnecourt, Saint-Nicaise at Reims, Lagny; and in the fourteenth century Prague Cathedral (designed in 1344 by Mathieu d'Arras). On this point, see above, Chapter VII, pp. 285–286.

36. Tongeren to the north-west of Liège, Bonn on the Rhine itself show that the style made deep inroads into the Mosan and Rhenish lands. Further south, it spread soon to the whole of Imperial Burgundy: Besançon, Salins, Geneva, Lausanne, going as far south as Lyon and the Viennois.

37. On this point, see above, Chapter V, pp. 158–172.

38. That loggia treatment of the upper story was repeated, with the same tribune elevation, at the destroyed abbey-church of St. Peter at Ghent (Blandinium), at Ghent again in the nave of Sint Niklaaskerk, and a little later at Limburg-an-der-Lahn. The direct prototype for these exterior passages was Tournai cathedral (nave and transepts); but the classic Gothic version of that idea, the tall open loggia of three equal arches per bay, was the creation of Cambrai, which can be treated as the point of departure for the Gothic series. The Noyon variant, with two arches only per bay, never gained much popularity. On the Lombard sources which can be perceived behind Tournai and which continued to act on some later buildings of that series, see R. Branner, "Sint-Leonardus at Zoutleeuw and the Rhein Valley in the Early Thirteenth Century," *Bulletin de la Commission Royale des Monuments et des Sites*, XIV, 1963, 257–268.

39. The same system of deep arches is found in the early thirteenth century choir of the church of Notre-Dame (which was a cathedral from 1561 to 1802) at Saint-Omer. See J. de Pas, "Saint-Omer, Cathédrale," *Congrès archéologique de France*, IC, (Amiens), 1936, 475–514.

40. See above, Chapter V, p. 178 and note 19, pp. 492–493.

41. See R. Branner, *Burgundian Gothic Architecture*, London, 1960.

42. In addition to R. Branner's book just mentioned, see J. Vallery-Radot, "Auxerre. La cathédrale Saint-Etienne. Les principaux textes de l'histoire de la construction," *Congrès archéologique de France*, CXVI, (Auxerre), 1958, 40–50. As at Chartres, the clerestory windows are composed of two fairly short lancets surmounted by an unusually large oculus, which fills the whole width of the bay at the top of the elevation.

43. See R. Branner, *Burgundian Gothic Architecture*, 54–62 and 132–133 (Notre-Dame, Dijon), 66–68 and 179–180 (Semur).

44. See A. Rhein, "La cathédrale de Dol," *Bulletin monumental*, LXXIV, 1910, 369–433. The nave of Dol was begun soon after 1203 with plain cylindrical columns; but construction was interrupted for a while after

the completion of the aisles, and the refined structure of the upper stories reflects the adoption of a new design. This is where new influences seem to have intervened.

45. The vaults over the nave were built somewhat later, in the mid-thirteenth century. That the clerestory was completed only then is proved by the change of style which takes place half-way up in the window jambs.

46. See J. Bony, "La technique normande du mur épais à l'époque romane," *Bulletin monumental,* XCVIII, 1939, 153–188.

47. The west bays of the nave of Worcester, rebuilt after the collapse of a tower in 1175, are dated ca. 1175–1180; St. Davids cathedral was begun in 1180. On these, see: H. Brakspear, "A Western School of Masons," *Archaeologia,* LXXXI, 1931, 1–18; W. M. Ede and H. Brakspear, *Worcester Cathedral,* 4th ed. revised, 1937, 50; E. W. Lovegrove, "The Cathedral Church of St. Davids," *Archaeological Journal,* LXXXIII, 1926, 254–283. At Kelso, the west transept and the west bays of the nave date also from the last quarter of the twelfth century: see: A. W. Clapham, "Kelso Abbey," *Archaeological Journal,* XCIII, 1936, 328–9; G. F. Webb, *Architecture in Britain: The Middle Ages* (Pelican History of Art), Harmondsworth and Baltimore, 1956, 53–55; *Royal Commission on Ancient and Historical Monuments of Scotland, Roxburghshire,* London, 1956, 241–245. On St. John's church at Chester, see: A. W. Clapham, *English Romanesque Architecture After the Conquest,* Oxford, 1934, 93; *id.,* "The Summer Meeting at Chester. St. John The Baptist," *Archaeological Journal,* XCIV, 1937, 307–308: on the basis of style, the adoption of a triforium design for the nave can be placed in the mid or late 1180s; the clerestory is of the early thirteenth century.

48. On the "ploughshare" shaping of the vaults, which is another French characteristic, see F. Bond, *Gothic Architecture in England,* London, 1905, 311.

49. R. Branner, *Burgundian Gothic Architecture,* London, 1960, 34–35 and 188.

50. R. Branner, "Westminster Abbey and the French Court Style," *Journal of the Society of Architectural Historians,* XXIII, 1964, 3–18.

51. This Burgundian series of the second quarter of the thirteenth century included also the nave of Saint-Seine-l'Abbaye, Prémery, Rougemont and Saint-Père-sous-Vézelay. In Lorraine the two-story elevation of the cathedral of Toul had probably been fixed upon in the early 1240s. The nave of Cuenca Cathedral in Spain (mid-thirteenth century) should be connected also with that Burgundian series. Many problems relating

to the two-story elevation are discussed in P. Héliot, "La suppression du triforium au début de la période gothique," *Revue archéologique,* 1964 (1), 131–168. On Toul cathedral, see A. Villes, "Les campagnes de construction de la cathédrale de Toul. Première partie: Les campagnes du XIIIe siècle," *Bulletin monumental,* CXXX, 1972, 179–189.

52. See my article "French Influences on the Origins of English Gothic Architecture," *Journal of the Warburg and Courtauld Institutes,* XII, 1949, 12. The nave of St. Davids in Wales, Nesles-la-Vallée near Pontoise, the choir of Avila Cathedral, the east bays of the nave of Geneva Cathedral are the earliest representatives that have survived of that split-bay pattern; they are all earlier than the central part of the choir of Vézelay, where this mannerism was introduced, as an afterthought, ca. 1207: see F. Salet, *La Madeleine de Vézelay,* Melun, 1948, 69–83. The origin of the series must surely have been a building of the 1170s situated somewhere in the Laon-Noyon area.

53. That distant westernmost part of Normandy had surprisingly strong stylistic links with the Paris region: the Abbaye Blanche at Mortain and, in the Cotentin proper, the churches of Picauville and Appeville point to direct Ile-de-France contacts. The case of Coutances choir is not so simple: the building appears in many ways a continuation of the Caen school of the first quarter of the thirteenth century; but it is the product of a wide synthesis in which the regional element combines not only with the spatial concept of Bourges but with many other classic Gothic formulas. On the connection of Coutances with the Bourges series, see Chapter VII, pp. 248–251.

54. Other examples of two-story elevations in Normandy are: Ardenne (near Caen), Longues (near Bayeux), the choir of Bernières, the north side of the nave of Saint-Gervais at Falaise.

55. In the present state of our knowledge, the first example is the nave of Melbourne (Derbyshire), begun ca. 1135–1140: see A. W. Clapham, *English Romanesque Architecture After the Conquest,* Oxford, 1934, pl. 22a, fac. 106. This precedes by about ten years the only Romanesque example existing in Normandy, the nave of Ouistreham, which displays many other signs of English influence. In the mid-1180s Deeping St. James (near Peterborough) still repeats a purely Romanesque type of two-story elevation. Was the appearance in Anglo-Norman naves of that kind of two-story elevation with upper passages in any way connected with the two-story treatment which had been given to Norman apses ever since Saint-Etienne at Caen and which had sometimes been extended to

the whole choir, as at la Trinité at Caen ca. 1120 or 1125? One would be tempted to think so, especially as an identical phenomenon can be observed at the end of the twelfth century in the lower Rhine area. The adoption from ca. 1185 in the churches of Cologne, and in the whole school that followed, of an alleviated version of the Norman double-wall apses, soon led to an extension of the same treatment to transeptal west halls, as at Xanten (ca. 1190), to whole choirs, as at Wetzlar, and to the nave itself, as at Bremen Cathedral (after 1224).

56. From 1185, the full sequence of English examples would be: Portsmouth (Hants.) St. Thomas, begun by 1189; Fountains (North Yorks.) choir, begun before 1211; Llandaff (South Glamorgan) nave, ca. 1215; Great Grimsby (Humberside) nave, ca. 1215–20; Boxgrove (West Sussex) choir, ca. 1220; Pershore (Hereford and Worcester) choir, ca. 1230; Southwell (Notts.) choir, 1234–41; Lanercost (Cumbria) nave, north side, ca. 1240; Netley (Hants.), begun 1244; then there follow in Scotland, four examples dated between 1250 and 1280: Dunblane cathedral, Pluscarden, Elgin cathedral and Sweetheart Abbey; and the series continues in England with eleven more examples between 1275 and 1350.

57. For the dating of Netley, see H. M. Colvin, ed., *The History of the King's Works, I. The Middle Ages,* London, 1963, 158, n.2.

58. In Normandy, in the second half of the thirteenth century, side by side with the flat Rayonnant elevations of the choirs of Sées and Evreux, a Rayonnant version of the two-story elevation with passages was adopted in the choirs of Saint-Wandrille and Jumièges. The same contrast is found in Brittany between the Parisian-looking choir of Saint-Malo and the choir of Quimper treated in the double-wall manner with two superposed interior passages. Similarly, in southern Champagne, two contrasting versions of the same type of two-story apse are given, at Troyes (Saint-Urbain) and at Mussy-sur-Seine; and in Burgundy the orthodox Rayonnant flatness of Varzy or Saint-Thibault makes a no less striking contrast with the deeply recessed two-passage elevations of the cathedrals of Nevers and Chalon-sur-Saône.

Notes: Chapter IX (pp. 357–405)

1. This means that rose-windows are normally restricted to west fronts and transept ends; but in buildings designed with a rectangular east end the rose-window may become the dominant motif at the end of the perspective of the nave. This started in Cistercian churches such as

Buillon (Doubs) or Kirkstall (Yorkshire) in the third quarter of the twelfth century. Saint-Vincent at Laon, ca. 1180, initiated a group which in the early thirteenth century spread from the Laon area (extended choir of Laon cathedral ca. 1205, church of Vaux-sous-Laon soon after) to the Paris region (Louveciennes) and to Champagne (Donnemarie-en-Montois). In the mid-thirteenth century, in a choir rebuilt between 1246 and 1269, the church of Saint-Denis at Reims (now destroyed) gave a Rayonnant version of that east end formula, which culminated in the new choir of Old St. Paul's in London, ca. 1258–1283.

2. The impact of the Rayonnant Style varied of course from country to country. The least profoundly affected was probably Italy: see W. Gross, *Die abendländische Architektur um* 1300, Stuttgart, 1948.

3. On the relationship between stained-glass and architecture, see: L. Grodecki, "Le vitrail et l'architecture au XIIe et au XIIIe siècles," *Gazette des Beaux Arts,* 6th ser., XXXVI, 1949, 5–24; *id., The Stained Glass of French Churches,* London, 1948; M. Aubert, A. Chastel, L. Grodecki, et al., *Le vitrail français,* Paris, 1958. Intensely colored glass in small medallions was the first answer to the fragmentation of surfaces that resulted from the use of tracery: e.g. at the Sainte-Chapelle glazed in 1247–1248. But the Rayonnant style was soon accompanied by a tendency toward reduced coloration through the use of grisaille either filling the whole window or, more commonly, surrounding panels of colored glass. Pure grisaille was used in the Lady Chapel of Saint-Germain-des-Prés in Paris, built by Pierre de Montreuil in the late 1240s. On the combination of grisaille with colored panels, see: J. Lafond, "Le vitrail en Normandie de 1250 à 1300," *Bulletin monumental,* CXI, 1953, 317–358; M. Parsons Lillich, "The Band Window, A Theory of Origin and Development," *Gesta,* IX:1, 1970, 26–33.

4. Among the most important of recent publications are: S. McK. Crosby, *L'abbaye royale de Saint-Denis,* Paris, 1953; H. Bober, "A Reappraisal of Rayonnant Architecture" in *The Forward Movement of the Fourteenth Century* (F. L. Utley, ed.), Columbus, 1961, 9–30; L. Grodecki, *Sainte-Chapelle,* Paris, 1962; and, by R. Branner, "Paris and the Origins of Rayonnant Gothic Architecture down to 1240," *Art Bulletin,* XLIV, 1962, 39–51; "Westminster Abbey and the French Court Style," *Journal of the Society of Architectural Historians,* XXIII, 1964, 3–18; *St Louis and the Court Style in Gothic Architecture,* London, 1965; "La place du 'Style de Cour' de Saint Louis dans l'architecture du XIIIe siècle" in *Le siècle de Saint Louis* (R. Pernoud & A. Chamson, eds.), Paris, 1970, 133–139.

5. This passage is published in the original Latin text in V. Mortet & P. Deschamps, *Recueil de textes relatifs à l'histoire de l'architecture et à la condition des architectes en France au moyen âge,* Paris, 1911–1929, II, 291.

6. The tomb used to be in the church of Saint-Nicaise, of which he had been the designer and the architect for over thirty years; it is now up against the north aisle wall in the nave of the cathedral.

7. See Chapter VII, pp 275–278.

8. On the development of architectural draughtsmanship in the mid-thirteenth century, see: H. R. Hahnloser, *Villard de Honnecourt. Kritische Gesamtausgabe des Bauhüttenbuches ms. fr* 19093 *der Pariser Nationalbibliothek,* Vienna, 1935; 2nd ed., Graz, 1972; R. Branner, "Drawings from a Thirteenth Century Architect's Shop: The Reims Palimpsest," *Journal of the Society of Architectural Historians,* XVII, 1958, 9–21; *id.,* "Villard de Honnecourt, Archimedes and Chartres," *Journal of the Society of Architectural Historians,* XIX, 1960, 91–96; *id.,* "Villard de Honnecourt, Reims and the Origins of Gothic Architectural Drawing," *Gazette des Beaux Arts,* series 6, LXI, 1963, 129–146; F. Bucher, "Design in Gothic Architecture: A Preliminary Assessment," *Journal of the Society of Architectural Historians,* XXV, 1968, 49–72.

9. On Bourges and its style of linearity, see above Chapter VI, p. 220.

10. See Chapter VII, pp. 288–295; for the dating and the stylistic analysis, refer to R. Branner, "Le maître de la cathédrale de Beauvais," *Art de France,* II, 1962, 77–92.

11. The windows of the chapels are similar to those of Reims cathedral both in type and in mode of construction. The shortened windows of the ambulatory clerestory also have their model at Reims, in the window which surmounts the east door of the north transept. The engaged piers which separate the chapels, although much thinner and differently treated (with applied monolithic shafts), are of the same *cantonné* type as at Reims. Finally the general silhouette of the chevet, with its straight vertical rise, is also derived from the Reims concept of alignment.

12. On this point see R. Branner, "Paris and the Origins of Rayonnant Architecture," *Art Bulletin,* XLIV, 1962, 43–44; *id., St Louis and the Court Style,* London, 1965, 25–28. Robert de Luzarches also brought with him to Amiens the new style of sculpture which had just been created in Paris: see W. Sauerländer, "Die kunstgeschichtliche Stellung der Westportale von Notre-Dame in Paris," *Marburger Jahrbuch für Kunstwissenschaft,* XVII, 1959, 1–56; *id., Gothic Sculpture in France* 1140–1270, London, 1972, 57, 466.

13. See R. Branner, *St Louis and the Court Style,* London, 1965, 31–37; *id.,* "Westminster Abbey and the French Court Style," *Journal of the Society of Architectural Historians,* XXIII, 1964, 3–18.

14. On the chronology of the thirteenth-century rebuilding of Saint-Denis, the changes of style, and the amount of work completed under Abbot Eudes (1228–1245), see: S. McK. Crosby, *L'abbaye royale de Saint-Denis,* Paris, 1953, 57–60; R. Branner, *St Louis and the Court Style,* 46–47. The type of piers used by the first architect, in the central area of what was preserved of the choir of Suger, does not relate only with the nave of Gonesse but also with two piers of the nave of Mantes which were remodeled ca. 1225–1230: see my article on Mantes in *Congrès archéologique de France,* CIV (Paris-Mantes), 1946, 187–189 (pier III south is closest to the Saint-Denis work).

15. See the conflicting opinions expressed by R. Branner, "A Note on Pierre de Montreuil and Saint-Denis," *Art Bulletin,* XLV, 1963, 355–357; *id., St Louis and the Court Style,* 143–146 (Appendix C), and L. Grodecki, "Pierre, Eudes et Raoul de Montreuil à l'abbatiale de Saint-Denis," *Bulletin monumental,* CXXII, 1964, 269–274. Grodecki is no doubt right in thinking that Pierre de Montreuil was in charge of the work at Saint-Denis in 1247; but this does not invalidate the argumentation of Branner concerning the authorship of the design of the 1230s. The work that was being done at Saint-Denis in the 1240s and 50s, specially in the chapels of the east end (new altars, retables, canopies or tabernacles above the altars), agrees perfectly with what is known of the style of Pierre de Montreuil: see J. Formigé, *L'abbaye royale de Saint-Denis, recherches nouvelles,* Paris, 1960, 120–148.

16. On this chapel, see: H. Verlet, "Les bâtiments monastiques de l'abbaye de Saint-Germain-des-Prés," *Paris et Ile-de-France,* IX, 1957–58, 9–68; R. Branner, *St Louis and the Court Style,* London, 1965, 68–71.

17. This is the system of revised chronology put forward by R. Branner in *St Louis and the Court Style,* 37–55. On the particular problem raised by the choir of Troyes cathedral, see *ibid.,* 41–45, where the author corrects the dating he had previously given in "Les débuts de la cathédrale de Troyes," *Bulletin monumental,* CXVIII, 1960, 113–114, and suggests that the rebuilding might have begun as early as 1229 or 1230. The details of execution, especially the groups of five shafts which rise all the way up on the face of the piers, indicate that the redesigning of Troyes relates with an early stage (probably no later than ca. 1235) in the development of the Saint-Denis style. A new study of these problems is at present being carried out by C. Bruzelius.

18. E.g., a middle mullion composed of three shafts instead of two; cusped circles of smaller diameter in the heads of the windows.

19. On the beginnings of that "linkage" between triforium and clerestory, see Chapter IV, pp. 147–149; on its history, see R. Branner, *St Louis and the Court Style*, 20–22. The English series begins (in the nave of St. Davids) some ten or fifteen years after Arras and Saint-Remi. A Cistercian variant of the concept appeared probably also in the 1170s in the west bays of the nave of les Vaux-de-Cernay, to the south of Paris.

20. The most precise document we have concerning the interior of Saint-Nicaise is a fairly rough sketch of one bay of the nave elevation. It has been published by Branner in his article of the *Art Bulletin*, XLV, 1963, pl. fig. 15, foll. 52, and in his book on *St Louis and the Court Style*, 31, fig. 3. This sketch indicates clearly that the triforium was cut in two in the middle of each bay by the continuation of the central mullion of the clerestory window.

21. The idea of giving light to the triforium story by piercing windows in its back wall had appeared in the mid-1220s in a variety of different guises: in the ambulatory of Beauvais cathedral, in the nave of Saint-Leu d'Esserent, at Chelles (now destroyed), then at Vaudoy-en-Brie, La Chapelle-sur-Crécy; the survival of one of these early forms of piercing can be observed in the 1240s in the choir of Tournai cathedral. See R. Branner, "Le maître de la cathédrale de Beauvais," *Art de France*, II, 1962, 83, n.18; *id., St Louis and the Court Style*, 22–23.

22. At first, in the straight bays of the choir, the new architect of Saint-Denis used compound piers made up of fourteen shafts, with a group of five set toward the central nave and continued upward to the vaults. But he soon changed to piers of slightly smaller section, reduced to twelve shafts, and with three shafts only toward the central nave: this new formula was used in the whole transept and nave. The shafts supporting the wall ribs were, from that moment, stopped at the base of the triforium story.

23. E. Panofsky, *Gothic Architecture and Scholasticism*, Latrobe, 1951; new ed. (Meridian Books), 1957, particularly 45–53.

24. See J. de Terline, "La tête de Saint Louis à Saint-Germain-en-Laye," *Monuments et Mémoires, Fondation E. Piot* (Académie des inscriptions et belles-lettres), XLV, 1951, 123–140; R. Branner, *St Louis and the Court Style*, 51–52.

25. This formula for the composition of a façade gives wider interior proportions than the Reims formula, which was based on the same

rule, but in which the upper compartment was heightened into a rectangle by the inscription of the rose within a pointed arch. At Saint-Denis the height of the clerestory even commands the height of the whole nave, since the measurements show that the combined height of the triforium and clerestory multiplied by two gives the full interior height.

26. See: C. Givelet, *L'église et l'abbaye Saint-Nicaise de Reims* (Travaux de l'Académie de Reims, 98), Reims, 1897; H. Deneux, "L'ancienne église Saint-Nicaise de Reims," *Bulletin monumental*, LXXXV, 1926, 117-142; and recently, M. Bideault and C. Lautier, "Saint-Nicaise de Reims. Chronologie et nouvelles remarques sur l'architecture," *Bulletin monumental*, CXXXV, 1977, 295-330.

27. The form is used commonly in Parisian triforia: choir of Brie-Comte-Robert, west bays of Saint-Séverin in Paris, choir of Cormeilles-en-Vexin; and it is found also on the façades of both Notre-Dame and Amiens: see R. Branner, *St Louis and the Court Style*, 18-19 and n.10. It should be noted that the rose part of the great west window owed its flamboyant tracery to a repair and redesigning of ca. 1540.

28. See E. B. Smith, *Architectural Symbolism of Imperial Rome and the Middle Ages*, Princeton, 1956; R. Krautheimer, *Early Christian and Byzantine Architecture*, (Pelican History of Art), Harmondsworth and Baltimore, 1965, 113-116. The process of formation of the Romanesque and Gothic two-tower façade cannot be reduced exclusively to the City-Gate or Palace-Gate sources which are at the origin of the Syrian type, and no doubt also of the pre-Carolingian examples which can be reconstructed in western Europe. In the Carolingian period and in the course of the tenth century, two other influences intervened: that of the complex *Westwerke* of the Corvey type on the one hand, which led to the storied inner structure of the later façade-blocks; and on the other hand that of the apse compositions with paired towers, of the Fulda type, which led to a tighter grouping of the towers. On these problems, see H. Schaefer, "The Origins of the Two-Tower Façade in Romanesque Architecture," *Art Bulletin*, XXVII, 1945, 85-108; and L. Grodecki, *Au seuil de l'art roman. L'architecture ottonienne*, Paris, 1958, 289-292. However, the City-Gate concept never lost its significance and was sometimes revived most literally, as at Lincoln Cathedral in the 1080s, where the pattern of a triple archway was based on the imitation of a triumphal gate of the type of the Golden Gate of Constantinople.

29. See: J. Mallion, *Chartres. Le jubé de la cathédrale*, Chartres, 1964; W. Sauerländer, *Gothic Sculpture in France* 1140-1270, London, 1972,

438–440, 498–499. The first mention of the choir-screen of Strasbourg appears in a document of 1261; the screen had probably been made only a few years before.

30. On these early gables used over the choir entrance in the middle of a choir screen, see: I. Petricioli, "La scultura pre-romanica figurativa in Dalmazia ed il problema della sua cronologia," *Stucchi e mosaici alto medioevali* (Atti del VIII Congresso di Studi sull'arte dell'alto Medioevo, 1959), Milan, 1962, I, 360–374 (on the church of St. Peter at Solin); E. Doberer, "Die ornamentale Steinskulptur an der karolingischen Kirchenausstattung," in W. Braunfels, ed., *Karl der Grosse,* Düsseldorf, 1965, III, 203–233 (on the Cortona fragment and on the chapel of St. Martin at Split). The source of this motif seems to be the arch within a pediment, of Syrian origin, used in Hadrians's Temple of Artemis at Ephesus, ca. 117–125, and repeated as a triumphal motif in Late Antique works such as the Missorium of Theodosius I of 388: see A. Boethius and J. B. Ward-Perkins, *Etruscan and Roman Architecture,* (Pelican History of Art), Harmondsworth & Baltimore, 1970, 393, 441; W. F. Volbach, *Early Christian Art,* New York, 1961, 322, and pl.53.

31. There seems to have been a late twelfth century rood-screen with large triangular frames of the gable type at Canterbury Cathedral, up to the rebuilding of the nave and transept in the late fourteenth and early fifteenth centuries. No final reconstruction of that screen has yet been reached, but fragments of carved decoration recovered at various dates have been interpreted as suggesting a pattern somewhat similar to that of the lower parts of the façade of Wells Cathedral. The west choir screen of Naumburg Cathedral, designed probably in the late 1250s, still conforms to a pattern of that type. See P. Brieger, *English Art* 1216–1307, Oxford, 1957, 35, n.1. This transfer of the choir screen treatment to façades has been fully analysed by C. M. Malone in an unpublished doctoral dissertation, "West English Gothic Architecture, 1175–1250," Berkeley, 1973. The Canterbury fragments have recently been discussed in the 1979 meeting of the British Archaeological Association at Canterbury.

32. See E. Lefèvre-Pontalis, "Abbaye de Longpont," *Congrès archéologique de France,* LXXVIII (Reims), 1911, I, 410–423. The Cistercian abbey of Longpont (Aisne), in the forest of Villers-Coterets, must not be confused with the Cluniac priory of Longpont (Essonne, formerly Seine-et-Oise), near Montlhéry, to the south of Paris.

33. On the choir of Cambrai, see essentially H. R. Hahnloser, *Villard*

Pariser Nationalbibliothek, Vienna, 1935; 2nd ed., Graz, 1972, 67–69, 226–228, 356–357, 386–387, pl.28c, Abb. 60, 61, 63. When it is published, the monograph of Cambrai Cathedral by J. Thiébaut will give a much better idea of the chronology of this choir and of its historical significance.

34. Lateral walls ending at the top in a series of gables had been fairly frequently used in Cistercian architecture: e.g. in England on the east side of the transept of Fountains (begun in 1135), around the east end of Abbey Dore (ca. 1200), and all along the aisles in the Gothic choir of Fountains (begun between 1203 and 1211); while at Bronnbach in Germany (dedicated in 1222) this gable treatment was extended to the whole building: see H. Feldtkeller, "Die Zistersienserkirche in Bronnbach o.d. Tauber und ihre ursprüngliche Dachlösung," *Zeitschrift für Kunstgeschichte,* XVIII, 1955, 199–211. A similar mode of roofing had been used as early as the 1120s over the tribunes of the nave of Durham and had been repeated in the 1170s at the east end of Arras cathedral. But these wider gables did not frame neatly the head of the windows as they did in the English Cistercian examples of the early thirteenth century, particularly in the choir of Fountains. For the use of a closely related solution in domestic architecture, see the reconstruction of the original state of Winchester Castle Hall (1222–1234), in H. M. Colvin, *Building Accounts of King Henry III,* Oxford, 1971, 16.

35. See P. Héliot, "Le choeur de la cathédrale de Tournai," *Académie royale de Belgique, Bulletin, Classe des Beaux-Arts,* XLV, 1963, 31–54.

36. See: L. Grodecki, *Sainte-Chapelle,* Paris, 1962; I. Hacker-Sück, "La Sainte-Chapelle de Paris et les chapelles palatines du moyen âge en France," *Cahiers archéologiques,* XIII, 1962, 217–257; R. Branner, "The Painted Medallions in the Sainte-Chapelle in Paris," *Transactions of the American Philosophical Society,* new series, LVIII:2, 1968, 3–42.

37. See: G. Durand, *Monographie de l'église Notre-Dame cathédrale d'Amiens,* Amiens & Paris, 1900–1901, I, 34, 274–275; R. Branner, "Westminster Abbey and the French Court Style," *Journal of the Society of Architectural Historians,* XXIII, 1964, 3–18; *id., St Louis and the Court Style,* London, 1965, 62–63 and 138–140 (Appendix A).

38. Star-shaped abaci of a simpler form (a five-point star) had been used also at Saint-Quentin, begun ca. 1215–1220, on top of the thin columns which support the triple-arch entrances to the ambulatory chapels. The origin of this star shape was the use of triangular abaci for individual

shafts (the French *tailloirs à bec*): a fashion which had started shortly before 1200 in the Laon-Soissons region.

39. The type of pier used at Strasbourg, in which five shafts rise from the ground to the vault, is that of Troyes and of the west bays of the choir of Saint-Denis. This means that Strasbourg was not influenced by the modified design already applied at Saint-Denis in the earliest bays of the transept (east side of the north transept). The pattern of the triforium is essentially the same as at Troyes and Saint-Denis, apart from the question of absolute linkage. See: H. Reinhardt. "La nef de la cathédrale de Strasbourg," *Bulletin de la Société des amis de la cathédrale de Strasbourg*, Ser.2, IV, 1937, 3–28; R. Branner, "Remarques sur la cathédrale de Strasbourg," *Bulletin monumental*, CXXII, 1964, 261–268; H. Reinhardt, *La cathédrale de Strasbourg*, Paris, 1972.

40. See A. Mussat, *Le style gothique de l'ouest de la France (XIIe–XIIIe siècles)*, Paris, 1963, 166–169. The choir of Tours cathedral is only about 28m (not quite 92′) high.

41. See M. Aubert, ed., *La cathédrale de Metz*, Paris, 1930.

42. See Chapter VII, pp. 288–295 and notes 40–45, pp. 508–509.

43. See: P. Clemen, *Der Dom zu Köln*, Düsseldorf, 1937 *(Kunstdenkmäler der Rheinprovinz, 6:3);* C. Pfitzner, "Die Anfänge des Kölner Dombaus und die Pariser Bauschule der erste Hälfte des 13. Jahrhunderts," *Zeitschrift des deutschen Vereins für Kunstwissenschaft*, IV, 1937, 203–217; R. Branner, *St Louis and the Court Style*, London, 1965, 128–132; A. Wolff, "Chronologie der ersten Bauzeit des Kölner Domes," *Kölner Domblatt*, XXVIII–XXIX, 1968, a work of particular importance, which could be considered a model of modern monographic method.

44. This applies essentially to the interior treatment of the choir of Cologne. On the exterior, at the level of the aisles and chapels, Cologne has a more refined touch than the Sainte-Chapelle, with thin framings of foliage which recall rather the style of Jean de Chelles at Notre-Dame.

45. See G. Durand, *Monographie de l'église Notre-Dame cathédrale d'Amiens*, Amiens & Paris, 2 vols., 1900–1901.

46. See Chapter X, pp. 421–423.

47. See R. Branner, *St Louis and the Court Style*, 76–79 (north transept), 101–106 (south transept); D. Kimpel, *Die Querhausarme von Notre-Dame zu Paris und ihre Skulpturen*, Bonn, 1971.

48. Among the characteristics of the late style of Pierre de Montreuil are new tracery forms, particularly the pointed trilobe inscribed in a curved ("spherical") triangle or placed upside down in the spandrel of an

arcading. Some of the new forms used in Paris in the 1260s are found also at Saint-Urbain at Troyes: see Chapter X, pp. 423–425.

49. The formula is Branner's: see *St Louis and the Court Style*, 57–59, which gives in a condensed form the most perceptive and most firmly supported presentation of the whole question.

50. The shrine of Saint Taurin seems to be the last survivor of the great Parisian shrines of the mid-thirteenth century. It was made under Abbot Gilbert, 1240–1255, and probably toward the end of his abbacy. See: G. Bonnenfant, *L'église Saint-Taurin d'Evreux et sa châsse,* Paris, 1926; J. Taralon, *Treasures of the Churches of France,* London, 1966, 280–281. The prototype for that new style of shrines, conceived as diminutive versions of the most recent architecture, was the Grande Châsse of the Sainte-Chapelle, datable to 1248: see R. Branner, "The Grande Châsse of the Sainte-Chapelle," *Gazette des Beaux-Arts,* 6th ser., LXXVII, 1971, 518.

51. The attempts to date the lower parts of the façade to the 1230s and 1240s have now been abandoned. It is generally admitted that the nave of Reims Cathedral was originally intended to be shorter by two bays; the planned façade would therefore have been situated two bays further to the east. The three westernmost bays of the cathedral, as it stands now, make an indissociable unit, built from the foundations to a revised design by Bernard de Soissons soon after he took over, ca. 1254. See: H. Deneux, "Des modifications apportées à la cathédrale de Reims au cours de sa construction du XIIIe au XVe siècle," *Bulletin monumental,* CVI, 1948, 121–140; R. Branner, "The Labyrinth of Reims Cathedral," *Journal of the Society of Architectural Historians,* XXI, 1962, 18–25; H. Reinhardt, *La cathédrale de Reims,* Paris, 1963; F. Salet, "Le premier colloque international de la Société française d'archéologie (Reims, ler-2 juin 1965). Chronologie de la cathédrale," *Bulletin monumental,* CXXV, 1967, 347–394.

52. For a variety of reasons, some authors in the last twenty years have tended to place the designing of the façade of Wells as late as ca. 1230, see: J. H. Harvey, *English Mediaeval Architects. A Biographical Dictionary down to* 1550, London, 1954, 170, 195, 354; L. Stone, *Sculpture in Britain: The Middle Ages* (Pelican History of Art), Harmondsworth and Baltimore, 1955, 108; G. F. Webb, *Architecture in Britain: The Middle Ages* (Pelican History of Art), Harmondsworth and Baltimore, 1956, 105. But the style of the lower parts of the façade and towers suggests a beginning date in the mid-1220s at the latest, supporting the chronology given by J. Bilson, "Notes on the Earlier Architectural History of Wells Cathedral,"

Archaeological Journal, LXXXV, 1928, 23–68. On these points of chronology and on the problems raised by the mode of treatment of the façade of Wells, see the unpublished dissertation by C. M. Malone mentioned above in note 31, p. 526.

53. It is well known that in the days of Abbot Anselm (1121–1148), Bury St Edmunds had been, under the leadership of Master Hugo, a center of experimentation on transfers between techniques and between media: from manuscripts to bronze, from doors and retables to fonts, from bronze panels to stone carving (choir-screen of Durham Cathedral). See: G. Zarnecki, *Later English Romanesque Sculpture* 1140–1210), London, 1953, 26–27, 32–33, 46; L. Stone, *Sculpture in Britain: The Middle Ages* (Pelican History of Art), Harmondsworth and Baltimore, 1955, 82, 104–105; G. Zarnecki, *English Romanesque Lead Sculpture,* London, 1957. Related phenomena had taken place also in architecture: the gable and pinnacles which frame the west arch of the gate tower at Bury St Edmunds (an insertion of the middle years of the century) show that English Romanesque builders were then beginning to play with reduced versions of large scale architectural forms. The west front of the great church, completed in its original state in the 1140s, seems to have had applied motifs of the same nature: the considerable projection of the buttresses of the upper zone of the façade (indicated by what remains of their rubble core) suggests that these buttresses may have ended at that level in the shape of pinnacles or miniature turrets set against the recessed wall face, see: A. B. Whittingham, "Bury St Edmunds Abbey. The Plan, Design and Development of the Church and Monastic Buildings," *Archaeological Journal,* CVIII, 1951, 168–187. An Irish building of ca. 1140, St Cronan's at Roscrea (county Tipperary), which can be related with Bishop Roger's work at Old Sarum, would seem to suggest that refinements of that order might also have been experimented with at Sarum in the 1130s: see R. A. Stalley, "A Twelfth-Century Patron of Architecture: A Study of the Buildings erected by Roger, Bishop of Salisbury 1102–1139," *Journal of the British Archaeological Association,* 3rd ser., XXXIV, 1971, 62–83.

54. See note 8, p. 522.

55. On the "hardness of metal," we must take care not to be deceived by anachronistic assumptions. For us, in an age of steel and machines, metal stands for dryness and rigidity of form. But for the medieval man, metal seems to have suggested a much wider range of potential properties, for metalwork commonly meant goldsmith's work, i.e. work in soft metals (in malleable sheets of gold and silver), as much as in the harder

gilt-bronze; and bronze itself, being fluid when cast, quite often keeps in its form the softness of wax or clay models. Metal must therefore be given back its variability of connotations.

Notes: Chapter X (pp. 411–463*)*

1. The idea of filling otherwise undecorated tympana with simple forms of tracery, such as two trefoiled arch heads surmounted by a quadrilobe, seems to have come from the Cistercians (Longpont, Royaumont); by the 1220s the idea had been adopted at Villeneuve-le-Comte and in some of the smaller Parisian churches (e.g. Saints-Côme-et-Damien, now destroyed). The fitting of rich sculptural decoration into such compartmented tympana was initiated in the doorways of Saint-Nicaise at Reims; but the more complex compositions of Saint-Urbain at Troyes and of the central doorway of Sens, with their patterns of sub-divided tracery, are no earlier than the 1270s. By that time Bernard de Soissons had adopted for the west façade of Reims Cathedral (designed most probably in the mid-1250s) the even more radical concept of the glazed tympanum, which did not become widespread until somewhat later.

2. E.g. the tomb of Louis de France (d. 1260), eldest son of Saint Louis, originally at Royaumont and now at Saint-Denis. See H. Goüin, *L'abbaye de Royaumont,* Paris, 1932, 17–19; S. McK. Crosby, *L'abbaye royale de Saint-Denis,* Paris, 1953, pl. 94; or the incised slab tombs illustrated in J. Guibert, ed., *Les dessins d'archéologie de Roger de Gaignières,* Paris, 1911–12, ser. 1, II, pl. 152; III, pl. 278. In wall tombs, the final formula does not seem to have been arrived at until the 1280s: the tomb of Dagobert at Saint-Denis (ca. 1260), in its sculptural richness, was only a first and rather atypical approximation of the concept.

3. Serialized into a gabled and pinnacled arcading, this framing motif had been used from ca. 1260 to enclose on the sides of tomb-chests little figures of virtues or of mourners, as on the tomb of Louis de France. It is this typical pattern of gabled arcading that is found, soon after 1268, on the dado zone on either side of the right-hand doorway of the west façade of Sens Cathedral.

All these refinements in concept and execution go with the new professionalism which manifests itself in the second half of the thirteenth century. On this point, see in particular R. Branner, "Villard de Honnecourt, Reims and the Origin of Gothic Architectural Drawing," *Gazette des Beaux-Arts,* 6th ser., LXI, 1963, 129–146.

4. In its earliest form the system of Rayonnant architectural framing can be observed in the Psalter of Saint Louis (B.N., Ms.Lat. 10525), which can be dated between 1253 and 1270: see: V. Leroquais, *Les psautiers manuscrits latins des bibliothèques publiques de France,* Mâcon, 3 vols., 1940–41, II, 101; Bibliothèque Nationale, *Manuscrits à peintures en France du XIIIe au XVIe siècle* (exhibition catalog), Paris, 1955, 12–14 (No. 11); J. Porcher, *Medieval French Miniatures,* New York, 1959, 45–46. More complex forms of framing had developed by the late 1280s: see for instance the Psalter and Hours of Yolande, Vicomtesse de Soissons (New York, Pierpont Morgan Library, Ms. M.729): Burlington Fine Arts Club, *Exhibition of Illuminated Manuscripts,* London, 1908, No. 139; W. D. Wixom, *Treasures from Medieval France,* Cleveland, 1967, 168–171.

5. On the development of thirteenth-century stained glass, see above, note 3, p. 521. Recent studies have stressed the two major new trends of the mid and late thirteenth century, the combination of grisaille with figures in full color: see M. Parsons Lillich, "The Band Window: A Theory of Origin and Development," *Gesta,* IX, 1970, 26–33; and the development of the architectural canopy: see R. Becksmann, *Die architektonische Rahmung des hochgotischen Bildfensters. Untersuchung zur oberrheinischen Glasmalerei von* 1250 *bis* 1350, (Forschungen zur Geschichte der Kunst am Oberrhein, 9–10), Berlin, 1967, who demonstrates the priority of the Strasbourg workshop but tends to date individual windows five to ten years early. The imaginary architectures of the stained glass artists of Strasbourg seem to have worked in turn on the imagination of Master Erwin, the designer of the Strasbourg façade.

6. See E. Lambert, "Bayonne: cathédrale et cloître," *Congrès archéologique de France,* CII (Bordeaux-Bayonne), 1939, 522–560, 568–570.

7. That recession of the central panel can be compared with the original design of the nave of Saint-Jacques at Reims, preserved in the eastern-most bay on the south side. As for the general arrangement of the window lights and of the triforium arches, it is related to window compositions found in the choirs of Essômes and Saint-Thierry (now destroyed). Essômes already has the window-within-a-window effect.

8. R. Branner in *St Louis and the Court Style,* London, 1965, 97–100, had corrected the date of the start of work at Clermont-Ferrand Cathedral from 1248 (date traditionally accepted on the basis of a late medieval reading of a lost inscription) to 1262 (when Saint Louis is said to have made a gift for the rebuilding). But V. Paul, in a recent reexamination of the building, tends to place again the start of work close to 1250.

9. See M. Aubert, "Abbaye de Valmagne," *Congrès archéologique de*

France, CVIII (Montpellier), 1950, 233–240. Also slightly earlier than Narbonne Cathedral are the choir and transept of Saint-Nazaire at Carcassonne (see pp. 427–428 and 447).

10. The immediate influence of these transept façades on the Ile-de-France workshops is demonstrated by the south doorway added in 1300 to the façade of Mantes.

11. On English architecture of the second half of the thirteenth century, see G. F. Webb, *Architecture in Britain: The Middle Ages* (Pelican History of Art), Harmondsworth & Baltimore, 1956, 107–125; P. Brieger, *English Art 1216–1307* (The Oxford History of English Art, 4), Oxford, 1957, 106–134, 183–199, 227–256; P. Kidson & P. Murray, *A History of English Architecture,* London, 1962, 86–101. On Westminster Abbey: W. R. Lethaby, *Westminster Abbey and the King's Craftsmen,* London, 1906; Royal Commission on Historical Monuments (England), *An Inventory of the Historical Monuments in London, I. Westminster Abbey,* London, 1924; W. R. Lethaby, *Westminster Abbey Re-examined,* London, 1925; G. F. Webb, "The Decorative Character of Westminster Abbey," *Journal of the Warburg and Courtauld Institutes,* XII, 1949, 16–20; H. M. Colvin, *The History of the King's Works. The Middle Ages,* London, 1963, I, 130–157, specially 141–144; R. Branner, "Westminster Abbey and the French Court Style," *Journal of the Society of Architectural Historians,* XXIII, 1964, 3–18. Work on the chapter house and the northeast section of the cloister was in progress by 1248 and had probably started in 1245; in 1253 canvas was purchased for the temporary stopping of the windows of the chapter house: the stone structure was therefore complete. The transept must have been finished by 1259, when work started on the second campaign of construction in the first five bays to the west of the crossing.

12. The nave of York Minster was begun in 1291. Its similarity with Clermont-Ferrand was noted by J. H. Harvey, *The English Cathedrals,* London, 1950, 58. The influence of York nave stimulated the appearance in Yorkshire of such purely Rayonnant compositions as the west front of Howden, added a little after 1300 to a nave of the 1290s. At Exeter, the easternmost bays of the choir (the presbytery bays), in their original two-story elevation, were begun ca. 1288; the west bays of the choir (choir bays proper), built from the start with triforium elevation, are dated ca. 1300–1310: see H. E. Bishop & E. K. Prideaux, *The Building of the Cathedral Church of St. Peter in Exeter,* Exeter, 1922.

13. On Strasbourg, Metz and Cologne, see above, Chapter IX, pp. 391–396.

14. On Utrecht cathedral, see E. J. Haslinghuis & C. J. A. C. Peet-

ers, *De Dom van Utrecht,* The Hague, 1965 (Nederlandse Monumenten van Geschiedenis en Kunst, II, 2). On Wimpfen, see H. Klotz, *Der Ostbau der Stiftskirche zu Wimpfen im Tal. Zum Frühwerk des Erwin von Steinbach,* (Kunstwissenchaftliche Studien 39), Munich & Berlin, 1967, a most useful work, even if the identification of the architect can be questioned. On the west front of Strasbourg, see below, n. 22.

15. See above, Chap. IX, p. 398. Master Arnold is first mentioned in the documents in 1271 but he may well have been at Cologne since about 1261, by which time the first architect, Gerard, had already vanished. The lower story of the choir is now considered to have been completed by 1268 and the upper stories by 1305. See A. Wolff, "Chronologie der ersten Bauzeit des Kölner Domes," *Kölner Domblatt,* Nos. 28–29, 1968.

16. On Regensburg Cathedral, see: F. Mader, *Regensburg,* (Kunstdenkmäler Bayerns, III. Oberpfalz, XXII, 1) Munich, 1933; G. Gall, "Zur Baugeschichte des Regensburger Domes," *Zeitschrift für Kunstgeschichte,* XVII, 1954, 61–78. On Meissen, see H. Küas, *Der Dom zu Meissen. Baukunst und Bildwerk,* Leipzig, 1938.

17. On Uppsala, see G. Boethius & A. Romdahl, *Uppsala Domkyrka 1258–1435,* Uppsala, 1935; and, for a more recent evaluation of the evidence, R. Zeitler, "Die Baugeschichte des Doms zu Uppsala," *Aspekte zur Kunstgeschichte von Mittelalter und Neuzeit, Karl Heinz Clasen zum 75. Geburtstag,* Weimar, 1971, 359–385. Etienne de Bonneuil arrived from Paris in 1287 with a team of assistants and workmen; by 1290 the walls of the church were rising and by 1310 the ambulatory and the choir chapels were completed. The text concerning the hiring of Etienne de Bonneuil can be found in V. Mortet & P. Deschamps, *Recueil de textes relatifs à l'histoire de l'architecture,* II, Paris, 1929, 305–306.

18. See: C. Enlart, *L'art gothique et la Renaissance en Chypre,* 2 vols., Paris, 1899; G. E. Jeffery, *A Description of the Historic Monuments of Cyprus. Studies in the Archaeology and Architecture of the Island,* Nicosia, 1918.

19. See: F. Salet, "Saint-Urbain de Troyes," *Congrès archéologique de France,* CXIII (Troyes), 1955, 98–122; R. Branner, *St Louis and the Court Style,* London, 1965, 106–108. It is very difficult to decide whether Jean Langlois (Johannes Anglicus), *civis Trecensis,* Master of the Works of Saint-Urbain, was merely the administrator of the fabric funds (which he certainly was) or was also at the same time the architect of the church. But from the tenor of the texts and from what is known of the Langlois family it seems unlikely that he was the actual architect.

20. This is often erroneously called the "triforium" of the apse of

Saint-Urbain, because that splitting up into two layers is similar to what happens currently in the Rayonnant treatment of the triforium story. But Saint-Urbain has no triforium story in an exact sense, and that duplication of tracery is here applied to a zone of the elevation which corresponds to the level of the aisle windows. The passage which runs there between the two planes of tracery is not a triforium passage but a Champenois passage.

21. On this point, see above, Chapter VIII, pp. 336–340.

22. Successive designs for the west façade on parchment are preserved in the *Musée de l'Oeuvre Notre-Dame* at Strasbourg. They are known as: *Riss* A, a purely Parisian design of ca. 1265 (attributed to Master Rudolf, who was then building the nave); *Riss* A¹, a slightly modified copy of *Riss* A, probably made ca. 1300; and *Riss* B, ca. 1276–77, which was the project according to which the façade was begun in 1277. Although his name is mentioned for the first time in 1284 only, there is every likelihood that Master Erwin (whose description as "von Steinbach" is probably legendary) was the author of *Riss* B. On the façade of Strasbourg, the basic work is still G. Dehio, "Das Münster Unserer Lieben Frau," in *Strassburg und seine Bauten,* Strasbourg (Architekten- und Ingenieur-Verein für Elsass-Lothringen), 1894, 141–204. The discovery of a further project of fourteenth century date, *Riss* C, known through an eighteenth-century copy, is reported in the most recent study on the Strasbourg façade: R. Wortmann, "Der Westbau des Strassburger Münsters und Meister Erwin," *Bonner Jahrbücher,* CLXIX, 1969, 290–318.

23. The chapel was probably begun in 1259. See A. Besnard, *L'église de Saint-Germer de Fly (Oise) et sa sainte chapelle,* Paris, 1913. It has a separate dado arcade. The continuation of mullions into the dado zone is restricted to the vestibule of ca. 1270.

24. See R. Branner, *St Louis and the Court Style,* London, 1965, 69.

25. On this chapel, see above, Chapter IX, p. 370 and n.16, p. 523.

26. The choir of Sées can be dated on the evidence of the stained-glass: if the clerestory windows were put up ca. 1280–1285, this means that the choir would have been begun before 1270, as it must have taken at least fifteen years to erect. See J. Lafond, "Les vitraux de la cathédrale de Sées," *Congrès archéologique de France,* CXI (Orne), 1953, 59–83. On Carcassonne: J. Poux, *La cité de Carcassonne. Précis historique, archéologique et descriptif,* Paris, 1925, 174–211; R. Branner, *St Louis and the Court Style,* London, 1965, 109–110. On Saint-Germain at Auxerre, see pp. 437–438 and n. 40 below, p. 538.

27. This was the first use of gables in a main arcade: it may have been suggested by the way in which Pierre de Montreuil had conceived the decoration of the inner face of the south transept façade at Notre-Dame (ca. 1261–1267), where the mullions of the triforium arcading are also continued on the wall face to the point where they meet the gables of the blind arches of the lower story. The gables over the main arcade on the east side of the transepts at Notre-Dame date only from ca. 1320.

28. This trend was particularly in evidence in the late 1260s and in the 1270s, but it continued well after that date as one of the basic options of the Rayonnant style, e.g.: choir of Saint-Thibault-en-Auxois (ca. 1290), Lady Chapel of Rouen Cathedral (1302), choir of Nevers Cathedral (from 1308), Chapelle de Navarre at Mantes (ca. 1325–1330).

29. See J. Vergnet-Ruiz & J. Vanuxem, "L'église de l'abbaye de Saint-Martin-aux-Bois," *Bulletin monumental,* CIII, 1945, 136–173, who suggest too late a date; a more likely dating is given by R. Branner, *St Louis and the Court Style,* London, 1965, 73–74.

30. See Chapter IV, pp. 149–154. The persistence of this austere mural tendency in the Parisian milieu into the 1240s is indicated by such works as the choir of Fontenay-en-Parisis. That, in a renewed form, it was still alive at the end of the century is proved by the cathedral of Uppsala, which was in all probability designed in 1287 by the Parisian master Etienne de Bonneuil.

31. Transoms were a common feature in domestic architecture: e.g. Winchester Castle hall, 1222–1235. In religious architecture, no transoms are found elsewhere until the very end of the thirteenth century or the first years of the fourteenth: in Provence, apse of Saint-Maximin, begun in 1295; in England, choir of Bristol Cathedral, begun in 1298; in Germany, apse of Oberwesel, begun in 1308.

32. There is no detailed enough study of the ruins of Hambye, which would require extensive investigation. The many inconsistencies of the plan reveal a complex architectural history, but the rustic roughness of the masonry makes it very difficult to detect the contact between successive campaigns of construction. In addition the stylistic autonomy of that part of Normandy leaves few reliable criteria for accurate dating. The crown of chapels at the east may have been begun in the later 1220s, when mention is made of works in progress (in 1228). But the straight bays and the central part of the choir are clearly later. The main arcade is much closer in style to the choir of Lonlay (dated in the second half of the thirteenth century) than to the nave of Mortain (of ca. 1220–1230); the

clerestory is of a type unknown before the 1240s; as for the crossing piers (which necessarily antedate the completion of the main arcade), their shape is so advanced as to suggest rather the 1250s or 1260s. The choir is likely to have been completed by 1266, when the number of monks was increased to 21 from 18 ten years before, but the transepts with their sharply pointed two-light windows cannot be much earlier than ca. 1280. See M. Thibout, "L'abbaye de Hambye," *Congrès archéologique de France*, CXXIV (Cotentin-Avranchin), 1966, 337–357.

33. Initiated at Clairvaux II in 1154, this type of Cistercian ambulatory plan had been repeated in the 1180s at Cherlieu and Pontigny II in Burgundy and had reached Normandy around 1190 (Savigny II, Bonport, Breuil-Benoît).

34. The comparative thinness of the walls and the rejection of the clerestory passage can to a certain extent be related with Cistercian practice. But there were also in that western part of Normandy, from the very first years of the thirteenth century, signs of direct contacts with Ile-de-France Gothic: e.g. the nave of Dol as originally designed, Mortain Abbey or further north, the church of Picauville. At Hambye the slim columnar piers (which recall the Ile-de-France-influenced choir of Rouen Cathedral) and the strong accentuation of the buttressing system (a most un-Norman feature also found at Picauville) underline the continuity of these contacts. See above, Chapter VIII, p. 346, and note 53, p. 519.

35. First and most famous of the Mendicant Orders were the Franciscans (Grey Friars) and Dominicans (Black Friars). Other orders of Friars were the Carmelites (White Friars), the Hermit Friars of Saint Augustine (Austin Friars—not to be confused with the Augustinian Canons, who represented one of the oldest forms of monasticism). There was also a variety of minor orders of Friars, some with a purely regional popularity.

36. The influence of Cistercian models is particularly in evidence in Germany (e.g. the church of the Dominicans at Regensburg, ca. 1260), but a similar phenomenon can be observed also in Italy (in Lombardy, in Florence, in Rome). See: R. Krautheimer, *Die Kirchen der Bettelorden in Deutschland*, Cologne, 1925; W. Gross, *Die abendländische Architektur um 1300*, Stuttgart, 1948. The Friars however were ready to experiment on almost any type of structure: see pp. 446–451 and 454–458.

37. The connections with the choir of Amiens should not be exaggerated: Branner has pointed out that the triforium of Saint-Thierry near Reims was much closer in type to that of Clermont-Ferrand; the nave of Evreux also has a triforium of gabled arches.

38. Even at Royaumont (begun in 1228), which was a big royal foundation, built rather like a cathedral and in some ways in the forefront of the stylistic development of its time, this narrow strip of wall was present at clerestory level. With its wide areas of wall, the ruined abbey of Lys near Melun (a work of the 1240s) is more typical of the traditional trends of Cistercian architecture in the middle years of the century.

39. The choir of Toulouse Cathedral had been begun by Jean des Champs in the same year as that of Narbonne, 1272; Limoges Cathedral was begun in 1273, Rodez in 1277. See R. Fage, *La cathédrale de Limoges,* Paris, 1926.

40. The axial chapel of Saint-Germain at Auxerre is a slightly enlarged version of the Carolingian octagon which stood on the same site and parts of which were incorporated into the Gothic structure at crypt level: see R. Louis, *Autessiodurum Christianum. Les églises d'Auxerre des origines au onzième siècle,* Paris, 1952. On the Gothic choir, see: J. Vallery-Radot, "Saint-Germain d'Auxerre. L'église haute," *Congrès archéologique de France,* CXVI (Auxerre), 1958, 26–39; R. Branner, *Burgundian Gothic Architecture,* London, 1960, 94–96 and 108–109. It should be noted that work proceeded slowly at Auxerre after 1279, the choir being completed only in the first quarter of the fourteenth century.

41. The prototype here was the Lady Chapel of Auxerre Cathedral, which was square in plan, not octagonal, but had the same triple entrance supported on thin isolated colonnettes, although without the vestibule bay which Saint-Germain inherited from the plan of its Carolingian crypt. Strangely enough all the elements of that spatial composition (rotunda-like chapel, triple entrance arches and bay-deep vestibule) were already present ca. 1180 in the east chapel of the south transept of Soissons cathedral, which suggests that the north of France may have had some Carolingian crypt arrangements similar to those of Auxerre or Flavigny in Burgundy.

42. This can be observed on the south transept façade in the blind arcading which runs immediately below the gallery of the triforium, and in the arches of the two gabled panels which flank the doorway.

43. The origins of the continuous order go back a very long way. Windows with a continuous framing were common in Syria in the late fifth and early sixth centuries, and the motif was revived with wide ornamental borders in early Mediterranean Romanesque (Arles-sur-Tech, S. Abbondio at Como). Arches without imposts, continuous with their supports, were common in Late Antique structures (e.g. the Trier "Basilica,"

S. Simpliciano in Milan); in the eighth and ninth centuries Islamic architecture had again made an extensive use of them (cistern of Ramla in
Palestine, Ribat of Sousse in Tunisia); and this continuous treatment
from arch to piers had been diffused in the early eleventh century from
Catalonia to Burgundy and central Italy, in the Mediterranean "First
Romanesque." Another variant of the same idea was applied between
1030 and 1060 in the multi-recessed doorway of Speyer Cathedral. In
England windows framed by a continuous roll seem to have made their
appearance shortly before the Norman Conquest; but it was after the
Conquest, in the 1080s and 1090s and particularly in the area of the West
Midlands, that the continuous order became a major element of stylistic
definition. Sometimes it was used in its bolder structural variant, as in the
lower story of the bishop's chapel at Hereford; more often it took the
form of continuous roll moldings, as in the ambulatory and chapels of the
choir of Gloucester; and from there it spread to all parts of England
during the first half of the twelfth century, taking its most spectacular
character after 1160 in the rich geometrical compositions of chevron-
decorated doorways (e.g. Middle Rasen, Lincs.; Iffley, Oxon.) and lend-
ing itself to all kinds of variations (e.g. Malmesbury, south porch, or St.
Albans, south transept door). From England the vogue of the continuous
order spread in the first half of the twelfth century first to Normandy (by
1120 on the exterior of Graville-Sainte-Honorine) and soon after to the
whole of northern France (ambulatory of Morienval ca. 1130; Airaines,
Chartres, Le Mans in the 1140s). But from the middle of the twelfth
century French Gothic practice tended to eliminate that continuity from
jamb to arch as a remnant of the formal looseness of late Romanesque;
and it was in England alone that a full transmission was made of the many
potential effects of that style of arch treatment from its Romanesque
forms to new Gothic variants. This process of transmission can be observed in action in the nave of St. Davids and the Lady Chapel of Glastonbury: see H. Brakspear, "A Western School of Masons," *Archaeologia,*
LXXXI, 1931, 1–18.

44. See E. W. Lovegrove, "Llanthony Priory," *Archaeologia Cambrensis,*
XCVII, 1943, 213–219.

45. At Troyes Cathedral and at Saint-Quentin the tierceron-type
crossing vaults date only from the late fourteenth century or from the
fifteenth. On the transept of Saint-Riquier and what remains there of the
construction of the years 1257–1292, see G. Durand, "Saint-Riquier,"
Congrès archéologique de France, IC (Amiens), 1936, 110. The type of the

539

regular tierceron vault had been created at Lincoln, probably in the late 1220s or early 1230s, and had been imitated almost at once in the choir of Ely (begun in 1238). By the time the tierceron vault reached Picardy, it was being used on a large scale in London, both at Westminster Abbey (in the east bays of the nave, dated 1258–1269) and at Old St. Paul's Cathedral (in the new choir begun in 1258).

46. As Geoffroy was called to Troyes in 1297 to advise on the work of the cathedral, this suggests that he had been active at Troyes before coming to build Mussy, thirty miles away. The founder of the new church at Mussy was in all probability Guillaume de Mussy, who held important administrative posts in the County of Champagne and must have spent many years of his life at Troyes. See: F. Salet, "L'église de Mussy-sur-Seine," *Congrès archéologique de France,* CXIII (Troyes), 1955, 320–337; R. Branner, *Burgundian Gothic Architecture,* London, 1960, 99–100 and 156.

47. See above, Chapter VIII, pp. 345–348.

48. As a stone must first be rough cut to a chamfered shape preparatory to its carving to any system of moldings based on the soffit roll, it is normal that plain chamfered profiles appeared first in England, where the soffit roll had been in current use since Late Saxon times. The chamfer came out of an effort to simplify profiles of the Durham type. Typical examples in England are: Calder Abbey and Lanercost in Cumberland, Brinkburn in Northumberland, North Luffenham in Rutland, Coleshill in Berkshire, etc.; in Normandy: the nave of Auffay, the choir of Hambye, the west bays of the ambulatory arcade in the choir of Coutances and, somewhat later, the choir of Lonlay-l'Abbaye. A slighter chamfering was occasionally used in North-French Gothic: crypt of Saint-Denis (1140), Orbais, Barzy (ca. 1200 to 1220). The single wide chamfer as used at Mussy has, as far as I know, only one precedent, the mid-thirteenth century nave of Woodchurch in Kent. See J. Newman, *West Kent and the Weald,* Harmondsworth & Baltimore, 1969, 586–588 and pl. 16.

49. This continuing of the chamfered arch into the pier was a Cistercian idea, probably initiated at Fountains in the late twelfth-century cellarium which occupies the whole lower story of the west range.

50. There are at Mussy other unusual details of design or workmanship: the tracery pattern used in the windows of the choir, both in the aisles and in the clerestory (three sharply pointed lights under a common arch) was very rare at that date outside England and Normandy. It had first appeared in Normandy around 1240, as a Norman alternative to the

Ile-de-France types of tracery: e.g. nave of Sées, Audrieu, inner ambulatory of the choir of Le Mans cathedral, etc.; after which this pattern was adopted in England, where it became quite common after ca. 1275. But F. Salet, in the *Congrès archéologique* of 1955 (328), lists three churches with related forms of tracery in the vicinity of Provins, the other capital of the county of Champagne, so that Mussy is no isolated exception on this point. Another striking element which may contribute to give Mussy an English look is the existence of a west tower planted in the axis of the nave; and certainly the west tower was common in England since late Saxon days; but at Mussy this feature is much more likely to have come, via Lorraine, from the Rhineland or the Netherlands than from England.

51. The strong emphasis which is placed up to triforium level on the central shaft in each bay is no longer present in the clerestory windows, which stress the first and third mullion rather than the second and therefore do not accord with the rest of the design. With their large central motif, the upper windows have a calm inner balance which relates them to the style of Saint-Bénigne at Dijon. On Saint-Thibault, see: L. Schürenberg, *Die kirchliche Baukunst in Frankreich zwischen 1270 und 1380*, Berlin, 1934, 172–174; R. Branner, *Burgundian Gothic Architecture*, London, 1960, 93–94 and 177–178.

52. The idea that certain French buildings of the second half of the thirteenth century anticipated some of the features of the Perpendicular Style and that these buildings were actually the starting point for the English developments that followed, was first formulated by Geoffrey Webb and Maurice Hastings in their joint investigation of the London Court Style of the 1290s. See: G. F. Webb, *Gothic Architecture in England*, London (British Council), 1951, 22–23; J. M. Hastings, *St. Stephen's Chapel and its Place in the Development of Perpendicular Style in England*, Cambridge, 1955, 96–99, 182–190 and 220. The first grid of mullions appeared in England probably only a few years after the designing of the choir of Saint-Thibault: the lower story of the Chapel of St. Stephen, built between 1292 and 1297 in the old palace of Westminster, was barred vertically on the outside by a downward continuation of the mullions of the upper windows. The artists working for the court of London in the early 1290s were obviously in close contact with the most recent developments of Continental Gothic, taking them as a point of departure for their own further speculations. The final steps in the creation of the Perpendicular came in the early 1330s: in 1332 William Ramsey began the construction of the chapter house of Old St. Paul's (known through

Hollar's engraving published in W. Dugdale, *The History of St. Paul's Cathedral in London,* London, 1658); and simultaneously work started at Gloucester on the remodeling of the south transept in a style which was extended to the whole choir from 1337.

53. See n. 26, p. 535. The transept was not completed until the 1320s.

54. See Chapter VIII, p. 306 and n. 7, p. 510.

55. See: A. Casademunt, *Santa Catalina,* Barcelona, 1886; L. Torres Balbas, *Arquitectura gótica* (Ars Hispaniae, 7), Madrid, 1952, 124; R. Branner, *St Louis and the Court Style,* London, 1965, 116.

56. On these two churches, see M. Durliat, "L'architecture gothique méridionale au XIIIe siècle," *Ecole Antique de Nîmes, Bulletin annuel,* new ser., VIII–IX, 1973–1974, 99–114. The new dating of the Jacobins has been established by M. Prin, "La première église des Frères Prêcheurs de Toulouse, d'après les fouilles," *Annales du Midi,* LXVII, 1955, 5–18, who has shown that the whole eastern part belongs to the last decades of the thirteenth century and that the rest of the church, further west, was progressively rebuilt as an extension of the same design in the course of the fourteenth century. It should be remembered that Toulouse was the birthplace of the Dominican movement, which had originated there in 1206, ten years before receiving pontifical approval as an order in 1216.

57. See: J. Laran, *La cathédrale d'Albi,* Paris, 1911; E. Mâle, *La cathédrale d'Albi,* Paris, 1950.

58. These spurred footings had recently been adopted in castle architecture. Dated examples in England are the gatehouse of St. Briavel in Gloucestershire (1292–1293), and Goodrich Castle in Herefordshire (begun in 1296): see H. M. Colvin, *The History of the King's Works, The Middle Ages,* London, 1963, I, 231; II, 822.

59. See: P. Lavedan, *L'architecture gothique religieuse en Catalogne, Valence et Baléares,* Paris, 1935; L. Torres Balbas, *Arquitectura gótica* (Ars Hispaniae, VII), Madrid, 1952, 189–197; A. Durán Sanpere, "La cathédrale de Barcelone," *Congrès archéologique de France,* CXVII (Catalogne), 1959, 28–36.

60. In Provence, in the mountain ranges to the north of Toulon, the Dominican church of Saint-Maximin, which does not seem to have been actively started until 1295, is a compromise between Court Style and monastic austerity. Founded by Charles II of Anjou, king of Naples, it combines with an arrangement of chapels and aisles analogous to that of Barcelona, typical northern French features: chevet à la Braine, transommullions like Saint-Martin-aux-Bois, and interior loftiness à la Reims.

61. On the beginning of the movement, see H. Thümmler, "Westfälische und italienische Hallenkirchen," *Festschrift Martin Wackernagel,* Cologne, 1958, 17–36; on its early development, see H. R. Rosemann, "Die westfälische Hallenkirche in der ersten Hälfte des 13. Jahrhunderts," *Zeitschrift für Kunstgeschichte,* I, 1932, 203–227. There had also been, at an even earlier date, some examples of Romanesque hall-churches in Bavaria, but the group was small and did not continue into the Gothic period.

62. On the diffusion of the hall church to Hesse and to eastern Saxony, see: R. Hamann and K. Wilhelm-Kästner, *Die Elisabethkirche zu Marburg und ihre künstlerische Nachfolge,* Marburg, 2 vols., 1924–29; G. Rudolf, "Mitteldeutsche Hallenkirchen und die erste Stufe der Spätgotik," *Jahrbuch für Kunstwissenschaft,* 1930, 137–175; W. Gross, "Die Hochgotik im deutschen Kirchenbau," *Marburger Jahrbuch für Kunstwissenschaft,* VII (1933), 290–346. The first step in that diffusion was the adoption of a hall-nave at the church of St. Elisabeth at Marburg, a decision taken at the latest by 1249, when the choir and transept were completed. In the 1260s and 1270s there followed: the nave of Wetzlar, Haina (a Cistercian church), Wetter, Minden Cathedral, the churches of Braunschweig, etc.; and by ca. 1280 the hall church had reached not only Erfurt (church of St. Severus), but Kolin and Olomouc in Bohemia and Heiligenkreuz in Austria (another Cistercian church, the hall choir of which was dedicated in 1295).

63. The basic work remains R. Krautheimer, *Die Kirchen der Bettelorden in Deutschland,* Cologne, 1925; the dating of some buildings has been corrected by H. Konow, *Die Baukunst der Bettelorden am Oberrhein,* Berlin, 1954 (Forschungen zur Geschichte der Kunst am Oberrhein, 6): nave of the Franciscan church at Freiburg im Breisgau redated to ca. 1310ff., nave of the Dominicans at Colmar advanced into the 1320s. The late date attributed by H. Konow to the Dominican church of Frankfurt-am-Main appears to be influenced by the author's conviction that Schwäbisch-Gmünd was the first hall-nave of that region; but Schwäbisch-Gmünd itself, with its light and originally unvaulted structure, is difficult to explain without some Mendicant prototype; which leaves the problem open.

64. An interior view of the church of the Dominicans at Colmar can be found in E. Gall, *Dome und Klosterkirchen am Rhein,* Munich, 1956, pl. 31.

65. The first example of this type of elevation in Germany seems to have been the Franciscan church of Würzburg.

66. On the position of Gothic architecture in Italy in the thirteenth century, see: R. Wagner-Rieger, *Die italienische Baukunst zur Beginn der*

543

Gotik,(Österreichisches Kultur-Institut in Rom, Publikationen, Abteilung für historische Studien, I, 2) Graz-Cologne, 2 vols., 1956; A. M. Romanini, *L'architettura gotica in Lombardia,* Milan, 2 vols., 1964; J. White, *Art and Architecture in Italy 1250 to 1400* (Pelican History of Art), Harmondsworth & Baltimore, 1966, 1-28. For central Italy: W. Krönig, "Hallenkirchen in Mittelitalien," *Kunstgeschichtliches Jahrbuch der Bibliotheca Hertziana,* II, 1938, 1-142; *id.,* "Note sull'architettura religiosa medioevale delle Marche," *Atti del XI Congresso di Storia dell'Architettura,* (Marche), 1959, 205-232, gives a full analysis of the situation at the end of the thirteenth century. The aisleless churches without diaphragms of S. Domenico and S. Francesco at Siena date only from the early fourteenth century (begun in 1309 and 1326 respectively). At first, in exceptional programs such as S. Francesco at Assisi or S. Francesco at Bologna, the Mendicants had decided on an eclectic use of Gothic formulas. It was only later in the thirteenth century that properly Mendicant trends became apparent.

67. On the churches of the Friars in Florence, see: W. Paatz, *Werden und Wesen der Trecento Architektur in Toskana,* Burg, 1937; W. Gross, *Die abendländische Architektur um 1300,* Stuttgart, 1947; W. & E. Paatz, *Die Kirchen von Florenz,* Frankfurt-am-Main, 1944-1955, I, 497-701 and III, 663-845.

68. One of these variants has been noted already in Germany: the unvaulted type which can be followed from the Franciscan church of Würzburg to that of Freiburg-im-Breisgau; another one, vaulted and with a somewhat tighter sequence of piers, is illustrated in the early fourteenth century by the two great Mendicant churches of Erfurt, particularly the church of the Dominicans (Predigerkirche). England had another significant variant, with a clerestory of two short windows per bay: see pp. 456-458. Related types in southern Europe culminate in the cathedrals of Palma in Majorca on the one hand, of Milan on the other.

69. On the general question of the architecture of the Mendicants in England and of its influence, see A. W. Clapham's chapter: "The Friars as Builders: The London Houses of Blackfriars and Whitefriars," in A. W. Clapham & W. H. Godfrey, *Some Famous Buildings and their Story,* London, 1913, 239-267. The church of the Austin Friars in London was under construction in 1354; it received a timber-built clerestory ca. 1475, but was a hall church until then. Another fourteenth century hall nave was that of the Whitefriars (Carmelites). The London churches of the Blackfriars (Dominicans) begun in 1279, and of the Greyfriars (Francis-

cans), begun in 1306, had totally vanished before the end of the seventeenth century, following the Dissolution of the Monasteries and the Great Fire. On the Blackfriars of Norwich, built between 1440 and 1470, see N. Pevsner, *North-East Norfolk and Norwich,* Harmondsworth & Baltimore, 1962, 260–261.

70. Most typical among the new towns is Winchelsea in East Sussex, where the wide (and fairly low) unvaulted hall church was begun in the 1290s. At Hull (Kingston-upon-Hull), another new town of Edward I, construction of the large clerestoried preaching-nave began only in the late fourteenth century. Impressive parish churches of that kind were built also in growing towns of older foundation, for instance Boston in Lincolnshire, where the very spacious nave dates from the mid-fourteenth century.

71. The parish churches of Boston and Hull are classic examples. Greyfriars in London, begun in 1306, may also have belonged to the type.

72. See A. W. Clapham, "Howden," *Archaeological Journal,* XCI (1934), 398–399. The college of canons was founded in 1267 by the Archbishop of York. The original choir (soon replaced) and the transept were built by 1290; the nave followed and was built in two stages, ca. 1290–1295 and ca. 1300–1310.

73. See: E. W. Godwin, "Bristol Cathedral," *Archaeological Journal,* XX, 1893, 38–63; N. Pevsner, "Bristol-Troyes-Gloucester," *Architectural Review* (London), CXIII, 1953, 88–98; G. F. Webb, *Architecture in Britain. The Middle Ages,* (Pelican History of Art) Harmondsworth & Baltimore, 1956, 138–140. On the whole movement of transformation, of which Bristol is such a significant example, see now J. Bony, *The English Decorated Style. Gothic Architecture Transformed* 1250–1350 (The Wrightsman Lectures, 10), Oxford & Ithaca, 1979.

74. The transverse barrel-vaulting of aisles was not practised only in Burgundy or in the Cistercian churches of the Bonmont-Fontenay type: the west of France had a long tradition of that constructional system, beginning ca. 1110 or 1120 with the church of the Ronceray at Angers, continuing through the twelfth century in the Limousin, Poitiers and occasionally Gascony; it was still in use at Bordeaux in the thirteenth century in the Gothic hall nave of Saint-Seurin.

75. The Bristol master was obviously conversant with the most advanced methods of timber construction, since he translated them into stone in the unique mode of vaulting he employed in the choir aisles. His familiarity with all kinds of constructional devices used in western France

in the twelfth and thirteenth centuries would be normal in the case of an architect who had, earlier in his career, been detailed to work for the king in Gascony.

76. The transformation of parish churches into preaching halls, so noticeable in England, was taking place also in the populous cities of Flanders. At Damme, the outer harbor of Bruges, a very large unvaulted hall choir was added shortly before 1300 to the mid-thirteenth-century nave: see L. Devliegher, *Kunstpatrimonium van West-Vlaanderen, V, Damme,* Tielt-Utrecht, 1971.

77. Louis IX was canonized in 1297. On that new church at Poissy, the first to be dedicated to the new saint, see: R. Branner, *St Louis and the Court Style,* London, 1965, 136–137; A. Erlande-Brandenburg, "La priorale Saint-Louis de Poissy," *Bulletin monumental,* CXXIX, 1971, 85-112.

78. On the Gothic rebuilding of Orléans Cathedral, see: G. Chenesseau, *Sainte-Croix d'Orléans; histoire d'une cathédrale gothique réédifiée par les Bourbons,* Paris, 2 vols., 1921; *id.,* "Orléans. Cathédrale Sainte-Croix," *Congrès archéologique de France,* XCIII (Orléans), 1930, 11–51. Work had started in 1287, but proceeded at a very slow pace, on a huge project (seven straight bays of choir, nine radiating chapels) which was a massive compilation of the forms current two generations before. It is worth noting that the next major building undertakings were to be abbey-churches: the Trinity at Vendôme (1306), Saint-Bertin at Saint-Omer (1311), Saint-Ouen at Rouen (1318).

79. The clerestory of Saint-Thibault, built in the early years of the fourteenth century, belongs to that new calm Burgundian style: see above, n. 51, p. 541.

80. The leadership may be said to have passed first to the South, in the 1280s, through the agency of the Mendicants, then to England around 1300, then to Germany in the second half of the fourteenth century.

81. That greater fluidity in the way of enclosing space can be illustrated by the retrochoir and Lady Chapel of Wells (begun ca. 1323), the Lady Chapel and Octagon of Ely (begun respectively in 1321 and 1322), the hexagonal north porch of St. Mary Redcliffe at Bristol (ca. 1325–1330), and the rebuilt ambulatory choir of Tewkesbury (ca. 1321–1344).

Selective Bibliography

ABEL, John F., R. Mark, and K. O'Neill, "Photoelastic and Finite Element Analysis of a Quadripartite Vault," *Experimental Mechanics*, XIII, 1973(8), 322–329.

——, *see also* ALEXANDER.

ABRAHAM, Pol, *Viollet-le-Duc et le rationalisme médiéval*, Paris, 1934.

ACHE, Jean B., "Le prieuré royal de Saint-Martin-des-Champs, ses rapports avec l'Angleterre et les débuts de l'architecture gothique," *Centre international d'études romanes, bulletin trimestriel*, 1963 (I), 5–15.

ADENAUER, Hanna, *Die Kathedrale von Laon*, Düsseldorf, 1934.

ADHEMAR, Jean, *Influences antiques dans l'art du moyen âge français* (Studies of the Warburg Institute, 7), London, 1939.

ALEXANDER, K. D., R. Mark, and J. F. Abel, "The Structural Behavior of Medieval Ribbed Vaulting," *Journal of the Society of Architectural Historians*, XXXVI, 1977, 241–251.

ALP, Emma, *Die Kapitelle des XII. Jahrhunderts im Entstehungs-gebiete der Gotik*, Detmold, 1927.

ANFRAY, Marcel, *L'architecture normande, son influence dans le nord de la France aux XIe et XIIe siècles*, Paris, 1939.

ANGLÈS, Auguste, "L'abbaye de Silvanès (Aveyron)," *Bulletin monumental*, LXXII, 1908, 41–60.

AUBERT, Marcel, *La cathédrale Notre-Dame de Paris. Notice historique et archéologique*, Paris, 1909; 2nd ed., 1919; new ed., 1950.

—— *Monographie de la cathédrale de Senlis*, Senlis, 1910.

—— *Notre-Dame de Paris, sa place dans l'histoire de l'architecture du XIIe au XIVe siècle*, Paris, 1920; 2nd ed., 1929.

—— "Rouen, la cathédrale," *Congrès archéologique de France*, LXXXIX (Rouen), 1926, 11–71.

—— *Notre-Dame de Paris. Architecture et sculpture*, Paris, 1928.

—— "Saint-Thibault," *Congrès archéologique de France*, XCI (Dijon), 1928, 252–266.

—— *La cathédrale de Metz*, Paris, 1930.

—— *L'abbaye des Vaux-de-Cernay* (monographie publiée pour le baron Henri de Rothschild), Paris, 1931.

—— "Les plus anciennes croisées d'ogives, leur rôle dans la construction," *Bulletin monumental,* XCIII, 1934, 5–67 and 137–237.

———— "Lyon. Cathédrale," *Congrès archéologique de France,* XCVIII (Lyon and Mâcon), 1935, 54–90.

———— "Le portail royal et la façade occidentale de la cathédrale de Chartres. Essai sur la date de leur exécution," *Bulletin monumental,* C, 1941, 177–218.

———— "L'abbaye de Valmagne," *Congrès archéologique de France,* CVIII (Montpellier), 1950, 233–240.

———— *La cathédrale de Chartres,* Paris and Grenoble, 1952.

———— "La construction au moyen âge," *Bulletin monumental,* CXVIII, 1960, 241–259; CXIX, 1961, 7–42, 81–120, 181–209 and 297–323.

———— "A propos de l'église abbatiale de Saint-Lucien de Beauvais," *Gedenkschrift Ernst Gall* (M Kühn and L. Grodecki, eds.), Berlin and Munich, 1965, 51–58.

AUBERT, Marcel, and G. de Maillé, *L'architecture cistercienne en France,* 2 vols., Paris, 1943.

————, and M. Minost, "La fenêtre occidentale du réfectoire de Saint-Germain-des-Prés, oeuvre de Pierre de Montreuil," *Bulletin monumental,* CXII, 1954, 275–280.

————, A. Chastel, L. Grodecki, J. J. Gruber, J. Lafond, F. Mathey, J. Taralon, and J. Verrier, *Le vitrail français,* Paris, 1958.

———— and S. Goubet, *Gothic Cathedrals of France and Their Treasures,* London, 1959.

————, J. A. Schmoll (gen. Eisenwerth), and H. H. Hofstätter, *The Art of the High Gothic Era,* New York, 1965.

BACH, Eugène, L. Blondel, and A. Bovy, *La cathédrale de Lausanne* (Kunstdenkmäler der Schweiz, 16: Monuments d'art et d'histoire du Canton de Vaud, 2), Basel, 1944.

BANDMANN, Günther, *Mittelalterliche Architektur als Bedeutungsträger,* Berlin, 1951.

BARBIER, Louis, "Etude sur la stabilité des absides de Noyon et de Saint-Germain-des-Prés," *Bulletin monumental,* LXXXIX, 1930, 515–529.

BARNES, Carl F., "The Cathedral of Chartres and the Architect of Soissons," *Journal of the Society of Architectural Historians,* XXII, 1963, 63–74.

———— "The Gothic Architectural Engravings in the Cathedral of Soissons," *Speculum,* XLVII, 1972, 60–64.

———— "The Documentation for Notre-Dame de Soissons," *Gesta,* XV, 1976, 61–70.

BARON, Françoise, "Histoire architecturale de l'abbaye de Vaucelles," *Cîteaux in de Nederlanden,* IX, 1958, 276–285.

———— "Les églises de Vaucelles," *Cîteaux in de Nederlanden,* XI, 1960, 196–208.

BAUDOT, Anatole de, and A. Perrault-Dabot, *Archives de la Commission des Monuments Historiques,* 5 vols., Paris, 1898–1903.

————, and A. Perrault-Dabot, *Les cathédrales de France,* 2 vols., Paris, 1905–1907.

BAUM, Julius, and H. Schmidt-Glassner, *German Cathedrals,* London and New York, 1956.

BAYLÉ, Maylis, *La Trinité de Caen, sa place dans l'histoire de l'architecture et du décor romans* (Bibliothèque de la Société française d'archéologie, 10), Geneva, 1979.

BEAUJOUAN, Guy, *L'interdépendance entre la science scholastique et les techniques utilitaires (XIIe, XIIIe et XIVe siècles),* Paris, 1957 (Université de Paris, Conférences du Palais de la Découverte, ser. D, 46).

BECKSMANN, Rüdiger, *Die architektonische Rahmung des hochgotischen Bildfensters. Untersuchung zur oberrheinischen Glasmalerei von 1250 bis 1350* (Forschungen zur Geschichte der Kunst am Oberrhein, 9–10), Berlin, 1967.

BÉGULE, Lucien, *La cathédrale de Sens. Son architecture, son décor,* Lyon, 1929.

——, and M.-C. Guigue, *Monographie de la cathédrale de Lyon,* Lyon, 1880.

BEHLING, Lottlisa, *Die Pflanzenwelt der mittelalterlichen Kathedralen,* Cologne, 1964.

BESNARD, A., *L'église de Saint-Germer de Fly (Oise) et sa sainte chapelle,* Paris, 1913.

BEVAN, Bernard, *History of Spanish Architecture,* London, 1938.

BIAŁOSTOCKI, Jan, "Late Gothic: Disagreements about the Concept," *Journal of the British Archaeological Association,* 3rd ser., XXIX, 1966, 76–105.

BIAUDET, Jean-Charles, H. Meylan, W. Stöckli, P. Jaton, M. Grandjean, C. Lapaire, E. J. Beer, and C. Bornand, *La cathédrale de Lausanne* (Bibliothèque de la Société d'Histoire de l'Art en Suisse, 3), Bern, 1975.

BIDEAULT, Maryse, and C. Lautier, "Saint-Nicaise de Reims. Chronologie et nouvelles remarques sur l'architecture," *Bulletin monumental,* CXXXV, 1977, 295–330.

BILSON, John, "The Beginnings of Gothic Architecture," *Journal of the Royal Institute of British Architects,* 3rd ser., VI (Nov. 1898—Oct. 1899), 259–319.

—— "The Architecture of the Cistercians, with Special Reference to some of their Earlier Churches in England," *Archaeological Journal,* LXVI, 1909, 185–280.

—— "Les voûtes de la nef de la cathédrale d'Angers," *Congrès archéologique de France,* LXXVII (Angers-Saumur), 1910, II, 203–223.

—— "The Norman School and the Beginnings of Gothic Architecture. Two Octopartite Vaults: Montivilliers and Canterbury," *Archaeological Journal,* LXXIV, 1917, 1–35.

—— "Durham Cathedral: The Chronology of its Vaults," *Ibid.,* LXXIX, 1922, 101–160.

BLOCH, Marc, "L'Ile-de-France (Les pays autour de Paris)," *Revue de Synthèse Historique,* XXV, 1912, 209–223, 310–339; XXVI, 1913, 131–193, 325–350.

BOASE, Thomas S. R., *English Art 1100–1216* (Oxford History of English Art, 3), Oxford, 1953.

BOBER, Harry, "A Reappraisal of Rayonnant Architecture," in *The Forward Movement of the Fourteenth Century* (F. L. Utley, ed.), Columbus, 1961, 9–30.

BOCK, Henning, *Der 'Decorated Style'* (Heidelberger Kunstgeschichtliche Abhandlungen, N.F.6), Heidelberg, 1962.

BOINET, Amédée, *Les églises parisiennes,* 2 vols, Paris, 1958–1962.

BOND, Francis, *Gothic Architecture in England,* London, 1905.

BONNENFANT, Georges, *La cathédrale d'Evreux,* Paris, 1925.

—— *L'église Saint-Taurin d'Evreux et sa châsse,* Paris, 1926.

BONY, Jean, "Tewkesbury et Pershore, deux élévations à quatre étages de la fin du XIe siècle," *Bulletin monumental,* XCVI, 1937, 281–290, 503–504.

—— "La technique normande du mur épais à l'époque romane," *Bulletin monumental,* XCVIII, 1939, 153–188.

—— "Gloucester et l'origine des voûtes d'hémicycle gothiques," *ibid.,* 329–331.

—— "Essai sur la spiritualité de deux cathédrales: Notre-Dame de Paris et Saint-Etienne de Bourges," *Chercher Dieu* (Rencontres, 13), Paris, 1943, 150–167.

—— "La collégiale de Mantes," *Congrès archéologique de France,* CIV (Paris-Mantes), 1946, 163–220.

—— *Notre-Dame de Mantes,* Paris, 1947.

—— "French Influences on the Origins of English Gothic Architecture," *Journal of the*

Warburg and Courtauld Institutes, XII, 1949, 1–15.

——— "Le projet premier de Durham: voûtement partiel ou voûtement total?" *Urbanisme et architecture, études écrites et publiées en l'honneur de Pierre Lavedan,* Paris, 1954, 41–49.

——— "The Resistance to Chartres in Early Thirteenth Century Architecture," *Journal of the British Archaeological Association,* 3rd ser., XX–XXI, 1957–58, 35–52.

——— "Les premiers architectes gothiques," in *Les architectes célèbres* (P. Francastel, ed.), 2 vols, Paris, 1959, II, 28–32.

——— "Origines des piles gothiques anglaises à fûts en délit," *Gedenkschrift Ernst Gall* (M. Kühn and L. Grodecki, eds), Berlin and Munich, 1965, 69–86.

——— Review of R. Branner, *La cathédrale de Bourges . . . ,* in *Art Bulletin,* XLVII, 1965, 521–525.

——— "Diagonality and Centrality in Early Rib-Vaulted Architectures," *Gesta,* XV, 1976, 15–25.

——— "The Genesis of Gothic: Accident or Necessity?" *Australian Journal of Art,* II, 1980, 17–31.

BONY J., M. Hürlimann, and P. Meyer, *French Cathedrals,* London, 1951, 2nd ed., 1967.

BORG, Alan, and R. Mark, "Chartres Cathedral: A Reappraisal of its Structure," *Art Bulletin,* LV, 1973, 367–372.

BOUET, Georges, "Analyse architecturale de l'abbaye de Saint-Etienne de Caen," *Bulletin monumental,* XXXI, 1865, 417–479.

BOUXIN, Auguste, *La cathédrale Notre-Dame de Laon,* Laon, 1890; 2nd ed., 1902.

BOWIE, Theodore, ed., *The Sketchbook of Villard de Honnecourt,* Bloomington, 1959.

BRANNER, Robert, "Drawings from a Thirteenth Century Architect's Shop: The Reims Palimpsest," *Journal of the Society of Architectural Historians,* XVII, 1958, 9–21.

——— "The Movements of Gothic Architects between France and Spain in the Early Thirteenth Century," *Actes du XIXe Congrès International d'Histoire de l'Art, Paris 8–13 Septembre 1958,* Paris, 1959, 44–48.

——— *Burgundian Gothic Architecture,* London, 1960.

——— "Villard de Honnecourt, Archimedes and Chartres," *Journal of the Society of Architectural Historians,* XIX, 1960, 91–96.

——— "Jean d'Orbais and the Cathedral of Reims," *Art Bulletin,* XLIII, 1961, 131–133.

——— *Gothic Architecture* (The Great Ages of World Architecture), New York, 1961.

——— "The North Transept and the First West Façades of Reims Cathedral," *Zeitschrift für Kunstgeschichte,* XXIV, 1961, 220–241.

——— "Historical Aspects of the Reconstruction of Reims Cathedral," *Speculum,* XXXVI, 1961, 23–37.

——— *La cathédrale de Bourges et sa place dans l'architecture gothique,* Paris-Bourges, 1962.

——— "The Labyrinth of Reims Cathedral," *Journal of the Society of Architectural Historians,* XXI, 1962, 18–25.

——— "Le maître de la cathédrale de Beauvais," *Art de France,* II, 1962, 77–92.

——— "Paris and the Origins of Rayonnant Gothic Architecture down to 1240," *Art Bulletin,* XLIV, 1962, 39–51.

——— "Gothic Architecture 1160–1180 and its Romanesque Sources," *Studies in Western Art, Acts of the Twentieth International Congress of the History of Art, New York, 1961,* Princeton, 1963, I, 92–104.

———— "Sint-Leonardus at Zoutleeuw and the Rhein Valley in the Early Thirteenth Century," *Bulletin de la Commission royale des monuments et des sites*, XIV, 1963, 257–268.

———— "Villard de Honnecourt, Reims and the Origin of Gothic Architectural Drawing," *Gazette des Beaux-Arts*, 6th ser., LXI, 1963, 129–146.

———— "Remarques sur la cathédrale de Strasbourg," *Bulletin monumental*, CXXII, 1964, 261–268.

———— "Westminster Abbey and the French Court Style," *Journal of the Society of Architectural Historians*, XXIII, 1964, 3–18.

———— *St Louis and the Court Style in Gothic Architecture*, London, 1965.

———— "The Transept of Cambrai Cathedral," *Gedenkschrift Ernst Gall* (M. Kühn and L. Grodecki, eds.), Berlin and Munich, 1965, 69–86.

———— "The Painted Medallions in the Sainte-Chapelle in Paris," *Transactions of the American Philosophical Society*, new ser., LVIII:2, 1968, 3–42.

———— ed., *Chartres Cathedral* (Norton Critical Studies in Art History), New York, 1969.

———— "La place du 'Style de Cour' de Saint Louis dans l'architecture du XIIIe siècle," *Le siècle de Saint Louis* (R. Pernoud and A. Chamson, eds.), Paris, 1970, 133–139.

———— "Die Architektur der Kathedrale von Reims im dreizehnten Jahrhundert," *Architectura*, I, 1971, 15–37.

BRANNER, Robert, and R. Gauchery, *see* R. GAUCHERY.

BRAY, Albert, "Moret-sur-Loing," *Bulletin monumental*, LXXXVIII, 1929, 437–449.

BRIEGER, Peter, *English Art 1216–1307* (Oxford History of English Art, 4), Oxford, 1957.

BRIGODE, Simon, *Les églises gothiques en Belgique*, Brussels, 1944.

———— *L'architecture religieuse dans le sud-ouest de la Belgique, I. Des origines à la fin du XVe siècle*, Brussels, 1960.

BROCHE, Lucien, *La cathédrale de Laon*, Paris, 1926.

BROSSE, Jacques, ed., *Dictionnaire des églises de France*, 5 vols., Paris, 1966–1971.

BRUZELIUS, Caroline A., "Cistercian High Gothic: The Abbey Church of Longpont and the Architecture of the Cistercians in the Early Thirteenth Century," *Analecta Cisterciensia*, XXXV, 1979, 3–204.

BUCHER, François, *Notre-Dame de Bonmont* (Berner Schriften zur Kunst, 7), Bern, 1957.

———— "Design in Gothic Architecture: A Preliminary Assessment," *Journal of the Society of Architectural Historians*, XXVII, 1968, 49–72.

———— "Medieval Architectural Design Methods, 800–1560," *Gesta*, XI:2, 1972, 37–51.

BUHOT DE KERSERS, Alphonse L. M., "Les chapelles absidales de la cathédrale de Bourges," *Bulletin monumental*, XL, 1874, 417–430.

CARLIER, Achille, *L'église de Rampillon*, Paris, 1930.

CARLSON, Eric G., "A Charter for Saint-Etienne, Caen: A Document and Its Implications," *Gesta*, XV, 1976, 11–14.

CERF, Charles, *Histoire et description de Notre-Dame de Reims*, 2 vols., Reims, 1861.

CHARDON DU RANQUET, Henry, *La cathédrale de Clermont-Ferrand*, Paris, 1913; 2nd ed., 1928.

CHARTRAIRE, Eugène, *La cathédrale de Sens*, Paris, 1930.

CHASTEL, André: *See* AUBERT et al., 1958.

CHENESSEAU, Georges, *Sainte-Croix d'Orléans*, 2 vols., Paris, 1921.

———— "Les fouilles de la cathédrale d'Orléans (Septembre-Décembre 1937)," *Bulletin monumental,* XCVII, 1938, 73–94.

CHOISY, Auguste, *L'art de bâtir chez les Romains,* Paris, 1873.

—— *L'art de bâtir chez les Byzantins,* Paris, 1883.

—— *Histoire de l'architecture,* 2 vols., Paris, 1899; reprinted 1929.

CHUECA GOITIA, Fernando, *Historia de la arquitectura española. Edad antigua y edad media,* Madrid, 1965.

CLAPHAM, Alfred W., *English Romanesque Architecture After the Conquest,* Oxford, 1934.

CLARK, William W., "The Nave of Saint-Pierre at Lisieux: Romanesque Structure in a Gothic Guise," *Gesta,* XVI:1, 1977, 29–38.

—— "Spatial Innovations in the Chevet of Saint-Germain-des-Prés," *Journal of the Society of Architectural Historians,* XXXVIII, 1979, 348–365.

—— and R. King, *The Cathedral of Notre-Dame at Laon,* London, (in press).

CLEMEN, Paul, *Der Dom zu Köln* (Kunstdenkmäler der Rheinprovinz, 6:3), Düsseldorf, 1937.

—— *Gotische Kathedralen in Frankreich,* Berlin, 1937.

COLMET-DAAGE, Patrice, *La cathédrale de Coutances,* Paris, 1933.

COLOMBIER, Pierre du, *Notre-Dame de Paris, mémorial de la France,* Paris, 1966.

—— *Les chantiers des cathédrales: ouvriers, architectes, sculpteurs,* Paris, 1953; 2n ed., 1973.

COLVIN, Howard M., ed., *The History of the King's Works, The Middle Ages,* 2 vols., London, 1963.

CONANT, Kenneth J., "The Third Church at Cluny," *Medieval Studies in Memory of A. Kingsley Porter* (W. R. W. Koehler, ed.), Cambridge (Mass.), 1939, II, 327–357.

—— *Carolingian and Romanesque Architecture 800 to 1200* (Pelican History of Art), Harmondsworth and Baltimore, 1959.

—— "The Pointed Arch—Orient to Occident," *Palaeologia,* VII, 1959, 267–270.

—— *Cluny. Les églises et la maison du chef d'ordre,* Cambridge (Mass.) and Mâcon, 1968.

—— and H. M. Willard, "Early Examples of the Pointed Arch and Vault in Romanesque Architecture," *Viator,* II, 1971, 203–209.

COTTINEAU, Lawrence H., *Répertoire topo-bibliographique des abbayes et prieurés,* 2 vols., Mâcon, 1935–1938.

CRESWELL, K(eppel) Archibald C., *A Short Account of Early Muslim Architecture,* Harmondsworth and Baltimore, 1958.

CROSBY, Sumner McK., "New Excavations in the Abbey Church of Saint-Denis," *Gazette des Beaux-Arts,* 6th ser., XXVI, 1944, 115–126.

—— "Fouilles exécutées récemment dans la basilique de Saint-Denis," *Bulletin monumental,* CV, 1947, 167–181.

—— "Early Gothic Architecture—New Problems as a Result of the St. Denis Excavations," *Journal of the Society of Architectural Historians,* VII:3–4, 1948, 13–16.

—— *L'abbaye royale de Saint-Denis,* Paris, 1953.

—— "Abbot Suger's St.-Denis. The New Gothic," *Studies in Western Art, Acts of the Twentieth International Congress of the History of Art, New York,* 1961, Princeton, 1963, I, 85–91.

—— "The Inside of St.-Denis' West Façade," *Gedenkschrift Ernst Gall* (M. Kühn and L. Grodecki, eds), Berlin and Munich, 1965, 59–68.

—— "Crypt and Choir Plans at Saint-Denis," *Gesta,* V, 1966, 4–8.

———— "The Plan of the Western Bays of Suger's New Church at St. Denis," *Journal of the Society of Architectural Historians*, XXVII, 1968, 39–43.

CURCIO, Luis C., *Estudios y reflexiones sobre estructuras medievales y equilibrio de la catedral gótica de Reims*, Buenos Aires, 1968.

DAVID, Marcel, "La fabrique et les manoeuvres sur les chantiers des cathédrales en France jusqu'au XIVe siècle," *Etudes d'histoire du droit canonique, dédiées à Gabriel Le Bras*, 2 vols., Paris, 1965, II, 1113–1130.

DEHIO, Georg G., "Das Münster Unserer Lieben Frau," *Strassburg und seine Bauten* (Architekten- und Ingenieur-Verein für Elsass-Lothringen), Strasbourg, 1894, 141–204.

———— *Handbuch der deutschen Kunstdenkmäler*, 3 vols., Berlin, 1905–1912; new ed., 8 vols., Munich, 1964–1974.

———— *Geschichte der deutschen Kunst*, 4 vols., Berlin and Leipzig, 1919–1921; 4th ed., 1930–1934.

———— and G. von Bezold, *Die kirchliche Baukunst des Abendlandes*, 2 vols. of text and 5 vols. of plates, Stuttgart, 1884–1901.

DELADREUE, Louis E., and Mathon, "Histoire de l'abbaye royale de Saint-Lucien (ordre de Saint Benoît)," *Mémoires de la Société académique d'archéologie, sciences et arts du département de l'Oise*, VIII, 1871–1873, 257–385, 541–704.

DELAPORTE, Yves, *La cathédrale de Chartres et ses vitraux*, Paris, 1943.

———— *Notre-Dame de Chartres*, Paris, 1957.

———— "Remarques sur la chronologie de la cathédrale de Chartres," *Bulletin de la Société archéologique d'Eure-et-Loir*, XXXI, 1959, 299–320.

———— and E. Houvet, *Les vitraux de la cathédrale de Chartres, histoire et description*, 4 vols., Chartres, 1926.

DEMAISON, Louis, *La cathédrale de Reims*, Paris, 1910.

DENEUX, Henri, "Signes lapidaires et épures du XIIIe siècle à la cathédrale de Reims," *Bulletin monumental*, LXXXIV, 1925, 99–130.

———— "De la construction en tas de charge et du point de butée des arcs-boutants au moyen âge," *Ibid.*, CII, 1943–1944, 241–256.

———— *Dix ans de fouilles dans la cathédrale de Reims*, 1919–1930 (Conférence donnée à la Société des amis du vieux Reims le ler juin 1944), Reims, n.d.

———— "Des modifications apportées à la cathédrale de Reims au cours de sa construction du XIIIe au XVe siècle," *Bulletin monumental*, CVI, 1948, 121–140.

———— "Des modifications apportées à la cathédrale de Reims au cours des restaurations effectuées du XVIe au début du XXe siècle," *Ibid.*, CVII, 1949, 125–142.

DERUELLE, Marcel I. J., *De Sint-Pietersabdij te Gent. Archeologische studie*, Ghent, 1933.

DESHOULIÈRES, François, "L'église Saint-Pierre de Montmartre," *Bulletin monumental*, LXXVII, 1913, 5–30.

DE SMIDT, Firmin, *De romaanse kerkelijke bouwkunst in West-Vlaanderen*, Ghent, 1940.

———— *De Sint-Niklaaskerk te Gent, archeologische studie* (Verhandelingen van de koninklijke Vlaamse Academie voor wetenschappen, letteren en schone kunsten van België, Klasse der schone kunsten, 23), Brussels, 1969.

DEVLIEGHER, Luc, "De opkomst van de kerkelijke gotische bouwkunst in West-Vlaanderen gedurende de XIIIe eeuw," *Bulletin van de koninklijke Commissie voor monumenten en landschappen*, V, 1954, 177–345; VII, 1956, 7–121.

———— "Het koor van de romaanse Sint-Donaaskerk te Brugge," *Bulletin van de koninklijke Commissie voor monumenten en landschappen,* XIV, 1963, 309–325.

———— "Enkele aantekeningen over de Scheldegotiek," *Bulletin van de koninklijke nederlandsche oudheidkundige bond,* 6th ser., XVII, 1964, 175–188.

DHANENS, Elisabeth, *Sint-Niklaaskerk, Gent* (Inventaris van het kunstpatrimonium van Oostvlaanderen, 3), Ghent, 1960.

Dictionnaire des églises de France, see BROSSE.

Dictionnaire d'histoire et de géographie ecclésiastiques (A. Baudrillart, ed.), Paris, 1912ff.

DIMIER, Anselme, *Recueil de plans d'églises cisterciennes,* 2 vols., Grignan and Paris, 1949.

———— *L'art cistercien, II. Hors de France* (La nuit des temps, 34), Saint-Léger-Vauban (Abbaye de la Pierre-qui-Vire), 1971.

———— and J. Porcher, *L'art cistercien, I. France* (La nuit des temps, 16), Saint-Léger-Vauban (Abbaye de la Pierre-qui-Vire), 1962.

DONAU, Victor, "L'église abbatiale de Mouzon (Ardennes)," *Bulletin monumental,* LXXIX, 1920, 137–164.

DONIN, Richard K., *Bettelordenskirchen in Österreich,* Baden, 1935.

DOW, Helen J., "The Rose Window," *Journal of the Warburg and Courtauld Institutes,* XX, 1957, 248–297.

DUBY, Georges, *The Europe of the Cathedrals,* 1140–1280, Geneva, 1966.

DURÁN SANPERE, Agustín, "La cathédrale de Barcelone," *Congrès archéologique de France,* CXVII (Catalogne), 1959, 28–36.

DURAND, Georges, *Monographie de l'église cathédrale Notre-Dame d'Amiens,* 2 vols., Amiens, 1901–1903.

DURAND, Paul, *Monographie de Notre-Dame de Chartres. Explications des planches* (Collection de documents inédits sur l'histoire de France, ser. 3), Paris, 1881: *see* LASSUS.

DURLIAT, Marcel, *L'art dans le royaume de Majorque,* Toulouse, 1962.

———— "L'architecture gothique méridionale au XIIIe siècle," *Ecole Antique de Nîmes, Bulletin annuel,* new ser., VIII–IX, 1973–1974, 63–132.

ENLART, Camille, *Origines françaises de l'architecture gothique en Italie,* Paris, 1894.

———— *Monuments religieux de l'architecture romane et de transition dans la région picarde. Anciens diocèses d'Amiens et de Boulogne,* Amiens, 1895.

———— *L'art gothique et la Renaissance en Chypre,* Paris, 1899.

———— *Manuel d'archéologie française depuis les temps mérovingiens jusqu'à la Renaissance. Première partie: Architecture religieuse,* Paris, 1902; 3rd ed., 3 vols., 1927–1930.

ERLANDE-BRANDENBURG, Alain, "La priorale Saint-Louis de Poissy," *Bulletin monumental,* CXXIX, 1971, 85–112.

———— "La cathédrale de Lisieux. Les campagnes de construction," *Congrès archéologique de France,* CXXXII (Bessin et Pays d'Auge), 1974, 139–172.

———— *Le roi est mort. Étude sur les funérailles, les sépultures et les tombeaux des rois de France jusqu'à la fin du XIIIe siècle* (Bibliothèque de la Société française d'archéologie, 7), Geneva, 1975.

———— "Le septième colloque international de la Société française d'archéologie (1er et 2 octobre 1974). La façade de la cathédrale d'Amiens," *Bulletin monumental,* CXXXV, 1977, 253–293.

ESCHER, Konrad, *Englische Kathedralen,* Munich, 1929.

EVANS, Joan, ed., *The Flowering of the Middle Ages,* London, 1966.

EYDOUX, Henri-Paul, *L'architecture des églises cisterciennes d'Allemagne,* Paris, 1952.

———— "L'abbatiale de Moreruela et l'architecture des églises cisterciennes d'Espagne," *Cîteaux in de Nederlanden,* V, 1954, 173–207.

———— *Saint Louis et son temps,* Paris, 1971.

FAGE, René, *La cathédrale de Limoges,* Paris, 1926.

FARCY, Louis de, *Monographie de la cathédrale d'Angers,* 4 vols., Angers, 1901–1910.

FELS, Etienne, "Die Grabung an der Fassade der Kathedrale von Chartres," *Kunstchronik,* VIII, 1955, 149–151.

FERNIE, Eric, "Historical Metrology and Architectural History," *Art History,* I, 1978, 383–399.

FIRMIN, Broeder, *see* DE SMIDT.

FITCHEN, John, "A Comment on the Function of the Upper Flying Buttresses in French Gothic Cathedrals," *Gazette des Beaux-Arts,* 6th ser., XLV, 1955, 69–90.

———— *The Construction of Gothic Cathedrals. A Study of Medieval Vault Erection,* Oxford, 1961.

FLEMING, John, H. Honour, and N. Pevsner, *The Penguin Dictionary of Architecture,* Harmondsworth and Baltimore, 1966.

FLEURY, Gabriel, *La cathédrale du Mans,* Paris, 1910.

FLIPO, Vincent, *La cathédrale de Dijon,* Paris, 1929.

FOCILLON, Henri, *Vie des Formes,* Paris, 1934; enlarged ed., 1939.

———— "Généalogie de l'unique (fragment)," *Actes du 2e Congrès international d'esthétique et de science de l'art,* Paris, 1937, II, 120–127.

———— *Art d'Occident. Le moyen âge roman et gothique,* Paris, 1938; 2nd ed., 1947; new ed., 1965.

———— "Le problème de l'ogive," *Recherche,* I, 1939, 5–28.

———— *The Life of Forms in Art,* New Haven, 1942; 2nd ed., New York, 1948.

———— *The Art of the West in the Middle Ages* (J. Bony, ed.), 2 vols., London and Greenwich (Conn.), 1963; 2nd ed., London and New York, 1969.

FOCKEMA ANDREAE, Sybrandus J., and E. H. Ter Kuile, *Duizend jaar bouwen in Nederland, I. De bouwkunst van de Middeleeuwen,* Amsterdam, 1948.

FORMIGÉ, Jules, *L'abbaye royale de Saint-Denis. Recherches nouvelles,* Paris, 1960.

FORSYTH, George H., *The Church of Saint-Martin at Angers: the Architectural History of the Site from the Roman Empire to the French Revolution,* 2 vols., Princeton, 1953.

FOSSARD, Albert, *Le prieuré de Saint-Leu d'Esserent,* Paris, 1934.

FOSSEY, Jules, *Monographie de la cathédrale d'Evreux,* Evreux, 1898.

FRACCARO DE LONGHI, Lelia, *L'architettura delle chiese cisterciensi italiane,* Milan, 1958.

FRANKL, Paul, "A French Gothic Cathedral: Amiens," *Art in America,* XXXV, 1947, 294–299.

———— "The Chronology of Chartres Cathedral," *Art Bulletin,* XXXIX, 1957, 33–47.

———— *The Gothic. Literary Sources and Interpretations through Eight Centuries,* Princeton, 1960.

———— "Reconsiderations on the Chronology of Chartres Cathedral," *Art Bulletin,* XLIII, 1961, 51–58.

———— *Gothic Architecture* (Pelican History of Art), Harmondsworth and Baltimore, 1962.

FRISCH, Teresa G., *Gothic Art 1140–c.1450*, Englewood Cliffs (N.J.), 1971.

FROIDEVAUX, Yves M., "L'abbatiale de Lessay," *Monuments historiques de la France,* new ser., IV, 1958, 139–149.

FYOT, Eugène, *L'église Notre-Dame de Dijon; monographie descriptive,* Dijon, 1910.

GAL, Ladislas, *L'architecture religieuse en Hongrie du XIe au XIIIe siècle,* Paris, 1929.

GALL, Ernst, "Neue Beiträge zur Geschichte vom Werden der Gotik, Untersuchungen zur Baugeschichte der Normandie," *Monatshefte für Kunstwissenschaft,* IV, 1911, 309–323.

———— *Niederrheinische und normannische Architektur im Zeitalter der Frühgotik: I. Die niederrheinischen Apsidengliederungen nach normannischem Vorbilde,* Berlin, 1915.

———— "Sankt-Georg in Limburg-an-der-Lahn und die nordfranzösische Frühgotik," *Festschrift für Adolf Goldschmidt,* Leipzig, 1923, 7–24.

———— "Die Abteikirche Saint-Lucien bei Beauvais," *Wiener Jahrbuch für Kunstgeschichte,* IV, 1926, 59–71.

———— *Die gotische Baukunst in Frankreich und Deutschland, Teil I: Die Vorstufen in Nordfrankreich von der Mitte des elften bis gegen Ende des zwölften Jahrhunderts,* Leipzig, 1925; 2nd ed., Braunschweig, 1955.

———— *Dome und Klosterkirchen am Rhein,* Munich, 1956.

GALL, Günter, "Zur Baugeschichte des Regensburger Domes," *Zeitschrift für Kunstgeschichte,* XVII, 1954, 61–78.

GANTNER, Joseph, *Kunstgeschichte der Schweiz, II. Die gotische Kunst,* Frauenfeld, 1947.

GAUCHERY, Robert, and R. Branner, "La cathédrale de Bourges aux XIe et XIIe siècles," *Bulletin monumental,* CXI, 1953, 105–123.

Gedenkschrift Ernst Gall, (M. Kühn and L. Grodecki, eds.), Berlin and Munich, 1965.

GIMPEL, Jean, *The Cathedral Builders,* New York, 1961.

GIRDLESTONE, Cuthbert M., "Thirteenth Century Gothic in England and Normandy, A Comparison," *Archaeological Journal,* CII, 1945, 111–133.

GIVELET, Charles de, *Le Mont-Notre-Dame. Histoire et description,* Reims, 1864; 2nd ed., Limé, 1893.

GLÜCK, Heinrich, *Der Ursprung des römischen und abendlandischen Wölbungsbaues,* Vienna, 1933.

GOETZ, Wolfgang, *Zentralbau und Zentralbautendenz in der gotischen Architektur,* Berlin, 1968.

GOUBET, Simone, *see* M. Aubert, 1959.

GOÜIN, Henry, *L'abbaye de Royaumont,* Paris, 1932.

GOÛT, Paul, *Le Mont Saint-Michel,* 2 vols., Paris, 1910.

GRANDJEAN, Marcel, "La construction de la cathédrale de Lausanne (fin XIIe—début XIIIe siècles): notes sur la chronologie et les maîtres d'oeuvre," *Genava,* new ser., XI, 1963, 261–287.

———— "La cathédrale actuelle: sa construction, ses architectes, son architecture," in J. C. Biaudet *et al., La cathédrale de Lausanne* (Bibliothèque de la Société d'Histoire de l'Art en Suisse, 3), Bern, 1975, 45–174.

GRIGSON Geoffrey, M. Hürlimann, and P. Meyer, *English Cathedrals,* London, 1950.

GRODECKI, Louis, *The Stained Glass of French Churches,* London, 1948.

————— "Le vitrail et l'architecture au XIIe et au XIIIe siècles," *Gazette des Beaux-Arts*, 6th ser., XXXVI, (1949), 5–24.

————— "The Transept Portals of Chartres Cathedral: The Date of their Construction according to Archaelological Data," *Art Bulletin*, XXXIII, 1951, 156–164.

————— "Chronologie de la cathédrale de Chartres," *Bulletin monumental*, CXVI, 1958, 91–119.

————— *Sainte-Chapelle*, Paris, 1962.

————— *Chartres*, Paris, 1963.

————— "Pierre, Eudes et Raoul de Montreuil à l'abbatiale de Saint-Denis," *Bulletin monumental*, CXXII, 1964, 269–274.

————— *Les vitraux de Saint-Denis. Etude sur le vitrail au XIIe siecle*, Paris, 1976.

GRODECKI, Louis, A. Prache, and R. Recht, *Gothic Architecture* (P. L. Nervi, ed., History of World Architecture), New York, 1977.

————— and J. Prinet, *Bibliographie Henri Focillon* (Yale Historical Publications in the History of Art, 15), New Haven, 1963.

—————, *See also* AUBERT *et al.*, 1958.

GROSS, Werner, "Die Hochgotik im deutschen Kirchenbau," *Marburger Jahrbuch für Kunstwissenschaft*, VII, 1933, 290–346.

————— *Die abendländische Architektur um 1300*, Stuttgart, 1948.

GRUBER, Jean-Jacques, *see* AUBERT et al., 1958.

GUIGUE, Marie-Claude, *see* BÉGULE, L.

HACKER-SÜCK, Inge, "La Sainte-Chapelle de Paris et les chapelles palatines du moyen âge en France," *Cahiers archéologiques*, XIII, 1962, 217–257.

HAHN, Hanno, *Die frühe Kirchenbaukunst der Zisterzienser, Untersuchungen zur Baugeschichte von Kloster Eberbach im Rheingau und ihren europaischen Analogien im 12. Jahrhundert* (Frankfurter Forschungen zur Architekturgeschichte, 1), Berlin, 1957.

HAHNLOSER, Hans R., *Villard de Honnecourt. Kritische gesamtausgabe des Bauhüttenbuches ms. fr 19093 der Pariser Nationalbibliothek*, Vienna, 1935; new ed., Graz, 1972.

HAMANN, Richard, *Deutsche und französische Kunst im Mittelalter. II. Die Baugeschichte der Klosterkirche zu Lehnin und die normannische Invasion in der deutschen Architektur des 13. Jahrhunderts*, Marburg, 1923.

————— and K. Wilhelm-Kästner, *Die Elisabethkirche zu Marburg und ihre künstlerische Nachfolge*, 2 vols., Marburg, 1924–1929.

HARVEY, John H., "The Mediaeval Office of Works," *Journal of the British Archaeological Association*, 3rd ser., VI, 1941, 20–87.

————— *The Gothic World 1100–1600. A Survey of Architecture and Art*, London, 1950.

————— *The English Cathedrals*, London, 1950.

————— *English Mediaeval Architects. A Biographical Dictionary down to 1550*, London, 1954.

————— "The Origins of Gothic Architecture: Some Further Thoughts," *Antiquaries Journal*, XLVIII, 1968, 87–99.

————— "The Tracing Floor in York Minster," *40th Annual Report of the Friends of York Minster for 1968*, York, 1969, 9–13.

————— *The Mediaeval Architect*, London, 1972.

HASLINGHUIS, Edward J., and C. J. A. C. Peeters, *De Dom van Utrecht* (Nederlandse

Monumenten van Geschiedenis en Kunst, II, 2), The Hague, 1965.

HASTINGS, J. Maurice, *St. Stephen's Chapel and its Place in the Development of Perpendicular Style in England*, Cambridge, 1955.

HAUG, Hans, R. Will, T. Rieger, V. Beyer, and P. Ahnne, *La cathédrale de Strasbourg*, Strasbourg, 1957.

HEARN, Millard F., "The Rectangular Ambulatory in English Mediaeval Architecture," *Journal of the Society of Architectural Historians*, XXX, 1971, 187–208.

HÉLIOT, Pierre, "Les Anciennes cathédrales d'Arras," *Bulletin de la Commission royale des monuments et des sites*, IV, 1953, 7–109.

—— "Remarques sur l'abbatiale de Saint-Germer et sur les blocs de façade du XIIe siècle," *Bulletin monumental*, CXIV, 1956, 81–114.

—— "La nef et le clocher de l'ancienne cathédrale de Cambrai," *Wallraf-Richartz-Jahrbuch*, XVIII, 1956, 91–110.

—— "Les oeuvres capitales du gothique français primitif et l'influence de l'architecture anglaise," *Wallraf-Richartz-Jahrbuch*, XX, 1958, 85–114.

—— "Les antécédents et les débuts des coursières anglo-normandes et rhénanes," *Cahiers de civilisation médiévale*, II, 1959, 429–443.

—— "Trois monuments disparus de la Flandre wallonne: l'abbatiale d'Anchin et les collégiales Saint-Pierre et Saint-Amé de Douai," *Revue belge d'archéologie et d'histoire de l'art*, XXVII, 1959, 129–173.

—— "La cathédrale de Tournai et l'architecture du moyen âge," *Revue belge d'archéologie et d'histoire de l'art*, XXXI–XXXIII, 1962–1964 (published 1969), 3–139.

—— "La suppression du triforium au début de la période gothique," *Revue archéologique*, 1964, I, 131–168.

—— "L'église abbatiale de Saint-Corneille à Compiègne," *Bulletin monumental*, CXXIII, 1965, 193–207.

—— "Deux églises champenoises méconnues: les abbatiales d'Orbais et d'Essomes," *Mémoires de la Société d'agriculture, commerce, sciences, et arts du département de la Marne*, LXXX, 1965, 87–112.

—— *La basilique de Saint-Quentin*, Paris, 1967.

—— "Du Carolingien au gothique, l'évolution de la plastique murale dans l'architecture religieuse du nord-ouest de l'Europe (IXe–XIIIe siècle)," *Mémoires présentés par divers savants à l'Académie des inscriptions et belles-lettres*, XV:2, 1967, 1–140.

—— "La collégiale Saint-Nicolas d'Amiens et l'architecture picarde," *Mélanges offerts à René Crozet* (Université de Poitiers, Centre d'Etudes Supérieures de Civilisation Médiévale), Poitiers, 1966, II, 985–992.

—— "Les églises de Cuis, de Rieux, et les passages muraux dans l'architecture gothique de Champagne," *Mémoires de la Société d'agriculture, commerce, sciences, et arts du département de la Marne*, LXXXII, 1967, 128–143.

—— "Les églises de l'abbaye Notre-Dame à Soissons et l'architecture romane dans le nord de la France capétienne," *Revue belge d'archéologie et d'histoire de l'art*, XXXVII, 1968, 49–88.

—— "Triforiums et coursières dans les églises gothiques de Bretagne et de Normandie," *Annales de Normandie*, XIX, 1969, 115–154.

—— "Les coursières et les passages muraux dans les églises du Midi de la France, d'Espagne et de Portugal aux XIIIe et XIVe siècles," *Anuario de estudios medievales*, VI, 1969, 187–217.

——— "Le choeur de l'abbatiale de Saint-Thierry et les débuts de l'architecture gothique en Champagne," *Bulletin de la Société nationale des antiquaires de France*, 1970, 336–358.

——— "Coursières et passages muraux dans les églises gothiques de la Belgique imperiale," *Bulletin de la Commission royale des monuments et des sites*, new ser., I, 1970–1971, 17–43.

——— "Coursières et passages muraux dans les églises gothiques de l'Europe centrale," *Zeitschrift für Kunstgeschichte*, XXXIII, 1970, 173–210.

——— "Passages muraux et coursières dans les églises gothiques du Nord-Est de la France médiévale, de la Lorraine et des pays du Rhône moyen," *Zeitschrift für Schweizerische Archäologie und Kunstgeschichte* (Revue Suisse d'Art et d'Archéologie), XXVII, 1970, 21–43.

——— "Coursières et passages muraux dans les églises romanes et gothiques de l'Allemagne du Nord," *Aachener Kunstblätter*, XLI, 1971 (Festschrift für Wolfgang Krönig), 211–223.

——— "Le chevet de la cathédrale de Laon, ses antécédents français et ses suites," *Gazette des Beaux-Arts*, 6th ser., LXXIX, 1972, 193–214.

——— "L'abbatiale de Saint-Michel-en-Thiérache, modèle de Saint-Yved à Braine, et l'architecture gothique des XIIe et XIIIe siècles," *Bulletin de la Commission royale des monuments et des sites*, new ser., II, 1972, 15–43.

——— and G. Jouven, "L'église Saint-Pierre de Chartres et l'architecture du moyen âge," *Bulletin archéologique du Comité des travaux historiques et scientifiques*, new ser., VI, 1970, 117–177.

HENDERSON, George, *Gothic*, Harmondsworth and Baltimore, 1967.

HENRIET, Jacques, "Le choeur de Saint-Mathurin de Larchant et Notre-Dame de Paris," *Bulletin monumental*, CXXXIV, 1976, 289–307.

HEYMAN, Jacques, "The Stone Skeleton," *International Journal of Solids and Structures*, II, 1966, 249–280.

——— "Beauvais Cathedral," *Transactions of the Newcomen Society*, XL, 1967–1968, 15–32.

——— "On the Rubber Vaults of the Middle Ages and Other Matters," *Gazette des Beaux-Arts*, 6th ser., LXXI, 1968, 177–188.

HOFSTATTER, Hans H., *see* AUBERT et al., 1965.

HONOUR, Hugh, *see* FLEMING *et al.*

HORN, Walter W., "Das Florentiner Baptisterium," *Mitteilungen des Kunsthistorischen Institutes in Florenz*, V, 1937–1940, 100–151; reprinted in *Die Fassade von Saint-Gilles. Das Florentiner Baptisterium*, Berkeley, 1974.

——— "On the Origins of the Mediaeval Bay System," *Journal of the Society of Architectural Historians*, XVII, 1958, 2–23; reprinted in a slightly abbreviated form in *Readings in Art History, I. Ancient Egypt through the Middle Ages* (H. Spencer, ed.), New York, 1969, 217–250.

HORN, Walter W. and E. Born, "New Theses About the Plan of St. Gall. A Summary of Recent Views," *Die Abtei Reichenau, Neue Beiträge zur Geschichte und Kultur des Inselklosters* (H. Maurer, ed.: Bodensee-Bibliothek, 20), Sigmaringen, 1974, 407–480.

——— and E. Born, *The Plan of St. Gall. A Study of the Architecture and Economy of, and Life in a Paradigmatic Carolingian Monastery,* 3 vols., Berkeley and Los Angeles, 1980.

HOUVET, Etienne, *Cathédrale de Chartres,* 7 vols., Chelles, 1919–1921.

——, *see also* DELAPORTE, 1926.

HUARD, Georges, *L'art en Normandie,* Paris, 1928.

HUBERT, Jean, *L'architecture religieuse du haut moyen âge en France,* Paris, 1952.

—— "Les fouilles de Saint-Lucien de Beauvais et les origines du plan tréflé," *Arte in Europa. Scritti di storia dell'arte in onore di Edoardo Arslan,* Milan, 1966, I, 229–235.

HUIZINGA, Johan, *The Waning of the Middle Ages,* Garden City (N.Y.), 1954.

HÜRLIMANN, Martin, *see* BONY *et al.;* and GRIGSON *et al.*

JALABERT, Denise, *L'art normand au moyen âge,* Paris, 1930.

JAMES, John, "The Contractors of Chartres," *Architectural Association Quarterly,* IV, 1972, 42–53.

JANTZEN, Hans, "Burgundische Gotik," *Sitzungsberichte der Bayerischen Akademie der Wissenschaften, Philosophisch-historische Klasse,* 1948 (5).

—— *Über den gotischen Kirchenraum* (Freiburger Wissenschaftliche Gesellschaft, 15), Freiburg i. Br., 1928; reprinted in *Über den gotischen Kirchenraum und andere Aufsätze,* Berlin, 1951, 7–20.

—— *High Gothic,* London, 1962.

JONES, Gwilym P., *see* KNOOP, 1931–1932.

JOUVEN, Georges, *see* HÉLIOT *et al.*

JUNGMANN Josef A., and E. Sauser, *Symbolik der katholischen Kirche* (Symbolik der Religionen, 6), Stuttgart, 1960.

KIDSON, Peter, "Canterbury Cathedral. The Gothic Choir," *Archaeological Journal,* CXXVI, 1969, 244–246.

—— and P. Murray, *A History of English Architecture,* London, 1962.

KIESOW, Gottfried, "Zur Baugeschichte des Florentiner Doms," *Mitteilungen des kunsthistorischen Instituts in Florenz,* X, 1961–1963, 1–22.

KIMPEL, Dieter, *Die Querhausarme von Notre-Dame zu Paris und ihre Skulpturen,* Bonn, 1971.

—— "Le développement de la taille en série dans l'architecture mediévale et son rôle dans l'histoire économique," *Bulletin monumental,* CXXXV, 1977, 195–222.

KING, Richard, see W. W. CLARK.

KING, Thomas H., *The Study-Book of Mediaeval Architecture and Art,* 4 vols., London, 1858–1868; 2nd ed., Edinburgh, 1893.

KLETZL, Otto, "Plan-Fragmente aus der deutschen Dombauhütte von Prag," *Veröffentlichungen des Archivs der Stadt Stuttgart,* III, 1939.

—— "Ein Werkriss des Frauenhauses von Strassburg," *Marburger Jahrbuch für Kunstwissenschaft,* IX, 1939, 103–158.

KLOTZ, Heinrich, *Der Ostbau der Stiftskirche zu Wimpfen im Tal. Zum Frühwerk des Erwin von Steinbach* (Kunstwissenschaftliche Studien, 39), Berlin and Munich, 1967.

KNOOP, Douglas, and G. P. Jones, "Masons and Apprenticeship in Mediaeval England," *Economic History Review,* III, 1931–1932, 346–366.

—— and G. P. Jones, *The Mediaeval Mason* (Publications of the University of Manchester, Economic History Series, 8), Manchester, 1933.

KÖLN, Zentral-Dombau-Verein, *Der Kölner Dom. Festschrift zur Siebenhundertjahrsfeier, 1248–1948,* Cologne, 1948.

KOEPF, Hans, *Die gotischen Planrisse der Wiener Sammlungen* (Studien zur österreichischen Kunstgeschichte, 4), Vienna, Graz and Cologne, 1969.

———— "Der Strassburger Fassadenriss Nr.289 der Wiener Sammlungen," *Alte und moderne Kunst,* XVI, No.119, 1971, 14–17.

KONOW, Helma, *Die Baukunst der Bettelorden am Oberrhein* (Forschungen zur Geschichte der Kunst am Oberrhein, 6), Berlin, 1954.

KRAUTHEIMER, Richard, *Die Kirchen der Bettelorden in Deutschland,* Cologne, 1925.

———— *Early Christian and Byzantine Architecture* (Pelican History of Art), Harmondsworth and Baltimore, 1965.

KRÖNIG, Wolfgang, "Hallenkirchen in Mittelitalien," *Kunstgeschichliches Jahrbuch der Bibliotheca Hertziana,* II, 1938, 1–142.

———— "Note sull'architettura religiosa medioevale delle Marche," *Atti del XI Congresso di Storia dell'Architettura* (Marche), 1959, 205–232.

———— *The Cathedral of Monreale,* Palermo, 1965.

———— "Caratteri dell'architettura degli ordini mendicanti in Umbria," *Atti del sesto convegno di studi Umbri, Gubbio,* 1968 (published 1971) 165–198.

KUBACH, Hans E., "Das Triforium. Ein Beitrag zur kunstgeschichtlichen Raumkunde Europas in Mittelalter," *Zeitschrift für Kunstgeschichte,* V, 1936, 275–288.

KUBLER, George, "A Late Gothic Computation of Rib Vault Thrusts," *Gazette des Beaux-Arts,* 6th ser., XXVI, 1944, 135–148.

KURMANN, Peter, *La cathédrale Saint-Etienne de Meaux. Étude architecturale* (Bibliothèque de la Société française d'archéologie, 1), Paris and Geneva, 1971.

———— and D. von Winterfeld, "Gautier de Varinfroy, ein 'Denkmalpfleger' in 13. Jahrhundert," *Festschrift fur Otto von Simson zum 65. Geburtstag,* Berlin, 1977, 101–159.

LA BORDE, Jean Benjamin de, *Description générale et particulière de la France ou Voyage pittoresque de la France . . . ,* see *Voyage pittoresque . . . .*

LAFOND, Jean, see AUBERT et al., 1958.

LAMBERT, Elie, "La cathédrale de Laon," *Gazette des Beaux-Arts,* 5th ser., XVI, 1926, 361–384.

———— *L'art gothique en Espagne aux XIIe et XIIIe siècles,* Paris, 1931.

———— "Caen roman et gothique," *Bulletin de la Société des Antiquaires de Normandie,* XLIII, 1935, 5–70.

———— "L'art gothique," in *Histoire de l'Art* (G. Huisman, ed.: Encyclopédie Quillet), Paris, 1938, II, 149–360; 2nd ed., 1957, I, 423–597.

———— "L'ancienne abbaye de Saint-Vincent de Laon," *Comptes-rendus de l'Académie des inscriptions et belles-lettres,* 1939, 124–138.

———— "La cathédrale de Toulouse," *Mémoires de la Société archéologique du Midi de la France,* XXI, 1947, 137–163; reprinted in E. Lambert, *Etudes médiévales,* Toulouse and Paris, 1956, II, 148–174.

———— "L'église de Saint-Martin d'Aumale," *Bulletin de la Société nationale des Antiquaires de France,* 1948–1949, 29–34.

——— *Etudes médiévales*, 4 vols., Toulouse and Paris, 1956–1957.

LAMPÉREZ Y ROMEA, Vicente, *Historia de la arquitectura cristiana española en la edad media*, Madrid, 2 vols., 1906–1908; 2nd ed., 3 vols., 1930.

LANFRY, Georges, "La salle capitulaire romane de l'abbaye de Jumièges," *Bulletin monumental*, XCIII, 1934, 323–340.

——— *La cathédrale dans la cité romaine et la Normandie ducale* (Cahiers de Notre-Dame de Rouen), Rouen, 1956.

——— *La cathédrale après la Conquête de la Normandie et jusqu'à l'occupation anglaise* (Cahiers de Notre-Dame de Rouen), Rouen, 1960.

LAPEYRE, André, *Des façades occidentales de Saint-Denis et de Chartres aux portails de Laon*, Paris, 1960.

LARAN, Jean, *La cathédrale d'Albi*, Paris, 1911.

LASSALLE, Monique, "Les fenêtres des chapelles de la nef de Notre-Dame de Paris," *Information d'histoire de l'art*, XVII, 1972, 28–32.

LASSUS, Jean-Baptiste A., and A. Duval, *Monographie de la cathédrale de Chartres. Architecture, sculpture d'ornement et peinture sur verre* (Collection de documents inédits sur l'histoire de France), Paris, 1842–1867: *see* DURAND.

LASTEYRIE, Robert de, *L'architecture religieuse en France à l'époque gothique*, 2 vols., Paris, 1926–1927.

LAUTIER, Claudine, *see* M. BIDEAULT.

LAVEDAN, Pierre, *L'architecture gothique religieuse en Catalogne, Valence et Baléares*, Paris, 1935.

——— *Histoire de l'art: II. Moyen-âge et temps modernes* (Clio, 10), Paris, 1944; 2nd ed., 1950.

LEBLOND, Victor, *La cathédrale de Beauvais*, Paris, 1933.

LECONTE, Emile, *Notre-Dame de Paris, recueil contenant 80 planches . . . et une notice archéologique . . . par Celtibère*, Paris, 1841–1843; new ed., retitled *Monographie de Notre-Dame de Paris et de la nouvelle sacristie de MM. Lassus et Viollet-le-Duc*, 1853.

LEFÈVRE-PONTALIS, Eugène A., *L'architecture religieuse dans l'ancien diocèse de Soissons au XIe et au XIIe siècle*, 2 vols., Paris, 1894–1896.

——— "Les architectes et la construction des cathédrales de Chartres," *Mémoires de la Société nationale des Antiquaires de France*, LXIV, 1905, 69–136.

——— "Saint-Leu d'Esserent," *Congrès archéologique de France*, LXXII (Beauvais), 1905, 121–128.

——— "Coutances. Cathédrale," *Ibid.*, LXXV (Caen), 1908, I, 247–271.

——— "Abbaye de Longpont," *Ibid.*, LXXVIII (Reims), 1911, I, 410–423.

——— "Cathédrale de Soissons," *Ibid.*, LXXVIII (Reims), 1911, I, 318–337.

——— "Eglise du Mont-Notre-Dame," *Ibid.*, LXXVIII (Reims), 1911, I, 250–258.

——— "Eglise de Saint-Martin-des-Champs à Paris," *Ibid.*, LXXXII (Paris), 1919, 106–126.

——— "L'origine des arcs-boutants," *Ibid.*, LXXXII (Paris), 1919, 367–396.

LELONG, Charles, "La nef de Saint-Martin de Tours," *Bulletin monumental*, CXXXIII, 1975, 205–231.

——— "Le transept de Saint-Martin de Tours," *Ibid.*, CXXXIII, 1975, 113–129.

LEMAIRE, Raymond, *De romaanse bouwkunst in de Nederlanden* (Verhandelingen van de koninklijke Vlaamse Academie voor wetenschappen, letteren en schone kunsten van België, Klasse der schone kunsten, 6), Brussels, 1952.

————, S. Leurs, and D. Roggen, *Bij het ontstaan der Brabantsche hooggotiek* (Verhandelingen van de koninklijke Vlaamse Academie voor wetenschappen, letteren en schone kunsten van België, Klasse der schone kunsten, 3), Brussels, 1944, 7–20.

LENOIR, Alexandre, *Statistique monumentale de Paris,* 3 vols., Paris, 1867.

LESUEUR, Frédéric, "L'église abbatiale Saint-Lomer de Blois," *Bulletin monumental,* LXXXII, 1923, 36–65.

LEURS, Stan, "L'architecture religieuse dans le sud-ouest de la Belgique, I. Des origines à la fin du XVe siècle," *Bulletin de la Commission royale des monuments et des sites,* I, 1949, 85–353.

LILLICH, Meredith P., "The Band Window: A Theory of Origin and Development," *Gesta,* IX:1, 1970, 26–33.

LITTLE, Lester K. "Saint Louis' Involvement with the Friars," *Church History,* XXXIII, 1964, 125–148.

LONGHI, Lelia Fraccaro de, *see* FRACCARO DE LONGHI.

LORENTE JUNQUERA, Manuel, "El ábside de la catedral de Toledo y sus precedentes," *Archivo Español de Arte y Arqueologia,* XIII, 1937, 25–36.

MAHIEU, Bernard, "Jean de Chelles et Notre-Dame de Paris au XIIIe siècle," *Paris et Ile de France,* XCIV–XCV, 1967–1968, 57–60.

MAILLÉ, Geneviève de, *Provins. Les monuments religieux,* 2 vols., Paris, 1939.

————, *see also* AUBERT et al., 1943.

MÂLE, Emile, *Art et artistes du moyen âge,* Paris, 1927.

———— *Notre-Dame de Chartres,* Paris, 1948.

———— *La cathédrale d'Albi,* Paris, 1950.

MALLION, Jean, *Chartres. Le jubé de la cathédrale,* Chartres, 1964.

MARK, Robert, "Gothic Cathedrals and Structural Rationalism," *Transactions of the New York Academy of Sciences,* 2nd ser., XXXIII, 1971, 607–624.

———— "The Structural Analysis of Gothic Cathedrals. A Comparison of Chartres and Bourges," *The Scientific American,* CCXXVII:5, November 1972, 90–99.

———— "Structural Experimentation in Gothic Architecture," *American Scientist,* LXVI, 1978, 542–550.

————, and R. A. Prentke, "Model Analysis of Gothic Structure," *Journal of the Society of Architectural Historians,* XXVII, 1968, 44–48.

————, and R. S. Jonash, "Wind Loading on Gothic Structure," *Journal of the Society of Architectural Historians,* XXIX, 1970, 222–230.

————, *see also:* ABEL, ALEXANDER, BORG, RAUCH, WOLFE.

MAYEUX, Albert, "Etude sur l'abside de la cathédrale de Chartres," *Mémoires de la Société archéologique d'Eure-et-Loir,* XII, 1901–1904, 49–62.

MEDDING-ALP, Emma, *see* ALP.

MEER, Frederik van der, *Atlas de l'ordre cistercien,* Paris and Brussels, 1965.

MEERSSEMAN, Gérard G., "L'architecture dominicaine au XIIIe siècle: législation et pratique," *Archivum Fratrum Praedicatorum,* XVI, 1946, 136–190.

MERLET, René, *La cathédrale de Chartres,* Paris, 1909.

MESSELET, Jean, "La collégiale Saint-Martin de Champeaux," *Bulletin monumental,* LXXXIV, 1925, 253–282.

MEYER, Peter, and M. Hürlimann, *Schweizerische Münster und Kathedralen des Mittelalters,* Zurich, 1945.

———, *see also* J. BONY *et al.,* and GRIGSON *et al.*

MEYER-BARKHAUSEN, Werner, *Das grosse Jahrhundert kölnischer Kirchenbaukunst,* Cologne, 1952.

MILLIN, Aubin L., *Antiquités nationales, ou Recueil de monumens pour servir à l'histoire générale et particulière de l'Empire françois,* 5 vols., Paris, 1790–1799.

MINOST, Maurice, *see* AUBERT, 1954.

MIROT, Léon, *Manuel de géographie historique de la France,* Paris, 1929; 2nd ed., 2 vols., 1947–1950.

MÖBIUS, Friedrich and Helga, *Sakrale Baukunst. Mittelalterliche Kirchen in der Deutschen Demokratischen Republik,* Berlin, 1963.

MOORE, Charles H., *Development and Character of Gothic Architecture,* London and New York, 1890; 2nd ed., 1899.

MORTET, Victor, *Etude historique et archéologique sur la cathédrale et le palais épiscopal de Paris du VIe au XIIe siècle,* Paris, 1888.

——— *Recueil de textes relatifs à l'histoire de l'architecture et à la condition des architectes en France au moyen âge, XIe–XIIe siècles,* Paris, 1911.

——— and P. Deschamps, *Recueil de textes relatifs à l'histoire de l'architecture et à la condition des architectes en France au moyen âge, XIIe–XIIIe siècles, Tome II,* Paris, 1929.

MURRAY, Stephen, "The Collapse of 1284 at Beauvais Cathedral," *Acta,* III, 1976, 17–44.

——— "The Gothic façade drawings in the Reims Palimpsest," *Gesta,* XVII:2, 1978, 51–55.

MUSSAT, André, *Le style gothique de l'ouest de la France (XIIe–XIIIe siècles),* Paris, 1963.

——— "La cathédrale Notre-Dame de Coutances," *Congrès archéologique de France,* CXXIV (Cotentin-Avranchin), 1966, 9–50.

MUSSET, Lucien, *Normandie romane* (La nuit des temps, 25 and 41), 2 vols., Saint-Léger-Vauban (Abbaye de la Pierre-qui-Vire), 1967–1974.

NICQ-DOUTRELIGNE, C., "L'abbaye de Vaucelles (Nord)," *Bulletin monumental,* LXXVIII, 1914, 316–328.

O'NEILL, K., *see* ABEL.

OURSEL, Charles, *L'art de Bourgogne,* Paris and Grenoble, 1953.

OZINGA, Murk D., *De gotische kerkelijke bouwkunst* (De Schoonheid van ons land, Bouwkunst, 2), Amsterdam, 1954.

PAATZ, Walter, *Werden und Wesen der Trecento Architektur in Toskana,* Burg, 1937.

———, and E. Paatz, *Die Kirchen von Florenz, Ein kunstgeschichtliches Handbuch,* 6 vols., Frankfurt, 1952–1955.

PANOFSKY, Erwin, *Abbot Suger on the Abbey Church of Saint-Denis and Its Art Treasures,* Princeton, 1946; 2nd ed., 1979.

——— *Gothic Architecture and Scholasticism,* Latrobe (Pa.), 1951; reprinted, Cleveland and New York, 1957.

PAQUET, Jean-Pierre, "La restauration de Saint-Leu d'Esserent. Problèmes de stabilité," *Monuments historiques de la France,* new ser., I, 1955, 9–19.

——— "Les tracés directeurs des plans de quelques édifices du domaine royal au moyen-âge," *Monuments historiques de la France,* new ser., IX, 1963, 59–84.

PAS, J. de, "Saint-Omer. Cathédrale," *Congrès archéologique de France,* IC (Amiens), 1936, 475–514.

PAUL, Vivian, "Le problème de la nef unique," in *La naissance et l'essor du gothique méridional au XIIIe siècle* (Cahiers de Fanjeaux, 9), Toulouse, 1974, 21–53.

Penguin Dictionary of Architecture, see FLEMING.

PÉROUSE DE MONTCLOS, Jean-Marie, F. Salet, and S. Stym-Popper, *Architecture. Méthode et vocabulaire* (Inventaire général des monuments et des richesses artistiques de la France, Principes d'analyse scientifique), 2 vols., Paris, 1972.

PERRAULT-DABOT, Anatole, *see* BAUDOT.

PEVSNER, Nikolaus, "The Term 'Architect' in the Middle Ages," *Speculum,* XVII, 1942, 549–562.

——— "Terms of Architectural Planning in the Middle Ages," *Journal of the Warburg and Courtauld Institutes,* V, 1942, 232–237.

——— *An Outline of European Architecture,* Harmondsworth and Baltimore, 1943; 7th ed., 1963, reprinted with revised bibliography, 1970.

——— *The Buildings of England,* 46 vols., Harmondsworth, 1951–1974.

——— "Bristol-Troyes-Gloucester," *The Architectural Review,* CXIII, 1953, 88–98.

——— *see also* FLEMING.

PFITZNER, Carlheinz, "Die Anfänge des Kölner Dombaus und die Pariser Bauschule der ersten Hälfte des 13. Jahrhunderts," *Zeitschrift des deutschen Vereins für Kunstwissenschaft,* IV, 1937, 203–217.

PINDER, Wilhelm, *Einleitende Voruntersuchung zu einer Rhythmik romanischer Innerräume in der Normandie,* Strasbourg, 1904.

POPE, Arthur U., "Possible Iranian Contributions to the Beginning of Gothic Architecture," *Beiträge zur Kunstgeschichte Asiens, In memoriam Ernst Diez* (O. Aslanapa, ed.), Istanbul, 1963, 1–29.

PORÉE, Charles, "Le choeur de la cathédrale d'Auxerre," *Bulletin monumental,* LXX, 1906, 251–262.

PORTER, A(rthur) Kingsley, *Medieval Architecture: Its Origins and Development,* 2 vols., New York, 1909.

——— *The Construction of Lombard and Gothic Vaults,* New Haven, 1911.

——— *Lombard Architecture,* 4 vols., New Haven, 1915–1917.

POUX, Joseph, *La Cité de Carcassonne, histoire et description,* 3 vols., Toulouse, 1922–1932.

——— *La Cité de Carcassonne. Précis historique, archéologique et descriptif,* Toulouse, 1923.

PRACHE, Anne, "Notre-Dame-en-Vaux de Châlons-sur-Marne. Campagnes de Construction," *Mémoires de la Société d'Agriculture, Commerce, Sciences et Arts du Département de la Marne,* LXXXI, 1966, 29–92.

——— *Saint-Remi de Reims. L'oeuvre de Pierre de Celle et sa place dans l'architecture gothique* (Bibliothèque de la Société française d'Archéologie, 8), Geneva, 1978.

——— , *see also* GRODECKI et al, 1977.

PRIN, Maurice, "La première église des Frères Prêcheurs de Toulouse, d'après les fouilles," *Annales du Midi,* LXVII, 1955, 5–18.

——— "L'église des Jacobins de Toulouse. Les étapes de la construction," in *La naissance et l'essor du gothique méridional au XIIIe siècle* (Cahiers de Fanjeaux, 9), Toulouse, 1974, 185–208.

PRINET, Jean, *see* GRODECKI *et al.,* 1963.

RANQUET, Henry du, *see* CHARDON DU RANQUET.

RAUCH, Thomas M., and R. Mark, "Model Study of Buttressing the Piers in Chartres Cathedral," *Gesta,* VI, 1967, 21–24.

RAVAUX, Jean-Pierre, "Les campagnes de construction de la cathédrale de Reims au XIIIe siècle," *Bulletin monumental,* CXXXVII, 1979, 7–66.

RAVE, Paul O., *Der Emporenbau in romanischer und frühgotischer Zeit* (Forschungen zur Formgeschichte der Kunst aller Zeiten und Völker, 8), Bonn and Leipzig, 1924.

RAVE, Wilhelm, *Westfälische Baukunst,* Münster in Westfalen, 1953.

RECHT, Roland, "Dessins d'architecture pour la cathédrale de Strasbourg," *L'oeil,* No. 174–175, June-July 1969, 26–33 and 44.

———— *L'Alsace gothique de 1300 à 1365,* Colmar, 1974.

————, *see also* GRODECKI *et al.,* 1977.

REINHARDT, Hans, "La nef de la cathédrale de Strasbourg," *Bulletin de la Société des amis de la cathédrale de Strasbourg,* 2nd ser., IV, 1937, 3–28.

———— *La cathédrale de Reims,* Paris, 1963.

———— *La cathédrale de Strasbourg,* Paris, 1972.

REY, Robert, *La cathédrale de Toulouse,* Paris, 1929.

———— *L'art gothique dans le Midi de la France,* Paris, 1934.

———— "La collégiale Saint-Paul de Narbonne," *Congrès archéologique de France,* CXII (Roussillon), 1954, 476–485.

RHEIN, André, "La cathédrale de Dol," *Bulletin monumental,* LXXIV, 1910, 369–433.

———— *Notre-Dame de Mantes,* Paris, 1932.

RIVOIRA, Giovanni T., *Roman Architecture and its Principles of Construction under the Empire,* Oxford, 1925.

ROHAULT DE FLEURY, Georges, *Gallia Dominicana. Les couvents de Saint Dominique au moyen âge,* 2 vols., Paris, 1903.

ROLLAND, Paul, "La technique normande du mur évidé et l'architecture scaldienne," *Revue belge d'archéologie et d'histoire de l'art,* X, 1940, 169–188.

ROMANINI, Angiola M., *L'architettura gotica in Lombardia,* 2 vols., Milan, 1964.

ROSE, Hans, *Die Baukunst der Zisterzienser,* Munich, 1916.

ROSEMANN Heinz R., "Die westfälische Hallenkirche in der ersten Hälfte des 13. Jahr-hunderts," *Zeitschrift für Kunstgeschichte,* I, 1932, 203–227.

ROSEROT, Alphonse, *Dictionnaire historique de la Champagne méridionale (Aube) des origines à 1790,* 4 vols., Troyes, 1942–1948.

RUPRICH-ROBERT, Victor M. C., *L'architecture normande aux XIe et XIIe siècles en Normandie et en Angleterre,* 2 vols., Paris, 1884–1889.

SAINT-PAUL, Anthyme, "Poissy et Morienval," *Mémoires de la Société historique et ar-chéologique de l'arrondissement de Pontoise et du Vexin,* XVI, 1894, 1–21.

SALET, Francis, "Saint-Loup-de-Naud," *Bulletin monumental,* XCII, 1933, 129–169.

———— "Notre-Dame de Corbeil," *Ibid.,* C, 1941, 81–118.

———— "Voulton," *Ibid.,* CII, 1943–1944, 91–115.

———— "Rozoy-en-Brie," *Congrès archéologique de France,* CIII (Ile-de-France), 1944, 282–294.

———— "Poissy, église Notre-Dame," *Ibid.,* CIV (Paris-Mantes), 1946, 221–268.

———— *La Madeleine de Vézelay,* Melun, 1948.

———— "Cathédrale de Tours," *Congrès archéologique de France,* CVI (Tours), 1948, 29–49.

———— "La cathédrale de Sens et sa place dans l'histoire de l'architecture médiévale," *Comptes-rendus de l'Académie des inscriptions et belles-lettres,* 1955, 182–187.

———— "L'église de Mussy-sur-Seine," *Congrès archéologique de France,* CXIII (Troyes), 1955, 320–337.

———— "Saint-Urbain de Troyes," *Ibid.,* CXIII (Troyes), 1955, 98–122.

———— "La cathédrale du Mans," *Ibid.,* CXIX (Maine), 1961, 18–58.

———— "Le premier colloque international de la Société française d'archéologie (Reims, 1 er-2 Juin 1965). Chronologie de la cathédrale," *Bulletin monumental,* CXXV, 1967, 347–394.

———— "Cluny III," *Ibid.,* CXXVI, 1968, 235–292.

———— "La cathédrale de Lausanne. A propos du septième centenaire de la consécration de 1275," *Ibid.,* CXXXV, 1977, 21–41.

———— *see also* PÉROUSE DE MONTCLOS.

SALMI, Mario, "L'architettura nell'Aretino: Il periodo gotico," *Atti del XII Congresso di storia dell'Architettura, Arezzo, 10–15 Settembre 1961: L'architettura nell'Aretino,* Rome, 1969, 69–103.

SALZMAN, Louis F., *Building in England down to 1540,* Oxford, 1952.

SANFAÇON, Roland, *L'architecture flamboyante en France,* Quebec, 1971.

SAUER, Joseph, *Symbolik des Kirchengebaudes und seiner Ausstattung in der Auffassung des Mittelalters,* Freiburg im Breisgau, 1924; 2nd ed., Münster in Westfalen, 1964.

SAUERLÄNDER, Willibald, "Die kunstgeschichtliche Stellung der Westportale von Notre-Dame in Paris," *Marburger Jahrbuch für Kunstwissenschaft,* XVII, 1959, 1–56.

———— *Gothic Sculpture in France 1140–1270,* London, 1972.

SAUSER, Ekkart, *see* JUNGMANN.

SCHLINK, Wilhelm, *Zwischen Cluny und Clairvaux: die Kathedrale von Langres und die burgundische Architektur des 12. Jahrhunderts* (Beiträge zur Kunstgeschichte, 4), Berlin, 1970.

SCHMIDT-GLASSNER, Helga, *see* BAUM.

SCHMOLL (gen. Eisenwerth), J. Adolf, "Zisterzienser-Romanik. Kritische Gedanken zur jüngsten Literatur," *Formositas Romanica. Beiträge zur Erforschung der romanischen Kunst, Joseph Gantner zugeeignet,* Frauenfeld, 1958, 151–180.

————, *see also* AUBERT *et al,* 1965.

SCHÜRENBERG, Lisa, *Die kirchliche Baukunst in Frankreich zwischen 1270 und 1380,* Berlin, 1934.

SEDLMAYR, Hans, *Die Entstehung der Kathedrale,* Zurich, 1950.

SÉJOURNÉ, Paul, *Grandes voûtes,* 3 vols., Bourges, 1913–1916.

SENÉ, Alain, "Un instrument de précision au service des artistes du moyen âge: l'équerre," *Cahiers de civilisation médiévale,* XIII, 1970, 349–358.

SERBAT, Louis, "L'église Notre-Dame-la-Grande à Valenciennes," *Revue de l'art chrétien,*

XLVI, 1903, 366–383; XLIX, 1906, 9–21 and 242–252.

——— "Narbonne. Monuments religieux," *Congrès archéologique de France,* LXXIII (Carcassonne and Perpignan), 1906, 79–102.

——— "Caen. Église Saint-Etienne et abbaye aux hommes," *Congrès archéologique de France,* LXXV (Caen), 1908, I, 21–52.

——— "Quelques églises anciennement détruites du nord de la France," *Bulletin monumental,* LXXXVIII, 1929, 365–435.

SEVERENS, Kenneth W., "The Early Campaign at Sens, 1140–1145," *Journal of the Society of Architectural Historians,* XXIX, 1970, 97–107.

SEYMOUR, Charles, *Notre-Dame of Noyon in the Twelfth Century, A Study in the Early Development of Gothic Architecture* (Yale Historical Publications, History of Art, 1), New Haven, 1939; new ed., New York, 1968.

SHELBY, Lon R., "Medieval Masons' Tools: The Level and the Plumb Rule," *Technology and Culture,* II, 1961, 127–130.

——— "The Role of the Master Mason in Mediaeval English Building," *Speculum,* XXXIX, 1964, 387–403.

——— "Medieval Masons' Tools: II. Compass and Square," *Technology and Culture,* VI, 1965, 236–248.

——— "Setting Out the Keystones of Pointed Arches: A Note on Medieval 'Baugeometrie'," *Ibid.,* X, 1969, 537–548.

——— "The Education of Medieval English Master Masons," *Mediaeval Studies,* XXXII, 1970, 1–26.

——— "Medieval Masons' Templates," *Journal of the Society of Architectural Historians,* XXX, 1971, 140–154.

——— "The Geometrical Knowledge of Mediaeval Master Masons," *Speculum,* XLVII, 1972, 395–421.

——— "The Practical Geometry of Medieval Masons," *Studies in Medieval Culture,* V, 1975, 133–144.

——— "The 'Secret' of the Medieval Masons" in Bert S. Hall and D. C. West, eds., *On Pre-Modern Technology and Science: Studies in Honor of Lynn White, Jr.* (Human Civilitas, 1), Malibu, 1976, 201–219.

——— *Gothic Design Techniques: The Fifteenth-Century Design Booklets of Mathes Roriczer and Hanns Schmuttermayer,* Carbondale, 1977.

SIMSON, Otto von, *The Gothic Cathedral, The Origins of Gothic Architecture and the Medieval Concept of Order,* London and New York, 1956.

——— *Das Mittelalter, II. Das Hohe Mittelalter* (Propyläen Kunstgeschichte, new ed., 6), Berlin, 1972.

SMIDT, Carl M., *Roskilde domkirkes middelalderlige bygningshistorie* (Nationalmuseets skrifter, Arkaeologisk-historik raekke, 3), Copenhagen, 1949.

SMITH, E(arl) Baldwin, *Architectural Symbolism of Imperial Rome and the Middle Ages,* Princeton, 1956.

SMITH, John T., "Medieval Aisled Halls and Their Derivatives," *Archaeological Journal,* CXII, 1955, 76–94.

——— "The Early Development of Timber Buildings: The Passing-Brace and Reversed Assembly," *Ibid.,* CXXXI, 1974, 238–263.

STEIN, (Frédéric A.) Henri, "Pierre de Montereau et la cathédrale de Paris," *Mémoires de la Société nationale des Antiquaires de France*, LXXI, 1911, 14–28.

———— *Le Palais de Justice et la Sainte-Chapelle de Paris, notice historique et archéologique,* Paris, 1912; 2nd ed., 1927.

———— *Les architectes des cathédrales gothiques,* Paris, 1911; 2nd ed., 1930.

STODDARD, Whitney S., *Monastery and Cathedral in France,* Middletown (Conn.), 1966; new ed. under title, *Art and Architecture in Medieval France,* New York, 1972.

STONE, Lawrence, *Sculpture in Britain: The Middle Ages* (Pelican History of Art), Harmondsworth and Baltimore, 1955.

STROBEL, Richard, *Romanische Architektur in Regensburg* (Erlanger Beiträge zur Sprach- und Kunstwissenschaft, 20), Nürnberg, 1965.

Studies in Western Art, Acts of the Twentieth International Congress of the History of Art, New York, 1961, I. Romanesque and Gothic Art, Princeton, 1963.

STYM-POPPER, Sylvain, *see* PÉROUSE DE MONTCLOS.

SUMMERSON John, *Heavenly Mansions and Other Essays on Architecture,* London, 1949.

SWOBODA, Karl M., *Peter Parler, der Baukünstler und Bildhauer,* Vienna, 1940.

TARALON, Jean, *Jumièges,* Paris, 1955.

———— *Treasures of the Churches of France,* London, 1966.

————, *see also* AUBERT *et al.,* 1958.

TER KUILE, Engelbert H., *De romaanse kerkbouwkunst in de Nederlanden,* Zutphen, 1975.

———— *see also* FOCKEMA ANDREAE.

TERLINE, Joseph de, "La tête de Saint Louis à Saint-Germain-en-Laye," *Fondation Eugène Piot, Monuments et Mémoires publiés par l'Académie des inscriptions et belles-lettres,* XLV, 1951, 123–140.

THIBOUT, Marc, "Les églises des XIIIe et XIVe siècles dans le département de la Manche," *Bulletin monumental,* XCVI, 1937, 5–43.

———— "L'église de Picauville. Une influence directe au XIIIe siècle de l'architecture d'Ile-de-France en Basse-Normandie," *Ibid.,* CII, 1943–1944, 117–127.

———— "La collégiale de Mortain," *Congrès archéologique de France,* CXI (Orne), 1953, 243–261.

———— "L'abbaye de Hambye," *Ibid.,* CXXIV (Cotentin-Avranchin), 1966, 337–357.

THIÉBAUT, Jacques, "L'église de Norrey-en-Bessin," *Congrès archéologique de France,* CXXXII (Bessin et Pays d'Auge), 1974, 240–285.

THIRION, Jacques, "L'ancienne église de Lamourguier à Narbonne," *Congrès archéologique de France,* CXII (Roussillon), 1954, 433–445.

———— "La cathédrale de Bayeux," *Ibid.,* CXXXII (Bessin et Pays d'Auge), 1974, 286–312.

THÜMMLER, Hans, "Die Anfänge der monumentalen Gewölbebaukunst in Deutschland und der besondere Anteil Westfalens," *Westfalen,* XXIX, 1951, 154–171.

———— "Westfälische und italienische Hallenkirchen," *Festschrift Martin Wackernagel zum 75. Geburtstag* (Kunstgeschichtliches Seminar der Universität Münster), Cologne, 1958, 17–36.

TOESCA, Pietro, *Storia dell'arte italiana, I. Il medioevo,* 2 vols., Turin, 1927.

TORRES BALBÁS, Leopoldo, *Arquitectura gotica* (Ars Hispaniae, 7), Madrid, 1952.

———— "Naves de edificios anteriores al siglo XIII cubiertas con armaduras de madera sobre arcos transversales," *Archivo Español de Arte,* XXXII, 1959, 109–119.

————— "Naves cubiertas con armadura de madera sobre arcos perpiaños a partir del siglo XIII," *Ibid.*, XXXIII, 1960, 19–43.

TOURNIER, René, *Les églises comtoises, leur architecture des origines au XVIIIe siècle*, Paris, 1954.

TRACHTENBERG, Marvin, *The Campanile of Florence Cathedral*, New York, 1971

UNGEWITTER, Georg G., *Lehrbuch der gotischen Konstruktionen*, 2 vols., Leipzig, 1859–1864; 4th ed., 1901–1903.

UTLEY, Francis L., ed., *The Forward Movement of the Fourteenth Century*, Columbus, 1961.

VALLERY-RADOT, Jean, *La cathédrale de Bayeux*, Paris, 1922; 2nd ed., 1958.

————— "Auffay," *Congrès archéologique de France*, LXXXIX (Rouen), 1926, 356–374.

————— "Fécamp, Eglise abbatiale," *Ibid.*, LXXXIX (Rouen), 1926, 405–458.

————— *L'église de la Trinité de Fécamp*, Paris, 1928.

————— *Eglises romanes. Filiations et échanges d'influences*, Paris, 1931.

————— "Introduction à l'histoire des églises de la Suisse romande des origines au milieu du XIIIe siècle," *Congrès archéologique de France*, CX (Suisse romande), 1952, 9–39.

————— "Auxerre. La cathédrale Saint-Etienne. Les principaux textes de l'histoire de la construction," *Ibid.*, CXVI (Auxerre), 1958, 40–50.

————— "Saint-Germain d'Auxerre. L'église haute," *Ibid.*, CXVI (Auxerre), 1958, 26–39.

VAN DER MEULEN, Jan, "Histoire de la construction de la cathédrale Notre-Dame de Chartres après 1194," *Bulletin de la Société archéologique d'Eure-et-Loir*, XXIII, 1965, 81–126.

————— "Die Querhausportale und die relative Chronologie der Kathedrale von Chartres mit Bezug auf das datum 1220," *Kunstchronik*, XIX, 1966, 286–287.

————— "Recent Literature on the Chronology of Chartres Cathedral," *Art Bulletin*, XLIX, 1967, 152–172.

VAN PELT, John V., ed., *Selected Monuments of French Gothic Architecture; one hundred plates from the Archives de la Commission des Monuments Historiques* (The Library of Architectural Documents, 3), New York, 1924.

VANUXEM, Jacques, *see* VERGNET-RUIZ.

VELGE, Henri, *La collégiale des Saints Michel et Gudule à Bruxelles*, Brussels, 1925.

VENABLES, Edmund, "On the Foundations of the East End of St. Hugh's Choir of Lincoln," *Archaeological Journal*, XLIV, 1887, 194–202.

VERBEEK, Albert, "Die ottonische Bautengruppe um Essen und Werden und die viergeschossige Wandgliederung," *Karolingische und ottonische Kunst: Werden, Wesen, Wirkung* (Forschungen zur Kunstgeschichte und christlichen Archäologie, 3), Wiesbaden, 1957.

VERGNET-RUIZ, Jean, and J. Vanuxem, "L'église de l'abbaye de Saint-Martin-aux-Bois," *Bulletin monumental*, CIII, 1945, 137–173.

VERHAEGEN, Pierre, "L'église Saint-Nicolas de Gand," *Bulletin monumental*, XCVI, 1937, 133–189.

————— *Les églises de Gand* (Ars Belgica, 7–8), 2 vols., Brussels, 1938.

VERLET, Hélène, "Les bâtiments monastiques de l'abbaye de Saint-Germain-des-Prés," *Paris et Ile-de-France*, IX, 1957–1958, 9–68.

VERMEULEN, Frans A. J., *Handboek tot de geschiedenis der Nederlandsche Bouwkunst*, I.

Voorgeschiedenis en Middeleeuwen, 2 vols., The Hague, 1928.

VERRIER, Jean, *La cathédrale de Bourges et ses vitraux,* Paris, 1941.

——, *see also* AUBERT *et al.,* 1958.

VERZONE, Paolo, *L'architettura religiosa dell'alto medioevo nell'Italia settentrionale,* Milan, 1942.

VILLES, Alain, "Les campagnes de construction de la cathédrale de Toul," *Bulletin monumental,* CXXX, 1972, 179–189; CXXXIII, 1975, 233–243; and CXXXV, 1977, 43–55.

VIOLLET-LE-DUC, Eugène E., *Dictionnaire raisonné de l'architecture française du XIe au XVIe siècle,* 10 vols., Paris, 1858–1868.

—— *Rational Building* (a translation of the article "Construction" in the *Dictionnaire raisonné* . . .), London and New York, 1895.

VOLBACH, Wolfgang, *Early Christian Art,* New York, 1961.

Voyage pittoresque de la France avec la description de toutes ses provinces par une société de gens de lettres, 8 vols., Paris, 1781–1796.

WAGNER-RIEGER, Renate, *Die italienische Baukunst zu Beginn der Gotik* (Publikationen des österreichischen Kulturinstituts in Rom, Abteilung für historische Studien, I, 2), 2 vols., Graz and Cologne, 1956–1957.

—— "Zur Typologie italienischer Bettelordenskirchen," *Römische historische Mitteilungen,* II, 1957–1958, 266–284.

WALTER, Joseph, *La cathédrale de Strasbourg,* Paris, 1933.

WAQUET, Henri, *Vieilles pierres bretonnes,* Quimper, 1920.

—— *L'art breton,* 2 vols., Grenoble, 1942; new ed., Paris, 1960.

WARD, Clarence, *Mediaeval Church Vaulting,* Princeton, 1915.

WEBB, Geoffrey F., "The Decorative Character of Westminster Abbey," *Journal of the Warburg and Courtauld Institutes,* XII, 1949, 16–20.

—— *Ely Cathedral,* London, 1951.

—— *Architecture in Britain. The Middle Ages* (Pelican History of Art), Harmondsworth and Baltimore, 1956.

WEBER, Helmut, *Das wechselseitige Verhältnis von Konstruktion und Formung an der Kathedralen Nordfrankreichs,* Hanover, 1957.

WEINBERGER, Martin, "The First Façade of the Cathedral of Florence," *Journal of the Warburg and Courtauld Institutes,* IV, 1940–1941, 67–79.

WEYRES, Willy, "Das System des Kölner Chorgrundrisses," *Kölner Domblatt,* XVI–XVII, 1959, 97–105.

WHITE, John, *Art and Architecture in Italy* 1250–1400 (Pelican History of Art), Harmondsworth and Baltimore, 1966.

WHITE, Lynn, *Medieval Technology and Social Change,* Oxford, 1962.

WHITTINGHAM, Arthur B., "Bury St. Edmunds Abbey. The Plan, Design and Development of the Church and Monastic Buildings," *Archaeological Journal,* CVIII, 1951, 168–187.

WILLIS, Robert, *The Architectural History of Canterbury Cathedral,* London, 1845.

WINTERFELD, Delhard von, *see* P. KURMAN.

WIXOM, William D., *Treasures from Medieval France,* Cleveland, 1967.

WOLFE, Maury I., and R. Mark, "Gothic Cathedral Buttressing: The Experiment at Bourges and Its Influence," *Journal of the Society of Architectural Historians,* XXXIII, 1974, 17–27.

——, and R. Mark, "The Collapse of the Vaults of Beauvais Cathedral in 1284," *Speculum,* LI, 1976, 462–476.

WOLFF, Arnold, "Chronologie der ersten Bauzeit des Kölner Domes," *Kölner Domblatt,* XXVIII–XXIX, 1968.

WOLFF METTERNICH, Franz, "Zum Problem der Grundriss- und Raumgestaltung des Kölner Domes," *Der Kölner Dom, Festschrift zur Siebenhundertjarhfeier* 1248–1948 (Cologne, Zentral-Dombau-Verein), Cologne, 1948, 51–77.

WORTMANN, Reinhard, "Der Westbau des Strassburger Münsters und Meister Erwin," *Bonner Jahrbücher,* CLXIX, 1969, 290–318.

ZARNECKI, George, *Later English Romanesque Sculpture* 1140–1210, London, 1953.

ZEITLER, Rudolf, "Die Baugeschichte des Doms zu Uppsala," *Aspekte zur Kunstgeschichte von Mittelalter und Neuzeit, Karl Heinz Clasen zum* 75. *Geburtstag* (H. Müller and G. Hahn, eds.), Weimar, 1971, 359–385.

ZIMMERMANN, Walther, *Das Münster zu Essen* (Die Kunstdenkmäler des Rheinlands, 3), Essen, 1956.

Index

duced to, 24–26, 145–149, 166; thick longitudinal, 167–168, 216, 238, 278, 332, 348, 498n19, 517n39; heavy transverse, 72; diaphragm, 84–85; in continuous order, 437–442, 538–539n43; with heavily molded profile, 27, 39; with chamfered profile, 441. *See also* Main arcade; Pointed arch; Quadrant arch buttressing

Architects: 259–260, 358–359, 361, 370–371, 421, 440, 456, 482n26, 511n11, 534n15, 540n46. *See also* Bernard de Soissons; Erwin; Hugh; Hugues Libergier; Jean le Loup; Jean des Champs; Jean d'Orbais; Pierre de Montreuil; Pierre des Champs; Renaud de Cormont; Robert de Luzarches; Thomas de Cormont; Villard de Honnecourt; William of Sens; William Ramsey; William the Englishman *(See under forenames.)*

Architecture: ages of, characterized by solutions to technical problems, 5; late 13th c., 411–463; listed as a science by Hugh of Saint-Victor, 478n13; relationship with music, 481n21. *See also* Constructional system; Engineering; Gothic architecture

Ardenne: on map, 298–299 (fig. 274), 351 (fig. 334); abbey church, 519n54

Arles: on map, 15 (fig. 13); church, 538n43

Armenia: rib vaults in, 466n8

Arnold, Master, builder of Cologne: 421, 534n15

Arnolfo di Cambio, architect of S. Croce in Florence: 456

Arras: 123; on map, 114–115 (fig. 113)
——Cathedral: 154; triforium passage, 110–111, 166; buttressing walls, 128; large cruciform plan, 135–137; late 18th c. drawing, 136 (fig. 129); exterior, 150–151; style of capital carving developed in, 161; exterior arcading of transept, 208; linkage between triforium and clerestory, 373; possible influence of Saint-Denis, 480n17; height of choir,

487n21, 488n27; oblong vaults, 499n26; gabled roofing of choir tribunes, 527n34
——St. Vaast: on map, 406–407 (fig. 384)

Articulated plan: *see* Cruciform plan; Plans, articulated; Trefoil plan

Ascoli Piceno: on map, 408–409 (fig. 385); hall church, 455

Ashlar masonry: in vaults, 16, 34

Assisi: on map, 300–301 (fig. 275); S. Francesco, 544n66

Audrieu: 541n50

Auffay: on map, 298–299 (fig. 274), 406–407 (fig. 384); church (chamfered profiles), 540n48

Augustinian Canons: 429, 537n35

Aumale: on map, 298–299 (fig. 274); Saint-Martin, 516n35

Austere trend in Rayonnant Style: 417, 429–437, 443; examples, on map, 406–407 (fig. 384); vs. linear abundance in Late Gothic, 445. *See also* Mussy-sur-Seine

Austin Friars: 537n35

Austria: *see* Heiligenkreuz

Auxerre: 437; on map, 112–113 (fig. 112), 114–115 (fig. 113), 298–299 (fig. 274), 300–301 (fig. 275), 350 (fig. 333), 406–407 (fig. 384), 408–409 (fig. 385)
——Cathedral: Romanesque cathedral, 66; Gothic choir, 336 (fig. 312), 336–339; (elevation) 336–338, (upper stories) 337 (fig. 314), (clerestory windows) 517n42, (Lady Chapel) 507n35, (Champenois passage) 337 (fig. 313), 337–338, 419n13, (revival of earlier style at) 338–339, (influence of) 373, 538n41
——Saint-Eusèbe: triforium, 484n6
——Saint-Germain abbey church: Carolingian crypts, 56; chevet, 428; choir, 438 (fig. 421), (continuous order in) 437–438, (dating of) 538n40; axial chapel on site of Carolingian octagon, 437, 538n40–41; entrance to Lady Chapel, 438 (fig. 422)

575

509n45; influence, 421; proportions, 275, 288; reconstructed plan in 1272, 290 (fig. 268); style of upper parts, (after 1250), 395; stylistic connections of first work, 364, 522n11; surprise effect of proportioning, 275, 281; triforium of ambulatory, 509n44, 524n21; triforium of hemicycle, 394 (fig. 372); verticality, 294–295

————Saint-Etienne: vaulting, 26, 27, 32; choir, 27; nave and south aisle, 28 (fig. 25); plan of pier, 34 (fig. 32); older parts, 312; north transept, 494n28

————Saint-Lucien abbey church (destroyed): 473n5, 486n17; height, 21–22; view of ruins, 23 (fig. 20); prototype of Gothic trefoil plan series, 135; mural style, 155; tribune elevation, 481n22

Beauvaisis: 35, 312

Belgium: A. Romanesque period: five aisled nave, 49; tribune churches and four-story elevation, 108–110, 481n22, 482n27; transmission of double wall structure, 110–111, 145–146, 470n23; single west tower, 505–506n28; multiple towers, 142–143, 487n22; use of dark marble, 159, 490n6
B. Gothic period: persistence of tribune elevation, 314, 513n17 and 20; Flemish connections of William of Sens, 161; variants of Braine-type elevations, 175, 178–179, 330–334, 509n2; diagonally planted chapels, 330, 492n16, 516–517n35; tall triforium, 214, 344, 497n18; double wall structure, 330–334, 517n36 and 38; hostility to flying-buttress, 332, 516n28; single west tower, 541n50; early Rayonnant works, 365, 386–388; late 13th c. spaciousness, 460, 546n76. See also Flanders; Tournai

Bernard, Saint: 429

Bernard de Castanet, bishop of Albi: 449, 451

Bernard of Soissons, architect of Reims Cathedral: 271, 401, 529n51, 531n1

Bernay, abbey church: 83, 470n22

Bernières: on map, 112–113 (fig. 112), 351 (fig. 334), 406–407 (fig. 384); church, 519n54

Berry: 247, 346; on map, 112–113 (fig. 112)

Berteaucourt: pointed arches used in, 21; on map, 112–113 (fig. 112)

Besançon: 517n36; on map, 298–299 (fig. 274), 300–301 (fig. 275), 351 (fig. 334)

————Cathedral: 346, 490n6

Beverley: on map, 300–301 (fig. 275)

————Minster: 505n23, 507n31, 515n27

Bilson, John: 10

Binham, priory church: 55

Black Friars: see Dominicans

Blanche of Artois: 440

Blandinium: see Ghent, Sint-Pieter

Blois: on map, 112–113 (fig. 112), 114–115 (fig. 113), 298–299 (fig. 274)

————Saint-Laumer (now Saint-Nicolas): choir, 56, 473n8, (pier with applied monoliths) 162 (fig. 152), 162–163; nave (Chartrain formula) 255–256

Bohemia, hall churches: 543n62

Boiscommun: on map, 298–299 (fig. 274); church, 516n31

La Boissière, Cistercian abbey church: 511n10

Bologna: on map, 300–301 (fig. 275)

————S. Francesco: 544n66

Bonmont: on map, 112–113 (fig. 112); vaulted Cistercian church, 512n14, 545n74

Bonn: on map, 298–299 (fig. 274), 300–301 (fig. 275), 350 (fig. 333); collegiate church, position in the movement of resistance to High Gothic, 335, 341, 517n36

de Bonneuil, Etienne: see Etienne de Bonneuil

Bonneval: 255; on map, 298–299 (fig. 274)

Bonport, Cistercian ambulatory plan: 537n33

Boquen, Cistercian church: 512n14

Bordeaux: on map, 300–301 (fig. 275), 408–409 (fig. 385)

579

mandy, 514–515n25; diffusion of Rayonnant style, 419; continuous order, 439, 539n43; chamfered profiles, 441, 540n48; influence of metalwork, 403–404; sense of pattern, 463; tierceron vaults, 420, 439; vaults of Angevin type, 511n11; transoms, 536n31; genesis of Perpendicular, 541n52; urge for spaciousness in late 13th c., 456, 458, 460–461; Mendicant orders and their influence, 458, 544n68; hall churches, 458, 544n69; influence on the development of Late Gothic in Europe, 462, 546n80. *See also* Norman Conquest

Epernon: on map, 112–113 (fig. 112), 114–115 (fig. 113)
———Saint-Thomas: choir, 65–66
Ephesus: St John, 486n18; Hadrian's Temple of Artemis, 526
Erfurt: on map, 408–409 (fig. 385)
———Church of the Dominicans (Predigerkirche), 544n68
———St. Severus, hall church, 543n62
Ernulf, prior of Canterbury: 506n30
Erwin, designer of Strasbourg façade: 425–426, 532n5, 535n22
L'Escale-Dieu, Cistercian church: 512n14
Essen: on map, 112–113 (fig. 112), 114–115 (fig. 113), 406–407 (fig. 384), 408–409 (fig. 385)
———Münster: 481n25, 482n26; choir, 24, 109, (elevation of double bay) 108 (fig. 107)
Essômes: church, 373, 532n7; on map, 298–299 (fig. 274), 406–407 (fig. 384)
Etampes: on map, 112–113 (fig. 112), 114–115 (fig. 113)
———Notre-Dame: nave, 21, 35–36, 36 (fig. 34), 48; choir, 121; dating, 471n30
———Sainte-Croix: 496n9
———Saint-Martin: 484n5–6, 496n9
Etienne de Bonneuil, architect of Uppsala Cathedral: 534n17, 536n30
Eu: 513n21; on map, 114–115 (fig. 113), 298–299 (fig. 274)
Eucharist, Cult of: 385

Eudes Clément, abbot of Saint-Denis: 366, 523n14
Europe: utilitarian timber architecture of northern part of, 81; map of Gothic Europe, 408–409 (fig. 385); diffusion of Rayonnant style, 415; artistic unity in later 13th c., 421
Evreux: on map, 14 (fig. 12), 112–113 (fig. 112), 114–115 (fig. 113), 406–407 (fig. 384), 408–409 (fig. 385)
———Cathedral: excavated Romanesque choir, 10, 465n2; Romanesque nave (main arcade story), 10, 27, 30 (fig. 28); Gothic nave (upper stories) 537n37; Gothic choir, 417, 419, 520n58
———Saint-Taurin: shrine, 401 (incl. fig. 380), 529n50
exedrae, in Late Antique and early Byzantine architecture: 24
Exeter: on map, 350 (fig. 333), 408–409 (fig. 385)
———Cathedral: presbytery and choir, 419, 420 (fig. 401), 463, 533n12

Façades: one axial tower, 281, 505–506n28, 541n50; two tower, 97, 135–136, 191–193, 384, 525n28 (*see also* all examples listed below under transept façades and west façades, except the transept façades of Notre-Dame de Paris); city-gate souces of, 385, 525n28; choir screen treatment of, 384–385, 526n30–31
———transept façades: of Laon, 135–136, 191 (incl. fig. 186); of Chartres, 201, 234–235, 499n27, 500n28; of Reims, 271–274, 272 (fig. 252), 273 (fig. 254); of 13th c. Saint-Denis, 378–380, 379 (fig. 356); of Notre-Dame de Paris, 356 (fig. 337), 365, 398 (fig. 377), 399–400, 404 (fig. 383); of Rouen Cathedral, 419
———west façades: of Saint-Denis, 37, 38 (fig. 36), 96 (figs. 88–89), 97–98; of Chartres Cathedral, 96–98, 97 (figs. 90–91), 198 (fig. 92), 480n18; of Senlis Cathedral, 190 (fig. 185), 191; of

Grez-sur-Loing: church, 20–21; on map, 112–113 (fig. 112), 114–115 (fig. 113)

Grisaille: 521n3, 532n5

Grodecki, Louis: 523n15

Groin vaults: 16, 18, 21, 51–52, 68, 466–467n10, 471–472n30; Cistercian series, 513n14

Guillaume de Mussy: 540n46

Hagia Sophia, Constantinople: 45. *See also* Istanbul

Haina, Cistercian hall church: 543n62

Hainault: 22, 108, 490n6, 505n28

Hall churches: on map, 114–115 (fig. 113), 298–299 (fig. 274), 300–301 (fig. 275), 406–407 (fig. 384), 408–409 (fig. 385); of Poitou and Anjou, 74, 308–309; of southern France and Catalonia, 447; of Germany, 452–454, 543n61–62; of northern Italy, 452, 455; Dominican, at Colmar, 454; of England, 458–459, 544n69

Hallenkirchen, the term: 475–476n23. *See also* Hall churches

Hambye: on map, 406–407 (fig. 384) ———Abbey church, 536–537n32; east end and choir, 431–432, 433 (figs. 415–416), (chamfered profiles) 540n48, (thin walls) 432, 537n34

Hans Stethaimer: 511n11

Hastings, Maurice: 541n52

Heavenly Jerusalem: 377–378, 384

Height: Gothic tendency towards, 21, 74, 76, 103; limited in first Gothic system, 124–126, 129, 131; of 13th c. churches, 212, 285, 294, 394, 396, 487n21, 488n27; of Amiens Cathedral, 275, 280, 361, 396, 509n45; of Mendicant churches of Toulouse, 449

Heiligenkreuz: on map, 408–409 (fig. 385); hall choir, 543n62

Heilsbronn: 512n14

Heisterbach: 285, 497n16

Hemicycle: definition, 6; seven-sided, 258, 260, 290, 498n21

Hénin-Liétard: 516n30; on map, 298–299 (fig. 274)

Henry I, king of England: 10

Henry II, king of England: 511n8

Henry III, king of England: 440

Henry I, count of Champagne: 121

Henri le Sanglier, archbishop of Sens: 66, 475n18

Herblay, church: 516n35

Hereford: on map, 408–409 (fig. 385); Bishop's Chapel, 539n43

Heresies: 446

Hermit friars of Saint Augustine (Austin Friars): 537n35

Hexham: 515n26; on map, 300–301 (fig. 275)

High Gothic: 5–7, 42, 195–295, 391–396, 401, 403, 411, 453; on map, 298–299 (fig. 274); the term, 246, 501n2; connection with rise of Capetian monarchy, 246–247; resistance to, 248, 323, 325–326, 330, 332, 502n4; heartland surrounded by peripheral Gothic movements, 300–301 (fig. 275), 341, 350 (fig. 333), 351 (fig. 334); temporary secession of Parisian milieu, 248, 325–326; chevet types, 297 (fig. 273 C, D, E)

Hochgotik: 501n2. *See also* High Gothic

Hollar, Wenceslaus: engraving of Old St. Paul's Cathedral, 418 (fig. 398), 541–542n52

Holy Roman Empire: 108–109; on map, 112–113 (fig. 112), 114–115 (fig. 113)

Horn, Walter W.: on bay design, 81, 476n3

Howden: on map, 351 (fig. 334), 408–409 (fig. 385); church, 533n12, 545n72, (nave) 458, 459 (fig. 446)

Hugh, architect of Bury St Edmunds: 530n53

Hugh of Saint-Victor: 478n13

Hugh of Semur, Saint, abbot of Cluny: 18

Hugues I, prior of Saint-Martin-des-Champs: 49

Hugues de Toucy, archbishop of Sens: 475n18

on map, 351 (fig. 334)

Melleray, Cistercian abbey church: 512n14

Melun: 123

Mendicant architecture: basic simplicity,
432–433, 446; Cistercian influence,
433, 537n36; unvaulted lightweight
construction, 433, 446, 448–449,
454, 455, 458; in Southern France
and Spain, 446–449, in Italy, 455–
456, 544n66, (the case of Florence)
456; in Germany, 454, 544n68; in
England, 458, 544–545n69; influence (in Southern France) 433–437,
449–451, (in Flanders) 460, 546n76,
(in England) 458–459, 545n70 and
71; one of the sources of Late Gothic,
462, 546n80

Mendicant Orders: their propagation and
action, 432–433, 446, 455; Principal
Orders, 537n35. *See also* Carmelites;
Dominicans; Franciscans; Mendicant
architecture

Mesopotamia: prototypes of Islamic rib
vaults, 466n8; use of pointed arch,
467n13

Messina: 468n14; on map, 408–409 (fig.
385)

Metalwork: relation to Rayonnant style,
400, 403, 405, 530n55

Metz: on map, 298–299 (fig. 274), 300–
301 (fig. 275), 351 (fig. 334), 406–407
(fig. 384), 408–409 (fig. 385)

———Cathedral: 394, 421

Michelangelo, dome of St. Peter's: 45

Middle Rasen (Lincs.): 539n43

Milan: 7, 470n22; on map, 14 (fig. 12)

———Cathedral: 544n68

———S. Ambrogio, nave: 7

———S. Lorenzo: 486n16; octagon of S.
Aquilino, 470n22

———S. Nazaro: 7

———S. Simpliciano, continuous order:
539n43

Minden: on map, 408–409 (fig. 385)

———Cathedral: hall nave, 453, 454 (fig.
441), 543n62

Missorium of Theodosius I: 526n30

Mobility: 171, 187–189, 193, 241–243,

260–265, 287, 397–398

Modularity: of ambulatory of Saint-
Denis, 90–94; of Notre-Dame de Paris,
137–141, (of façade of Notre-Dame)
239, 500n31

Moissac: lower story of porch tower, 12 (fig.
10); on map, 14 (fig. 12), 15 (fig. 13)

Mons-en-Laonnois: 516n35

Monte Cassino: 11th c. abbey church, 17;
on map, 15 (fig. 13)

Montierender: 123; on map, 114–115
(fig. 113), 298–299 (fig. 274), 300–
301 (fig. 275)

Montierneuf: *see* Poitiers

Montivilliers: 511n12

Le Mont Notre-Dame: east end, 104,
189, (water color) 105 (fig. 101); nave
piers, of Soissons type, 256; tower
bases opening onto nave, 491n15; on
map, 114–115 (fig. 113), 298–299
(fig. 274)

Le Mont Saint-Michel: nave (climax of
thin wall construction) 471n28, (elevation) 101 (fig. 95), (triforium type)
71, 83, 100, 480n20; on map, 15 (fig.
13), 112–113 (fig. 112), 114–115 (fig.
113), 298–299 (fig. 274)

Moret: choir, 325–326; on map, 298–299
(fig. 274), 300–301 (fig. 275)

Morienval: on map, 14 (fig. 12), 112–113
(fig. 112)

———Priory church: ambulatory, 20, 26,
27, 31 (fig. 29), 539n43; interior of
choir, 29 (fig. 26); east end, 30 (fig.
27)

Mortain: on map, 298–299 (fig. 274)

———Abbey church: 519n53, 536n32,
537n34

Mozarabic architecture: 466n9

Much Wenlock, Cluniac Priory: church,
343; Chapter House, 93 (blind arcading) 93 (fig. 85); on map, 300–301
(fig. 275), 350 (fig. 333)

Mullions: 234, 357, 361–362, 373–374,
377, 400, 411, 415–416, 419–420,
424, 428–429, 431, 541n52, 542n60;
downward extension of, 426–429,
524n20, 536n27

599

471n29; influence of Sens, 131, 488n29; west façade, 190 (fig. 185), 191, 494n28

Sens: on map, 14 (fig. 12), 15 (fig. 13), 112–113 (fig. 112), 114–115 (fig. 113), 406–407 (fig. 384)

———Cathedral: 119, 257; dating and changes of design, 66–68, 98–100, 475n18; chapel of Saint Jean, 66 (fig. 62); ambulatory, 67 (fig. 63); sources, (antique) 64, 68, 475n19, (Norman) 66, 71–72, 100, (Lombard) 68, 70, 72, (regional) 65–66, 68, 71, (influence of Saint-Denis) 72; plan without transept, 64 (fig. 60), 65, 121, 131; dimensions, 65, 68, 475n19 and 21; interior spaciousness, 64–72, (nave) 67–68, 69 (fig. 64), 99 (fig. 93), 102 (fig. 98), (spatial units) 68–70, 72, 100, 121, 475n21; wide and squat proportions of building, 106, 121; alternating supports, 68, 71–72, 100, 102–103, 484n5, (stronger piers) 72, 471n29, (twin columns) 64, 474n13; sexpartite vaults, 71–72, 100, 102–103, 120–121, 479n16, 499n26; elevation, 98–103, (principle of organization) 100–102; triforium type, 71, 100, 121, 322, 480–481n20, 484n6; influence, 70, 155, 488n29, 500n30, (type of plan) 120–121, 131–133, (type of elevation) 103, 120–121, 327, (English series) 322–323; west façade, 531n1, (traceried tympanum) 531n3

———Saint-Pierre-le-Vif (chronicle): 66

Sens group: 65–66, 70, 120–121, 484n5 and 6; Paris school, 103, 131–133; Le Mans sub-group, 70, 102–103; Saint-Père at Chartres, 65, 121, 122 (fig. 116B). See also Southern Group of Early Gothic

Seraincourt: crossing, 20 (fig. 17); vaults, 21; on map, 112–113 (fig. 112)

Sexpartite vault: functioning, 493n22; sexpartite vs. oblong, 499n26; Early Gothic use, 71–72, 100, 103, 121, 182, 488n29; Parisian type, 206–207,

497n12; split bay type, 346, 492–493n19, 507n34; 13th c. Gothic, 206–207, 293, 316, 339, 346, 507n34

Shrines: 400–401, 529–50

"Shrine treatment": 44, 400–404

Sicily: 17, 468n14

Siena: on map, 408–409 (fig. 385)

———Mendicant churches (S. Domenico and S. Francesco): 455, 544n66

Sigüenza: on map, 300–301 (fig. 275); Cathedral, 513n15

Silvanès Cistercian Abbey church: 306, 510n6; on map, 300–301 (fig. 275)

Simplification, movements towards: in plan, (Sens) 65, 68, (Bourges) 200–201, 209; in Cistercian architecture, 312; at Braine, 172–175; at Chartres, 221, 225–227, 233, 239; at Reims, 266, 274–275. See also Aisleless naves; Hall churches; Mendicant architecture

Skeletonization: 6–7, 22–24, 128, 157–158, 437. See also Double Wall; Openness

Soffit roll: 27, 472n32, 540n48

Soignies: on map, 112–113 (fig. 112)

———Saint-Vincent: nave, 481n22; west tower, 506n28

Soissons: on map, 15 (fig. 13), 112–113 (fig. 112), 114–115 (fig. 113), 298–299 (fig. 274), 406–407 (fig. 384); architecture of region of, 104, 124, 189, 255, 260, 527–528n38; diocese of, 124

———Cathedral: A. 12th c. work (south transept): trefoil plan, 132 (fig. 126 D), 134; interior elevation, 148 (fig. 143), 149, 172; chapel entrance, 507n35, 538n41; use of shafts en délit, 163, 164 (fig. 155), 165 (fig. 156), 166; double wall treatment of chapel walls, 169, 340; flying buttresses, 183. B. 13th c. work (choir and nave): typical High Gothic work, 5–6, 42, 323; dating, 255, 465n1; plan of chevet (shallow chapels), 285, 386; chevet composition, 196 (fig. 189), 323, 325 (fig. 298); flying buttresses,

Westminster Abbey: *(continued)*
tures, 418 (fig. 397), 419; influence of Coronation ritual, 503–504n15; tierceron vaults in east bays of nave, 539–540n45

———Palace: Hall (wall passage) 490n12; St. Stephen's Chapel, 541n52

Westphalia, hall churches: 311, 452–454, 476n23, 512n13, 543n61–62

Westwerke, Corvey type: 525n28

Wetter, hall church: 543n62

Wetzlar: 520n55, 543n62

Whitby: on map, 300–301 (fig. 275)

———Abbey: 319 (fig. 293), 321, 515n25–26

White Friars (or Carmelites): 537n35

Width, as a recurrent ideal in Gothic: at the very beginning, 49, 60, 64–65, 68, 72, 103, 475n19 and 21; in Early Gothic, 121, 137, 147, 488n29; in High Gothic, 198, 200–201, 209–216, 221–224, 265, 361; in the Peripheral milieux, 305–311, 354; in mid 13th c. Rayonnant, 391; in the late 13th c., 446–460, 462–463

William of Sens: 159, 161, 164, 322, 480n17, 491n13, 506n30

William Ramsey: 541–542n52

William the Englishman: 159, 164, 178, 335, 342, 480n17, 515n27

Wimpfen: transept, 421; on map, 408–409 (fig. 385)

Winchelsea: parish church, 545n70; on map, 406–407 (fig. 384)

Winchester: on map, 14 (fig. 12), 112–113 (fig. 112), 114–115 (fig. 113)

———Castle Hall: 527n34, 536n31

———Cathedral: 486n18, 487n22, 491n12, 511n11

Windows: in continuous sequences, 57–58, 60, 90; materializing the metaphysics of light, 117–118; repeated on multiple levels, 134, 141–142, 166–167, 271–272; increased in size, 62, 117, 227, 329; trefoil-headed, 491n13; triangular, 280, 389; round, 151, 154 (fig. 148), 272; twin, 100, 167; in triplets, 147, 149, 332; com-

posed, 227, 270–273, 325–326, 329; traceried (*see* Tracery; Window tracery); short clerestory type, 125–126, 129, 133, 141, 149, 207, 225, 328, 330, 336, 341, 348, 451, 454, 456, 458; tall clerestory type, 221, 225–227, 243, 255, 270–271, 287, 336, 339, 346, 361, 375, 377, 394; squared at the top, 378–379; with continuous framing, 538–539n43; recessed, 426; topped with gables, 386–388, 397, 424–425; set above doorways, 280, 381; running through two or three stories, 235, 383, 423–424, 429, 431, 525n27. *See also* Clerestory; Mullions; Rose windows; Stained glass; Window tracery

Window tracery: beginnings, 271, 361–363, 365; early formulations, 154, 375, 377–379, 383, 405, 411, 434, 521n3, 531n1, 540–541n50; at Amiens, 361, 363 (fig. 340), 389; at Saint-Denis, 80, 372 (fig. 350), 377–378; at Troyes Cathedral, 377; at the chapel of the château of Saint-Germain-en-Laye, 379; at the Sainte-Chapelle, 389; diffusion in the third quarter of the 13th c., 394–395, 415–420, 423–425, 428–429, 434, 528–529n48, 532n7; at Metz Cathedral, 394; at León Cathedral, 416, 532n7; at Westminster Chapter House, 419; in the late style of Pierre de Montreuil, 528–529n48; at Saint-Urbain of Troyes, 424; at Saint-Germain of Auxerre, 437; at Mussy-sur-Seine, 540n50; at Saint-Thibault, 444–445; linkage with triforium, 373–375, 524n21; influence on stained glass, 521n3; transoms, 431, 536n31, 542n60; late 13th c. developments, 437–438, 443–445, 447, 449, 453, 463, 541n52. *See also* Tracery; Triforium story

Woodchurch: 540n45; on map, 406–407 (fig. 384)

Wooden structures: *see* Timber architecture

622